E/2004/75/Rev.1/Add.1
ST/ESA/291/Add.1

Department of Economic and Social Affairs

World Economic and Social Survey 2004

International Migration

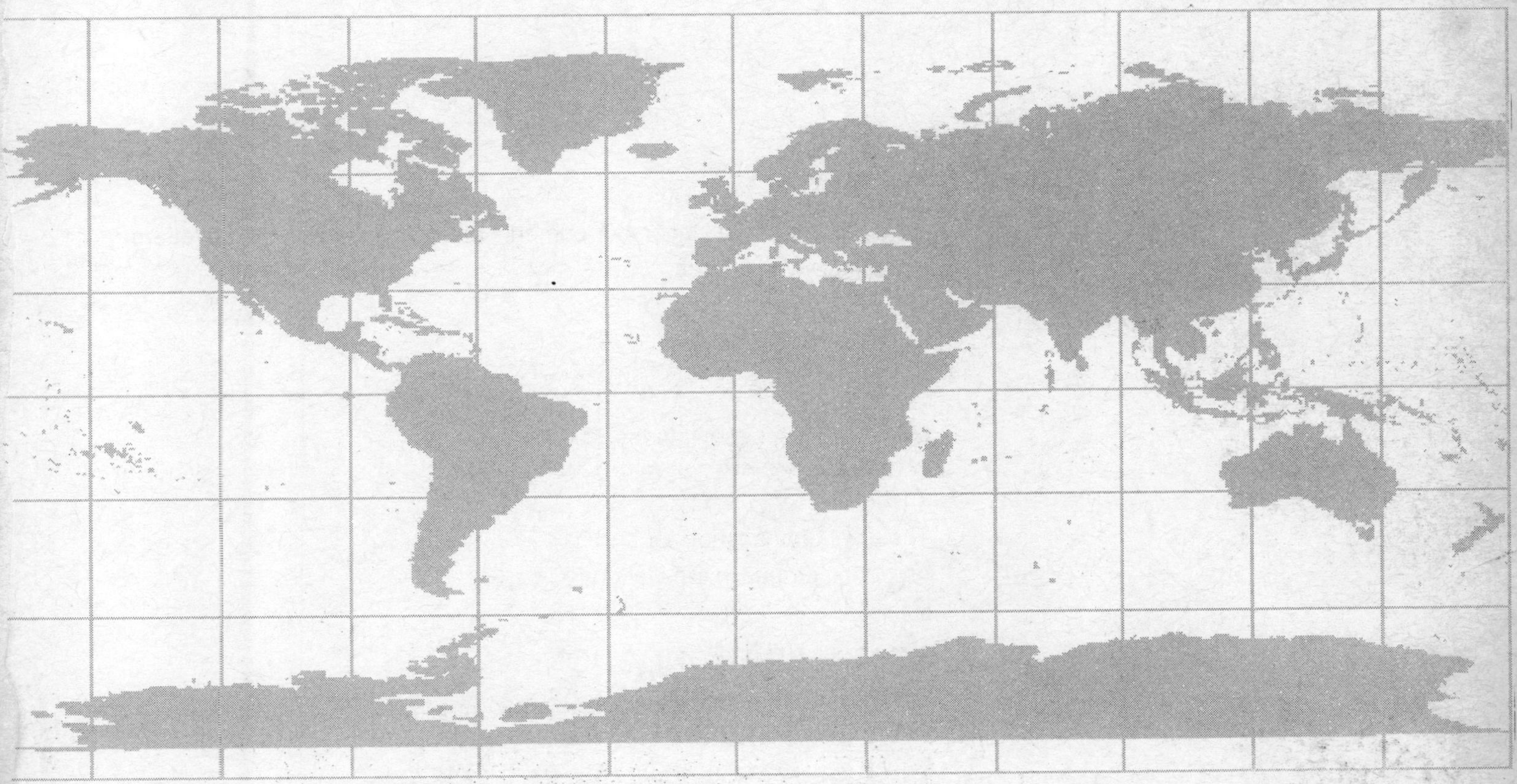

The work is published for
and on behalf of the United Nations

AF
ACADEMIC FOUNDATION

DESA

The Department of Economic and Social Affairs of the United Nations Secretariat is a vital interface between global policies in the economic, social and environmental spheres and national action. The Department works in three main interlinked areas: (i) it compiles, generates and analyses a wide range of economic, social and environmental data and information on which States Members of the United Nations draw to review common problems and to take stock of policy options; (ii) it facilitates the negotiations of Member States in many intergovernmental bodies on joint courses of action to address ongoing or emerging global challenges; and (iii) it advises interested Governments on the ways and means of translating policy frameworks developed in United Nations conferences and summits into programmes at the country level and, through technical assistance, helps build national capacities.

Note

Symbols of United Nations documents are composed of capital letters combined with figures.

UNITED NATIONS PUBLICATION

The work is published for and
on behalf of the United Nations
by

ACADEMIC FOUNDATION

4772 / 23 Bharat Ram Road, (23 Ansari Road),
Darya Ganj, New Delhi - 110 002.

Tel : +91-11-23245001 / 02 / 03 / 04
Fax : +91-11-23245005
e-mail : academic@vsnl.com
www.academicfoundation.com

ISBN 81-7188-460-1

This edition is printed in India in 2005.

Preface

This part of the ***World Economic and Social Survey 2004*** deals with a subject that profoundly affects the economic and social fabric of all nations—international migration.

More people live outside their country of origin today than at any time in history, and the numbers of people who move across international borders in search of a new home are expected to rise in the future. At the same time, there is growing awareness in many countries of the impact of migration, and it has become a matter of intense policy debate.

This is only to be expected. After all, migration brings with it many complex challenges—including issues of human rights and economic opportunity, of labour shortages and unemployment, of brain drain and brain gain, of multiculturalism and integration, of refugee flows and asylum-seekers, of law enforcement and human trafficking, of human security and national security.

We cannot ignore the real policy difficulties posed by migration. But neither should we lose sight of its immense potential to benefit migrants, the countries they leave and those to which they migrate. And we must ensure that, in our approach to this issue, we uphold the values of tolerance and respect for human rights.

If States work together in that spirit—as many are already doing—the benefits of migration can be maximized, and its problems minimized. I have no doubt that, through strengthening multilateral cooperation, States can find rational, creative and principled ways to protect the rights of migrants, and promote their shared interest in the better management of emigration, immigration and transit.

In this context, I particularly welcome the decision of a group of developed and developing countries to establish a Global Commission on International Migration, and look forward to its report next year. I am also glad that the United Nations General Assembly is to convene a high level dialogue on international migration in 2006.

The present volume provides a comprehensive review of developments in international migration, and of the diverse issues involved. It is a collaborative effort of the United Nations Department of Economic and Social Affairs, the United Nations Conference on Trade and Development and the Office of the United Nations High Commissioner for Refugees. I hope that the information and analysis in this volume will assist all concerned with international migration, and advance our joint responsibility to manage this issue for the benefit of all.

KOFI A. ANNAN
Secretary-General

Overview

International migration is one of the central dimensions of globalization. Facilitated by improved transportation and communications and stimulated by large economic and social inequalities in the world, people are increasingly moving across national borders in an effort to improve their own and their family's well-being. In the past few decades, international movements of people have increased alongside, though less strongly than, the expanded international flows of goods and capital. International migration is an increasingly worldwide phenomenon, involving a growing number of States as countries of origin, destination or transit of migrants. The forces underlying these trends are unlikely to reverse so that these international movements of people will continue—and most probably increase—in the future.

The increased mobility of people across national borders has affected not only the migrants themselves but also the lives and welfare of many peoples and societies, as well as the functioning of States and groups of States. As with increasing flows of goods and capital, it is necessary for Governments—and the international community—to decide how to address this facet of global development. The present publication examines the background and the nature of the increase in international migration and its wide-ranging impacts, and identifies the policy challenges posed by these developments.

International migration in the nineteenth and in the early twentieth century

The period between the Napoleonic wars and the First World War, from 1820 to 1914, was characterized by freer international movement of goods, capital and labour and has been referred to as the "first global century". Innovations in both transoceanic shipping and transcontinental railways made possible major intercontinental flows of people seeking better lives in the expanding economies.

The most important component of the migratory flows during this period encompassed those that occurred between two parts of today's developed world. The rapid economic growth in the Americas and Oceania attracted European workers in numbers that, relative to the population of the destination countries, have not been surpassed since. Available data indicate that about 52 million Europeans migrated to the main destination countries in the Americas between 1820 and 1932, of whom 32 million were admitted by the United States of America alone. An additional 3.5 million migrated to Australia and New Zealand. These migration flows tended to accelerate in the last decades of the nineteenth and in the early twentieth century, as "new" source countries in Southern, Central and Eastern Europe replaced the earlier sources of migration flows, largely countries in Northern Europe.

These large flows of people played a major role in the population growth of some of the countries of destination during this period. In Argentina, for instance, migration between 1870 and 1910 increased the population by 60 per cent and the labour force by almost 90 per cent. On the emigration side, Europe lost 11 per cent of its population and 13 per cent of its labour force to migration, with a few countries (Ireland and Italy) losing as much as 30 per cent of their labour force. International migration helped tie

Western Europe to the economies of Northern America, southern Latin America and Oceania, creating what is referred to as the Greater Atlantic economy.

The large movements of workers, whose major incentive for emigration was the large difference in wages and economic opportunities between the countries of origin and the countries of destination, did have an effect on these relative wages. Indeed, migration was the major reason for a convergence in wages across the Greater Atlantic economy between 1880 and 1920, particularly with respect to the Western European countries of origin of migrants on the one hand and the United States and other destination countries on the other. One estimate is that, between 1870 and 1910, emigration increased real wages in the countries of origin by nearly 9 per cent and lowered them by 8 per cent in the countries of destination, with the magnitudes of the effects in individual countries being directly related to relative migratory flows. Despite this narrowing of wage differentials across countries, the rapid economic growth of the countries of destination, which was supported by—and, indeed, could hardly be understood in the absence of—large migration flows, caused the real wages of low-income migrants in destination countries to improve over time.

The nineteenth century also witnessed large flows of migrants among developing countries, notably the flows of contract labour from China and India who moved to other developing countries to work on estates and plantations. The vast majority of Indian migrants to other developing countries were indentured and otherwise assisted, whereas Chinese emigration occurred under the coolie system with individual contracts that were often exploitive. The differences between wages of workers in the export enclaves and those of estate and plantation workers were higher than they were within the Greater Atlantic economy. However, migration between developing countries was constrained by its high cost in relation to incomes: incomes in China and India were so low that few unskilled workers could secure the funds to pay for the move. It was also constrained by the relative immobility of labour in most traditional rural societies. Thus, relative to the population of the source countries, migration flows were much smaller than those that characterized the European countries of emigration; return migration was also more important, particularly to India.

The demand for labour in estates and plantations was driven by the improvement in the terms of trade of tropical primary goods that lasted for more than a half-century. When prices of exports declined (as did those of sugar in the 1880s and those of other major commodities in the following decades), the recruitment of contract labour for the estates and plantations declined as well. Assisted migration between the developing countries thus came to an end largely for economic reasons. The most exploitative forms of indenture were also subject to political opposition and eventually abolished.

These two flows of migration ran largely parallel to each other, owing to the open discrimination against Asian migrants in the countries of settlement in America and Oceania. The high segmentation of European and non-European migration flows became a major source of North-South inequalities which built up during this period.

In the main countries of destination for European migrants, increasingly restrictive immigration policies and public hostility towards migrants emerged towards the end of the nineteenth century, and became harsher after the First World War. In the United States, restrictive legislation targeted immigrants from "new" source countries in Southern, Central and Eastern Europe. These restrictive immigration policies could be understood as a reaction of political authorities in destination countries in defense of the economic interests of their unskilled workers. Although transatlantic migration resumed briefly during the 1920s, it dropped again to very low levels during the Great Depression.

Migration during the current period of globalization

After a period of relative stability, international migration increased markedly over the last decades of the twentieth century, particularly after 1970 (see table 1). The number of international migrants in the world had risen from 76 million in 1960 to 82 million in 1970, reached 100 million in 1980 and increased to 154 million in 1990; the sharp increase in the 1980s was largely owing to the fact that internal migrants in the former Union of Soviet Socialist Republics (USSR) had become international migrants when the country disintegrated. By 2000, an estimated 175 million persons were living outside their country of birth (see table 2). Of these, about 158 million were deemed international migrants; approximately 16 million were recognized refugees fleeing out of a well-founded fear of persecution; and 900,000 were asylum-seekers.

Most countries have not been countries of immigration or countries of emigration for lengthy periods. Between 1950 and 2000, only seven countries consistently experienced net positive migration while 16 experienced steady negative net migration. Some countries of emigration have become destination countries, while in others, economic and political events have led to large fluctuations in migration trends.

Table 1.
International migrants in the main countries and regions of destination, 1910-2000

Thousands	1910			1930			1960			2000		
	Population	Migrants	Share[a]	Population	Migrants	Share[a]	Population	Migrants	Share[a]	Population	Migrants	Share[a]
Australia	4 455	787	17.7	6 630	356	5.4	10 276	1 701	16.6	19 153	4 705	24.6
Canada	7 207	1 587	22.0	10 377	2 308	22.2	17 909	2 766	15.4	30 769	5 826	18.9
New Zealand	1 008	306	30.3	1 534	77	5.0	2 372	334	14.1	3 784	850	22.5
United States	91 972	13 516	14.7	122 775	14 204	11.6	186 158	9 735	5.2	285 003	34 988	12.3
Sub-total: traditional countries of immigration	104 642	16 196	15.5	141 316	16 945	12.0	216 715	14 537	6.7	338 709	46 369	13.7
Argentina	7 885	2 358	29.9	10 922	2 828	25.9	20 616	2 615	12.7	37 074	1 419	3.8
Uruguay	1 080	181	16.8	..	..	..	2 538	192	7.6	3 342	89	2.6
Western Europe[b]	143 099	3 348	2.3	158 583	4 233	2.7	151 902	7 002	4.6	183 502	18 836	10.3
Total	256 706	22 083	8.6	310 821	24 006	7.7	391 771	24 346	6.2	562 627	66 713	11.9

Source: International Labour Office, *World Statistics of Aliens: A Comparative Study of Census Returns 1910-1920-1930*, Studies and Reports, Series O (Migration), No. 6. (Geneva, International Labour Office, 1936) and United Nations, *Trends in Total Migrant Stock: The 2003 Revision* (POP/DB/MIG/Rev.2003 and ESA/P/WP.188), data in digital form.

Note: Two dots (..) indicate that data were unavailable.

a Percentage.

b Comprising Belgium, France, Germany, Italy, Luxembourg and Switzerland only.

Table 2.
International migrants by region of destination, 1960-2000

Millions					
Region	1960	1970	1980	1990	2000
World	75.9	81.5	99.8	154.0	174.9
Developed countries	32.1	38.3	47.7	89.7	110.3
Developed countries excluding USSR	29.1	35.2	44.5	59.3	80.8
Developing countries	43.8	43.2	52.1	64.3	64.6
Africa	9.0	9.9	14.1	16.2	16.3
Asia[a]	29.3	28.1	32.3	41.8	43.8
Latin America and the Caribbean	6.0	5.8	6.1	7.0	5.9
Northern America	12.5	13.0	18.1	27.6	40.8
Oceania	2.1	3.0	3.8	4.8	5.8
Europe[b]	14.0	18.7	22.2	26.3	32.8
USSR (former)	2.9	3.1	3.3	30.3	29.5

Source: United Nations, *Trends in Total Migrant Stock: The 2003 Revision* (POP/DB/MIG/Rev.2003 and ESA/P/WP.188), data in digital form.

a Excluding Armenia, Azerbaijan, Georgia, Kazakhstan, Kyrgyzstan, Tajikistan, Turkmenistan and Uzbekistan.

b Excluding Belarus, Estonia, Latvia, Lithuania, the Republic of Moldova, the Russian Federation and Ukraine.

Reflecting the increasingly global nature of migration, there has been greater diversity both in the countries from which international migrants originate and in their countries of destination. This is because the dominant trend since the 1970s has been the growing migration flows from the developing to the developed countries. Intercontinental flows of migrants mostly from Europe to a few traditional countries of immigration have waned as migrants from many developing countries, particularly in Asia and Latin America and the Caribbean, have become more numerous throughout Western Europe and Northern America. Europe is now home to the largest number of international migrants, followed by Asia and Northern America. In relative terms, Oceania has the largest ratio of migrants to total population, followed by Northern America, Europe and Africa. Reflecting the increased diversity in destinations, the number of countries in which migrants exceeded 10 per cent of the population, which had been 43 in 1960, rose to 70 in 2000 (although most of these were small countries). Geographical proximity is important in determining migrants' countries of destination, with historical ties, especially colonial links, becoming of diminished importance in this respect.

One break with past patterns was the increase in flows of migrants from Eastern Europe to the West during the transition following the end of communist rule in Eastern Europe and the break-up of the former USSR. This break-up also produced important flows of migrants among the successor States of the former USSR, driven in part by the return of some ethnic groups to their newly independent countries of origin. These new trends have modified the major poles of attraction in Europe, with a number of countries of Southern Europe being transformed from net sources of migrants to net receivers.

Although migration flows in the last decades of the twentieth century were, relative to population, weaker than during the last decades of the nineteenth and the first decade of the twentieth century, they have played a significant role in demographic change in the developed world owing to the low fertility rates of these countries. Without inflows of migrants, Europe would have experienced a population decline between 1995 and 2000 since, even with about 5 million immigrants in this period, its population increased by only 600,000. Northern America experienced positive natural population growth during the same period, but net migration accounted for 43 per cent of the total increase in population. In contrast, the negative net migration from developing countries has had only a small effect on overall population trends. In 1995-2000, the net migration rate of the developing countries was -0.6 per thousand annually, small in relation to the rate of natural increase of 16.7 per thousand.

Unauthorized migration is, by its very nature, not well reflected in official statistics, but it is still possible to gain some insight into its magnitude. In the United States, combined evidence from various sources suggests that there were at least 7 million unauthorized migrants at the time of the census in 2000, out of a total of 31 million foreign-born persons in the country who were not US citizens at the time of birth. Of the unauthorized, an estimated 4.8 million were Mexican. In Europe, the International Organization for Migration (IOM) has estimated that the number of unauthorized migrants was about 3 million in the late 1990s. However, estimates for individual countries vary widely. In particular, little is known about the levels of unauthorized migration in countries of Central and Eastern Europe; during the 1990s, these were countries of transit for unauthorized migrants heading to Western Europe, but they also became de facto destinations for those migrants who could not proceed in their westward journey.

That the growth in the number of international migrants who settle in the developing world has been slow is not because migration between developing countries has ceased, but rather because migration flows are to large extent temporary spurts associated with economic booms in destination countries or political events in countries of origin. Increases in the number of migrants in some developing countries have also been counterbalanced by declines in immigration in other developing countries as a result of economic crises or the normalization of political events in a specific region. Following the increase in oil prices in 1973, the oil-producing countries of Western Asia began recruiting large numbers of foreign workers and Venezuela became a large pole of attraction for workers from neighbouring countries. The rapidly industrializing countries of Eastern and South-eastern Asia also emerged as destinations for migrant workers in the 1980s and 1990s. However, in the 1990s, the increases in economically motivated migration in Asia were offset by the repatriation of refugees in Africa, Central America and South-central Asia.

These recent return flows are a reflection of the importance of involuntary international displacements in some parts of the developing world, caused mostly by conflict but also by natural disasters. In Africa, Central America and in certain parts of Asia, movements of refugees have been a major—and, in some cases, the main—component of international migration flows among developing countries. The number of refugees under the mandate of the Office of the United Nations High Commissioner for Refugees (UNHCR) had increased from 2 million in 1975 to 16 million in 1990, but declined during the 1990s as a number of long-standing conflicts came to an end. By 2000, the number of refugees reported by UNHCR had dropped to 12 million. In addition, there were some 4 million Palestinian refugees receiving assistance from the United Nations Relief and Works Agency for Palestine Refugees in the Near East (UNWRA).

Another group of "involuntary" migrants are asylum-seekers endeavouring to escape the threats that they face in their home country. In contrast with the mass movements of refugees, these flows consist largely of individuals or families that are more inclined to move to developed than to developing countries.

Global economic effects of international migration

As a result of restrictions imposed on immigration, the effects of international migration on population growth, labour supply and labour markets are smaller today than they were during the first global century. The universal restrictions on immigration also contrast with the current increasingly unrestricted environment for international flows of foreign direct investment (FDI) and financial capital. This asymmetry in the mobility of different factors of production has an adverse distributive impact on the less mobile factor, labour. This effect, together with the small effect that migration flows have on population and labour-force growth in the developing countries as a whole, implies that, even if the general trends are similar, international migration is unlikely to have the same effect in terms of income convergence that it had during the first global century. In addition, the tendency of developed countries to favour the admission of skilled migrants reinforces the segmentation of labour markets in terms of skills and may be generating a distributive effect worldwide in favour of the more mobile form of labour (skilled labour) but directed against the less mobile one (unskilled labour).

For individual countries of origin and of destination, migration has a number of tangible positive and negative economic effects (table 3). In some cases, the benefit to a country of origin (destination) has its counterpart in an equal but opposite cost to the country of destination (origin), as in the case of remittances. Even in such cases, however, the effects may not be equal in magnitude and opposite in sign because the same financial

Table 3.
"Balance sheet" of economic effects of migration on countries of origin

Positive effects	Negative effects
• Provides opportunities to workers • not available in the home country. • May ease the effect on the domestic market of the supply of excess labour. • Inflow of remittances and foreign exchange. • Technology transfer, investments and venture capital contributed by diasporas. • Can contribute to increased trade flows between sending and receiving countries. • Stimulus to investment in domestic education and individual human capital investments. • Return of skilled workers may increase local human capital, transfer of skills and links to foreign networks.	• Loss of highly skilled workers and reduced quality of essential services. • Reduced growth and productivity because of the lower stock of highly skilled workers and its externalities. • Lower return from public investments in public education. • Selective migration may cause increasing disparities in incomes in the home country. • Loss of fiscal revenue from taxation of workers. • Remittances may diminish over time.

Source: UN/DESA, partly based on Piyasiri Wickramasekara, "Policy responses to skilled migration: retention, return and circulation", *Perspectives on Labour Migration, 5E* (Geneva, International Labour Office, 2002).

resources may be put to very different uses in the two countries. This difference may be more marked with respect to the international transfer of human capital that migration involves: the consequences of the loss of a skilled person for the country of origin may be greater than the benefit to the country of destination.

Economic impacts of international migration on countries of origin

The adverse effects of the "brain drain" are the most common concern regarding migration for countries of origin. The country of origin of a skilled migrant loses both its earlier investment in the education and training of the person who emigrates and the future contributions that person would have made to the economic development of the home country, including future tax payments. The significance of the brain drain for development is underscored by the "new growth theory" which argues that a person's knowledge not only provides a direct benefit in terms of available skills but also has positive effects on the productivity of others. Emigration of those with skills eliminates this indirect benefit to the economy at large.

This phenomenon underlies the incoherence that characterizes development policies and immigration policies in developed countries. Development assistance is frequently invested in education, training, health and advanced technologies for developing countries while, at the same time, the immigration policies of developed countries encourage the departure of those trained, including persons with critical skills, such as health personnel. Aware of the detrimental effects of such emigration, some developed countries have introduced policies and measures to reduce their intake of personnel whose skills are needed for the development of the countries of origin.

Standing in contrast with the loss of human resources embodied in brain drain is the financial transfer to the home country represented by the remittances sent by migrants to their families. Data on remittances are incomplete and almost certainly underestimate the true magnitude of such transfers because they do not accurately reflect funds flowing through informal channels. Nevertheless, available data show that remittances have grown in parallel with the number of international migrants and are estimated to have reached $130 billion in 2002, $79 billion of which went to developing countries (figure I). Although the different uses of flows make the comparison imprecise, for developing countries as a group, remittances have become the second largest financial flow, smaller than FDI but surpassing official development assistance (ODA). Most remittance flows to developing countries go to Latin America and the Caribbean, followed by Eastern and Southern Asia (figure II). Sub-Saharan Africa receives only 1.5 per cent of remittance flows. The European Union (EU) is the largest source of remittance payments, followed by the United States and countries in the Middle East.

Remittances are most often used for the consumption that satisfies basic subsistence needs, but they also encourage investment, particularly in human capital, through health and education expenditures. Remittances may also be turned into savings and investment, through the purchase of land, tools or machinery, or by helping to start a business. A noteworthy development has been the formation of hometown associations in countries of destination through which migrants collect funds to send back to the community of origin for the financing of local development projects.

Figure 1.
Selected financial flows to developing countries, 1980-2003

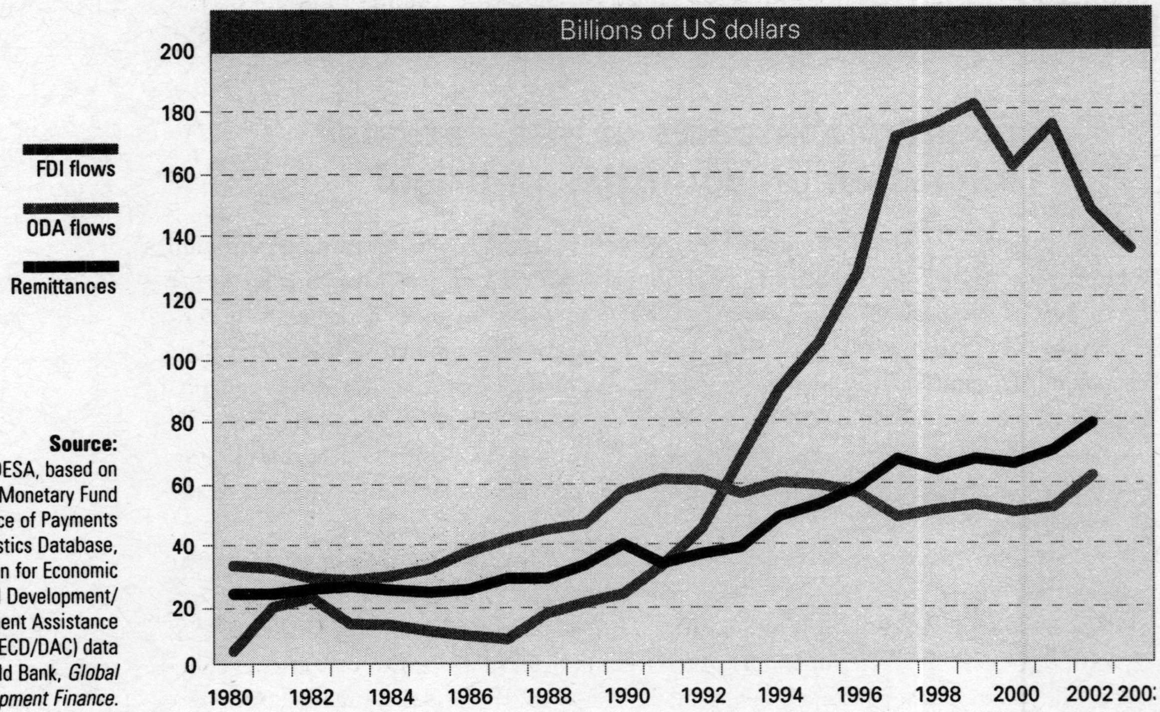

Source: UN/DESA, based on International Monetary Fund (IMF), Balance of Payments Statistics Database, Organization for Economic Cooperation and Development/ Development Assistance Committee (OECD/DAC) data and World Bank, *Global Development Finance.*

Figure 2.
Inflows of remittances by region, 1980 and 2002

Source: UN/DESA, based on International Monetary Fund (IMF), Balance of Payments Statistics Database, Organization for Economic Cooperation and Development/ Development Assistance Committee (OECD/DAC) data and World Bank, *Global Development Finance.*

In addition to sending remittances, there are other, broader forms of contact that migrants are likely to maintain with their country of origin. These may generate flows of knowledge, investment and trade to and from that country. For instance, approximately 70 per cent of total FDI flows to China originate among the Chinese community abroad, especially among those living in South-East Asia. Some migrants return to their home country, bringing with them new skills and experience that may improve domestic productivity and accelerate growth. These types of positive impacts of international migration have encouraged Governments in some countries of origin to facilitate emigration. Several countries of origin have arrangements to facilitate contacts between migrants abroad and their families, friends, business and academic communities in the country of origin, and to make it easier for migrants to use their skills and benefit from investment opportunities when they return home.

Economic impacts on destination countries

In destination countries, the main economic concern with respect to international migration is its impact on the labour market. The fear of losing jobs or of reduced wages owing to the influx of migrants is often widespread among the native population, particularly among those occupying jobs at the lower end of the labour market. Despite the efforts of destination countries to attract skilled migrants, many temporary and unauthorized migrants are unskilled and occupy those lower-end jobs. However, empirical studies show that migrants have only a modest impact on wages and employment. Even historical cases of large inflows of migrants during a short period of time —as exemplified by the return of settlers to France from Algeria in 1962 and to Portugal from Angola and Mozambique in 1974, as well as by the entry of Cubans into Miami in 1980—were not marked by a major impact on the local labour market of the developed countries involved. However, where labour markets are less flexible, the absorption of migrants may be more difficult and the negative effects on native workers may be more pronounced.

The major reason why migrants do not have a significant impact on the labour market, particularly over the medium term, is that they increase not only the labour supply but also the demand for goods and services. In addition, some use their entrepreneurial abilities to set up businesses. These activities, together with their dynamic and multiplier effects, increase the demand for labour, offsetting the initial increase in the labour supply that migrants represent. Because of such effects, migration inflows have been identified as a factor that increases economic growth to the benefit of the destination country and all its citizens. This is particularly the case if inflows of skilled workers relieve shortages in important sectors of the labour market. They may also increase the supply of labour in low-skilled occupations that domestic residents are unwilling to fill, thus complementing rather than substituting for domestic labour.

Studies also show that migrants tend to be net contributors to fiscal revenue: what migrants, on the whole, pay in taxes is greater than what they cost the State in welfare payments, education and additional infrastructure. Because migrants tend to be of working age, they also relieve the fiscal burden of future generations in low-fertility countries. However, migration cannot be the answer to the fiscal challenges created by an ageing population: Governments cannot rely on a constantly renewing and rapidly increasing group of migrants to generate the fiscal revenue needed to pay for the health costs and pension benefits of the elderly.

It is sometimes argued that international migration has contributed to the increase in economic inequality observed in several destination countries. However, other factors, such as skill-based technological progress, declining labour union membership, weakening social protection systems and the expansion of trade with labour-rich countries, have played a more important role.

Social integration of migrants

Migration affects the social fabric of both home and host societies. The dynamics of social relationships among migrants, and home and host societies are complex but the overriding challenge for host countries is to integrate migrants into local society. There have been two predominant approaches to the integration of migrants: assimilation and multiculturalism. Assimilation implies that migrants adopt the language, culture, values and beliefs of the host society. Multiculturalism recognizes ethnic, racial and cultural differences and promotes diversity within the host society. The policies and programmes to promote integration adopted by the Governments of destination countries vary according to the approaches pursued.

Since the 1970s, a multicultural approach has been favoured over assimilation in most developed countries. The increasing multiculturalism of many destination countries has improved the prospects for beneficial social interaction between migrants and the host society. Nevertheless, the social integration of migrants depends largely on the migrant's command of the host-country language, the migrant's ability to obtain employment that provides sufficient income, the migrant's legal status, her or his participation in the civil and political life of the host society, his or her access to social services and the likelihood of family reunification.

Recently, however, disenchantment with multicultural principles has arisen in some destination countries where there is increasing debate about ways of making migrants conform to national norms. Official reports suggest that migrants should be required to have some knowledge of the local language and to adopt local values, including acquiring civic knowledge. Some countries have also prohibited migrants from maintaining or practising certain national customs. More generally, there continues to be broad scope for increased action to promote respect of cultural, religious and ethnic diversity in most destination countries.

These trends indicate that, although migrants enrich destination communities socially and culturally by bringing with them different ideas, customs, languages, cultural values and religions, their presence may also be a source of discomfort and division in host societies. Almost every new and numerous migrant group has elicited some degree of opposition, if not outright stigmatization, as it integrates. The experience of some migrants today is reminiscent of the hostility that Huguenots once faced in England, that Germans, Italians or Irish experienced in the United States, or that Chinese confronted in the United States and Australia. Harmful public perceptions are reinforced if the media focuses only on the negative aspects of international migration, such as the persistence of unauthorized migration, criminal activities by migrants or problems related to integration. On the other hand, a lack of information may reinforce public perceptions that international migration and its social consequences are beyond the control of State authorities and may give rise to anti-immigrant political parties.

Networks of migrants are a valuable source of assistance and support, particularly for new migrants. With the emphasis that the immigration policies of developed countries put on family reunification, families are often the crucial unit for support, but support may also be provided by neighbours and colleagues at work. Potential migrants may receive information on life and jobs abroad from these networks even before they migrate and may be provided with guidance, information and support when they arrive in the host country. As a special form of network, hometown associations in host countries, in addition to serving as a financial conduit, help maintain the culture of migrants and assist with integration by providing a bridge to the host society. They also facilitate the exchange of information, goods and funds between the home and host countries.

National migration policies

National policies on international migration have been adopted to address an array of concerns, including the effects of low fertility and population ageing, unemployment, the protection of human rights, social integration, xenophobia, national security, the brain drain and the brain gain, remittances, the granting of asylum, undocumented movements and trafficking in persons. These concerns have led to a re-examination of international migration policies and of the potential benefits and disadvantages of international migration to countries of origin, destination and transit.

Immigration policies are mainly intended to have a bearing on the size and composition of international migration flows. The number of Governments adopting measures to restrict international migration has increased significantly in recent decades: by 2003, one-third of all countries had policies to lower immigration, compared with only 7 per cent of all countries in 1976. Moreover, there is now a similarity between developed and developing countries with respect to their propensity to pursue lower levels of immigration: in both groups, about one-third of the countries aim to reduce immigration.

Although most countries are gradually imposing tighter controls on immigration, restrictions based on nationality are much less important today than they were in the early and mid-twentieth century. For the majority of developed countries, family reunification has become a major factor for accepting migrants. At the same time, a growing number of developed countries are seeking to alleviate labour shortages by promoting the immigration of highly skilled workers and have thus introduced admission criteria that stress skills. As a result, migrants legally admitted to the major destination countries in the developed world for reasons other than family reunification have increasingly been skilled workers, but in many countries they are admitted only on a temporary basis. Except when it relates to migration for the family reunification of citizens, the concept of permanent migration is embraced only by the traditional countries of immigration (Australia, Canada, New Zealand and the United States).

Although admission policies have become more restrictive, destination countries are giving greater attention to policies that focus on the integration of non-nationals living in their midst. In 2003, 61 countries reported that programmes were in place for the integration of non-nationals, up from 52 countries in 1996. Policies for the integration of non-nationals are more common in developed than in developing destination countries. Measures to promote the integration of migrants include programmes to improve linguistic and vocational competence, steps to combat discrimination, measures to facilitate naturalization, the recognition of dual citizenship and, in a few countries, granting migrants the right to vote in local elections.

An important trend has been the development of policies in countries of origin to enhance the benefits that they derive from international migration and to reduce the costs they incur. Such policies include measures to facilitate migrants' remittances; support to networks that link migrants to their country of origin; the facilitation of return migration; the strengthening of consular services; and, in a few countries, dual citizenship and the right of emigrants to vote abroad in national elections.

Multilateral policy initiatives

The complexity of international migration and its growing scale have compelled Governments to move from a unilateral approach to the development of enhanced international cooperation in the management of migration, as a complement to the aforementioned policy initiatives at the national level. Consequently, the 1990s witnessed a renewed willingness of Governments to undertake cooperative efforts at the bilateral, regional and international levels to find novel ways of ensuring orderly migration.

Bilateral arrangements on international migration, which are a useful means of responding rapidly to changing migration trends or to specific issues, are not new; but there has been an upsurge in the number of agreements concluded since 1990. In addition, the range of issues covered by bilateral agreements has broadened to include temporary labour migration, the control of irregular migration, border management, the return of migrants in an irregular situation and the management of remittances. The bilateral approach, although effective for advancing the interests of two Governments, has generally a narrow geographical focus and thus makes a limited contribution to the regional or global management of international population mobility.

Managing international migration has also become a high priority of regional and subregional groups. EU has been at the forefront of regional initiatives, having adopted a phased approach to reaching agreement on the free movement of persons and workers among its member States. Elsewhere, a number of regional consultative processes on international migration were initiated in the 1990s and such arrangements now exist in most areas of the world, as exemplified by the Migration Dialogue for Southern Africa (MIDSA) and the Migration Dialogue for Western Africa (MIDWA), the Manila and Bali Processes in Asia, and the Puebla and Lima Processes in Latin America. Regional consultative processes offer a context for the development of common approaches to migration management, as they typically revolve around a particular issue, such as undocumented migration or trafficking in persons, on which consensus can be achieved relatively easily. By providing a venue for repeated contact and informal dialogue among policy makers in a region, these have become viable mechanisms of cooperation.

At the international level, the United Nations system and other multilateral institutions have undertaken a variety of activities through which to address international migration issues. The United Nations system has contributed to the formulation and adoption of legal instruments on international migration (see table 4) and has provided forums for intergovernmental dialogue on international migration issues. The United Nations Secretariat, including the regional commissions, has contributed to the collection, analysis and dissemination of information on international migration. Various other intergovernmental bodies and organizations have also been increasingly active in these areas, particu-

Table 4.
Legal instruments relevant to international migration

Instrument	Year adopted	Countries ratified[a]		*Of which:* Countries with net immigration at the time of ratification	
		Number	Percentage[b]	Number	Percentage[c]
Migrant workers					
ILO Convention concerning Migration for Employment (Revised 1949) (No. 97)	1949	42	21.5	12	28.6
ILO Convention concerning Migrations in Abusive Conditions and the Promotion of Equality of Opportunity and Treatment of Migrant Workers (Supplementary Provisions) (No. 143)	1975	18	9.2	8	44.4
International Convention on the Protection of the Rights of All Migrant Workers and Members of Their Families	1990	26	13.3	2	7.7
Smuggling and trafficking					
Protocol to Prevent, Suppress and Punish Trafficking in Persons, Especially Women and Children[d]	2000	54	27.7	16	29.6
Protocol Against the Smuggling of Migrants by Land, Air and Sea[d]	2000	48	24.6	14	29.2
Refugees					
1951 Convention relating to the Status of Refugees	1951	142	72.8	39	27.5
1967 Protocol relating to the Status of Refugees	1967	141	72.3	47	33.3

a As of 1 September 2004. The number includes non-member States of the United Nations and the Governments of Cook Islands and Niue.
b Of States Members of the United Nations.
c Of countries that have ratified.
d Supplementing the United Nations Convention against Transnational Organized Crime.

larly contributing to the formulation of global norms on migration management. The 1951 Convention relating to the Status of Refugees and the 1967 Protocol thereto have been ratified by a large number of countries, and the more recent protocols against the trafficking in persons have received increasing attention. Nevertheless, the conventions regarding the rights of migrant workers and their families have been ratified by only a limited number of countries and, particularly, by very few destination countries. Most importantly, however, there is no global institutional framework within which to address the full spectrum of international migration issues in a comprehensive and systematic manner.

Prospects and future role for international migration

Like the newly industrializing economies of the nineteenth century, many of the developed countries of the twenty-first century face shortages of labour, although the reasons and their consequences—low fertility rates and population ageing, resulting in a natural decline of population and rapidly rising support ratios—differ from those of the past. Many developed countries also face labour scarcity in a variety of specific areas, including highly skilled work in information and communication technologies (ICT), skilled labour in service activities and manual labour in agriculture, manufacturing and construction. Without increased migration, many of the demands for such labour will not be met and economic output and personal well-being in these countries will suffer. A less restrictive migration policy can contribute to overcoming these demographic and labour demands.

Migrants move today predominantly from developing to developed countries, but the need for migrant labour is also present in some developing countries, including the newly industrializing economies of South-East Asia and the oil-rich countries of the Gulf Cooperation Council (GCC). As noted above, however, migration policies in a growing number of developing countries are also becoming more restrictive. Such countries also need to give greater consideration to the benefits that a more liberal admission policy might produce.

Future trends in international migration are more difficult to predict than the other determinants of national population growth, particularly because, as the first half of the twentieth century showed, they can be directly and substantially affected by changes in migration policy in destination countries. At present, no radical or widespread shifts in policy are anticipated and the economic forces prompting migration are also expected to remain relatively unchanged. Under these assumptions, the migration trends of the past 40 years can reasonably be used to project migration flows over the next 40 years.

Combined with population projections to 2050, such extrapolations suggest that net emigration will continue to have only a small impact on the total population growth of developing regions in the future. Without migration, the increase in the population of developing regions from 2000 to 2050 is projected to be nearly 3 billion. With net emigration, the increase would be reduced to 2.8 billion. The reduction of population growth because of net emigration will be largest for Latin America and the Caribbean (13 per cent) but will be relatively small for Asia (5 per cent) and, particularly, for Africa (1 per cent) (see figure III).

In contrast, the natural increase in population in developed regions is expected to be negative and net migration is expected to be positive. Without net migration, the population of the more developed regions would decline from 1.2 billion in 2000 to 1.0 billion in 2050 but net international migration is expected to more than counterbalance the natural decline and a slight increase in the population will result. Among developed regions, the population decline due to an excess of deaths over births would be most acute in Europe—its population would decline by 139 million between 2000 and 2050. With the levels of international migration projected, Europe's population is still expected to decline, but by only 96 million.

Sustained positive levels of net international migration can play a role in offsetting natural reductions of the overall population or in the working-age population, but migration inflows should not be seen as an antidote to population ageing. The levels of

Figure 3.
Contribution of net international migration to population change, by region, 1995-2000 and 2045-2050

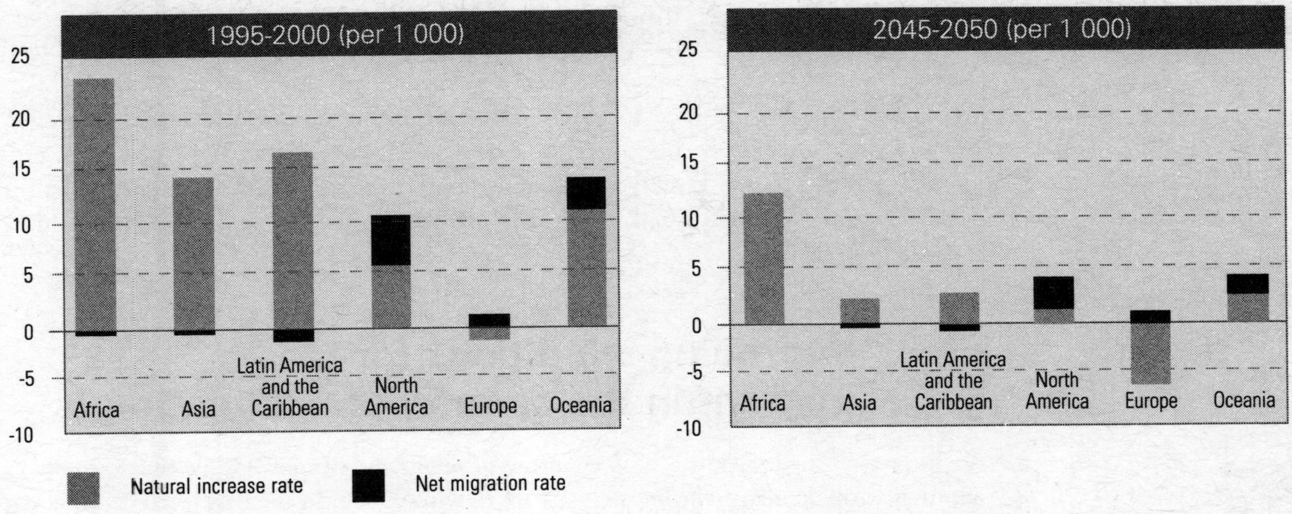

international migration needed to maintain the potential support ratio are high and unlikely to be socially or politically acceptable or sustainable for any society. For instance, the number of migrants required to maintain the potential support ratio constant in 2003 in the 15 States members of EU during 2000-2050 would be 13.5 million persons per year, some 20 times higher than recently recorded levels. By 2040-2050, the equivalent of about half of the world's annual population growth would have to emigrate to EU in order to maintain its present support ratio. Maintaining the size of the working population constant would require close to 1.6 million migrants a year, about three times the recent levels.

These estimates indicate that sustained or, better, rising migration flows can play a role in preventing reductions of the working-age population in developed countries. Nevertheless, the challenge of ageing population will require a comprehensive strategy that should also include reassessing the age of retirement and retirement benefits and increasing the labour-force participation of the working-age population.

One possibility for reducing the gaps between the demand and supply of labour in developed countries would be to increase temporary migrant flows. For destination countries, temporary migration might present fewer difficulties of social integration. For countries of origin, temporary work could reduce domestic unemployment and be a source of remittances (and, possibly, also of a capital gain in the form of repatriated assets); it might also reduce the impact of the brain drain if temporary migrants returned to their country of origin and use their newly acquired skills there.

The temporary movement of unskilled workers from developing to developed countries promises to bring the greatest gains because it is with regard to these two groups of countries that the difference between factor prices is greatest and the gaps between demand and supply are often the largest in absolute terms. The bilateral arrangements between Mexico and Canada, and Mexico and the United States, regarding the temporary movement of workers provide useful examples. Some oil-exporting developing countries also have well-defined schemes for temporary migration that exclude the possibility of long-term settlement.

There is also a demand for the temporary movement of skilled workers which may or may not include the highly skilled. Reflecting this demand, a multilateral framework for short-term movement is already in place in the form of Mode 4 of the General Agreement on Trade in Services under the World Trade Organization. Mode 4 illustrates the advantages of security and predictability that are provided by a binding multilateral instrument, such as the General Agreement on Trade in Services, compared with the bilateral agreements that are used to govern temporary flows of unskilled labour. However, Mode 4 could usefully be liberalized in a number of respects and the Doha work programme provides an opportunity for doing so. Simplifying some of the technicalities in the implementation of Mode 4 and broadening it to encompass less skilled labour would be major improvements.

Improving conditions for the migrant in the country of destination

At the level of the individual, both countries of origin and countries of destination need to ensure that the human rights of migrants are fully respected. In the first instance, all countries should take decisive action to eliminate smuggling and trafficking in migrants. Having been legally admitted into a country, migrants should obey national laws but should also be given protection by national legislation, especially to prevent discrimination, in accordance with international agreements relating to the protection of migrants. Governments should ensure that migrant workers are not exploited. Special protection may need to be accorded to migrant women, including illegal migrants, who have been subject to exploitation.

Governments of destination countries need to take measures to facilitate the integration of migrants in a manner that both protects their human rights and dignity and fosters mutual understanding between migrants and the host society. Such programmes and policies should be developed in partnership with associations of migrants, employers and trade unions. Offering appropriate education and labour training that allow all groups of migrants to access labour markets will also enhance the integration process. As part of this process, special attention should be accorded to measures that facilitate the naturalization of those migrants who have undergone a long period of residence in their country of destination. The decision of some countries to allow long-term migrants to vote in local elections should also be seen as a welcome development.

Public attitudes in a number of countries remain hostile to migrants. In several States, policies and programmes addressing migrants are unclear, enabling the issue of migration to become highly politicized and spurring the formation of anti-immigration movements. Governments should actively seek to reverse this trend by highlighting the benefits that migrants bring to the host country, promoting tolerance and understanding, and combating all forms of xenophobia.

One area of explicit social inequity in many countries is the non-portability of migrants' acquired retirement benefits. In addition to being in the interest of the migrant, this portability may foster the return of older migrants to their countries of origin. It is also of interest to employers wishing to attract internationally mobile workers with needed skills. Increasing the recognition of foreign educational and professional qualifications, skills and experience would be a further improvement in policy in countries of destination. The lack of such recognition often forces qualified migrants to work in jobs at a level well below their potential, resulting in a waste of human capital.

During the 1990s, as a result of both the proliferation of conflict in some areas of the world and the increasingly restrictive admission policies in developed countries, the number of persons seeking asylum in those countries increased. Recognition rates among asylum-seekers, however, remained low, suggesting that the asylum system was being used as a means of back-door entry by migrants. In order to reduce such potential abuse of the system, measures to expedite the processing of asylum claims have been introduced. It is important, however, to ensure that cases are adjudicated openly and fairly, with full respect for the human rights of those concerned, and that no person is forced to return to a situation where her or his life is in danger.

Increasing the benefits and reducing the costs of international migration for countries of origin

The flurry of attention being given to remittances by policy makers provides an opportunity to increase the benefits they provide. An immediate goal should be to reduce the transaction costs of remittances through a mix of improved regulation and enhanced competition, including making more information available about alternative means of transferring remittances. However, a balance has to be struck between efforts to facilitate the transfer of remittances and those to reduce money-laundering and other illegal financial practices. Countries of origin need to improve their financial environment to ensure that remittances are put to effective use. The measures needed to that end are similar to those required to promote development, although additional attention may need to be given to enhancing financial services, particularly in the rural communities from which many migrants originate.

Policies to facilitate the transfer of migrants' remittances should be part of broader policies in countries of origin to enhance the benefits from international migration, one of the most positive trends in recent years, as we have seen. Such policies should also include support to hometown associations, and business and academic networks that link migrants to their country of origin; the facilitation of return migration; the promotion of exports of idiosyncratic products destined to communities of migrants; and mechanisms that allow the political participation of migrants in the life of their countries of origin and dual citizenship.

The loss of skilled personnel by developing countries (brain drain) is related to the migration policies of destination countries wishing to attract persons with needed skills. To reduce the negative effects of the brain drain, destination countries should ensure that the selection of skilled migrants does not end up removing a critical proportion of the skilled personnel of individual developing countries, particularly in areas such as health, education and information technology. Coordination in this respect is crucial. For that reason, efforts to reduce the outflow of essential personnel from developing countries should be taken at the multilateral level. A complementary and useful approach would be for destination countries to defray the training costs involved if they continue attracting migrants in critical fields. For their part, countries of origin should monitor the extent of skilled emigration and, if necessary, take measures to address it, inter alia, by training more personnel in areas where there is an excessive outflow.

Towards improved international cooperation on migration

Since international migration is not likely to decrease in volume or importance in the foreseeable future, Governments have an interest in continuing to seek new and effective forms of international cooperation in migration management. While bilateral, regional and multilateral approaches each have their own strengths and limitations, the achievement of orderly migration calls for efforts at all levels, but preferably in the context of an overarching, universally agreed and applied international framework. Broad-based ratification of existing conventions and protocols would be a first major step in that direction.

A first responsibility in managing international migration flows requires an improvement in conditions and opportunities for potential migrants in their home countries and a reduction in the enormous gap between the well-being of the average individual in a developed country and that of most inhabitants of poorer countries. The international community's overall development agenda is therefore one essential component of the overall effort to manage international migration. Improving human well-being in the developing countries by achieving the Millennium Development Goals should, for example, reduce the large numbers of people who would emigrate if they had the opportunity.

At the same time, international migration is itself increasingly seen as a development issue. However, national and international migration policies do not yet fully reflect this development perspective and are sometimes inconsistent with other dimensions of development policy, particularly in the developed countries. It is therefore necessary to integrate migration policy into development policy, ensuring complete consistency and coherence between the two. Within both countries of origin and countries of destination, migration is usually not dealt with by the same ministry or ministries that deal with development policy; changes in institutional arrangements at the national level may therefore be needed if this divide is to be crossed.

From a development perspective, the present policy stances on international migration appear to be limiting the benefits that all could derive from larger migration flows. To overcome this limitation, it is important to ensure that all concerned—countries of destination, countries of origin, transit countries, the individuals who migrate and those left behind—recognize that well-managed international migration can be mutually advantageous. With such recognition, a process could be developed to ensure that the gains related to international migration are maximized, that the costs are minimized and that both gains and costs are shared appropriately.

In order to improve the necessary analysis and policy formulation, data on migration need to be improved. Concepts and definitions vary across countries and data collection is not universal. The most comprehensive data relate to the stock of migrants but they are not available for all countries. Data on flows of migrants are even scarcer, yet they are becoming increasingly important with the growing number and complexity of flows. To address some of these problems, the United Nations Statistics Division has issued a set of recommendations on how to improve international migration statistics. While the scarcity of resources for such purposes is recognized, it would be highly desirable to achieve nonetheless some improvement in international reporting on migration flows.

In addition to addressing the issue of international reporting, individual countries—particularly developed countries, since they are the destination of most migrants—may wish to consider producing national reports on international migration. These could indicate, for instance, the number of international migrants and such characteristics as age, sex, country of birth, citizenship, type of migration status, length of stay, type of employment, and nature and extent of financial and other resource flows to the countries of origin.

In terms of legislative actions, all countries should become parties to the international conventions and protocols on trafficking of persons, and on the rights of migrant workers and their families. In particular, many countries, including most destination countries, have yet to ratify the International Convention on the Protection of the Rights of All Migrant Workers and Members of their Families, which was adopted by the United Nations General Assembly in 1990 and entered into force in 2003.

International policies also need to address the situation of those who feel compelled to leave their home country out of fear for their safety. At the end of 2003, almost three quarters of the world's refugees were living in developing countries. To reduce the burden that large refugee flows impose on those countries, the international community needs to improve the mechanisms for burden-sharing, as called for by the Convention Plus initiative launched by the United Nations High Commissioner for Refugees.

Beyond existing conventions and protocols, the international community lacks a comprehensive international framework that addresses the wide range of issues pertaining to international migration. EU is at the forefront in addressing these matters within its region, primarily in terms of the harmonizing of policies and coordinating of actions that are being undertaken by its members cooperating as a group of destination countries. Migration is a global and transnational phenomenon involving various parties with differing perspectives and interests. It therefore calls for a global approach and a global framework.

There remains a need for cooperation, in the area of movements of people, as in that of flows of goods and capital, between countries of origin and countries of destination to ensure that the large international imbalances between the supply and demand for labour at all skill levels do not cause economic and social disruption at either the national, the regional or the global level. However, multilateral cooperation regarding international flows of labour has been negligible, particularly in comparison with the progress made in respect of international flows of goods and capital. This gap in international cooperation must be bridged, through an international framework that looks after the interests of both migrants and host communities.

The creation of the Global Commission on International Migration marks an important recent step in addressing international migration from a global perspective. Within the United Nations General Assembly, there have been calls for an international conference on migration, although no agreement has been reached. The high-level dialogue on international migration and development that will take place in the Assembly in 2006 will provide an opportunity to discuss all aspects of international migration with a view to maximizing its development benefits and minimizing its negative impacts. It will also create a valuable opportunity to integrate the results of various national, regional and international migration processes, so as to enhance cooperation among the members of the international community on this issue of global importance.

José Antonio Ocampo
Under-Secretary-General for Economic and Social Affairs
July 2004

Contents

Boxes

Figures

Tables

Explanatory Notes

The following symbols have been used in the tables throughout the report:

.. **Two dots** indicate that data are not available or are not separately reported.

– **A dash** indicates that the amount is nil or negligible.

- **A hyphen (-)** indicates that the item is not applicable.

- **A minus sign (-)** indicates deficit or decrease, except as indicated.

. **A full stop (.)** is used to indicate decimals.

/ **A slash (/)** between years indicates a crop year or financial year, for example, 1990/91.

- **Use of a hyphen (-)** between years, for example, 1990-1991, signifies the full period involved, including the beginning and end years.

Reference to "dollars" ($) indicates United States dollars, unless otherwise stated.

Reference to "tons" indicates metric tons, unless otherwise stated.

Annual rates of growth or change, unless otherwise stated, refer to annual compound rates.

In most cases, the growth rate forecasts for 2004 and 2005 are rounded to the nearest quarter of a percentage point.

Details and percentages in tables do not necessarily add to totals, because of rounding.

The following abbreviations have been used:

APEC	Asia-Pacific Economic Cooperation
ASEAN	Association of Southeast Asian Nations
CEMAC	Central African Economic and Monetary Community
CIS	Commonwealth of Independent States
COMESA	Common Market for Eastern and Southern Africa
ECE	Economic Commission for Europe
ECLAC	Economic Commission for Latin America and the Caribbean
ECOWAS	Economic Community of West African States
ENT	economic needs test
ESCAP	Economic and Social Commission for Asia and the Pacific
ESCWA	Economic and Social Commission for Western Asia
EU	European Union
Eurostat	Statistical Office of the European Communities
FDI	foreign direct investment
GCC	Gulf Cooperation Council
GDP	gross domestic product
GNP	gross national product
HTA	hometown association
ICMPD	International Centre for Migration Policy Development
IGC	Intergovernmental Consultations on Asylum, Refugee and Migration Policies in Europe, North America and Australia
ILO	International Labour Organization
IMF	International Monetary Fund
IOM	International Organization for Migration
IRCA	Immigration Reform and Control Act (United States)
MERCOSUR	Southern Common Market
MFN	most favoured nation
MIDA	Migration for Development in Africa
MIDSA	Migration Dialogue for Southern Africa
MIDWA	Migration Dialogue for Western Africa

MRAs	mutual recognition arrangements
NAFTA	North American Free Trade Agreement
NBER	National Bureau of Economic Research (Cambridge, Massachusetts)
OAS	Organization of American States
ODA	official development assistance
OECD	Organization for Economic Cooperation and Development
OSCE	Organization for Security and Cooperation in Europe
SAARC	South Asian Association for Regional Cooperation
SOPEMI	Continuous Reporting System on Migration (OECD)
TOKTEN	Transfer of Knowledge through Expatriate Nationals (UNDP)
UNCTAD	United Nations Conference on Trade and Development
UN/DESA	Department of Economic and Social Affairs of the United Nations Secretariat
UNDP	United Nations Development Programme
UNFPA	United Nations Population Fund
UNHCR	Office of the United Nations High Commissioner for Refugees
UNICEF	United Nations Children's Fund
UNITAR	United Nations Institute for Training and Research
UNRWA	United Nations Relief and Works Agency for Palestine Refugees in the Near East
WHO	World Health Organization

The designations employed and the presentation of the material in this publication do not imply the expression of any opinion whatsoever on the part of the United Nations Secretariat concerning the legal status of any country, territory, city or area or of its authorities, or concerning the delimitation of its frontiers or boundaries.

The term "country" as used in the text of this report also refers, as appropriate, to territories or areas.

For analytical purposes, the following country groupings and subgroupings have been used:[a]

Developed economies:

Europe, excluding the European transition economies
Canada and the United States of America
Japan, Australia and New Zealand.

European Union:[b]

Austria, Belgium, Cyprus, Czech Republic, Denmark, Estonia, Finland, France, Germany, Greece, Hungary, Ireland, Italy, Latvia, Lithuania, Luxembourg, Malta, Netherlands, Poland, Portugal, Slovakia, Slovenia, Spain, Sweden, United Kingdom of Great Britain and Northern Ireland.

Economies in transition:

Central and Eastern European transition economies:

Albania, Bulgaria, Romania and the following successor States of the Socialist Federal Republic of Yugoslavia: Bosnia and Herzegovina, Croatia, Serbia and Montenegro, the former Yugoslav Republic of Macedonia.

Commonwealth of Independent States (CIS)

Armenia, Azerbaijan, Belarus, Georgia, Kazakhstan, Kyrgyzstan, Republic of Moldova, Russian Federation, Tajikistan, Turkmenistan, Ukraine, Uzbekistan.

Developing economies:

Africa

Asia and the Pacific (excluding Japan, Australia, New Zealand and the member States of CIS in Asia)

Latin America and the Caribbean.

Subgroupings of Asia and the Pacific:

Western Asia:

Bahrain, Cyprus, Iran (Islamic Republic of), Iraq, Israel, Jordan, Kuwait, Lebanon, Oman, Qatar, Saudi Arabia, Syrian Arab Republic, Turkey, United Arab Emirates, Yemen.

Eastern and Southern Asia:

All other developing economies in Asia and the Pacific (including China, unless listed separately). This group has in some cases been subdivided into:

China

South Asia: Bangladesh, India, Nepal, Pakistan, Sri Lanka
East Asia: all other developing economies in Asia and the Pacific.

Subgrouping of Africa:

Sub-Saharan Africa, excluding Nigeria and South Africa (commonly contracted to "sub-Saharan Africa"):

All of Africa except Algeria, Egypt, Libyan Arab Jamahiriya, Morocco, Nigeria, South Africa, Tunisia.

---

a Names and composition of geographical areas follow those of "Standard country or area codes for statistical use" (ST/ESA/STAT/SER.M/49/Rev.3), with one exception, namely, Western Asia, which in the *Survey* includes the Islamic Republic of Iran (owing to the large role of the petroleum sector in its economy) and excludes the transition economies of the region. Also, "Eastern Europe", as used in this *Survey*, is a contraction of "Central and Eastern Europe"; thus the composition of the region designated by the term differs from that of the strictly geographical grouping.

b Reflects membership of the European Union up to 30 April 2004. Ten additional countries joined the Union on 1 May 2004.

International Migration

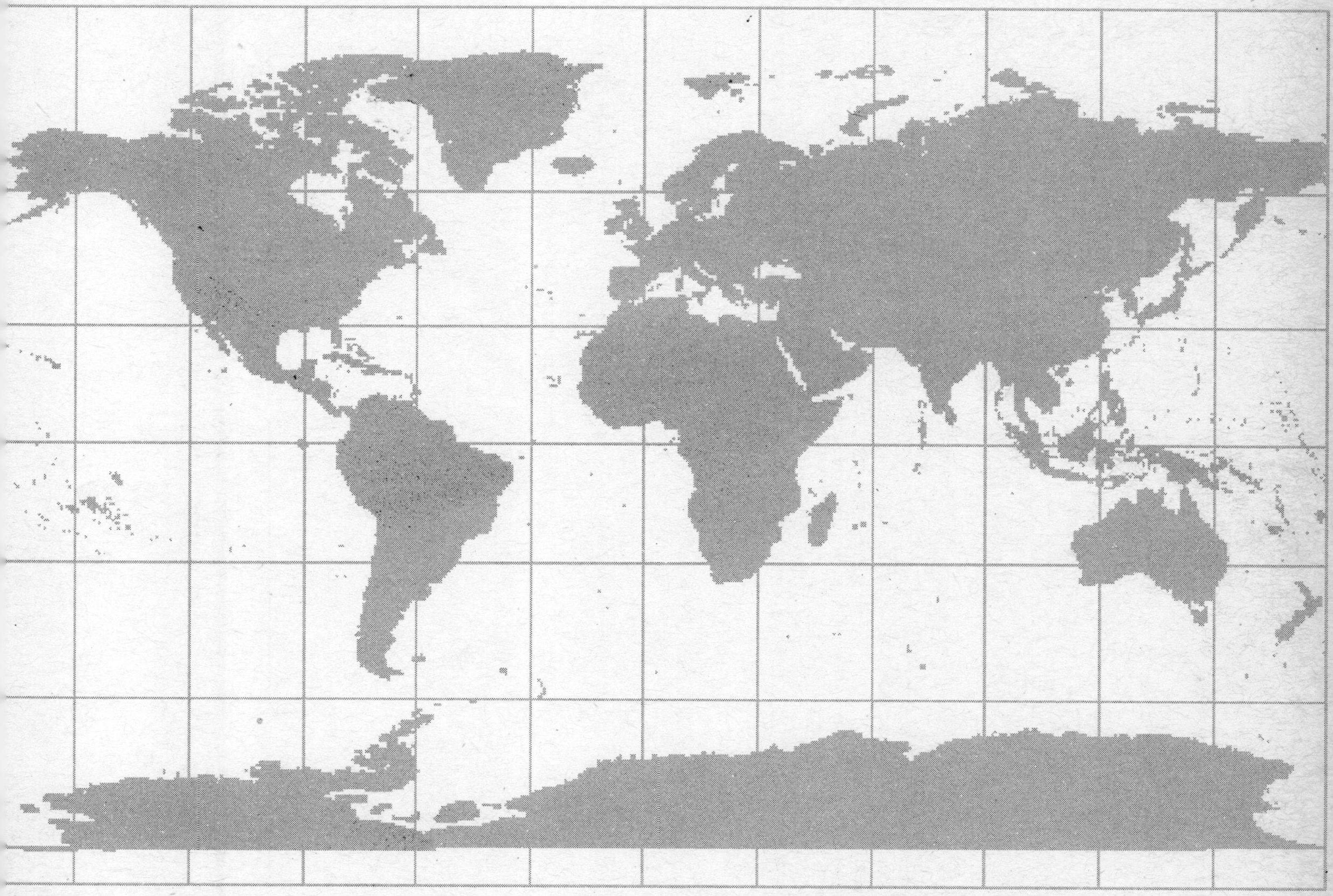

Chapter I
Migration during 1820-1920, the First Global Century

Introduction

Part two of the World Economic and Social Survey 2004 examines the consequences of international migration, a phenomenon that has largely determined the course of human history. Although humankind has always been migratory, large intercontinental migration began in the sixteenth century during the age of European expansion. The settlement of the colonies required the relocation of significant numbers of subjects of the colonial powers. This process gained momentum during the eighteenth century as the British Empire expanded and the settlement of overseas colonies accelerated.

In Latin America, labour needs during the colonial period were at first met by forcing the native population into servitude, but the expansion of the plantation economy in the eighteenth century, especially in Brazil, the French, English and Netherlands colonies of the Caribbean and South America, and the southern United States of America, required more workers than could be secured locally and led to the forced migration under slavery of workers from Africa. At least 10 million African workers were forcefully transferred to the Americas during the period 1700-1850, the majority of whom had originated on the western coast of Africa and in Madagascar (Potts, 1990).

A major component of the first great wave of intercontinental migration was the 10 million or more Africans transported as slaves to the Americas

Despite British efforts to suppress the slave trade, it continued to expand in the early part of the nineteenth century and was abolished only in the second part of that century in countries that had depended heavily on slave labour, such as Brazil and Cuba, and in the southern United States. With the gradual dismantling of the slave trade, other methods of securing needed labour were developed. Known under the general term of the coolie system, they involved the transportation of workers, often over long distances, to perform agricultural or infrastructure work at destination under a variety of binding contract arrangements, all of which involved the obligation to work for the contractor for a period of time. Between 1830 and 1930, at least 12 million persons, mostly from India and China, were traded as coolie labour (Potts, 1990).

The slave trade was succeeded by a system whereby 12 million or more persons were transported as indentured workers

The nineteenth century, particularly the period 1820-1920, also witnessed major intercontinental flows of people seeking better lives in the expanding economies of the Americas and Oceania. The rapid economic growth experienced by those regions attracted European workers in numbers that, relative to the population of the receiving countries, have not been surpassed since. Available data indicate that about 52 million Europeans migrated to the main receiving countries in the Americas between 1820 and 1932, 32 million of whom were admitted by the United States alone (Thomas, 1959). An additional 3.5 million migrated to Australia and New Zealand (ibid.).

During the nineteenth century, some 52 million Europeans emigrated to the Americas

The first global century, which started after the Napoleonic wars and ended with the First World War, was characterized by freer movement of goods, capital and labour. It witnessed relative peace in Europe and unprecedented economic growth linked to an expansion of trade and rapid technological progress which included a revolution in transportation. Although the late 1800s had witnessed a rise in protectionism and increasing restrictions on immigration, transatlantic migration peaked during the first decade of the twentieth century. Over the course of the first global century, migration helped tie Western Europe, where a large proportion of migrants had originated, to the major economies of North America, South America and Oceania, creating what we shall refer to as the Greater Atlantic economy.

The present chapter provides an overview of international migration during the first global century in order to provide a historical basis for the discussion of recent experience.[1] Although migration during the second half of the twentieth century differed in many respects from migration in the nineteenth and early twentieth centuries, the fact that both occurred during an era of increasing globalization permits parallels to be drawn between them, particularly with regard to economic aspects.

The economic context of mass migration in the nineteenth century

Industrialization and the demand for raw materials

During the nineteenth century, industrialization and demographics helped spur migration from Europe

During the nineteenth century, several European countries and the United States underwent a rapid process of industrialization. Furthermore, over the course of the century, improvements in nutrition, hygiene and preventive medicine led to reductions of mortality, particularly among the young, which increased population growth. These demographic changes contributed to increasing the labour supply in Europe and creating a context favourable to emigration.

A decline in the terms of trade of industrialized countries was accompanied by increased demand for primary products and falling transportation costs, ...

The industrialization that had led to the unprecedented rates of economic growth in the countries of origin and in some of the receiving countries, especially the United States, resulted in lower prices of manufactured products in both domestic and foreign markets, which in turn led to a decline in the terms of trade of industrialized countries, as exemplified by the case of the United Kingdom (fig. I.1). Some countries located in the periphery of European countries of origin and of the major countries of destination also benefited from the economic boom because it triggered increased demand for agricultural products, mineral resources and raw materials. The very favourable terms of trade that accompanied this boom lasted for more than a half century, until about 1895, as illustrated by the experience of Latin America (fig. I.2). It should be noted, however, that although such a trend was the obverse of the decline in the terms of trade of industrialized countries, falling transportation costs tended to improve the terms of trade of all countries.

... which in turn stimulated international migration

International migration helped the periphery generate the exports needed to fuel the expansion of the Greater Atlantic economy. The improvement of the terms of trade provided price incentives that set in motion this process in the resource-rich parts of the periphery. While the United States did become a major industrialized power over the course of the nineteenth century, it still shared some characteristics with countries of the periphery, particularly by being a supplier of food and raw materials to the industrialized countries of Europe.

Figure I.1.
Terms of trade, United Kingdom, 1820-1872

Source:
Jeffrey G. Williamson, "Williamson Data Appendix", Department of Economics, Harvard University, Cambridge, Massachusetts, 2004.

Figure I.2.
Terms of trade, Latin America, 1820-1938

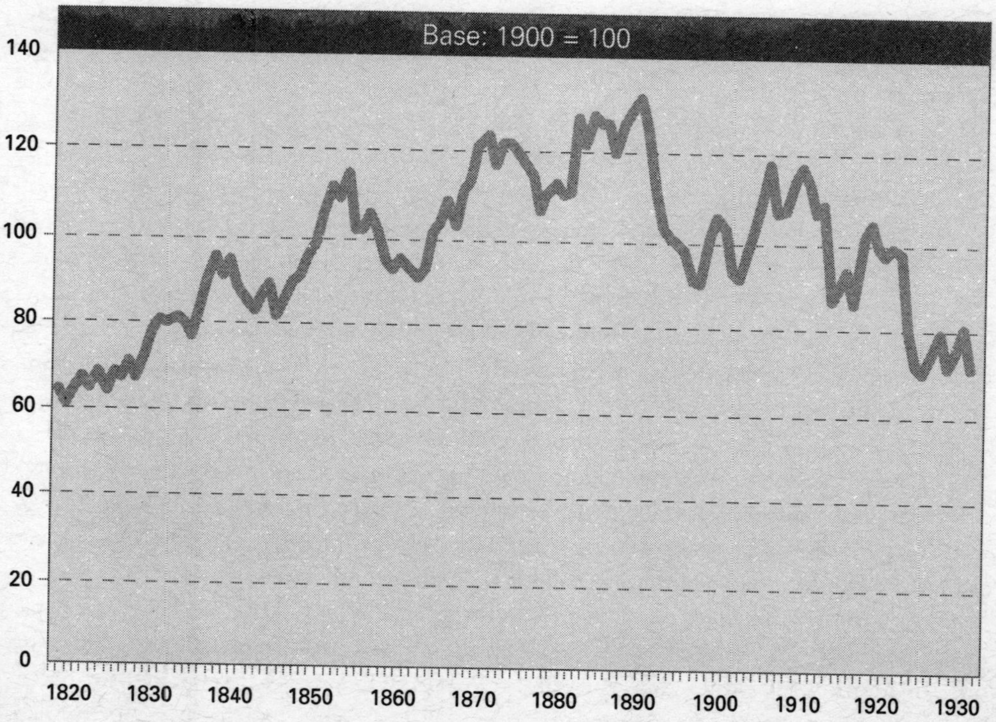

Source:
Jeffrey G. Williamson, "Williamson Data Appendix", Department of Economics, Harvard University, Cambridge, Massachusetts, 2004.

The transport revolution and the convergence of prices

Beginning around 1820, technological innovation led to rapid declines in transportation costs

Innovations in transportation, in terms of both transoceanic shipping and transcontinental railways, made possible both the mass migrations of the nineteenth century and the movement of the goods and raw materials needed to fuel the Greater Atlantic economy. Transportation costs had dropped rapidly between 1820 and 1860 and continued to decline during the rest of the century. For instance, between 1882 and 1914, the shipping rate for transporting rice from Rangoon to Europe fell from 74 to 18 per cent of the Rangoon price of rice, and the freight rate on sugar between Java and Amsterdam fell by 50 to 60 per cent (O'Rourke and Williamson, 1999, chap. 3). There were equally dramatic reductions in transportation costs between cities in the periphery. The freight rate on coal between Nagasaki, Japan, and Shanghai, China, fell by 76 per cent between 1880 and 1910.

The reduction of transportation costs contributed to reducing price differences between markets. For instance, wheat prices in Liverpool had exceeded those in Chicago by 58 per cent in 1870 but by only 18 per cent in 1895. Price convergence would appear even greater if account was taken of the collapse in price differences between Midwestern farm gates and Chicago markets, as well as between Liverpool prices and those paid by British consumers. This price convergence in Anglo-American wheat markets was paralleled by a similar one for the prices of other foodstuffs between markets such as London, Buenos Aires, Montevideo and Rio de Janeiro. Markets in the Russian Empire and the rest of the eastern European periphery also experienced a convergence to world prices: wheat price differences between Odessa and Liverpool, for instance, which had stood at about 40 per cent in 1870, had virtually disappeared by 1906. Commodity prices also converged in the eastern Mediterranean. The price difference on Egyptian cotton between Liverpool and Alexandria dropped from a high plateau after the 1860s. Thus, Liverpool price quotes exceeded those in Alexandria by 63 per cent in 1837-1846, by 41 per cent in 1863-1867 and by just 5 per cent in 1890-1899 (Issawi, 1966, pp. 447-448).

Transportation cost declines underpinned the growth of globalized markets

Reductions in transportation costs from a country's interior to a port and from ports to Europe ensured that African and Asian export-oriented enclaves would become more integrated into world markets. Thus, the price difference for raw cotton between Liverpool and Mumbai fell from 57 per cent in 1873 to 20 per cent in 1913, and that for jute in London and Calcutta fell from 35 to 4 per cent. The same changes were taking place even further east, involving Burma (now Myanmar) and the rest of South-East Asia: the price difference for rice between London and Rangoon fell from 93 to 26 per cent between 1870 and 1913. These trends had a profound impact on the emergence of an Asian market for wheat and rice, as well as of a truly global market for grains (Latham and Neal, 1983).

Later in the nineteenth century, transportation cost declines also began to benefit passengers, including migrants

Before the nineteenth century, overseas production had been largely determined by the needs of overseas populations. In the nineteenth century, with the reduction of transport costs, the resources of overseas countries could be profitably exploited by the industrializing countries of Europe, but a larger supply of overseas workers was needed to do so. Since Europe had those workers, emigration was encouraged, starting with the protection of passengers on board ship provided by the statutes of 1819 (Ferenczi and Willcox, 1929). Yet, until well into the nineteenth century, the transatlantic voyage continued to be long and risky. It had not been uncommon for from 1 to 10 per cent of emigrants to perish either on board ship or soon after landing. The multiplication of steamships and modified navigation techniques improved the situation. By 1870, use of sailing vessels to transport emigrants was rare. In addition, steamship companies and transportation agents actively recruited potential emigrants by providing rosy information on the many opportunities available overseas. Government assistance to emigrants also contributed to an increase in emigration.

Greater Atlantic migration during the first global century

The migration boom

Overseas migration within the Greater Atlantic economy increased over the course of the nineteenth century as industrialization proceeded and transport costs fell. Until around 1850, migration had been determined mainly by conditions in European countries because the lands beyond the sea were not well known or attractive. Moreover, the transatlantic journey was still costly and risky. Nevertheless, by the 1840s, emigration was increasing in parallel with the dismantling of legal restrictions placed on emigration. Periodic economic depressions and the ensuing rise in unemployment fuelled emigration. This was the case for Germany where a depression in the 1840s had led to the emigration of about 1.2 million Germans during 1844-1854 (Ferenczi and Willcox, 1929). Similarly, the potato famine that devastated Ireland in 1846-1847 caused a sharp rise in emigration. During 1835-1850, over 1.4 million Irish left their country (ibid.). Such high numbers of Irish contributed to making British citizens the dominant group among overseas European emigrants until the late 1870s.

The Greater Atlantic migration flows began in earnest around 1840

Between 1820 and 1910, the majority of British intercontinental passengers left for the United States. Perhaps three fifths of all British emigrants went to the United States. The second most important destination of British emigrants was Canada, followed by Australia and New Zealand. Emigrants to the British dominions in Oceania benefited from State aid in paying for the trip. Before 1840, Australia had mostly been regarded as a penal colony by the British Government. Between 1787 and 1860, about 131,000 criminals were forcefully transported to the colony to serve their sentences there (Ferenczi and Willcox, 1929). By the 1840s, the voluntary departure of settlers to Australia was rising and high numbers of British emigrants left for Australia in the 1850s after the discovery of gold in the colony.

It is estimated that during 1815-1924, about 18 million British subjects emigrated overseas. During the same period, between 5 million and 6 million Germans left Europe. These two groups plus the 2-3 million emigrants from the Scandinavian countries of Denmark, Finland, Norway and Sweden had constituted the major contingents of settlers going to transatlantic destinations until the 1880s. After 1890, emigration from southern, central and eastern Europe (the "new" sources of emigrants) became dominant, particularly that originating in Austria-Hungary, Italy, Poland, Portugal, the Russian Empire and Spain (fig. I.3).

Great Britain was the leading country of origin during the first phase (up to the 1880s) of the Greater Atlantic migration, followed by Germany and the Scandinavian countries; during the second phase, the leading countries of origin were located in Eastern and Southern Europe

The change in sources of emigrants coincided with the migration boom that occurred towards the end of the first global century. Indeed, during 1881-1915, average annual immigration to the major countries of destination reached 1,047,000, having risen from an annual average of 378,000 in 1851-1880 and from 188,000 in 1821-1850 (Kenwood and Lougheed, 1999, chap. 3). Yet migration levels did not remain uniformly high during 1881-1915 because an economic depression in the United States in the mid-1890s caused a drop in immigration. Recovery was swift, however, and immigration levels remained high until they were interrupted by the outbreak of hostilities during the First World War (fig. I.4).

Figure I.3.
New and old sources of immigration to the United States of America

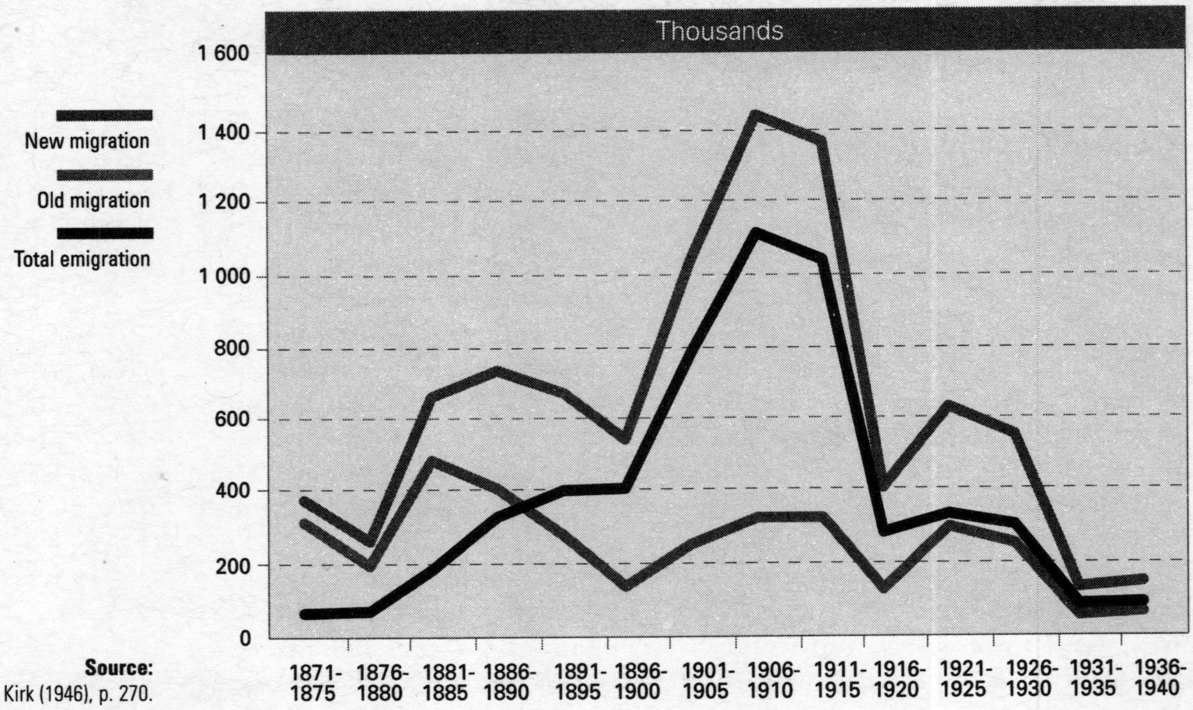

Source:
Kirk (1946), p. 270.

Figure I.4.
Immigration to chief New World destinations, 1881-1938

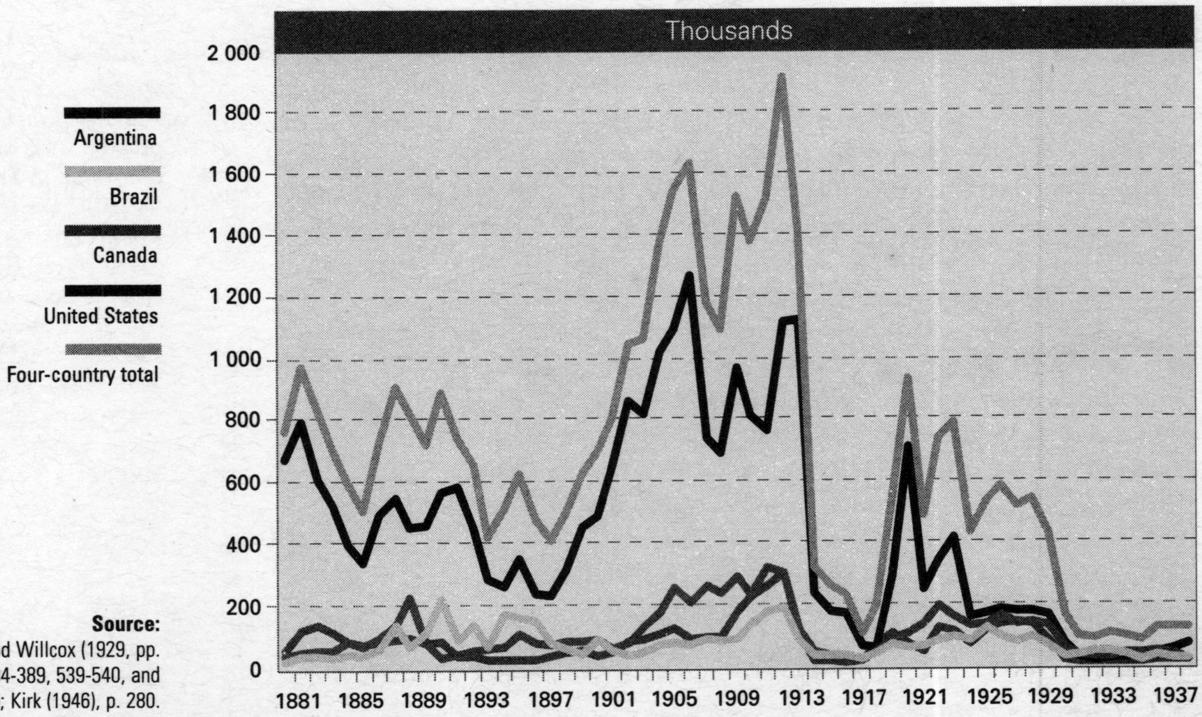

Source:
Ferenczi and Willcox (1929, pp. 361, 384-389, 539-540, and 550); Kirk (1946), p. 280.

As for the major destinations of overseas emigrants, the majority went to destinations in the Americas, where the United States was the major attraction pole. Argentina, Brazil and Canada were the other important countries of destination in the Americas (fig. I.4). Between 1890 and 1900, Argentina and Brazil each attracted a greater share of immigrants to the Americas than Canada, and Argentina was the second most important receiving country in the Americas during 1900-1924. Other Latin American countries receiving small but significant numbers of European migrants included Chile, Cuba, Uruguay and Venezuela. In Africa, South Africa was also a significant country of destination.

The leading country of destination was the United States, with Argentina, Brazil and Canada being other important countries of destination

Migration made major contributions to the population growth of some overseas countries. In Argentina, for instance, the population increased by 60 per cent between 1870 and 1910 and its labour force rose by 86 per cent (table I.1). Canada's population rose by 32 per cent and its labour force by 44 per cent in the same period. For the United States, the proportional increase was smaller because it had a larger base population, but its population rose by 17 per cent and its labour force by 24 per cent during 1870-1910. In total, the population of the New World (according to the definition adopted in table I.1) increased by 29 per cent and its labour force rose by 40 per cent. Concomitantly,

The first Greater Atlantic migration had a heavy demographic impact both on some countries of origin and on some countries of destination

Table I.1.
Cumulative impact of mass migration, 1870-1910

	Persons		Labour force	
	Net migration rate 1870-1910	Cumulative 1910 impact (percentage increase)	Net migration rate 1870-1910	Cumulative 1910 impact (percentage increase)
Argentina	11.74	60	15.50	86
Australia	6.61	30	8.73	42
Brazil	0.74	3	0.98	4
Canada	6.92	32	9.14	44
United States	4.03	17	5.31	24
New World	6.01	29	7.93	40
Belgium	1.67	7	2.20	9
Denmark	-2.78	-11	-3.67	-14
France	-0.10	0	-0.13	-1
Germany	-0.73	-3	-0.96	-4
Great Britain	-2.25	-9	-2.97	-11
Ireland	-11.24	-36	-14.84	-45
Italy	-9.25	-31	-12.21	-39
Netherlands	-0.59	-2	-0.78	-3
Norway	-5.25	-19	-6.93	-24
Portugal	-1.06	-4	-1.40	-5
Spain	-1.16	-5	-1.53	-6
Sweden	-4.20	-15	-5.55	-20
Old World	-3.08	-11	-4.06	-13

Source: Taylor and Williamson (1997), tables 1, 3 and 4).
Note: Migration rates are per thousand per annum. Minus denotes emigration. The New World and Old World averages are unweighted.

Ireland and Italy saw their populations decline by 36 and 31 per cent, respectively, and the decline exceeded 10 per cent in three Scandinavian countries. Overall, Europe (the Old World) lost 11 per cent of its population and 13 per cent of its labour force to migration. Even the major migration flows experienced by certain countries since 1980 or 1990 have not had similar effects on population or labour-force size. For instance, whereas the annual immigration rate for the United States was 11.6 per thousand in 1900-1910, it reached only 4 per thousand in 1990-1995. Similarly, for Mexico, one of the major countries of emigration, the proportion of the population that has emigrated is comparable with the proportion emigrating from Scandinavian countries at the turn of the nineteenth century and has certainly been much smaller than the proportion that emigrated from Ireland or Italy at that time.

Economic aspects of transatlantic migration

Although some States subsidized the costs of emigration, the majority of emigrants had to cover those costs by themselves, often with the assistance of relatives already established abroad. Other support mechanisms included parishes and philanthropic or charitable societies and individuals. The British Government provided support to emigrants going to Australia and New Zealand during the 1840s and 1850s: the Colonial Land and Emigration Administration defrayed most of the costs involved in transporting close to 340,000 migrants, including convicts. Germany also provided subsidies to emigrants from Baden (Kenwood and Lougheed, 1999, chap. 3).

The migrants of the first wave tended to be young, male, more able and ambitious, and to have more resources

As in most migration streams, transatlantic migrants had been positively selected from the rest of the population, as they tended to be younger, more able and ambitious and to have more resources (see, for example, Chiswick, 2000). Just as today, those who were really poor did not emigrate because they could not afford the cost of passage. However, as incomes rose and transportation costs fell, more persons could afford to emigrate. In addition, successful emigrants often financed the emigration of relatives (Hatton and Williamson, 1994). Migration selectivity was also evident in the higher participation of men than of women in migration. Among immigrants to the United States, for instance, about 4 of every 10 were female; and the proportion female; and was generally lower among immigrants to other countries of destination.

The major incentive for migration was the large wage gap between countries of origin and countries of destination

Undoubtedly the major incentive for emigration was the large difference between wages in the country of origin and those in the country of destination. In the 1850s, the biggest gap in wages was that subsisting between Norway and overseas countries of destination, since average wages in the former were 27 per cent of the latter. The corresponding figures for the better-off European countries ranged from 44 per cent for Ireland to 59 per cent for England. The potential gains to be derived from emigration were therefore substantial.

Part of the change in the sources of migrants over the course of the nineteenth century can be explained by the increases in real terms in the wages in Germany and the United Kingdom as they industrialized and their labour surpluses diminished. Real wages in those countries tended to approach, even if they did not exceed, real wages in the main countries of destination, which were themselves industrializing rapidly. Thus, international migration contributed to raising real wages both in Western Europe and, although more moderately, in the overseas countries of destination. The attraction of these countries diminished, however, as real wages converged. Yet, for workers from Southern, Central and Eastern European countries, where wages remained low, overseas emigration remained attractive.

Differences in wages do not explain completely the emigration rates for different countries. The development of family and social networks in the country of destination was also a significant factor in maintaining migration flows even after the economic incentive had diminished. Furthermore, the situation in the country of origin often compelled people to emigrate, as in the case of the Irish during the famine years or Jews who were subject to persecution in Eastern Europe. Before the First World War, shifts in the countries of origin of the main immigrant flows resulted from a combination of rising incomes in the older countries of origin, the effect of accelerated population growth in Europe, falling transport costs, the self-reinforcing attraction of transnational communities and the crises affecting certain countries or populations in particular regions of origin.

In addition, some migrants crossed the Atlantic to escape agricultural crises or persecution

During most of the nineteen century, there had been little concern about matching the skills of migrants with existing needs. Immigrants, however, did not totally lack needed skills. Many possessed skills that were in particular demand in the countries of destination. For instance, many of the Germans migrating to the United States during 1850-1895 were experienced agricultural workers, specializing particularly in the dairy business and possessing the skills of artisans and tradesmen that were in demand in the urban areas of the United States (Grant, 2003). At the turn of the century, large numbers of immigrants with similar skills but with lower reservation wages arrived from Southern, Central and Eastern Europe. Moreover, the territory open to settlement in the United States moved west towards the more arid areas which were less well suited to dairy farming. The result of these changes combined with the rapid growth of the German economy after 1895 was a sharp drop in German immigration to the United States, from 123,000 in 1881-1895 to slightly under 30,000 in 1896-1910, with Germany being transformed from a net sender into a net receiver of migrants.

Nineteenth century transatlantic migrants broadly matched the needs for both skilled and unskilled workers in the countries of destination

As the century progressed, the greatest demand for labour became increasingly concentrated in urban areas where manufacturing industries were located. As a result, unskilled migrants flocked to factories and the construction industry. Yet, skilled immigrants continued to arrive. In the 1880s, for instance, skilled Belgian workmen developed the plate glass industry, new to the United States. The United Kingdom also supplied many of the skills needed for the industrialization of the United States. Because of its own industrialization and the concentration of heavy industry on the Clyde River, Scotland was disproportionately the source of immigrant labour to the United States. Skilled immigrants also played a crucial role in the development of manufacturing in Latin America, even in countries that did not receive large overseas immigration flows.

A major effect of transatlantic migration was to absorb the surplus labour generated in Europe by the combination of the agricultural and industrial revolutions and the demographic transition in Europe. Migration contributed, in turn, to the rapid expansion of the industrializing countries of the New World, where inflows of labour were complemented by equally massive inflows of capital and the availability of underutilized agricultural land. In all the major receiving countries, but particularly in those growing fastest, such as Argentina and the United States, the economic growth achieved would have been impossible without mass immigration.

The transatlantic migration flows also absorbed the surplus labour generated in Europe by technological and demographic changes

In general, nineteenth century transatlantic migration increased real wages in countries of origin and lowered them in countries of destination

Given the large movement of labour involved, the relative wage effects were clearly significant. One estimate is that, between 1870 and 1910, immigration increased real wages by nearly 9 per cent in the countries of origin and lowered them by 8 per cent in the receiving countries. The effects were larger the larger the immigration. Thus, real wages in Ireland and Italy increased by some 30 per cent as the result of emigration but those in Argentina decreased by 20 per cent. According to this analysis, migration was the major source of wage convergence across the Greater Atlantic economy during 1880-1920, particularly with respect to the core group of Western European countries experiencing rapid industrialization on the one hand and the United States and other major overseas receiving countries on the other. As a consequence, there were positive distribution effects on the former but adverse distribution effects on the latter, which were enhanced by the effects of skill differentials generated by the relatively larger flows of unskilled workers that characterized the last phase of immigration (O'Rourke and Williamson, 1999, chap. 8).

Nonetheless, between around 1880 and 1920, the adverse real wage effects on immigration were fairly small and were overshadowed by its effect on labour supply. Thus, real wages increased in Argentina by 1 per cent from 1880 to 1915 and at a much faster rate of 7.5 per cent during the renewal of immigration during the 1920s (Cortés-Conde, 2000, chap. 9). The adverse distributive effects that immigration may have had in the receiving countries were complemented by similar or even stronger factors, such as the increase in rental/wage ratios in countries specializing in resource-intensive goods, the rising concentration of wealth during the Golden Age in the United States, and the high concentration of land in the hands of oligarchies in Argentina.

Unlike the nineteenth century transatlantic migrants, Asians faced far greater resistance and ultimately exclusion from most of the Americas

While some of the immigrants from the new source countries in Europe met with discrimination in the receiving countries, they did not suffer from the same level of discrimination facing Asian migrants. In fact, immigrants from Asia were effectively excluded from the Greater Atlantic economy. Early in the nineteenth century, several countries of European settlement had resorted to Indian and Chinese labour: New South Wales in the 1840s, Victoria in the early 1850s and Queensland and Natal a few years later; but resistance against "coloured" immigrants increased leading to the adoption of legislation restricting the inflow (Huttenback, 1976, p. 75) and eventually culminating in the total exclusion of Chinese and Indian migrant workers. Victoria led the way in 1857 with a residence tax and in the 1880s all the Australian colonies moved to increase the ratio of shipping tonnage to the number of coloured immigrants who were allowed to land, backing this practice up with heavy fines. Similarly, small flows of Chinese immigrants to California led to the Chinese Exclusion Act of 1882. In British Columbia, the response was similar, although the Government in Ottawa used the tonnage ratio rule, with heavy fines for violations, before a law providing for the complete exclusion of Chinese immigrants was enacted in 1903.

The inflows of European and non-European migrants were thus strictly segmented. Non-European migration flourished in places where contract labour could be restricted to plantation economies distant from white settlement—particularly on islands like Cuba, the West Indies, Mauritius, Réunion and Fiji. In places where Asian contract workers could potentially infiltrate settler economies and compete head-on with workers of European origin, their migration was fiercely and, for the most part, successfully resisted. As a result, migration tended to generate two wage levels, one relative to the European flows in the Greater Atlantic economy and another associated with South-South migration. As W. Arthur Lewis (1978) emphasized, this dualism in world migration flows also affected price formation in commodity markets and became a major cause of the North-South inequalities that shaped the world economy during the first global century.

Policy and the demise of the North-North mass migration

While steps had been taken early on to exclude Asian immigrants from the New World, there was also a more general though gradual drift away from a positive view of migration towards one conducive to more restrictive migration policies after the 1880s. This drift can be illustrated by the evolution of migration policy in the United States, but similar developments took place in Argentina and Australia in the 1890s and in Canada in the early part of the twentieth century (O'Rourke and Williamson, 1999, chap. 10). In 1891, the United States Congress made polygamists, persons suffering from contagious disease and those convicted of a "misdemeanor involving moral turpitude" ineligible for immigration. Later, after the assassination of President McKinley by a Polish anarchist, the Anarchist Exclusion Act of 1901 established that immigrants could be excluded on the basis of their political opinion. The depression of 1893-1898 was accompanied by a further reaction against immigration. A debate on immigration began in the House of Representatives in 1895 and led to the first House roll-call thereon in 1897 where 86 per cent of Representatives voted for restriction. The Immigration Act adopted in 1907, established a tax of US$ 4 per immigrant and permitted the exclusion of, among others, paupers or those likely to become paupers.

By the end of the nineteenth century, increasingly restrictive immigration policies and public hostility towards migrants had appeared in the main countries of destination

Legislative changes reflected broader shifts in public opinion against not only Asian migrants but also immigrants from Southern, Central and Eastern Europe. This antagonism was manifested in "hate crimes" committed against immigrants and in overtly racist statements made against them (see Jaret, 1999). Beatings and murders of Chinese miners were frequent in the western United States, Pennsylvania militia killed and wounded dozens of Slavic and Polish miners during labour disputes in the 1890s, and hundreds of Italian immigrants were burned out of their homes, clubbed and expelled from West Frankfort, Illinois, in 1920. Degrading statements about immigrants from the Mediterranean, the Balkans and Poland were common even among serious writers and concern about a changing racial balance was openly expressed.

With the start of the First World War in 1914, European immigration to the New World had begun to dry up: overseas immigration to the United States fell from 1.1 million annually in 1913-1914, to 60,000 in 1918. Potential immigrants in Europe found it difficult to reach the ports and the ports themselves shut down to commercial activity. As the war in the trenches dragged on, economic hardship made it increasingly difficult for potential emigrants to find the resources necessary to finance migration. Post-war recession and unemployment kept immigration low during 1919-1920. With economic recovery in 1921, 702,000 immigrants reached the United States, a level comparable with those recorded between 1885 and 1900; but the recovery proved to be temporary. Between 1922 and 1929, the annual average number of immigrants was 232,000, about a third of the average annual level during 1881-1914. The Great Depression further depressed immigration, which averaged about 50,000 a year during the 1930s.

With the start of the First World War, transatlantic migration began to dry up

The collapse in global migration in the 1930s is depicted in figures I.3 and I.4. Three central facts stand out. First, the migration flows of the 1920s were never able to recover the levels of the 1880s, let alone those of 1900-1914, and they fell to much lower levels in the 1930s. By the 1950s, the United States was no longer a nation of immigrants, but rather a closed economy whose youth was mostly native-born. Second, most of the collapse in immigration was due to the sharp drop of emigration from the "new" source countries located in Southern, Central and Eastern Europe. Emigration from the "old" sources in North-

Greater Atlantic migration resumed briefly during the 1920s, then dropped to very low levels during the Great Depression

western Europe reached levels in the 1920s comparable with those prior to the First World War and fell only in the 1930s. Third, the recovery of immigration in the 1920s was relatively stronger in Argentina than in the United States but the strong recession of the 1930s in the former put an end to the era of mass migration (Cortés-Conde, 2000).

Changes in immigration policy in the United States occurred in major but discrete steps, often after long and acrimonious debates (Timmer and Williamson, 1998). In 1917, Congress passed an Immigration Act that increased the tax per immigrant to US$ 8 and, more significantly, imposed a literacy test on immigrants. Admission was henceforth contingent on proving that one could read and write in one's own language. In addition, the 1917 Immigration Act included an "Asian barred zone" provision that effectively excluded all immigrants from Asia.

Anti-immigration legislation continued to grow in the United States during the 1920s

In 1921, the Emergency Quota Act (Johnson Act) set limits to immigration according to national origin. This Act was adopted in a rush after 700,000 European immigrants had arrived that year (easily satisfying the literacy requirement). The Act limited the annual number of immigrants of a given nationality to no more than 3 per cent of the population of that nationality living in the United States; as enumerated by the 1910 Census. Under the 1921 Act, the number of immigrants from Northern and Western Europe could not surpass 198,000 and the number from all other source countries—mainly in Southern, Central and Eastern Europe—could not surpass 158,000, thus setting an upper limit for European migration of about 356,000. The legislation was clearly targeted at limiting the number of immigrants from the newer countries of origin who, as the pre-war Dillingham Immigration Commission had argued, were considered harder to assimilate, were a source of poverty and a potential welfare burden on the State, and became poor citizens, or failed to become citizens at all. Annual quotas for Southern, Central and Eastern European countries were in all cases less than a quarter of the numbers admitted before the First World War. The Asian barred zone remained in place until the late 1940s but was definitely discarded with the Immigration Act of 1965.

Under United States immigration legislation, transatlantic migration was increasingly restricted, while immigration from within the Americas was not

The 1921 Act also had a pro-western hemisphere bias since immigration from other countries in the Americas was not subject to numerical limitations. This provision passed because there appeared to be no reason to set quotas on immigration from neighbouring countries and South America was too poor and distant to become a viable pool of migrants. Furthermore, Canada was a member of the British family and Canadians had mostly European origins. Lastly, farm interests in the South-west lobbied to have access to cheap Mexican unskilled labour to work the fields and produce the agricultural products that were being supplied to national and international markets. As a consequence, migrants poured over the border from Canada and Mexico but remained outside the regulated flow. In some cases, migrants trying to sidestep the quotas on European migration or the restrictions placed on Asian migration entered through the border with neighbouring countries. As in recent times, estimates of the numbers crossing the land borders of the United States involved were high. In any case, the share of legal immigrants to the United States from Canada and Mexico rose from 12.9 per cent in 1910-1919 to 45.4 per cent in 1920-1929. Mexican immigration alone rose by about 320,000 over the decade, a harbinger of things to come later in the century.

The category of family reunification entered United States immigration law in 1921

Lastly, the 1921 Act had also introduced a migration category outside the quota and based on individual characteristics (rather than nationality) that would come to represent the "family reunification" component of United States immigration; that is to say, wives and children of United States citizens were exempted from the quota and consequently the number of persons of any given national origin actually admitted annually during the 1920s was considerably higher than that set by the quota. By 1929, actual immigration to the United States from Southern, Central and Eastern Europe was more than three times the prevailing quota (Gemery, 1994, p. 182, table 9.4).

Yet the 1921 Act was not restrictive enough for some anti-immigration interests and their power in Congress was on the rise. Thus, the Act was revised in 1924 (Johnson-Reid Act), lowering the worldwide quota from 356,000 to 165,000, by reducing the upper limit for Southern, Central and Eastern European countries from 158,000 to 21,000 (Bernard, 1982, p. 96, table 3.1). The 1924 Act set the annual quotas at 2 per cent of the foreign-born by nationalities as enumerated in the 1890 Census.

During the 1920s, there was a shift in the composition of migration to the United States from predominantly workers to dependants

Because of family reunification, the share of females among all immigrants rose from 30.3 per cent in 1906-1910 to 43.5 per cent in 1921-1924 and to above 50 per cent in the 1930s. Concomitantly, the proportion of immigrants who were not in the labour force (being mainly women and children) rose steadily, nearly doubling between 1910-1920 and the 1930s. The result was that, after nearly a century in which immigrants had been mostly workers, the new policies transformed the migration stream into one comprising mainly dependants.

In the 1930s, it was the Great Depression that caused the final collapse of mass migration to the United States. The clearest evidence is that even the low quotas set by the 1924 Act remained unmet during the 1930s. Most of the countries in Southern, Central and Eastern Europe were at most able to fill 40 per cent of their quotas during 1932-1937 (Gemery, 1994, figure 9.1).

Throughout the period 1860-1930, migration policy was most consistently shaped by changing labour-market conditions

An analysis of immigration policy during 1860-1930 indicates that labour-market conditions had a consistent influence on immigration policy and did so through the absolute and relative income performance of unskilled workers. The most consistently significant explanatory variable was the ratio of the unskilled wage to per capita income, or of income near the bottom to income in the middle of the distribution. Rising inequality was associated with an increasingly restrictive immigration policy. Whereas rising relative labour scarcity had encouraged more open immigration policies, declining relative labour scarcity encouraged more restrictive immigration policies. Receiving countries acted to defend the economic interests of their unskilled workers. At the same time, unskilled immigrants from the new countries of origin who were competing with existing unskilled workers were seen as less desirable than the "old" immigrants, and so nativist and xenophobic arguments reinforced pressures to restrict immigration from the new source countries.

The collapse in world migration had a major impact on receiving countries. The United States, as the largest market for immigrant labour, experienced the largest decline in immigration after 1914. The annual rate of growth of the labour force in the United States was effectively cut in half, falling from 2.29 per cent during 1880-1910 to 1.14 per cent during 1910-1940.

The end of immigration into the United States produced increased opportunities for African Americans

One consequence of the drop in immigration was an increase in opportunities for unskilled workers in the United States, especially African Americans. Thus, whereas after emancipation only about a half-million African Americans had migrated from the southern States to the urban centres of the North during 1870-1910, about 3.5 million made the northward journey during 1910-1950. By 1950, one fifth of all the African Americans born in the southern States lived in northern States. This mass internal migration helped improve both the economic lives of the migrants and the wages of those who remained in the southern States, since the wage gap between the northern and southern States declined sharply (Wright, 1986). Thus, it would appear that immigration from Europe had crowded out southern African Americans from better jobs in the urban North and, symmetrically, the end of mass immigration allowed them access to those jobs.

Since the migration northward greatly improved the relative income position of African Americans between 1910 and 1950, it helps account for the levelling of incomes in the middle third of the twentieth century, and indicates how changes in European migration contributed to achieving that levelling. However, immigration was only one among many factors affecting income distribution. The interwar period witnessed significant improvements in income distribution throughout the industrialized world (see, in this regard, Bourgignon and Morrison, 2002), which can also be traced to the gradual building up of the modern welfare State.

South-South migration in the periphery

Government and private assisted migration in the periphery

Labour-force needs grew in some countries of the periphery during the first half of the nineteenth century, just as the slave trade was being progressively suppressed

The increasing demand and the relative price boom for the exports of tropical products had increased the demand for labour in those parts of the periphery that attempted to fulfill that demand after 1820. Prior to 1820 —at a time when the potential immigrant could not afford the costs of passage and there existed no credit market to lend him or her the fare—the problem of supplying needed labour from other parts of the South had been solved in the most obscene way—by African slavery. That option began to disappear in 1807 when Parliament banned all British subjects from engaging in the slave trade. In 1834, slavery was abolished in the British colonies, and the rest of the world followed suit over subsequent decades—although those countries that depended heavily on slave labour did so very slowly. The alternative to slavery lay in something between it and free labour, namely, contracts whereby the investor funded the cost of passage, and the migrant agreed to work for that investor (or whomever he represented) for a number of years and at somewhat below-market wage. In theory, the agreement allowed the investor to recoup, and obtain a market return on, his investment while the migrant was allowed to collect the remaining wage gains from the move.

Some form of indenture was increasingly used to meet labour-market needs

The most famous contractual arrangement was indentured servitude, but there were a variety of other arrangements in which the most important condition was contract length. The higher the cost of passage and recruitment, the longer the time necessary to recoup the investment with an adequate market return. By the 1850s, "five-year contracts became the norm in ... British colonies ... with migrants in those closer to their homelands having the right to a free return passage after five years" (Northrup, 1995, p. 116). Since political rhetoric in the mid-nineteenth century correctly viewed long contracts as too close to slavery and a source of abuse, progressive legislation constantly pushed for shorter contracts. The progressives met with less and less resistance as steerage costs fell across the century.

The vast majority of Indian emigrants were assisted under contracts that varied by length, the really short-term arrangements being typical of moves within South and South-East Asia. This was called the *kangani* system and was common for emigration to nearby areas (Davis, 1951, p. 104). Emigration to Ceylon (now Sri Lanka), Burma (now Myanmar) and Malaya (in 1963, the name of the Federation of Malaysia was changed to Malaya) presented a marked contrast to migration to the West Indies. All the emigrants to Ceylon and Malaya were from the South and the migrants were recruited by headmen known as *kangani*. The Indians worked on the tea, coffee and rubber plantations. During the period 1852-1937, 1.5 million Indians went to Ceylon, 2 million to Malaya and 2.5 million to Burma. After 1920, the *kangani* system of labour recruitment was discontinued owing to a fall in demand for the Indian labour.

Plantation employment requirements were driven by demand. As the terms of trade of tropical economies improved, the quest for contract labour gained in intensity; when export prices declined, so did recruitment of contract labour for the estates and plantations. These migrations offer a classic example of elastic labour supplies that goes back to the writings of W. Arthur Lewis.

While the vast majority of Indian migrants were indentured and otherwise assisted, the vast majority of Chinese migrants, similar to the European migrants, moved freely (Northrup, 1995, p. 52). Perhaps the explanation for the difference lies in the fact that Chinese workers had been migrating to South-East Asia for centuries, and thus new emigrants could secure funding from previous pioneer emigrants established abroad; or perhaps the Chinese coolie market was sufficiently old to have become much more professional and efficient compared with the newer Indian market, as illustrated by the ubiquitous "lodging house" system; or perhaps the explanation lies in the fact that the move from the south China provinces of Fukien and Kwangtung to South-East Asia was much shorter in time and distance and thus less costly than the move from major Indian sending regions.

The vast majority of nineteenth century Indian migrants were indentured; the vast majority of Chinese emigrants moved as free individuals

Wage gaps and costs of moving in the nineteenth century periphery

The average Indian indentured immigrant in British Guiana, a sugar-growing area in the north-east shoulder of South America, earned a monthly wage of $4.45 in 1869 (Northrup, 1995, p. 129); if he had stayed home in the Madras Presidency to work as a rural labourer, he would have made about $1.50 per month, making the ratio of his monthly wages in Guiana to his monthly wages back home 3 to 1. However, the wage received by the indentured worker in Guiana was over and above the lodging, board, medical care and some of the clothing furnished by his employer. For a poor unskilled coolie in those times, expenses on food, clothing and lodging would have almost exhausted his income back home in Madras. Thus, it seems fair to say that when income in kind is added to his wage income in Guiana, his monthly wage would have been $8 or more, and the ratio to monthly wages back home in India would have been 5 or more. According to this Guiana-Madras example from 1869, these wage gaps—measures of relative labour scarcity between the export enclaves and one of the two main labour surplus sources of the estate and plantation workers—were far higher around the periphery than they were around the Greater Atlantic economy.

An individual who signed an indenture agreement could increase his earnings manyfold

Applying the same calculation to other regions yields similar, or even more spectacular, results: wages in the West Indies in 1870 implied a ratio of 4.8; Trinidad in 1870, a ratio of 7.8; Hawaii in 1870, a ratio of 9 (Northrup, 1995, p. 130; Tinker, 1974, p. 186). There is additional evidence supporting the existence of a large wage gap: indentured Indian migrants returning from Mauritius in the late 1870s brought back cash equal to, on average, about four years of income at home, a figure that must understate the accumulated gains from the move, since so many used postal savings to remit earnings while in Mauritius and brought home gold, silver and jewellery (Northrup, 1995, p. 137).

Chinese migrants, who more typically moved as free individuals, could also substantially increase their earnings

The distances from south India to the Caribbean or Hawaii were very large, while those for the Chinese coolie trade connecting the South China provinces to South-East Asia were much shorter. Yet a wage gap still existed. In the 1870s, the unskilled labour wage ratios between Thailand and China were almost 3 (assuming no real change in Chinese real wages in the period 1873-1909) (Williamson, 2000, table 1.1).

But along with the increased earnings, nineteenth century South-South migrants also often faced extremely harsh conditions of life ...

This benign description of the gains from migration as an indentured worker should not imply a rejection of the abundant evidence documenting poverty and hard times for these migrants, as well as abuse of their contracts (Lewis, 1978; Tinker, 1974, chap. 6; Northrup, 1995, chap. 5). Mortality rates on ships transporting indentured Chinese and Indian migrants were much higher than for those carrying non-indentured passengers on the same routes and at the same time. On the other hand, non-indentured passengers were financially much better off and thus had had much lower mortality rates back home too. Furthermore, ship mortality rates declined sharply between mid-century and the 1870s.

In the plantation enclaves, indentured labourers worked under harsh restrictions. Policy towards Indian immigrants in Natal was often severe. In an effort to make the previously indentured immigrants re-contract, they were taxed £3 annually until they re-contracted, although 69 per cent did not (Northrup, 1995, p. 133). Further discriminatory restrictions imposed on Indian immigrants led to protests, including those led by the young Mohandas K. Gandhi, and some violence, so much so that many left for home after 1908. Things might have been even worse in Mauritius where, in addition to a tax of £2 18s imposed on the "free" Indian immigrant, they were harassed by vagrancy laws and licences that intended to reduce economic alternatives available to them upon the termination of their indentured contracts. Racial prejudice against the Indian immigrants was frequent in many countries.

... though working conditions may have been even worse in the countries of origin

In any case, while health and working conditions were certainly very bad in the estates and plantations abroad, those conditions may well have been worse at home. While the authorities and reformers pointed to examples of physical cruelty, restricted freedom, arbitrary wage deductions and penal sanctions, they scrutinized the coolie trade far more critically than they did the abject conditions in the regions whence the migrants came.

During the century following 1834, some 30 million left India, while some 24 million returned

Given wage differentials like those cited above, "the miracle is that there was not an even greater exodus" (Davis, 1951, p. 102). While 30.2 million had left India, 23.9 million returned, so that only 6.3 million left India for good between 1834 and 1937. India was and is a huge country, so small percentages imply large numbers, but a figure of 6.3 million making permanent moves abroad is surprisingly small, especially given the enormous incentive to move.

Most Indian emigrants went to South or South-East Asia

Most of these Indian migrants went to south or South-East Asia: about 42.2 per cent of them went to Burma, another 24.9 per cent to Ceylon and another 19.3 per cent to British Malaya (Davis, 1951, pp. 99, 101). The rest, 13.6 per cent, went to the Caribbean, the Pacific and Africa. However, all of these net migrations over the century between the 1830s and the 1930s involved only 9.4 per cent of India's 1900 population, a low proportion relative to those of European countries (Davis, 1951, p. 98, table 34). Moreover, significant migrations were taking place within India that were driven by much the same forces: migration to the tea, coffee and rubber estates in Mysore and Assam; and migration to the Punjab and Sind where government investment in irrigation created an enormous addition to hectarage. The movements to Assam, which were the largest and the most similar to the international migrations, were also driven by substantial wage gaps.

Nineteenth century Chinese emigration was similarly predominantly South-South

The mass migration data for the other main labour surplus area, China, are not as good, but 8.2 million Chinese were residing abroad in 1922 (Ferenczi and Willcox, 1929, p. 149). As was the case for India, most of China's emigrants were in Asia: Formosa, Hong Kong and Macao, 32.4 per cent; Java, the Straits Settlements and the Philippines, 28.3 per cent; Siam, 18.3 per cent; Annam, Burma and Ceylon, 16.6 per cent; and elsewhere, the remaining 4.4 per cent. While 8.2 million is a large number, it was less than 2 per cent of China's 1910 population, a very small emigration share indeed, at least compared with the European experience. This represented a significantly larger share of the male population than of the female population, since few women moved: in 1900-1903, almost 89 per cent of the Chinese immigrants entering Singapore were men (Huff, 1994, pp. 154, 402-403). Furthermore, it comprised an even larger share of males in the coastal regions whence most of the Chinese emigrants originated. Still, the numbers for these emigrations were small compared with the sending country populations.

The question arises why South-South migration over the century after 1820 was so low compared with North-North migration. It was not a result of a policy of forbidding migration: migration was not shut off by policy at the origin, either in China or in India.

South-South migration in the nineteenth century was impeded by strong ties of peasants to the land and by high moving costs

A first answer, and probably the most important one, is that labour was still largely tied to the land in most of the periphery, which is to say that, contrary to Europe, the institution of a "free labour market" was less established there.[2] A second answer, one that is fully consistent with experience of the European mass emigrations, is that the cost of the move was so large, and the living standards in India and China were so low, that few unskilled workers could possibly secure the funds to invest in the move and thereby obtain the high returns available abroad. The largest ratio of passenger fare to annual income per capita at home for European emigrants heading for the United States in the early nineteenth century had been about 0.4-0.6 for British emigrants. With the subsequent transport revolution, these ratios for British emigrants had fallen to 0.1 by the end of the century. The ratios of passage fare to home annual per capita income were much higher for workers pondering emigration from India and China (Galenson, 1984, table 1): for indentured Chinese immigrating to the West Indies in 1859-1880, 5.3-9.9; for indentured Chinese immigrating to Hawaii in 1877-1880, 6.8; for contract Chinese labour immigrating to California in 1877-1880, 5.5-6.8; and for indentured Indian labour immigrating to the West Indies in 1859-1901, 3.6-11.8. These figures are at minimum 10 times those for the Greater Atlantic economy.

Few poor Indian or Chinese labourers could have made the move under these cost conditions given their inability to obtain loans to finance the move. However, estates in the export enclaves, or their recruiters, were ready to make the investment, especially as transport costs had fallen after 1820 and as the soaring terms of trade had raised the labour costs facing these estates and plantations. Indeed, an index of the ratio of moving costs for an indentured migrant (recruitment, board en route and passenger fare) to the wage at the export enclave fell from 4 to 1 between 1852-1874 and 1881-1909.

Another part of the explanation for the relatively small numbers involved in South-South migration lies in the purpose of migration. In the case of, say, Canada or the United States, the intention of the United States or Canadian authorities in encouraging immigration from Europe was to fill "empty" spaces with permanent settlers. In the case of movement of labour from, say, India to Malysia, the intention of the colonial authorities in permitting the entry of indentured labour was to supply labour for specific needs in what were enclave industries, not to fill empty spaces.

The end of assisted migration in the periphery

Economic incentives for indentured migration weakened greatly by the end of the nineteenth century, and most countries of origin moved to regulate and then to abolish it

In the 1870s, China moved first to regulate and then to abolish the indentured migrant trade. Portuguese officials in Macao agreed to join the movement, and stopped the trade from that port in 1874; and Cuba, Peru and the United States supported the move. British officials continually intervened to shut down the indentured migrant trade from India whenever abuses were reported. All of this culminated in the Government's decision to end the Indian trade as of March 1916 (Galenson, 1984, pp. 144-145).

Economic factors can largely explain the end of assisted migration. First, net emigration of all Indian workers—assisted and unassisted—fell off very sharply from the early 1890s to the First World War, from 790,000 in 1891-1895 to 383,000 in 1906-1910, and to 59,000 by 1936-1937 (Davis, 1951, p. 99). This sharp drop was likely induced by poor economic conditions in the estates and plantations, manifested by the secular decline in their terms of trade after the peak in the 1870s and 1880s. Second, the migration of indentured labour fell off much earlier and even more steeply than did total migration. Indian indentured migration had reached a peak in the 1850s and Chinese indentured migration had reached a peak in the 1860s. The decade totals of indentured immigration from all sources—African, Chinese, Indian, Japanese and others—had risen from about 34,000 in the 1830s to almost 420,000 in the 1850s, but never came close to regaining that level thereafter, dropping to 212,000 in the 1880s. It peaked in the 1850s in Mauritius and Réunion, and in the 1860s in Cuba, Peru and the Caribbean; and only the peaks in Africa and the Pacific came late enough to have been cut off by policy. In short, the share of the Indians and Chinese migrating under indentured contracts had fallen sharply after the 1850s and 1860s, long before restrictive legislation was passed and implemented.

Although some vestiges of contract labour survived into the interwar period, it had largely been abolished during or immediately after the First World War. Sharp declines in the price of sugar in the 1880s cut the pace of recruitment to the sugar plantations. Other primary product producing plantations elsewhere in the tropics followed suit. In addition, from the turn of the century the level of protest increased in India and throughout the British Empire. If the political tide had been moving against indentured labour and the demand for it was ebbing, the War-induced shipping shortage was the event that ultimately brought it to a halt by 1917. High wartime transport costs coincided with demonstrations in India, both factors stopping recruitment on the supply side. The Indian Government invoked the formal abolition of recruitment for British Guiana in 1919, for Fiji in 1920 and for Mauritius in 1921.

Economics and idealism combined to bring an end to the indentured labour system. Economics and backlash combined to reduce, more generally, the mass migrations in the poor periphery. These fundamental forces had often cumulated over long periods before sudden shocks caused a radical change in policy, as was true for the frontiers of European settlement. Declining demand was the key fundamental at work, but it was helped by a rising backlash, as manifested by a discriminatory reaction to post-indentured labourers in the poor periphery, and by their outright exclusion from most of the Greater Atlantic economy. Late nineteenth century immigrant backlash was on the rise in both center and periphery.

Conclusions

Given the major role that migration played during the first global century in shaping the Great Atlantic economy, it would be worthwhile to determine what lessons that experience holds for today's world and to attempt to draw parallels between the effects of the mass migration that had occurred during 1880-1920 and those produced by the large movements of migrants that took place during the last two decades of the twentieth century.

The differences between conditions in the first global century and the current situation are considerable. In the nineteenth century, European countries were able to export the surplus labour that had resulted from their agrarian and industrial revolutions and their demographic transition to countries that needed to increase their workforce and their population. This option is not open at present to developing countries experiencing high unemployment and underemployment rates. Likewise, there is no country ready to accept large numbers of immigrants for settlement. The history of Europe and of the world would have been different if the industrializing countries of Europe had had to rely on their own resources to absorb their surplus labour during the nineteenth century and if there had been no New World to absorb their emigrants. In this sense, it is difficult to imagine what would have been the counterfactual to the mass migrations in the Greater Atlantic economy of 1820-1920.

The migration experience of the nineteenth century is not an exact template for that of our own era

The experience of the first global century indicates that immigration can affect the wage levels and income distribution of both sending and receiving countries. At the international level, largely owing to the improvement in per capita incomes of workers in Europe during the nineteenth century, average incomes in the region nearly caught up with the levels in the United States and the other receiving countries, although this process was strong enough only in the most industrialized centres of Europe, or in those countries, like Ireland and Italy, that sent abroad a large proportion of their population. At the same time, the high segmentation of European and non-European migration flows became a major source of the North-South inequalities that built up during this period.

The countries that developed during the nineteenth century could export surplus labour; the developing countries of today cannot

Several key differences explain why the effects of immigration are unlikely to be similar today. First, restrictions on immigration are universal, generating an asymmetry between constrained flows of labour and mobile financial capital, which generates an adverse distributive impact on those factors of production that are less mobile (see Rodrik, 1997; Ocampo and Martin, eds., 2003). This effect is likely to reduce the impact of migration on income convergence, even if the general tendencies are similar. Second, as a result of existing restrictions, the impact of migration on population growth and labour supply is smaller today than in the Greater Atlantic economy during the first global century. Furthermore, population trends in the receiving countries are radically different; and in Europe, migration is largely compensating the currently low or even negative rates of growth of the native populations (see chap. II). Third, the national economies of receiving countries are more integrated than they were in the nineteenth century. This integration can neutralize the possible adverse impacts of immigrants on particular industries or locations by allowing the absorption of redundant workers in other industries or locations, and making the impact of migration modest, as suggested by the evidence presented in chapter IV.

Several key conditions in the modern world combine to constrain the impact of migration on wage levels and income distribution in both countries of origin and countries of destination

Curiously, the effects of segmentation in migration flows seem as important as in the first global century but segmentation itself now has a different character. Instead of being associated with a cleavage between North migration and South migration, segmentation today is based on skills, since receiving countries, particularly those in the industrialized world, favour the admission of skilled migrants (see chap. III). This segmentation

At the same time, contemporary labour-markets favour skilled migrant wages, but do little for the unskilled

may be generating a distributive effect worldwide in favour of the more mobile factor (skilled labour) but to the detriment of the less mobile one (unskilled labour). While skilled workers may find it easier to migrate to industrialized countries with the resulting brain drain pushing up the incomes of skilled workers in the countries of origin, the restricted mobility of unskilled workers limits the effect of their migration on average wages for unskilled workers worldwide. The latter effect is reinforced by the fact that unskilled labour migration is small relative to the labour surplus in developing countries. Furthermore, though most labour migration occurs within the legal framework established by the receiving State, a significant proportion of all unskilled migration is undocumented and wages for undocumented migrants tend to be lower than those for migrants in regular situations. Both facts tend to reduce the possible effects on wages in the countries of origin. The effects of segmentation in terms of skill differentials in migration interact with other factors, particularly those of a technological character, to push up skills premiums in the global labour market.

Deteriorating labour markets and growing inequality may precipitate a backlash against immigration

During the mass migration of 1880-1920, the natives of receiving countries protested that immigrants from Asia and Southern, Central and Eastern Europe had crowded out unskilled native workers in the job market. According to some analysts, the presence of these immigrants and the widening income gaps between unskilled and skilled workers, combined with economic depression, led eventually to the adoption of restrictive immigration laws by the receiving countries during the 1920s (Hirschman, 2001, pp. 7221-7226). In this sense, history offers support for the proposition that relatively poor labour-market conditions and rising inequality played an important role in precipitating a backlash against immigration. Although at the present time the impact of the inflows of immigrants on native workers or on income distribution has been modest, economic reality does not necessarily form the basis for policy-making. The growing sense in receiving countries that migrants may have negative effects on wages and foster income inequality can set the context within which to justify further restrictive measures regarding migration.

The first period of mass migration ended with the First World War, which also put an end to the first global century; but it is difficult to imagine a seriously disruptive event of such magnitude occurring again in the near future. Consequently, despite concerns and even open antagonism towards immigration, the expectation is that relatively high migration levels will continue and that migration issues will remain an important item in international debates.

Notes

1 The present chapter draws heavily from a background paper prepared by Timothy J. Hatton, Australian National University, and Jeffrey G. Williamson, Harvard University, and from their forthcoming book (Hatton and Williamson, 2005), as well as from Williamson (2004). However, some interpretations differ from those of these authors. The chapter focuses mainly on transatlantic migration. It does not cover, among others, the Russian migrations to Siberia and the eastern territories, nor the Chinese migrations to Mongolia and the northern territories.

2 This is also one reason why the most dynamic export economies had to rely on migrant labour rather than on their domestic agricultural labour, which was much less mobile. See, for example, Cárdenas, Ocampo and Thorp (2000, chap.1) for the effects that use of different forms of labour mobilization had on the relative experiences of Latin American countries.

Chapter II
International migration trends

The major transatlantic migration flows originating in Europe were first disrupted by the First World War and then dampened by the Great Depression. Although data are sparse, international migration worldwide seems to have reached a low point during the 1930s. International migration increased during the Second World War, as the German Reich mobilized millions of people to serve as slave labour in German factories and millions more were displaced or forcefully relocated in Europe, the Union of Soviet Socialist Republics (USSR) and Asia as a result of the War. At the end of the War, there were from 7 million to 8 million foreign civilian workers and prisoners of war working for the Reich (Potts, 1990) and 1.9 million Koreans who had been forced to move to and work in Japan.

The Second World War also had repercussions on migration flows in the Americas. The need for labour during the War had prompted the United States of America to allow the admission of temporary workers from Mexico under the Bracero Programme, which started in 1942. When the Programme ended in 1964, the number of unskilled migrant workers from Mexico living in the United States had increased significantly both as a result of admissions under the Programme and because of the undocumented migration that developed parallel to it.

The population dislocations that occurred during the Second World War led to major resettlement flows once the War was over. It is estimated that about 6 million migrants were resettled, 4 million of whom moved to the immigration countries of the time (Argentina, Australia, Brazil, Canada, Israel, New Zealand, South Africa, the United States and Venezuela). In addition, about 1 million persons moved within Europe. The data available do not reflect with accuracy other major movements that occurred in Africa and Asia as persons who had moved or been forced to move because of the War relocated. Furthermore, the process of decolonization also resulted in major population movements between the newly independent States. The partition of India, for instance, led to the mass movement of from 7 million to 8 million persons between India and Pakistan in 1949 (Thomas, 1959).

During the 1950s, as the economies of countries in Western Europe had begun to recover from the devastation of war, demand for workers grew and was initially met by the admission of workers from Southern European countries (Greece, Portugal and Spain) or from the colonies or former colonies (for example, Algeria in the case of France; India, Pakistan and colonies or ex-colonies in the West Indies in the case of the United Kingdom of Great Britain and Northern Ireland). By the 1960s, both the labour-importing countries of Europe and the overseas countries of immigration had become the major attraction poles in the world. By that time, the greater availability of census data on the foreign-born population enumerated in each country made possible a better accounting of the number of international migrants in the world. The next section discusses worldwide trends in terms of changes in the number of international migrants estimated for each country of the world from 1960 to 2000.

Global trends since 1960

The rising levels of international migration after the Second World War had resulted from the growing interdependence among countries, the continued and even growing income disparities between them, cheaper and more accessible means of transportation, and growing demographic disparities, particularly between the developed and the developing world. These forces led to increasing international mobility, especially after 1970.

Estimates of the number of international migrants derived mostly from census information on the number of foreign-born persons enumerated in each country[1] indicate that the number of international migrants in the world had increased by only 6 million from 1960 to 1970, passing from 76 million to 82 million, and by 18 million from 1970 to 1980, reaching 100 million in 1980 (table II.1). During 1980-1990, the estimated increase in the number of international migrants was sharper, at 54 million. However, at least half of that increase was caused by the disintegration of the former USSR, the effects of which, for comparison purposes, have been "backdated" to 1990 in the estimates presented in table II.1. It is estimated that in 1991, when the former Soviet Union broke up into 15 independent States, the number of international migrants increased by 27 million,

Table II.1.
Indicators of the stock of international migrants by major area, 1960-2000

	Number of international migrants (millions)					Average annual rate of growth of the number of international migrants (percentage)				International migrants as a share of the population (percentage)		Distribution of international migrants by region (percentage)	
Major area	1960	1970	1980	1990	2000	1960-1970	1970-1980	1980-1990	1990-2000	1960	2000	1960	2000
World	75.9	81.5	99.8	154.0	174.9	0.7	2.0	4.3	1.3	2.5	2.9	100.0	100.0
Developed countries	32.1	38.3	47.7	89.7	110.3	1.8	2.2	6.3	2.1	3.4	8.7	42.3	63.1
Developed countries excluding USSR	29.1	35.2	44.5	59.3	80.8	1.9	2.3	2.9	3.0	4.0	8.3	38.4	46.2
Developing countries	43.8	43.2	52.1	64.3	64.6	-0.1	1.8	2.1	0.0	2.1	1.3	57.7	36.9
Africa	9.0	9.9	14.1	16.2	16.3	0.9	3.6	1.4	0.0	3.2	2.0	11.8	9.3
Asia[a]	29.3	28.1	32.3	41.8	43.8	-0.4	1.4	2.6	0.5	1.8	1.2	38.6	25.0
Latin America and the Caribbean	6.0	5.8	6.1	7.0	5.9	-0.5	0.7	1.3	-1.7	2.8	1.1	8.0	3.4
Northern America	12.5	13.0	18.1	27.6	40.8	0.4	3.3	4.2	3.9	6.1	12.9	16.5	23.3
Oceania	2.1	3.0	3.8	4.8	5.8	3.5	2.1	2.3	2.1	13.4	18.8	2.8	3.3
Europe[b]	14.0	18.7	22.2	26.3	32.8	2.9	1.7	1.7	2.2	3.3	6.4	18.5	18.7
USSR (former)	2.9	3.1	3.3	30.3	29.5	0.5	0.5	22.3	-0.3	1.4	10.2	3.9	16.8

Source: United Nations, *Trends in Total Migrant Stock: The 2003 Revision* (POP/DB/MIG/ Rev. 2003), data in digital form.

a Excluding Armenia, Azerbaijan, Georgia, Kazakhstan, Kyrgyzstan, Tajikistan, Turkmenistan and Uzbekistan.

b Excluding Belarus, Estonia, Latvia, Lithuania, the Republic of Moldova, the Russian Federation and Ukraine.

as persons who had used to be considered internal migrants because they had moved from their Soviet republic of birth to another Soviet republic became international migrants when their respective republics of birth gained independence. A similar discontinuity in the evolution of the number of international migrants occurred with the disintegration of the former Czechoslovakia and the former Yugoslavia, although the numbers involved were smaller. The reverse transformation also occurred when, for instance, the former German Democratic Republic and the Federal Republic of Germany reunited in late 1990. By backdating the disintegration of the former USSR to 1990, the stock of international migrants rises sharply from 1980 to 1990 and more moderately—by 21 million—from 1990 to 2000. Excluding the effects of such disintegration, the number of international migrants worldwide would have risen by 18 million from 1970 to 1980, 27 million from 1980 to 1990, and 21 million from 1990 to 2000.

In 2000, 175 million persons were living outside of their country of birth, making 1 in every 35 persons on earth an international migrant, up from 1 in every 40 in 1960. In 1910, just after the period of high international migration that had characterized the early twentieth century, an estimated 33 million persons were living in countries other than their own,[2] meaning that 1 out of every 48 persons could be considered an international migrant (International Labour Office, 1936); that is to say, between 1910 and 2000, the number of international migrants in the world had increased fivefold, whereas the world population had been multiplied by less than four, passing from 1.6 billion to 6.1 billion. As a result, international migrants, who had represented 2.1 per cent of the world population in 1910, accounted in 2000 for 2.9 per cent of the world's population. Furthermore, whereas it had taken 50 years for the number of international migrants to increase by a factor of 2.3—from some 33 million in 1910 to 76 million in 1960—a similar increase occurred over the next 40 years—from 76 million in 1960 to 175 million in 2000.

In 2000, 175 million persons were living outside of their country of birth

To set these numbers in perspective, note that in India the number of persons living in a district other than that in which they had been born amounted to 75 million in 1981 and among them, 24 million were living outside the State in which they had been born; that is to say, inter-district migrants accounted for 11 per cent of the Indian population in 1981, whereas interstate migrants accounted for 3.4 per cent. Clearly, the longer distances and costs involved in interstate migration reduced considerably the number of persons involved in that type of relocation. In that light, the finding that international migrants have accounted for at least 2.5 per cent of the world population since 1960 indicates that the prevalence of international migration is comparable with that of interstate movers in a large and complex society such as that of India.

The estimates of the number of international migrants by major development group indicate that the distribution between developed and developing countries of increments in the number of international migrants worldwide has changed considerably. Excluding the former USSR, developed countries gained 6 million international migrants from 1960 to 1970, 9 million from 1970 to 1980, nearly 15 million from 1980 to 1990, and over 21 million from 1990 to 2000; that is to say, in the 1960s, developed countries had accounted for virtually the full increase in the number of international migrants worldwide, but in the 1970s they absorbed only about half of the increase in that number. During the 1980s, when the number of international migrants worldwide increased by 27 million (excluding the effects of the disintegration of the former USSR), developed countries accounted for 55 per cent of that growth; but by the 1990s, they accounted once more for the full increase in the number of international migrants worldwide, leaving the migrant stock in developing countries in effect unchanged.

The nearly unchanging overall number of international migrants in the developing world from 1990 to 2000 does not mean, however, that migration between developing countries ceased. Many of the poles of attraction that emerged during the 1970s and 1980s in the developing world have persisted, and the flows of refugees and other types of international migrants between developing countries continue. Nevertheless, during the 1990s, the increases in the number of international migrants in certain developing countries were largely counterbalanced by declines in the numbers of migrants in other developing countries, leading to a stable overall number of international migrants in the developing world. This overall stability masks the dynamism of recent international migration flows in the developing world, where the repatriation of refugees in Africa, for instance, counterbalances the increases in economically motivated migration in Asia, or where the repatriation of migrant workers from oil-producing countries in Western Asia during the Gulf war was followed by new inflows once the war had ended.

In 2000, 37 per cent of all international migrants lived in a developing country, down from 58 per cent in 1960

As a result of these trends, the concentration of international migrants in the developed world has increased. Whereas in 1960, 38 per cent of all international migrants lived in developed countries other than the USSR and 58 per cent lived in developing countries, by 2000, 46 per cent of all international migrants lived in the first set of countries and just 37 per cent lived in developing countries (table II.1). With the inclusion of the former USSR among the developed countries, the proportion of international migrants in the developed world rises to 42 per cent in 1960 and to 63 per cent in 2000. Even taking account of the fact that some of the successor States of the former USSR are now classified as developing countries, the proportion of all international migrants in the developed world remains at nearly 60 per cent in 2000.

Twenty-three per cent of all international migrants lived in Northern America in 2000...

Furthermore, the concentration of international migrants in certain regions has also risen. Northern America's share of international migrants grew from 17 per cent in 1960 to 23 per cent in 2000 and that of the former USSR increased from 4 per cent in 1960 to 17 per cent in 2000. Yet the share of all other regions declined, with reductions being particularly marked in Asia, whose share of all international migrants dropped from 39 per cent in 1960 to 25 per cent in 2000, and in Latin America and the Caribbean, whose share was cut by more than half from 1960 to 2000—from 8 to 3.4 per cent.

The sharp rise in the number of international migrants in Northern America is noteworthy, since that number more than tripled from 1960 to 2000, passing from 13 million to 41 million, and increasing at an average rate of 3.2 per cent per year. The United States, whose foreign-born population more than tripled—from 10 million in 1960 to 35 million in 2000—accounted for most of the regional increase. As a result, the proportion of international migrants among the total population of Northern America more than doubled: from 6 per cent in 1960 to 13 per cent in 2000.

... replacing Europe as the leading region of destination

In Europe, excluding the former USSR, the number of international migrants also increased significantly, particularly in the 1990s. In the period from 1960 to 2000, it rose from 14 million to 33 million, and the number of international migrants as a proportion of the total population increased from 3.3 to 6.4 per cent; thus, whereas in 1960, Europe had 4 million more international migrants than the United States, by the end of the century, there were more international migrants in the United States than in Europe, excluding the former USSR.

The majority of refugees in the world have found asylum in developing countries, particularly in Africa and Asia. In 2000, refugees accounted for 23 per cent of all international migrants in Asia and for 22 per cent of those in Africa. The number of refugees under the mandate of the Office of the United Nations High Commissioner for Refugees (UNHCR) has been rising since the late 1970s, passing from 2 million in 1975 to 16 million in 1990. During the 1990s, as long-standing conflicts, particularly in Africa and Latin America and the Caribbean, came to an end, the repatriation of large numbers of refugees became possible. By 2000, the number of refugees reported to UNHCR had dropped to 12 million and an additional 5 million refugees were under the mandate of the United Nations Relief and Works Agency for Palestine Refugees in the Near East (UNRWA).

Available estimates of the number of international migrants by sex show that the volume of international migration has been nearly equal for men and women. In 2000, females constituted almost 49 per cent of all international migrants, up from 47 per cent in 1960 (table II.2). The proportion of females among international migrants has tended to be higher in the developed regions than in the developing world. In 1960, female migrants had constituted 49 per cent of the migrant stock in developed countries, whereas they accounted for 45 per cent of the migrant stock in developing countries. By 2000, female migrants were slightly more numerous than their male counterparts in developed countries—51 versus 49 per cent—but their share of the international migrant stock in developing countries had declined somewhat, to just under 45 per cent; that is to say, although there has been an overall increase in the worldwide proportion of female migrants, that increase has not been universal. In particular, the share of female migrants declined in Asia, from 46.4 per cent in 1960 to 43.3 per cent in 2000. Nevertheless, by the end of the twentieth century, females were more numerous than males among the international migrants in Latin America and the Caribbean, Northern America, Oceania, Europe and the former USSR, although they remained underrepresented among international migrants in Africa and Asia.

There are approximately equal numbers of women and men in the world's stock of international migrants

Table II.2.
Females in the stock of international migrants by major area, 1960 and 2000

Percentage	1960	2000
World	46.7	48.6
Developed countries	48.7	51.0
Developed countries excluding USSR	48.7	50.6
Developing countries	45.3	44.6
Africa	42.3	46.7
Asia[a]	46.4	43.3
Latin America and the Caribbean	44.7	50.2
Northern America	49.8	50.3
Oceania	44.4	50.5
Europe[b]	48.5	51.0
USSR (former)	48.5	52.1

Source: United Nations, Trends in Total Migrant Stock: The 2003 Revision (POP/DB/MIG/Rev. 2003), data in digital form.

a Excluding Armenia, Azerbaijan, Georgia, Kazakhstan, Kyrgyzstan, Tajikistan, Turkmenistan and Uzbekistan.

b Excluding Belarus, Estonia, Latvia, Lithuania, the Republic of Moldova, the Russian Federation and Ukraine.

About 50 per cent of all international migrants were economically active in 2000

The International Labour Organization (2004a) estimates that about 50 per cent of all international migrants, that is to say, 86 million, were economically active in 2000, with 32 million in developing countries and 54 million in developed countries. Labour-force participation rates among foreign men in 23 developed countries were higher than those of men who were nationals or natives, but the opposite tended to be true of foreign women in relation to national or native women (see below). In most developed countries, unemployment rates were higher for foreigners, particularly foreign women, than for nationals. Although the majority of international migrants in the labour force of developed countries were unskilled or semi-skilled, a significant number were in professional or managerial occupations. During the 1990s, receiving countries put greater emphasis on admitting migrants on the basis of their skills, and countries experiencing shortages of skilled personnel adopted policies that promoted the admission of persons with the required skills.

Distribution of international migrants at the country level

During the twentieth century, no country was closed to international migration. Accordingly, the proportion of international migrants in all countries was greater than zero. Nevertheless, many countries hosted small proportions of migrants both in 1960 and in 2000, and the concentration of international migrants in countries with relatively high proportions of migrants increased during the period.

While in 1960 there had been 43 countries where the share of international migrants in the population exceeded 10 per cent, that number had risen to 70 countries in 2000 (figs. II.1 and II.2). Countries or areas where international migrants constituted more than 60 per cent of the population in 2000 included Andorra, Macao Special Administrative Region of China, Guam, Monaco, Qatar and the United Arab Emirates.

However, most of the countries or areas with high proportions of international migrants have fewer than a million inhabitants. Among the 40 countries with more than 10 million inhabitants in 1960, only in 4—Argentina, Australia, Canada and Pakistan—had the proportion of international migrants surpassed 10 per cent. By 2000, that number had increased to 9 out of the 78 countries with 10 million inhabitants or more—Australia, Belarus, Canada, Côte d'Ivoire, France, Kazakhstan, Saudi Arabia, Ukraine and the United States. In 1960, the four populous countries with the highest proportions of international migrants accounted for less than 18 per cent of all international migrants in the world, whereas in 2000, the nine countries listed accounted for 40 per cent of all international migrants.

International migrants are concentrated in relatively few countries

International migrants remain concentrated in relatively few countries. Thus, just 22 countries, representing 10 per cent of all countries in 1960, accounted for over three quarters of all international migrants in that year; and in 2000, just 28 countries, representing 12 per cent of all countries in that year, accounted for the same proportion (table II.3). There has been a marked concentration of international migrants in the major receiving country, the United States, whose share of all international migrants increased from 13 per cent in 1960 to 20 per cent in 2000. Other countries whose share of all international migrants increased substantially include Australia, Canada, France, Germany and the United Kingdom. In addition, several countries that had not made the list of major receiving countries in 1960 occupied prominent places in the list for 2000, including Kazakhstan, Pakistan, the Russian Federation, Saudi Arabia and Ukraine.

Figure II.1.
International migrants as a proportion of total population, by region, 1970

Percentage

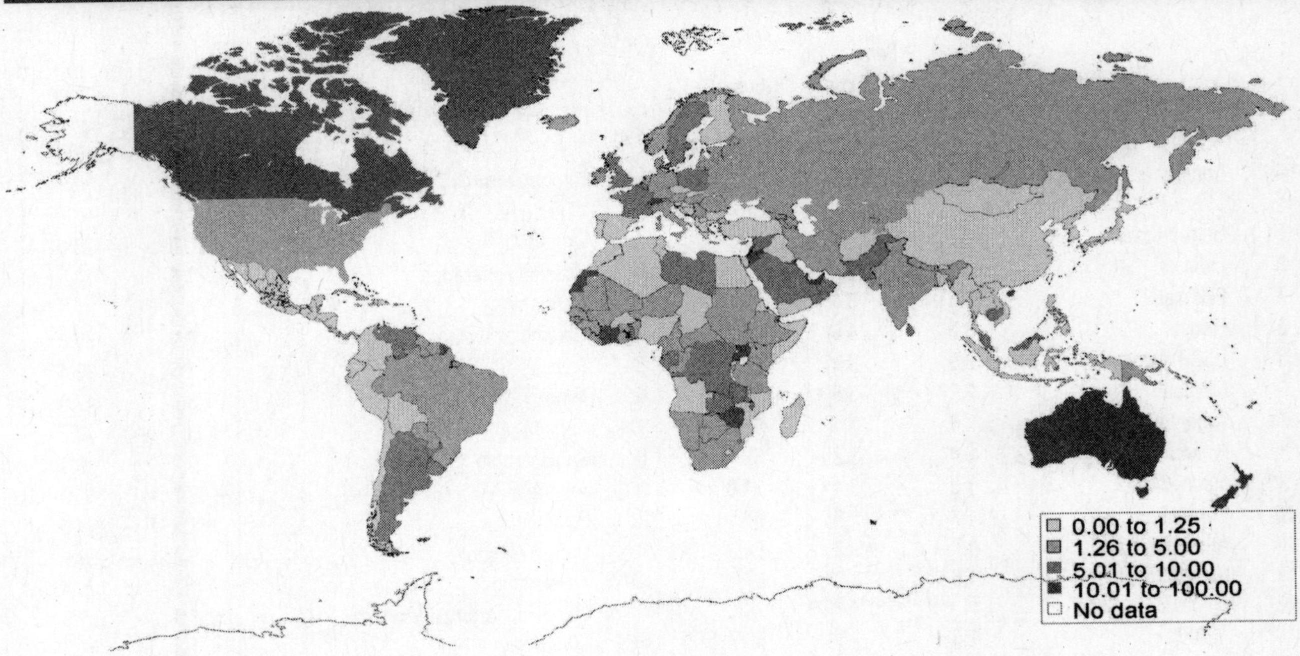

Figure II.2.
International migrants as a proportion of total population, by region, 2000

Percentage

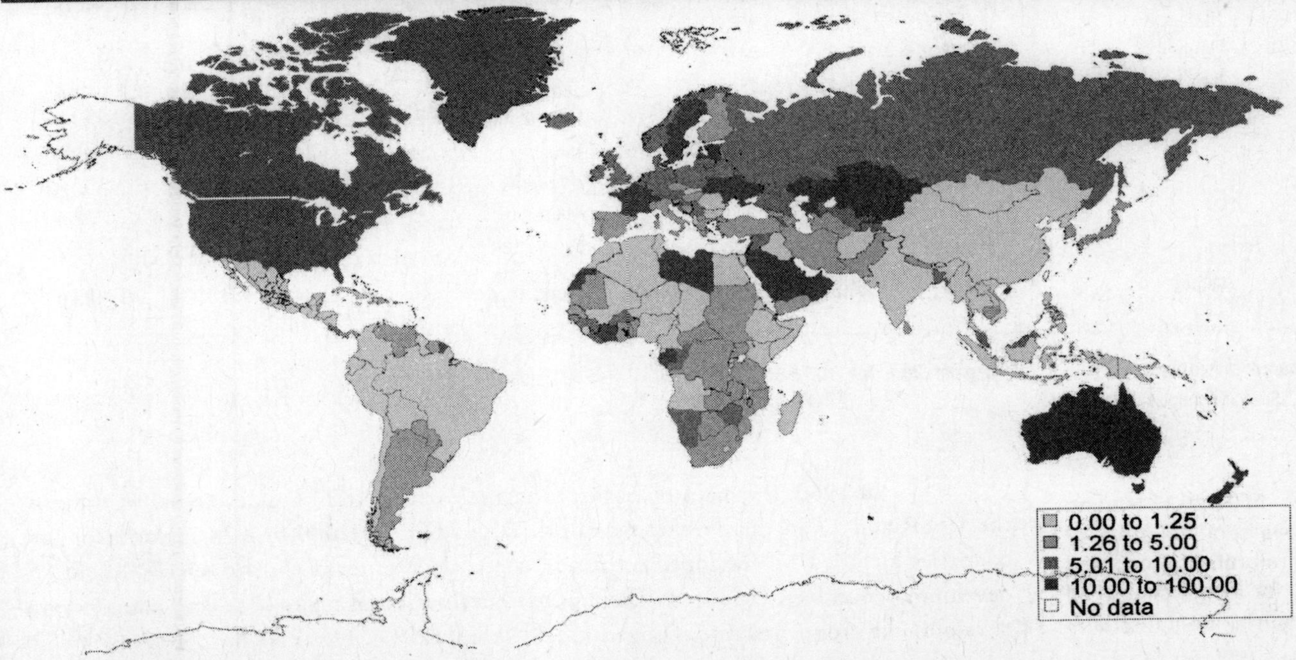

Table II.3.
Leading host countries for international migrants, 1960 and 2000

1960					2000				
Rank	Country or area	Migrant stock (millions)	Percentage of the world's migrant stock	Cumulated percentage	Rank	Country or area	Migrant stock (millions)	Percentage of the world's migrant stock	Cumulated percentage
1	United States	9.7	12.8	12.8	1	United States	35.0	20.0	20.0
2	India	9.4	12.4	25.2	2	Russian Federation	13.3	7.6	27.6
3	Pakistan	6.3	8.4	33.6	3	Germany	7.3	4.2	31.8
4	France	3.5	4.6	38.2	4	Ukraine	6.9	4.0	35.8
5	USSR (former)	2.9	3.9	42.1	5	France	6.3	3.6	39.4
6	Canada	2.8	3.6	45.7	6	India	6.3	3.6	43.0
7	Argentina	2.6	3.4	49.2	7	Canada	5.8	3.3	46.3
8	Poland	2.4	3.2	52.4	8	Saudi Arabia	5.3	3.0	49.3
9	Indonesia	1.9	2.4	54.8	9	Australia	4.7	2.7	52.0
10	Germany	1.7	2.3	57.1	10	Pakistan	4.2	2.4	54.4
11	Australia	1.7	2.2	59.3	11	United Kingdom	4.0	2.3	56.7
12	United Kingdom	1.6	2.2	61.5	12	Kazakhstan	3.0	1.7	58.4
13	China, Hong Kong SAR[a]	1.6	2.1	63.7	13	China, Hong Kong SAR[a]	2.7	1.5	59.9
14	Brazil	1.4	1.8	65.5	14	Côte d' Ivoire	2.3	1.3	61.2
15	Israel	1.2	1.6	67.1	15	Iran (Islamic Republic of)	2.3	1.3	62.5
16	Sri Lanka	1.0	1.3	68.4	16	Israel	2.3	1.3	63.8
17	Democratic Republic of the Congo	1.0	1.3	69.7	17	Poland	2.1	1.2	65.0
18	Turkey	1.0	1.3	71.0	18	Jordan	1.9	1.1	66.1
19	South Africa	0.9	1.2	72.2	19	United Arab Emirates	1.9	1.1	67.2
20	Malaysia	0.9	1.1	73.3	20	Switzerland	1.8	1.0	68.2
21	Uganda	0.7	1.0	74.3	21	Occupied Palestinian Territories	1.7	1.0	69.2
22	Italy	0.7	1	75.3	22	Italy	1.6	0.9	70.1
					23	Japan	1.6	0.9	71.0
					24	Netherlands	1.6	0.9	71.9
					25	Turkey	1.5	0.9	72.8
					26	Argentina	1.4	0.8	73.6
					27	Malaysia	1.4	0.8	74.4
					28	Uzbekistan	1.4	0.8	75.2
	World	81.5	100.0	100.0		World	174.9	100.0	100.0

Source: United Nations, *Trends in Total Migrant Stock: The 2003 Revision* (POP/DB/MIG/Rev. 2003), data in digital form.
a Special Administrative Region.

In 2000, 11 leading developed countries of immigration accounted for 41 per cent of all international migrants

In 1960, the main receiving countries included 8 in the developed world plus the USSR and 13 in the developing world (table II.3). By 2000, the 28 major receiving countries included 11 developed countries, 4 successor States of the former USSR and 13 developing countries. However, although the distribution of major receiving countries by development group had not changed much, there was a substantial shift in the share of international migrants corresponding to each group. Thus, in 2000, the 11 major receivers in the developed world accounted for 41 per cent of all international migrants, up from the 30 per cent share of the 8 developed countries in the list in 1960. Concomitantly, the share of the 13 developing countries had declined markedly, from 40 per cent in 1960 to 20 per cent in 2000, with most of the gain going to the main receivers among the successor States of the former USSR, whose share had risen from 4 to 14 per cent between 1960 and 2000.

These changes point to the declining importance, in relative terms, of international migration for developing countries of destination. Although sizeable numbers of international migrants exist in a number of developing countries, their weight both as a proportion of the global migrant stock and in relation to the population of developing countries as a whole is declining. Accordingly, international migrants as a proportion of the population of developing countries dropped from 2.1 per cent in 1960 to 1.3 per cent in 2000, illustrating a trend that contrasts with that in developed countries, where the share of international migrants in the population rose from 3.4 to 8.7 per cent over the same period (table II.1).

By the end of the twentieth century, international migration accounted for two-thirds of all population growth in the developed regions; it reduced slightly the rate of population growth in the developing regions

The significance of international migration in developed countries also stems from the role it plays in population growth. In the period 1960-1965, the rate of natural increase[3] in the more developed regions as a whole had been 10.4 per thousand, whereas the net migration rate was 0.5 per thousand; hence, when net migration was added to the rate of natural increase, this yielded a growth rate of 10.9 per thousand (table II.4); that is to say, the contribution of net migration to population growth in the more developed regions was small. In the less developed regions, where the rate of natural increase was 24 per thousand, the contribution of negative net migration, at -0.2 per thousand, had been negligible in the early 1960s. However, in the period 1995-2000, the relative impact of international migration on the growth of the more developed regions increased markedly, with net migration

Table II.4.
Contribution of net international migration to population change, by major region, 1960-1965 and 1995-2000

	Per thousand					
	1960-1965			1995-2000		
Major area	Rate of natural increase	Net migration rate	Population growth rate	Rate of natural increase	Net migration rate	Population growth rate
More developed regions	10.4	0.5	10.9	1.2	2.2	3.4
Less developed regions	23.7	-0.2	23.5	16.7	-0.6	16.1
Africa	25.6	-1.0	24.6	24.0	-0.5	23.5
Asia	22.0	0.0	22.0	14.5	-0.4	14.1
Latin America and the Caribbean	28.6	-1.1	27.5	16.8	-1.2	15.6
Northern America	13.2	1.4	14.6	6.1	4.6	10.7
Europe	9.4	0.2	9.6	-1.2	1.4	0.2
Oceania	15.9	5.2	21.1	11.1	3.0	14.1

Source: *World Population Prospects: The 2002 Revision, vol. I: Comprehensive Tables* (United Nations publication, Sales No. E.03.XIII.6).

nearly doubling the contribution of natural increase (2.2 per thousand versus 1.2 per thousand). In the less developed regions, net migration, at -0.6 per thousand, was still reducing the rate of natural increase (16.7 per thousand) by a very small percentage.

In the absence of immigration, the population of Europe would have declined during the last years of the twentieth century

In other words, although developing countries as a whole have been consistently losing population because of international migration, their overall rate of natural increase is still so high that net emigration has had only a small impact on population trends. In sharp contrast, the rising net inflows of international migrants to developed countries have been and will continue to be crucial in increasing levels of population growth or, in some cases, preventing population reductions from taking place. Europe, in particular, would have experienced a population decline of 4.4 million during 1995-2000 had it not been for migrant inflows, since the population of Europe gained about 5 million migrants between 1995 and 2000 while its population increased by just 600,000 people. As shown in table II.4, the net migration rate of Europe in 1995-2000 at 1.4 per thousand has been barely high enough to offset the negative rate of natural increase of -1.2 per thousand experienced during that period. The contribution of net migration to population growth has also gained significance in Northern America, where net migration's contribution to population growth rose from 10 per cent in 1960-1965 to 43 per cent in 1995-2000. In contrast, the relative contribution of net migration to population growth declined in Oceania, from 25 per cent in 1960-1965 to 21 per cent in 1995-2000. At the country level, Germany's population would have been declining since at least 1970 had it not been for the net migration gains the country has experienced. In the late 1990s, positive net international migration made major contributions to the growth of countries such as Austria, Denmark, Greece, Italy, Luxembourg, Spain and Switzerland, where it contributed at least three quarters of overall population growth.

In sum, the number of international migrants is increasingly being concentrated in developed countries and relatively few countries account for the majority of international migrants in the world (28 in 2000). Virtually all the increase in the international migrant stock during the 1990s was absorbed by developed countries, especially those in Northern America, Oceania and Western Europe. Although the number of countries where international migrants constitute at least 10 per cent of the population had increased markedly, reaching 70 in 2000, the vast majority of those countries had small overall populations and small numbers of international migrants. The impact of international migration is particularly important for Western Europe and the overseas countries of immigration, not only because they are attracting more international migrants than the rest of the world, but also because international migration is contributing significantly to raising their low rates of population growth. Lastly, the primacy of the United States as a migrant-receiving country has increased markedly. In 2000, 1 out of every 5 international migrants in the world lived in the United States.

An analysis of net migration

Whereas the international migrant stock measured in terms of the number of foreign-born persons in each country is a useful indicator of the cumulative impact of international migration on a population, the dynamics of international migration can best be assessed by considering measures of international migration flows. Ideally, one would have access to estimates of the number of immigrants arriving in and the number of emigrants departing from each country over a particular period. In practice, those estimates do not exist. Yet estimates of net migration, which represents the difference between the number of immigrants and the number of emigrants, are available for all countries or areas with at least 150,000 inhabitants in 2000 for each five-year period between 1950 and 2000 (United Nations, 2003e). Such estimates permit an assessment of the migration status of countries by considering whether they have experienced positive or negative net migration consistently or whether—and, if so, how often—net migration has changed sign, from positive to negative or vice versa, during the period 1950-2000.

According to table II.5, among the 109 countries with 5 million inhabitants or more in 2000, 16 had experienced consistently negative net migration during each five-year period between 1950 and 2000, and just 7 had experienced consistently positive net migration; that is to say, 16 countries (including India, Indonesia, Bangladesh and Mexico, in order of decreasing population size) were consistently countries of emigration and 7 (the United States, France, Canada, Australia, Côte d'Ivoire, Sweden and Israel, in order of decreasing population size) were consistently countries of immigration.

Among the other 86 countries, net migration had changed sign or been zero at least once since 1950. The last column of table II.5 presents a classification of each country according to whether it was mostly a country of emigration (E) or a country of immigration (I). In general, countries experiencing three or more periods of negative net migration were classified as countries of emigration. Exceptions include mostly countries in Europe and Asia that used to be countries of emigration but have become receiving countries in recent years, namely, Greece, Italy, Portugal, Slovakia and Spain, which used to be the main sources of migrant workers for the rest of Europe in the 1950s and 1960s but have become important destinations of migrants since the late 1980s; Finland, which was a source of workers for neighbouring Sweden until the 1970s; the United Kingdom, which was a major source of overseas emigrants before it became mainly a destination for migrants from the Commonwealth and other countries; Malaysia, whose workers provided labour for Singapore but which is now importing workers from other countries in South-East Asia; Japan, which has become an important attraction pole for ethnic Japanese from Latin America and workers from Asia; the Russian Federation, which is experiencing the return or repatriation of ethnic Russians from other member States of the Commonwealth of Independent States (CIS); and the Czech Republic and Hungary, which, as new members of the European Union (EU), will likely continue to be attractive destinations for migrants from other Eastern and Central European countries.

Countries with at most one or two periods of negative net migration were generally classified as countries of immigration, the only exception being Ecuador, which has become a country of emigration. In addition, the Democratic People's Republic of Korea is exceptional because it is the only country that still restricts international mobility and is largely closed to international migration.

For many countries, international migration can and does shift from a net inflow to a net outflow, and vice versa

According to table II.5, international migration is a volatile phenomenon whose direction can and often does change, implying that, for most countries, it is not possible to postulate that a lengthy period of sustained negative net migration will necessarily be followed by a period of sustained positive net migration. As the discussion that follows will show, the economic and political causes of international migration do not change smoothly and, consequently, they often lead to wide and rapid fluctuations in international migration trends.

Table II.5.

Countries or areas with 5 million inhabitants or more in 2000, by net migration status, 1950-2000

Number of periods with negative net migration	Number of periods with positive net migration	Country or area	1950-1955	1955-1960	1960-1965	1965-1970	1970-1975	1975-1980	1980-1985	1985-1990	1990-1995	1995-2000	Total net migration 1950-2000 (millions)	Population in 2000 (millions)	Migration type
10	0	Nicaragua	-1	-1	-1	-1	-1	-1	-1	-1	-1	-1	-0.4	5	E
		Haiti	-1	-1	-1	-1	-1	-1	-1	-1	-1	-1	-0.8	8	E
		Bulgaria	-1	-1	-1	-1	-1	-1	-1	-1	-1	-1	-0.9	8	E
		Bolivia	-1	-1	-1	-1	-1	-1	-1	-1	-1	-1	-0.6	8	E
		Tunisia	-1	-1	-1	-1	-1	-1	-1	-1	-1	-1	-0.9	10	E
		Cuba	-1	-1	-1	-1	-1	-1	-1	-1	-1	-1	-1.0	11	E
		Mali	-1	-1	-1	-1	-1	-1	-1	-1	-1	-1	-1.4	12	E
		Burkina Faso	-1	-1	-1	-1	-1	-1	-1	-1	-1	-1	-1.5	12	E
		Syrian Arab Republic	-1	-1	-1	-1	-1	-1	-1	-1	-1	-1	-0.4	17	E
		Nepal	-1	-1	-1	-1	-1	-1	-1	-1	-1	-1	-0.6	24	E
		Poland	-1	-1	-1	-1	-1	-1	-1	-1	-1	-1	-1.4	39	E
		Colombia	-1	-1	-1	-1	-1	-1	-1	-1	-1	-1	-2.4	42	E
		Mexico	-1	-1	-1	-1	-1	-1	-1	-1	-1	-1	-8.7	99	E
		Bangladesh	-1	-1	-1	-1	-1	-1	-1	-1	-1	-1	-0.9	138	E
		Indonesia	-1	-1	-1	-1	-1	-1	-1	-1	-1	-1	-2.2	212	E
		India	-1	-1	-1	-1	-1	-1	-1	-1	-1	-1	-4.4	1 017	E
9	0	Chile	-1	-1	-1	-1	-1	-1	-1	-1	0	-1	-0.5	15	E
	1	El Salvador	-1	-1	-1	1	-1	-1	-1	-1	-1	-1	-1.0	6	E
		Benin	-1	-1	-1	-1	-1	-1	-1	-1	1	-1	-0.6	6	E
		Burundi	-1	-1	-1	-1	-1	-1	1	-1	-1	-1	-1.2	6	E
		Azerbaijan	-1	1	-1	-1	-1	-1	-1	-1	-1	-1	-0.7	8	E
		Malawi	-1	-1	-1	-1	-1	-1	-1	1	-1	-1	-0.4	11	E
		Yemen	-1	-1	-1	-1	-1	-1	-1	-1	1	-1	-0.4	18	E
		Romania	1	-1	-1	-1	-1	-1	-1	-1	-1	-1	-1.2	22	E
		Morocco	1	-1	-1	-1	-1	-1	-1	-1	-1	-1	-1.8	29	E
		Algeria	-1	-1	-1	-1	-1	-1	1	-1	-1	-1	-2.1	30	E
		Republic of Korea	1	-1	-1	-1	-1	-1	-1	-1	-1	-1	-0.4	47	E
		Turkey	-1	-1	-1	-1	-1	-1	1	-1	-1	-1	-1.8	68	E
		China	-1	-1	-1	1	-1	-1	-1	-1	-1	-1	-5.5	1 275	E

Table II.5 (cont'd)

Number of periods with negative net migration	Number of periods with positive net migration	Country or area	1950-1955	1955-1960	1960-1965	1965-1970	1970-1975	1975-1980	1980-1985	1985-1990	1990-1995	1995-2000	Total net migration 1950-2000 (millions)	Population in 2000 (millions)	Migration type
8	0	Dominican Republic	0	0	-1	-1	-1	-1	-1	-1	-1	-1	-0.6	8	E
		Guatemala	0	0	-1	-1	-1	-1	-1	-1	-1	-1	-1.2	11	E
		Sri Lanka	0	0	-1	-1	-1	-1	-1	-1	-1	-1	-1.3	19	E
	2	Paraguay	-1	-1	-1	-1	-1	1	-1	1	-1	-1	-0.3	5	E
		Niger	1	-1	-1	-1	-1	-1	-1	-1	1	-1	-0.1	11	E
		Zimbabwe	-1	-1	-1	-1	-1	-1	1	1	-1	-1	-0.1	13	E
		Egypt	-1	1	1	-1	-1	-1	-1	-1	-1	-1	-3.5	68	E
7	0	Madagascar	0	0	0	-1	-1	-1	-1	-1	-1	-1	-0.1	16	E
		Philippines	0	0	0	-1	-1	-1	-1	-1	-1	-1	-4.2	76	E
	1	Papua New Guinea	-1	-1	-1	1	-1	-1	-1	-1	0	0	0.0	5	E
	3	Georgia	1	1	-1	1	-1	-1	-1	-1	-1	-1	-0.4	5	E
		Tajikistan	-1	-1	1	1	1	-1	-1	-1	-1	-1	-0.7	6	E
		Honduras	1	1	1	-1	-1	-1	-1	-1	-1	-1	-0.2	6	E
		Guinea	-1	-1	-1	-1	-1	1	-1	1	1	-1	-0.2	8	E
		Portugal	-1	-1	-1	-1	1	1	-1	-1	-1	1	-1.8	10	EI
		Angola	-1	-1	-1	-1	-1	1	1	-1	1	-1	-0.3	12	E
		Cambodia	-1	-1	-1	-1	-1	-1	-1	1	1	1	-0.4	13	E
		Mozambique	-1	-1	-1	-1	-1	1	-1	-1	1	1	-0.9	18	E
		Iraq	-1	1	-1	-1	-1	-1	-1	-1	1	1	-0.5	23	E
		Iran (Islamic Republic of)	-1	-1	-1	-1	-1	1	1	1	-1	-1	-0.2	66	E
		Pakistan	-1	-1	-1	-1	-1	1	1	1	-1	-1	-0.3	143	E
6	3	Ethiopia	0	-1	-1	-1	-1	-1	1	1	1	-1	0.1	66	E
	4	Slovakia	1	1	-1	-1	-1	-1	-1	-1	1	1	-0.1	5	EI
		Hungary	1	-1	1	1	-1	-1	-1	-1	-1	1	-0.4	10	EI
		Belarus	-1	-1	-1	1	-1	-1	1	-1	1	1	-0.8	10	E
		Serbia and Montenegro	1	-1	-1	-1	-1	1	-1	1	1	-1	-0.1	11	E
		Kazakhstan	1	1	1	1	-1	-1	-1	-1	-1	-1	-1.4	16	E
		Spain	-1	-1	-1	-1	-1	1	-1	1	1	1	0.1	41	EI
		Italy	-1	-1	-1	-1	-1	1	-1	1	1	1	-0.8	58	EI
		United Kingdom	-1	-1	1	-1	-1	-1	-1	1	1	1	0.3	59	EI
		Nigeria	1	1	1	-1	-1	1	-1	-1	-1	-1	-0.2	115	E
		Japan	-1	-1	-1	-1	-1	-1	1	1	1	1	0.5	127	EI

Table II.5 (cont'd)

Number of periods with negative net migration	Number of periods with positive net migration	Country or area	1950-1955	1955-1960	1960-1965	1965-1970	1970-1975	1975-1980	1980-1985	1985-1990	1990-1995	1995-2000	Total net migration 1950-2000 (millions)	Population in 2000 (millions)	Migration type
5	0	Peru	0	0	0	0	0	-1	-1	-1	-1	-1	-1.1	26	E
		Viet Nam	0	0	0	0	0	-1	-1	-1	-1	-1	-1.8	78	E
	3	Rwanda	0	0	-1	1	-1	-1	-1	1	-1	1	-0.1	8	E
		Kenya	0	0	-1	-1	-1	-1	1	1	1	-1	0.1	31	E
		Sudan	0	0	-1	-1	1	1	1	-1	-1	-1	0.0	31	E
	4	Ghana	1	1	0	-1	-1	-1	1	-1	1	-1	-0.8	20	E
	5	Finland	-1	-1	-1	-1	1	-1	1	1	1	1	-0.2	5	EI
		Lao People's Democratic Republic	-1	1	1	1	1	-1	-1	1	-1	-1	-0.3	5	E
		Greece	-1	-1	-1	-1	-1	1	1	1	1	1	0.6	11	EI
		Ukraine	-1	-1	1	1	1	-1	-1	1	1	-1	0.9	50	E
		Russian Federation	-1	-1	-1	-1	-1	1	1	1	1	1	2.9	146	EI
4	1	Afghanistan	0	0	0	0	0	-1	-1	-1	1	-1	-3.1	21	E
		Brazil	1	0	0	0	0	0	-1	-1	-1	-1	0.1	172	E
	2	Thailand	0	0	0	0	1	1	-1	-1	-1	-1	-1.0	61	E
	3	Chad	0	0	0	-1	-1	-1	-1	1	1	1	-0.1	8	E
	4	Uganda	0	0	1	1	-1	-1	-1	1	1	-1	0.0	23	E
	6	Czech Republic	1	1	-1	-1	-1	1	1	-1	1	1	0.2	10	EI
		Malaysia	1	1	1	-1	-1	1	-1	-1	1	1	0.6	23	EI
		Uzbekistan	1	1	1	1	1	1	-1	-1	-1	-1	-0.4	25	E
3	1	Myanmar	0	0	0	0	0	0	-1	-1	-1	1	-0.3	48	E
	2	Somalia	0	0	0	0	0	1	-1	-1	-1	1	-0.5	9	E
	4	Cameroon	0	0	0	1	1	1	-1	1	-1	-1	0.0	15	E
	7	Libyan Arab Jamahiriya	-1	1	1	1	1	1	1	-1	-1	1	0.4	5	I
2	0	Ecuador	0	0	0	0	0	0	0	0	-1	-1	-0.2	12	E
	5	Zambia	0	0	0	-1	1	1	1	1	-1	1	0.2	10	I
	6	United Republic of Tanzania	0	0	1	1	1	-1	1	1	1	-1	0.7	35	I
	7	Democratic Republic of the Congo	0	1	1	1	1	1	-1	1	1	-1	0.0	49	I
	8	Jordan	1	1	1	1	-1	-1	1	1	1	1	1.3	5	I
		Denmark	-1	-1	1	1	1	1	1	1	1	1	0.2	5	I
		Switzerland	1	1	1	1	-1	-1	1	1	1	1	1.1	7	I
		Austria	-1	-1	1	1	1	1	1	1	1	1	0.5	8	I
		Senegal	1	1	1	1	1	1	1	1	-1	-1	0.2	9	I
		Netherlands	-1	-1	1	1	1	1	1	1	1	1	0.8	16	I
		Saudi Arabia	-1	1	1	1	1	1	1	1	-1	1	4.1	22	I

Table II.5 (cont'd)

Number of periods with negative net migration	Number of periods with positive net migration	Country or area	1950-1955	1955-1960	1960-1965	1965-1970	1970-1975	1975-1980	1980-1985	1985-1990	1990-1995	1995-2000	Total net migration 1950-2000 (millions)	Population in 2000 (millions)	Migration type
1	0	Democratic People's Republic of Korea	-1	0	0	0	0	0	0	0	0	0	-0.9	22	N
	9	China, Hong Kong SAR[a]	1	1	1	-1	1	1	1	1	1	1	1.9	7	I
		Belgium	1	1	1	1	1	1	-1	1	1	1	0.5	10	I
		Venezuela	1	1	1	1	1	1	-1	1	1	1	1.2	24	I
		Argentina	1	1	1	1	1	-1	1	1	1	1	1.2	37	I
		South Africa	1	1	1	1	1	1	1	1	1	-1	1.0	44	I
		Germany	1	1	1	1	1	1	-1	1	1	1	9.5	82	I
0	10	Israel	1	1	1	1	1	1	1	1	1	1	1.7	6	I
		Sweden	1	1	1	1	1	1	1	1	1	1	0.7	9	I
		Côte d'Ivoire	1	1	1	1	1	1	1	1	1	1	2.2	16	I
		Australia	1	1	1	1	1	1	1	1	1	1	4.4	19	I
		Canada	1	1	1	1	1	1	1	1	1	1	5.8	31	I
		France	1	1	1	1	1	1	1	1	1	1	4.7	59	I
		United States	1	1	1	1	1	1	1	1	1	1	32.1	285	I

Source: *World Population Prospects: The 2002 Revision*, data sets in Excel and PDF formats (United Nations publication, Sales No. E.03.XIII.8).

Note: For each period, a value of 1 indicates net migration was positive, a value of -1 indicates that net migration was negative and a value of 0 indicates that net migration was zero. The migration type is coded as E if the country is considered mainly a country of emigration, I if the country is mainly a country of immigration, EI when the country has changed position over time but is considered a country of immigration in recent times, and N if the country has essentially been closed to migration.

a Special Administrative Region.

The traditional countries of immigration

In Canada, Australia and New Zealand, the numbers of foreign-born has approximately doubled over the past 40 years

Australia, Canada, New Zealand and the United States are among the few countries in the world admitting immigrants for permanent settlement. Consequently, the number of international migrants in these four countries increased markedly between 1960 and 2000, passing from 14.5 million to 46.4 million. The United States registered the major increase, amounting to over 25 million migrants, as its foreign-born population rose from 9.7 million to 35 million.[4] Canada registered a net gain of 3 million migrants during the period, Australia another 3 million, and New Zealand about half a million. By 2000, Canada was hosting 5.8 million foreign-born persons, Australia, 4.7 million and New Zealand, 850,000.

Immigration to these countries has been shaped by the admission policies adopted by each. In 1965, the United States modified its admission system by eliminating the quotas by region of origin that had been used until then and substituting for them selection criteria based mainly on family ties with United States citizens or permanent residents (see chap. III). In the 1970s, Australia and Canada had followed suit, eliminating their selection systems based on national origins and adopting instead their respective versions of a "points system" whereby various attributes of prospective immigrants are graded and weighed in making selections for admission. In 1987, New Zealand enacted new immigration legislation that no longer used country of origin as an explicit basis for immigrant selection. As a result of these changes, all four countries experienced a diversification of immigration flows. Yet there have been significant differences in the trends in immigrant admissions experienced by each (table II.6). Australia and Canada, just like receiving countries in Western Europe, experienced fairly low levels of immigration in 1975-1984. Since 1985, trends in the two countries diverged, as immigration to Canada rose above the levels recorded in 1970-1974 and reached an average annual level of 236,000 in 2000-2002, a level above the range adopted by planning authorities (between 200,000 and 225,000). In contrast, the average annual number of immigrants to Australia remained below 100,000 throughout the 1990s.

There were about 7 million unauthorized migrants in the United States in 2000

Trends in immigrant admissions by the United States were different: between 1960 and 1995, the average annual number of immigrants admitted increased steadily. The slight decline recorded in 1995-2000 was due to delays in processing applications. During the 1990s, the United States admitted an annual average of over 750,000 immigrants and by the early twenty-first century that number had grown to nearly 1 million immigrants per year. In fact, the actual number of immigrants processed during 1989-1994 was higher than that listed in table II.6 because the table excludes the 2.7 million immigrants whose status was regularized as a result of the Immigration Reform and Control Act (IRCA) of 1986, of whom 75 per cent were Mexican. As a result of that regularization, the number of migrants in an irregular situation in the United States declined from an estimated 4 million in 1986 to an estimated 2.5 million in 1989. However, unauthorized migration appears to have continued unabated during the 1990s, especially as the United States economy boomed. The number of unauthorized migrants in the United States in January 2000 has been estimated at 7 million,[5] 4.8 of whom were Mexican (United States Immigration and Naturalization Service, 2003).

In New Zealand, the average annual number of arrivals of permanent and long-term immigrants has increased steadily since 1975 but net gains from international migration have been much lower because the number of departures of permanent and long-term migrants has also been high (see figure II.3). The net number of migrants was negative during 1975-1989. Since 1990, New Zealand has again been recording net gains of permanent and long-term immigrants, averaging about 12,000 a year during 1990-2003.

Table II.6.
Admissions of immigrants to Australia, Canada, New Zealand and the United States, and their distribution by region of birth, 1960-2002

Region of birth	Receiving country	1960-1964	1965-1969	1970-1974	1975-1979	1980-1984	1985-1989	1990-1994	1995-1999	2000-2002
	Annual average (thousands)									
All regions	Australia	115	147	142	71	95	115	99	87	92
	Canada	102	182	159	130	114	138	236	204	236
	New Zealand[a]	31	31	55	41	43	45	56	68	84
	United States	284	359	385	460	565	606	770	746	993
	Distribution by region of birth (percentage)									
Developing countries	Australia	6	9	19	40	39	53	60	55	53
	Canada	11	21	42	56	62	71	78	78	78
	United States	41	56	70	81	85	87	79	82	81
Eastern and Central Europe	Australia	8	7	12	5	7	5	7	9	6
	Canada	9	7	5	5	9	10	11	12	12
	United States	7	6	5	3	4	4	11	11	11
Developed countries excluding Eastern and Central Europe	Australia	86	85	69	55	53	42	32	36	41
	Canada	80	72	52	40	29	19	11	10	10
	United States	52	38	25	19	11	10	10	7	8
Asia	Australia	4	6	12	29	31	41	51	43	40
	Canada	4	11	22	32	44	40	49	54	54
	United States	8	14	29	37	45	43	41	33	30
Latin America and the Caribbean	Canada	3	6	15	17	13	16	13	8	8
	United States	34	41	40	41	35	40	35	42	42

Sources: United Nations, *South-to-North International Migration* (POP/1B/MIG/2001/1), data in digital form; SOPEMI (Continuous Reporting System on Migration), *Trends in International Migration: Annual Report, 2003 Edition* (Paris, OECD, 2004); and United States Department of Homeland Security, Office of Immigration Statistics. *2002 Yearbook of Immigration Statistics* (Washington, D.C., United States Government Printing Office, 2003).

a Data referring to the period 1960-2003, a complete time series of data classified by place of birth is not available.

Countries of origin were far more diverse in Australia, Canada, New Zealand and the United States in 2000 than they had been in 1960

In all countries of immigration, the flows of immigrants have become more varied in terms of origin. Data for Australia, Canada and the United States show that the proportion of immigrants originating in developing countries increased in all of them, but especially in Australia, where it passed from 6 per cent in 1960-1964 to 60 per cent in 1990-1994, and in Canada, where the corresponding increase was from 11 to 78 per cent. In the United States, the proportion of immigrants originating in developing countries had already been higher than in Australia or Canada in 1960-1964 (41 per cent) and after having risen to 87 per cent in 1985-1989, has remained close to 80 per cent since 1990. In fact, if the migrants who regularized their status in the United States as a result of the Immigration Reform and Control Act had been included in the statistics for the early 1990s, the proportion originating in developing countries would have risen considerably.

Figure II.3.
Permanent and long-term migration, New Zealand, 1950-2003

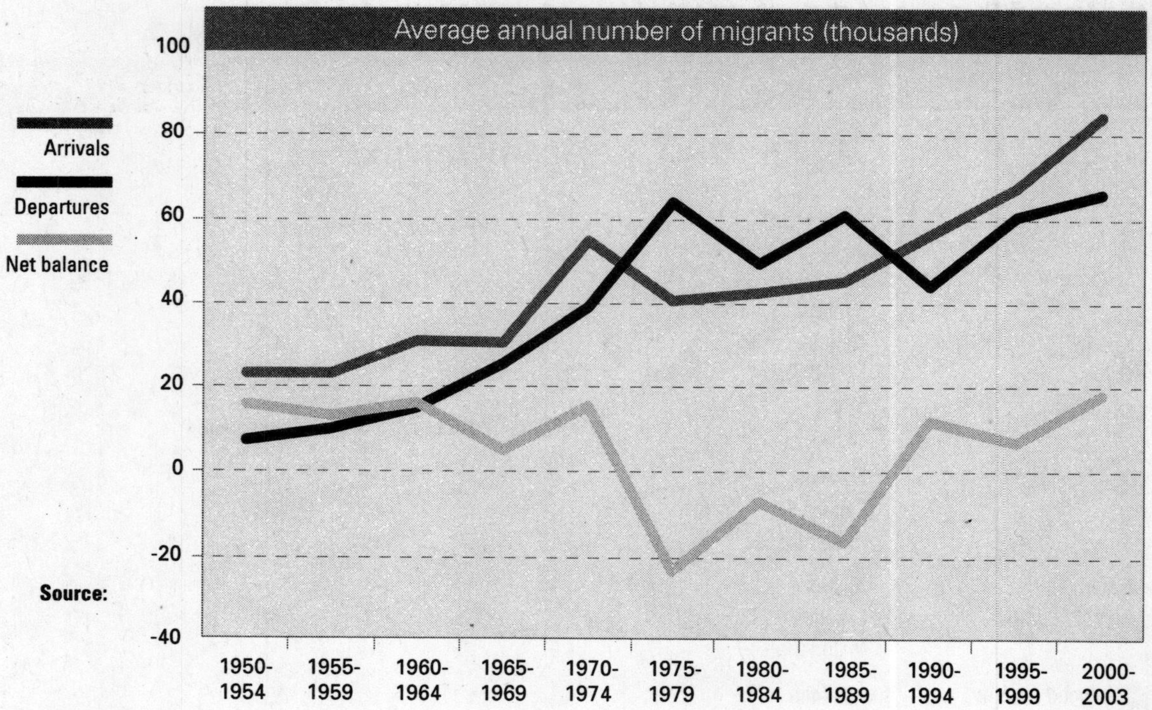

Source:

In all three countries, there has been a tendency for the proportion of immigrants originating in Eastern and Central European countries to increase, but the rise occurred earlier in Canada (early 1980s) than in the United States (1990s). In Australia, the increase at the end of the 1990s does not seem to have been sustained after 2000. In addition, in Australia, the proportion of immigrants originating in developed countries rose significantly after 1990-1994.

Immigrants from Asia are a growing share of the foreign-born in all four countries of immigration, especially Canada

Immigrants from Asia have accounted for a growing share of the immigrant intake in all four countries of immigration, but particularly Canada, where over half of the immigrants admitted since 1995 originated in Asia. In Australia, the highest relative levels of Asian migration were recorded in 1990-1994 and a similar trend was experienced by New Zealand where immigration from Asia, especially from Hong Kong Special Administrative Region of China, Taiwan Province of China and the Republic of Korea increased sharply following the introduction of a points-based selection system in 1991 (Bedford, 2003). In the United States, high proportions of immigrants from Asia date to 1980-1984 when important contingents of refugees from Indo-China were being resettled.

Immigrants from Latin America and the Caribbean have generally constituted very high proportions of the immigrant admissions to the United States. During the 1990s, their proportion surpassed the share of Asia, especially if the admissions that resulted from the regularization established by the Immigration and Reform Control Act of 1985 are taken into account. Even in the absence of that regularization, Mexico would still have been the major source of immigrants to the United States since at least 1980.

There has been considerable diversity in the sources of immigrants to the countries of immigration. However, Canada and the United States tended to have a more diversified immigrant intake than Australia or New Zealand. Among the immigrants admitted during 1990-1994, 26 countries of origin accounted for three quarters of those admitted by the United States, 24 for those admitted by Canada and just 12 for those received by Australia. A major component of immigration to Australia and New Zealand is the free movement of citizens between the two countries made possible by the Trans-Tasman Travel Arrangement.

International migration in Europe

Changes in the international migration landscape have been particularly sharp in Europe since the 1960s. Propelled by post-war reconstruction during the 1950s, the market economies of Western Europe experienced a rapid economic expansion that increased labour demands and led to labour shortages. To relieve such shortages, Governments actively recruited foreign workers, especially those from neighbouring countries, from current or former colonies, and from Southern Europe. Greece, Italy, Portugal and Spain became major sources of workers for other European countries. The active recruitment of foreign workers continued during the 1960s and involved an expanding number of countries, including Morocco, Turkey and the former Yugoslavia. When the recession caused by the sharp increases in oil prices that occurred in 1973 began, the Governments of countries that had fostered the admission of foreign workers during previous decades decided to stop further recruitment and permit the continued stay of migrant workers already present in their territories while facilitating their reunification with immediate family members. Therefore, the "oil crisis" marked the beginning of the settlement phase of migrant populations. The overall migrant population in Europe increased from 18.7 million in 1970 to 22.2 million in 1980 (table II.1). Flow statistics for Belgium, Denmark, Germany, the Netherlands and Sweden indicate that the levels of net migration in those countries remained low or even became negative between 1975 and 1984. In most of them, negative net migration was the result of losses with respect to other developed countries, while gains continued to be recorded with respect to developing countries (Zlotnik, 1998). Family reunification contributed to maintaining a positive net migration with developing countries, whereas the return of migrant workers to their countries of origin during 1975-1984 more than counterbalanced further inflows from other European countries.

By the 1990s, Italy, Spain, Greece and Portugal shifted from being countries of net emigration to having net inflows from other EU countries and elsewhere

By the early 1980s, the economic configuration of Europe was changing. The European Community had approved the membership of Greece in 1981. Although Greek workers were granted the right to free movement only in 1988, the admission of Greece into the Community was a sign that the country was no longer considered a supplier of labour. Moreover, the further enlargement of EU to include Portugal and Spain did not lead to rising migration from those countries to other member States when workers were granted the right to free movement in 1992. In all three cases, as in that of Italy in the 1960s, free movement rights within the Community had been granted when the new member States were no longer likely to produce major outflows of workers. In fact the reverse happened, as Italy, Spain and, to a lesser extent, Greece and Portugal became poles of attraction for citizens from other member States and migrants from developing countries who generally remained in an irregular situation. In Italy, for instance, the number of foreigners increased from 183,000 in 1980 to 781,000 in 1990, while in Spain the increase occurred mostly in the 1990s, with the number of foreigners having risen from 279,000 in 1990 to 1.1 million in 2001. In Europe as a whole, the number of international migrants rose by 4.1 million in the 1980s, reaching 26.3 million in 1990 (table II.1).

Inflows to Europe increased and diversified in the mid-1980s, when the Communist regimes in some Eastern and Central European countries began to dismantle restrictions on travel abroad or became more lenient with regard to the emigration of certain ethnic groups (for example, Jews, Pontian Greeks and ethnic Germans). Germany, in particular, registered major increases in the net intake of migrants from Eastern and Central Europe and the former USSR, mainly because of the admission of *Aussiedler*, that is to say, ethnic Germans, who had the right to German citizenship upon their entry into the country. Most *Aussiedler* had originated in Kazakhstan, Poland and the Russian Federation. During 1985-1989, Germany gained an annual average of 284,000 persons as returning citizens or migrants from Eastern and Central Europe and the former USSR and by 1990-1994, that number had risen to about half a million (Zlotnik, 1998). By the late 1990s, the net inflow from that region dropped again to about 280,000 persons annually as the number of ethnic Germans abroad declined and the Government of Germany took measures to slow the inflow.

Other relevant flows of ethnic migrants were those of Greeks from Albania and the successor States of the former USSR to Greece, of Hungarians from Romania and Slovakia to Hungary, and of Jews to Israel and the United States, and the repatriation of Russian nationals from various successor States of the former USSR to the Russian Federation. The easing of emigration restrictions by the former USSR had resulted in the emigration of 469,000 Jews from 1985 to 1991, of whom 75 per cent migrated to Israel (United Nations, 1995). Over the next decade, from 1992 to 2002, a further 592,000 persons left the former USSR to settle in Israel. For the Russian Federation, such outward flows were more than counterbalanced by the inflow of 3.7 million persons, from 1992 to 1998, from other member States of CIS and the Baltic States. Nearly 80 per cent of those migrants were ethnic Russians.

During the 1990s, the countries of Western Europe received more than 2 million applications for asylum from citizens of Eastern and Central European countries

In addition, from 1990 to 2000, the countries of Western Europe received more than 2 million applications for asylum from citizens of Eastern and Central European countries. The contentious disintegration of the former Yugoslavia—the war in Croatia in 1991 and the confrontation that began in Bosnia and Herzegovina in 1992, in particular—generated outflows of almost half a million persons per year between 1990 and 1994 (United Nations, 2002a). Although refugee status was granted to only a small proportion of applicants, many were allowed to stay legally in the countries of asylum for humanitarian reasons. However, flows of persons seeking asylum had become controversial because, as the main armed conflicts subsided, the reasons for admitting large numbers of refugees and asylum-seekers waned. Although most member States of EU had tightened their asylum regulations by the mid-1990s, countries such as Belgium, France, the Netherlands, Sweden and the United Kingdom experienced increases in asylum applications in the late 1990s which continued until the early part of the twenty-first century as conflicts in Afghanistan, Western Asia and several countries of sub-Saharan Africa continued to rage. These trends, together with developments in the former USSR, produced a significant increase in the proportion of refugees among all international migrants in Europe and the former USSR, from 2.3 per cent in 1990 to 3.9 per cent in 2000 (table II.7).

The number of international immigrants in Western Europe reached 32.8 million by 2000

As a result of these developments and the improved economic climate in most countries of Western Europe in the late 1990s, the number of international migrants in Europe rose by 6.5 million in the 1990s, reaching 32.8 million by 2000. Increases occurred not only in terms of the foreign-born population but also with respect to those who remained foreigners, that is to say, non-citizens of the countries in which they resided. As table II.8 shows, increases in the number of foreigners were particularly marked after 1990,

Table II.7.
International migrants and refugees by major area, 1970-2000

	Number of international migrants excluding refugees (millions)				Number of refugees (millions)				Proportion of refugees (percentage)			
Major area of destination	1970	1980	1990	2000	1970	1980	1990	2000	1970	1980	1990	2000
World	77.2	90.2	135.0	158.3	4.3	9.5	19.0	16.6	5.3	9.6	12.3	9.5
Developed countries	37.1	46.2	87.6	107.1	1.2	1.5	2.0	3.2	3.1	3.1	2.2	2.9
Developing countries	40.1	44.0	47.4	51.2	3.1	8.1	17.0	13.5	7.3	15.5	26.4	20.8
Africa	8.9	10.5	10.9	12.7	1.0	3.6	5.4	3.6	10.1	25.6	33.0	22.0
Asia	26.1	28.0	31.3	33.9	2.0	4.3	10.4	9.8	7.1	13.3	25.0	22.5
Under UNHCR	..	..	..	..	0.2	2.0	7.4	5.1	0.6	6.1	17.7	11.6
Under UNRWA	..	..	..	..	1.9	2.3	3.1	4.8	6.6	7.2	7.3	10.9
Latin America and the Caribbean	5.6	6.0	5.8	5.9	0.1	0.1	1.2	0.0	1.9	2.4	17.1	0.8
Northern America	12.5	17.4	27.0	40.2	0.5	0.6	0.6	0.6	4.0	3.6	2.1	1.6
Oceania	3.0	3.4	4.6	5.8	0.0	0.3	0.1	0.1	1.5	8.4	2.3	1.1
Europe and former USSR	21.2	24.9	55.4	59.8	0.6	0.5	1.3	2.4	2.9	2.1	2.3	3.9

Source: United Nations, *Trends in Total Migrant Stock: The 2003 Revision* (POP/DB/MIG/Rev. 2003), data in digital form.
Note: The hypen (-) signifies the item is not applicable.

especially in countries that had not been among the major destinations of migrant workers in the 1960s. Thus, the number of foreigners residing in Finland, Ireland, Italy, Portugal and Spain increased substantially, generally doubling or more between 1990 and 2000. In Spain, as mentioned above, the foreign population increased fourfold. More moderate increases were observed in Austria, Denmark, Luxembourg and the United Kingdom. In contrast, the number of foreigners remained unchanged or declined in Belgium, France, the Netherlands and Sweden, mostly owing to naturalization. More than 1 million foreigners acquired French nationality between 1991 and 2000; more than half a million persons naturalized in the Netherlands and some 350,000 did so in Belgium and Sweden (SOPEMI (Continuous Reporting System on Migration), 2004). In Germany, the country with the largest number of foreigners in Europe, the growth of the foreign population depends not only on international migration but also on natural increase, since persons of foreign parents born in Germany do not have the right to German citizenship, although naturalization is possible after some period of continuous legal residence (its length had been 15 years before 1 January 2000 and became 8 years after that date). Between 1990 and 2001, 2.6 million foreigners acquired German citizenship by naturalization. Thus, both the reduction in the number of foreigners in France and the modest increase of their number in Germany owe much to the large number of naturalizations occurring in each country during the 1990s.

During the 1990s, 1 million foreigners were naturalized in France and 2.6 million in Germany

Table II.8.
Foreigners in selected European countries, 1980-2001

Thousands					
Country	1980	1985	1990	1996	2001
Austria	209	309	456	728	711
Belgium	887	847	905	912	847
Denmark	98	117	161	238	267
Finland	13	17	27	74	99
France	3 634	3 670	3 597	3 371	3 193
Germany	4 453	4 379	5 343	7 314	7 336
Ireland	29	45	80	118	182
Italy	183	423	781	1 096	1 363
Luxembourg	95	98	113	143	167
Netherlands	520	553	692	680	690
Norway	82	102	143	158	186
Portugal	42	67	108	173	224
Spain	183	242	279	539	1 109
Sweden	413	389	484	527	476
Switzerland	893	940	1 100	1 338	1 419
United Kingdom	1 739	1 731	1 723	1 934	2 681
Total	13 474	13 926	15 990	19 340	20 948

Sources:
SOPEMI (Continuous Reporting System on Migration), *Trends in International Migration: Annual Report, 1993* and *2003 Editions* (Paris, OECD, 1994 and 2003).

Migrant stocks in Europe are becoming increasingly diversified in origin

There have been significant changes in the countries of origin of international migrants to European countries. One way of assessing the extent of those changes is to consider the countries of citizenship of the majority of foreigners in each of the major receiving countries. Table II.9 provides the numbers of citizens from the main countries of origin who were living between 1980 and 2001 in those countries of Western Europe listed in table II.8. Over that period, the number of Poles in those countries tripled, the number of Moroccans rose by 74 per cent and the number of British citizens, Turks and citizens from the successor States of the former Yugoslavia increased by about 40 per cent each. In contrast, very small increases or even outright reductions were evident among the expatriate populations of Greeks, Italians, Portuguese and Spaniards, nationalities that in the 1960s and 1970s had constituted the bulk of migrants workers in other European countries. There was also a reduction in the number of Algerians and little change in that of United States citizens. Table II.9 also indicates that the total number of foreigners of all the major nationalities of origin accounted for a decreasing proportion of the total foreign population in the countries of Western Europe during the period 1980-2001, implying that there was an increasing diversification of the origins of migrants to those countries. More detailed information suggests that the numbers of migrants from Brazil, China, the Dominican Republic, Peru, Senegal, Sri Lanka and Romania have been rising.

Despite the growing diversification of sources of international migrants, there has not been a similar diversification of the destinations to which migrants from a given origin gravitate. As table II.10 indicates, virtually all Algerian migrants are in France, while most Greeks, Poles and Turks are in Germany. There is somewhat greater diversification in the European destinations of migrants from Italy, Morocco, Portugal, Spain, the former Yugoslavia and the United States. Yet over half of all Portuguese migrants and 45 per cent

Table II.9.

Foreigners of the major nationalities of origin, residing in the main countries of destination in Europe, by country of citizenship, 1980-2001

Country of citizenship	1980	1985	1990	1996	2001
Number of citizens in Europe (thousands)					
Italy	1 833	1 595	1 557	1 504	1 474
Portugal	1 001	914	929	1 009	1 037
Spain	738	616	542	488	436
Greece	319	287	345	382	378
United Kingdom	..	328	364	420	449
United States	..	361	340	381	384
Former Yugoslavia	930	949	1 156	1 628	1 293
Poland	142	198	336	379	457
Turkey	1 845	1 879	2 333	2 696	2 606
Algeria	816	738	625	529	459
Morocco	640	785	1 030	1 082	1 116
Total number of foreigners, all countries	13 474	13 926	15 990	19 340	20 948
Percentage of total foreigners					
Italy	13.6	11.5	9.7	7.8	7.0
Portugal	7.4	6.6	5.8	5.2	4.9
Spain	5.5	4.4	3.4	2.5	2.1
Greece	2.4	2.1	2.2	2.0	1.8
United Kingdom	..	2.4	2.3	2.2	2.1
United States	..	2.6	2.1	2.0	1.8
Former Yugoslavia	6.9	6.8	7.2	8.4	6.2
Poland	1.1	1.4	2.1	2.0	2.2
Turkey	13.7	13.5	14.6	13.9	12.4
Algeria	6.1	5.3	3.9	2.7	2.2
Morocco	4.7	5.6	6.4	5.6	5.3
Total foreigners of major nationalities of origin as percentage of total foreigners	61.3	62.1	59.8	54.3	48.2

Source:
SOPEMI (Continuous Reporting System on Migration), *Trends in International Migration: Annual Reports, 1993* and *2003 Editions* (Paris, OECD, 1994 and 2004), chart 1.2.

Note:
Two dots (..) signify that the data are unavailable.

of all Moroccans are in France, and over 40 per cent of Italians and citizens from the successor States of the former Yugoslavia are in Germany. Spaniards are somewhat more evenly distributed between France and Germany as are citizens of the United States, between Germany and the United Kingdom. The tendency of persons of certain nationalities to cluster in a few European countries of destination reflects the strong migration ties existing between the countries of origin and those of destination, and suggests that diversification of destinations, though possible, needs time to take root.

Table II.10.
Main nationalities of origin of immigrants by country of destination, 2000

Country of citizenship	Main country of destination	Proportion of all immigrants in country of destination in 2000 (percentage)	Cumulative proportion (percentage)
Algeria	France	98.4	98.4
Greece	Germany	95.3	95.3
Poland	Germany	78.8	78.8
Turkey	Germany	73.4	73.4
	France	8.1	81.4
Portugal	France	52.2	52.2
	Switzerland	13.1	65.3
	Germany	12.6	77.9
Yugoslavia (former)	Germany	47.7	47.7
	Austria	24.9	72.6
	Switzerland	15.1	87.6
Morocco	France	44.5	44.5
	Spain	16.8	61.4
	Italy	13.4	74.8
Italy	Germany	41.3	41.3
	Switzerland	21.3	62.6
	France	13.0	75.6
Spain	France	34.8	34.8
	Germany	29.2	64.0
	Switzerland	18.6	82.6
United States	Germany	29.4	29.4
	United Kingdom	28.4	57.8
	Italy	11.4	69.1
	France	6.7	75.9

Source:
SOPEMI (Continuous Reporting System on Migration), *Trends in International Migration: Annual Report, 2003 Edition* (Paris, OECD, 2004).

Many European countries have used amnesties as one means of dealing with undocumented migration

The data presented so far are derived from official statistical sources that usually cover only migrants in a regular situation. Unauthorized migration, by its very nature, is not well reflected in official statistics. Nevertheless, there are some statistical sources that shed light on the magnitude of irregular migration. The results of regularization programmes provide such statistics. Italy and Spain, for instance, have conducted a number of regularization drives since the late 1980s. In Spain 44,000 applications for regularization were lodged in 1985-1986 and 133,000 in 1991, of which 110,000 were regularized (SOPEMI (Continuous Reporting System on Migration), 1998). Nationals from Argentina, the Dominican Republic, Morocco and Peru constituted the major groups applying for regularization. More recently, almost 600,000 applications were filed in Spain during two exceptional regularization programmes implemented in 2000 and 2001 (SOPEMI (Continuous Reporting System on Migration), 2004). In Italy, 105,000 migrants had regularized their status under a drive carried out in 1987-1988 and 216,000 obtained temporary residence permits through a regularization programme implemented in 1990. The largest groups regularized were citizens of Morocco, Tunisia, Senegal, the Philippines and the former Yugoslavia, in order of importance (United Nations, 1998e). The most recent regularization in Italy took place in 2002 when 700,000 applications were lodged during the first three months of the programme. By 2000, migrants who had regularized their status were estimated to have accounted for 4 per cent of all migrants in France, 14 per cent of those in Portugal and Spain and 25 per cent of those in Greece and Italy (Salt, 2002).

Estimates of the overall level of unauthorized migration in Western Europe vary considerably. The International Organization for Migration (IOM) put the number at 3 million in the late 1990s (International Organization for Migration and United Nations, 2000). The International Labour Office argues that, if irregular migrants are assumed to have constituted 15 per cent of the foreign population in Western Europe, there would have been 3.3 million migrants with an irregular status in 2000 when the region was estimated to have had 22 million foreign residents (International Labor Organization, 2004a). Europol is reported to believe that about half a million undocumented migrants enter EU annually (ibid.).

It is estimated that there were some 3.3 million migrants in irregular status in Western Europe in 2000,...

In addition, estimates of unauthorized migration in individual countries vary widely. For instance, the number of unauthorized migrants in France in the late 1990s was estimated to have been either 140,000 or 500,000 (Delaunay, 1998; International Organization for Migration and United Nations, 2000). Recent estimates of the number of irregular workers in Switzerland range from 70,000 to 180,000 (Piguet and Losa, 2002). In the Russian Federation, the Ministry of the Interior estimated that in September 2003, there were 5 million foreigners whose legal status was unclear, of whom 1.5 million were "clearly unauthorized" (International Labor Organization, 2004a).

...but such estimates can vary widely for individual countries

With the easing of travel restrictions in Eastern and Central European countries during the 1980s, several of them became countries of transit for unauthorized migrants heading west, if not de facto destinations for those migrants who failed to proceed on their westward journey. The Czech Republic, Hungary and Poland served as countries of transit but their recent admission to EU is expected to strengthen their capacity to keep unauthorized migrants out. The eastern expansion of EU is also expected to reduce the short-term visits of citizens from neighbouring countries who engage in petty trade and other unauthorized economic activities. Although these movements did not qualify as migration, they appeared to be an important source of income for people in the countries involved (Okólski, 1998).

Bases for admission and characteristics of migrants in developed countries

A common feature of the traditional countries of immigration is their recognition of the importance of family ties in the selection of immigrants (see chap. III). Admissions on the basis of family reunification are therefore a major component of the immigrant intake of those countries. Nevertheless, as table II.11 shows, there are still wide differences among them in respect of the importance assigned to family reunification. In the United States, family reunification accounts for 70 per cent or more of total immigration, while its share in Canada is somewhat higher than 60 per cent and in Australia, considerably below 50 per cent. A comparison with European countries indicates that Denmark, France and Sweden also admit between 50 and 70 per cent of their long-term migrants on the basis of family reunification. In addition, because refugees also constitute high proportions of the migrant intake of those countries, the share of economically based migration (that is to say, of workers admitted) is relatively low, ranging from 2 per cent in Sweden to between 20 and 30 per cent in Denmark and France. The pattern of admissions is different in Switzerland and the

Family reunification is the leading criteria for entry into developed countries, ...

Table II.11.
Immigrants and long-term migrant admissions by category, selected developed countries, 1991 and 2001

Percentage						
	Workers		Family reunification		Refugees	
Receiving country	1991	2001	1991	2001	1991	2001
Australia	45	55	47	33	8	12
Canada	18	26	64	62	18	12
United States	10	19	75	70	15	11
Denmark	20	22	60	53	20	25
France	27	20	58	69	15	11
Sweden	2	2	62	65	36	33
Switzerland	47	55	51	42	2	3
United Kingdom	49	54	42	35	9	11

Source: SOPEMI (Continuous Reporting System on Migration), *Trends in International Migration: Annual Report, 1998* and *2003 Editions* (Paris, OECD, 1998 and 2004), chart I.2.

United Kingdom, where the proportions of long-term migrants admitted for work purposes are high and the share of those admitted for family reunification generally remains below 50 per cent. Furthermore, trends in these countries are similar to those in Australia in that the share of family-based admissions has declined in favour of admissions of workers. Thus, not only is there considerable variation among the traditional countries of immigration regarding the types of immigrants admitted but the variability of circumstances resembles that found between countries in Europe, suggesting that there are growing similarities in the management of migration between these two groups of countries.

... but employment skills are becoming increasingly important

The admission of skilled workers is another area of convergence among receiving countries in the developed world. Thus, the number and percentage of persons formally admitted as immigrants in the skilled categories of the traditional countries of immigration tended to increase between the early and the late 1990s, and similar trends have characterized admissions of skilled personnel in Sweden and the United Kingdom (table II.12). By 2001, skilled immigrants and their family members constituted over half of the immigrant intake in Australia, Canada and New Zealand and nearly one third of long-term migrants admitted by the United Kingdom.

Another means of having recourse to foreign skilled workers is by admitting them under temporary visas or permits. All traditional countries of immigration allow for such temporary admission and, as shown in table II.13, they all have been importing a growing number of temporary skilled workers. Increasing trends in the temporary admission of skilled personnel are also evident in the cases of France and the United Kingdom. There are, however, striking differences among countries in the level of admissions, with over half a million having been reported by the United States in 2000; over 100,000 each for Australia and the United Kingdom; slightly less than 100,000 in Canada; and nearly 50,000 in New Zealand. France, with less than 10,000, is an anomaly. Lack of data comparability may be the cause of such a variety of outcomes, but it is still clear that the temporary migration of skilled workers is very significant and is making a major contribution to the migration intake of the main receiving countries of the developed world.

Significant differences exist as well among developed countries in the educational attainment of international migrants. According to information from censuses and other household-based inquiries, the proportion of migrants holding a tertiary education

Table II.12.
Skilled immigrants in selected countries, 1991, 1999 and 2001

	Number (thousnds)			Share of all immigrants (percentage)		
Country	1991	1999	2001[a]	1991	1999	2001[a]
Australia[b]	41	35	54	37	42	60
Canada[c]	41	81	137	18	47	55
New Zealand	..	13	36	..	47	68
United States[d]	12	57	175	18	22	17
Sweden	0	3	4	6	8	10
United Kingdom	4	32	40	7	33	32

Sources: SOPEMI (Continuous Reporting System on Migration) *Trends in International Migration; Annual Report, 1992, 2001* and *2003. Editions* Paris, OECD, 1992, 2001 and 2004); Organization for Economic Cooperation and Development (2001); United States Department of Justice, Immigration and Naturalization Service (1991, 1999); and United States Department of Homeland Security, Office of Immigration Statistics (2003).

Note: Two dots (..) signify data unavailable.

a Data for the United States referring to 2002.
b Skilled category including family members with certain tested professional qualifications and linguistic aptitudes.
c Skilled worker category including assisted relatives who are not point-tested.
d Employment-based preferences category including family members of skilled workers.

Table II.13.
Temporary workers admitted under the skills-based categories, selected countries, 1992-2000

	Thousands				
Country	1992	1997	1998	1999	2000
Australia	41	82	93	100	116
Canada	70	75	80	85	94
New Zealand	..	27	30	39	48
United States[a]	143	..	343	423	505
France	5	5	4	6	8
United Kingdom	54	80	89	98	124

Sources: SOPEMI (Continuous Reporting System on Migration), *Trends in International Migration: Annual Report, 1992, 2001 and 2003 Editions* (Paris, OECD, 1992, 2001 and 2004). Organization for Economic Cooperation and Development, 2001; United States Department of Justice, Immigration and Naturalization Service (1991, 1999); and United States Department of Homeland Security, Office of Immigration Statistics (2003).

a Statistics reflect the number of admissions under H-IB visas, not the number of persons. Double-counting is possible if a person enters the United States more than once during a fiscal year.

In 1990, about one fourth of all migrants in Australia, Canada and the United States had tertiary education degrees

degree is higher in Australia (27 per cent in 1996), Canada (25 per cent in 1996) and the United States (23 per cent in 1990) than in EU (15 per cent in 2001) (United Nations, 2003d). However, while the foreign-born were as well educated as natives in Australia and Canada in 1996, they were clearly less well educated than natives in the United States in 1990. These differences have been attributed to the different criteria for admission applied by these countries as well as to the differences in the distribution of immigrants by country of origin (Borjas, 1994; Duleep and Regets, 1992). The educational attainment of foreigners was also significantly below that of nationals in some of the main receiving countries of Western Europe, namely, Belgium, France, Germany and the Netherlands.

The proportion of the labour force who are foreigners is increasing in Europe

Foreign workers remain an important part of the labour force of many developed countries. According to table II.14, foreign workers constitute at least 5 per cent of the labour force in 8 of the 16 European countries listed. In small Luxembourg, 62 per cent of the total labour force is foreign; but in more populous Switzerland, the proportion foreign is 18 per cent and in Austria, 11 per cent. Furthermore, in virtually all countries with trend data, the proportion of the labour force constituted by foreign workers increased between 1990 and 2000. That increase was particularly marked, in relative terms, among the newer countries of destination—Ireland, Italy, Norway, Portugal and Spain. High participation in

Table II.14.
Foreign participation in the labour force in selected European countries, 1990 and 2001

Percentage

Country	Proportion of foreign population active in the labour force		Foreign labour as a proportion of the total labour force	
	1990	2001	1990	2001
Austria	50.3	50.6	7.4	11.0
Belgium	..	47.1	..	9.1
Denmark	42.8	37.7	2.4	3.5
Finland	..	46.0	..	1.7
France	43.1	50.7	6.2	6.2
Germany	..	49.3	..	9.1
Ireland	42.5	45.2	2.6	4.6
Italy	35.2	58.8	1.2	3.8
Luxembourg	74.9	..	45.2	61.7
Netherlands	28.5	..	3.1	..
Norway	32.3	63.6	2.3	5.0
Portugal	48.1	46.8	1.0	2.0
Spain	30.6	54.7	0.6	3.4
Sweden	50.9	47.7	5.4	5.1
Switzerland	60.8	52.1	18.9	18.1
United Kingdom	51.2	45.8	3.3	4.4

Sources: SOPEMI (Continuous Reporting System on Migration), *Trends in International Migration. Annual Report, 2003 Edition* (Paris, OECD; 2004).

Note: The first column has as denominator the total foreign population and not the foreign population of working age.
Two dots (..) signify data unavailable.

the labour force characterizes the foreign populations of most European countries. Among the countries with data, all but one had 45 per cent or more of its foreign population in the labour force in 2001. In Austria, France, Italy, Norway, Spain and Switzerland, over half of the foreign population was economically active, validating the view that economic considerations continue to be an important reason for migration to Western Europe.

There are important differences in the labour-force participation rates of foreign men and foreign women as well as between the labour-force participation rates of nationals and foreigners in the developed countries. Table II.15 presents average labour-force participation rates for persons aged 15-64 classified by sex and citizenship. The countries are listed according to the difference between the labour-force participation rate of their male nationals and that of their male foreigners, starting from the country with the highest negative difference and ending with the country with the greatest positive differ-

Table II.15.
Labour-force participation by nationality and sex, selected developed countries, average 2000-2001

Percentage

	Labour-force participation rate					
	Men			Women		
Country	Nationals	Foreigners	Difference	Nationals	Foreigners	Difference
Italy	73.6	87.7	-14.1	46.6	50.7	-4.1
Greece	76.2	89.2	-13.0	49.0	56.0	-7.0
Hungary (2001)	67.6	77.8	-10.2	52.2	51.8	0.4
Czech Republic	78.7	87.8	-9.1	63.3	56.3	7.0
Spain	77.3	85.4	-8.1	50.9	59.1	-8.2
Austria	78.9	85.1	-6.2	62.4	63.3	-0.9
Luxembourg	74.0	79.7	-5.7	47.7	57.7	-10.0
United States[a]	80.7	85.6	-4.9	71.4	61.7	9.7
Finland	79.4	83.1	-3.7	74.6	60.2	14.4
Portugal	79.0	81.5	-2.5	64.0	65.3	-1.3
Slovakia	76.9	79.4	-2.5	63.2	51.8	11.4
France	75.1	76.6	-1.5	63.3	48.6	14.7
Switzerland	89.2	89.5	-0.3	73.3	68.6	4.7
Belgium	73.3	72.4	0.9	57.0	41.0	16.0
Germany	78.9	77.6	1.3	64.7	50.7	14.0
Ireland	79.2	77.0	2.2	55.9	56.2	-0.3
Norway	84.6	82.1	2.5	76.8	67.2	9.6
Canada (1996)[a]	73.8	68.4	5.4	60.2	52.9	7.3
United Kingdom	83.1	75.6	7.5	68.4	55.8	12.6
Australia[a]	75.0	67.0	8.0	59.1	48.2	10.9
Denmark	84.1	71.2	12.9	76.2	53.0	23.2
Sweden	78.0	63.1	14.9	74.2	60.3	13.9
Netherlands	84.9	69.5	15.4	67.2	49.0	18.2

Source: SOPEMI (Continuous Reporting System on Migration), *Trends in International Migration: Annual Report, 2003 Edition* (Paris, OECD; 2004).

Note: Data cover the labour force aged 15-64 years, with the exception of Australia and Canada (15 years or over) and the United States (16 years or over).

a Referring to the native and foreign-born populations.

ence. Among the 23 countries listed, in 13, male foreigners had higher labour-force participation rates than nationals. Differences of 8 percentage points or greater existed in the Czech Republic, Greece, Hungary, Italy and Spain, all recent destinations of migrant workers. Yet even in the United States, the major migrant destination of the world, male foreign-born men had a labour-force participation rate that exceeded that of natives by 5 percentage points. In Canada and Australia, in contrast, foreign-born men had lower labour-force participation rates than natives, and in both, the difference between the two was high (at least 5 percentage points). Other countries where the labour-force participation rate of nationals exceeded that of foreigners by more than 5 percentage points include Denmark, the Netherlands, Sweden and the United Kingdom.

In the developed countries, labour-force participation rates are higher for men than for women, especially among foreigners

In the 23 developed countries considered, the labour-force participation rates of men were higher than those of women, and the differences between the sexes were particularly marked among foreigners. In addition, foreign women are generally less economically active than women who are citizens. Thus, in only 7 of the 23 countries considered did the labour-force participation rates of foreign women exceed those of their national counterparts. In Greece, Italy, Luxembourg and Spain, the labour-force participation rates of foreign women surpassed those of female citizens by at least 4 percentage points. Yet there were 10 countries where the difference between the two was at least 10 percentage points in favour of female citizens. Even in Australia, Canada and the United States, the labour-force participation rates of native women surpassed those of foreign-born women by substantial margins. In many of these countries, the overall labour-force participation rates of foreigners are lower than those of nationals because of the large difference between the labour-force participation rates of national and foreign women.

Labour migration in Asia

In 2000, some 25 per cent of the world's migrant stock lived in an Asian country

In 1960, Asia had accounted for 39 per cent of the world's migrant stock (table II.1). By 2000, that share had been reduced to 25 per cent, although Asia had experienced a major increase in the number of refugees (from 2 million in 1970 to 9.8 million in 2000) and had seen the number of other types of international migrants in its midst rise from 26 million to 34 million (table II.7). However, international migration trends differ significantly by country and subregion in this vast and diverse continent. Indeed, most of the growth in the number of international migrants from 1960 to 2000 occurred in Western Asia and the newly industrialized economies of Eastern and South-eastern Asia.

In 2000, between 25 and 70 per cent of the populations of the Gulf Cooperation Council countries were foreign-born

Following the sharp increase in oil prices in 1973, the oil-producing countries of Western Asia accelerated the recruitment of foreign workers who were needed to build infrastructure. The number of international migrants in the six member States of the Gulf Cooperation Council (GCC)—Bahrain, Kuwait, Oman, Qatar, Saudi Arabia and the United Arab Emirates—had increased from an estimated 1 million in 1970 to 4 million in 1980 and further to 9.6 million in 2000, of which 5.3 million resided in Saudi Arabia (table II.16). It is estimated that by 2000, international migrants constituted 38 per cent of the population in Bahrain, 49 per cent in Kuwait, 26 per cent in Oman, 70 per cent in Qatar, 24 per cent in Saudi Arabia and 68 per cent in the United Arab Emirates (United Nations, 2004c). Over time, workers were recruited from increasingly distant locations. While in the 1970s, migrant workers had been imported mostly from other Arab countries, by the late 1970s, workers were being recruited in Bangladesh, India and Pakistan and then in several Eastern and South-eastern Asian countries, especially the Republic of Korea, the Philippines and, later, Indonesia, Sri Lanka and Thailand.

Table II.16.
International migrants in the members of the Gulf Cooperation Council, 1970-2000

Thousands					
Country	1960	1970	1980	1990	2000
Bahrain	27	38	103	173	254
Kuwait	91	468	964	1 560	1 108
Oman	32	40	180	450	682
Qatar	12	63	157	345	409
Saudi Arabia	64	303	1 804	4 220	5 255
United Arab Emirates	2	62	737	1 556	1 922
Total	228	974	3 946	8 305	9 630

Source:
United Nations, *Trends in Total Migrant Stock: The 2003 Revision* (POP/DB/MIG/Rev. 2003), data in digital form.

Iraq's invasion of Kuwait in August 1990 had a significant effect on the foreign population in GCC. During the first four months of the invasion, more than 2 million foreigners were estimated to have left Iraq, Kuwait and Saudi Arabia (Russell, 1992). Soon after the end of the war in 1991, foreign workers began returning to Kuwait and Saudi Arabia. However, changes in political alignments during the crisis led to the repatriation of important groups of foreigners, including Jordanians, Palestinians and Yemenis, and to the recruitment of workers from Egypt, as well as from the main sending countries in Eastern and South-eastern Asia, to fill the jobs left vacant by those departing.

Women make up an increasing proportion of the foreign labour force in the Gulf Cooperation Council countries

During the past 30 years, labour migration to the member States of GCC evolved in terms of the occupations involved and with respect to the participation of women. Once the construction of infrastructure was over, migrant workers began moving from construction jobs to services. As part of the rising demand for service workers, women began to be recruited as migrant workers, mainly as domestic workers in private homes. Consequently, their numbers increased, although the foreign labour force in the GCC countries remained primarily male. Thus, in the early 1990s, women constituted 25 per cent of the foreign labour force in Kuwait, 10 per cent in Oman and 9 per cent in Qatar (United Nations, 2003a, p. 21, table 10).

Another important pole of attraction in Western Asia has been Israel, which had been admitting Jewish immigrants for permanent settlement since its establishment in 1948. During the 1960s, a majority of immigrants to Israel originated in Northern Africa, particularly in Morocco, and to a lesser extent in Eastern Europe (United Nations, 2003a). However, since the 1970s, the major source of new settlers has been the former USSR, especially during the early 1990s as the outflow of Soviet Jews increased sharply with the disintegration of the USSR. Between 1989 and 1991, nearly 350,000 Soviet Jews had arrived in Israel, increasing the population of the country by 7 per cent (United Nations, 1998e). In total, 925,000 Soviet Jews migrated to Israel from 1990 to 2002. In addition to admitting Jewish immigrants, Israel had begun to admit foreign workers in the late 1980s, partly in order to reduce its dependence on Palestinian workers. By 1994, there were about 30,000 foreign workers in Israel and their number increased to some 88,000 in 2001. The main countries of origin of these workers, who were employed mainly in construction and agriculture, were the Philippines, Romania and Thailand.

Labour migration is increasing substantially into the countries of Eastern and South-eastern Asia that have higher rates of economic growth

In the 1980s, the sustained economic growth of Japan and of the newly industrialized countries of Eastern and South-eastern Asia began attracting foreign workers from less prosperous countries in the region. Hong Kong Special Administrative Region (SAR) of China, and Singapore, which had long been importers of migrant workers, as well as Japan, Malaysia, the Republic of Korea and Taiwan Province of China, provided an alternative destination to unskilled workers from countries such as China, Indonesia, the Philippines and Thailand. As in other settings, migrant workers inserted themselves mostly in construction and in certain manufacturing industries, such as the automotive industry in Japan and the electronics sector in the Republic of Korea and Taiwan Province of China. Labour migration within Eastern and South-eastern Asia involved a high participation of women who found employment mainly in the service sector, typically as domestic workers.

By 2001, there were 1.8 million legal foreign residents in Japan

Japan deserves especial attention because, until the early 1980s, it had achieved rapid economic growth without resorting to foreign workers. However, as Japanese workers became more affluent and shunned certain low-paying jobs, foreign workers flowed in to fill them. Between 1975 and 2001, the number of legally resident foreigners in Japan more than doubled, passing from 750,000 to 1.8 million (SOPEMI (Continuous Reporting System on Migration), 1992 and 2004). Increases in the number of foreigners of Japanese descent, originating mostly in Brazil and Peru, accounted for almost half of the growth of the migrant stock in Japan between 1985 and 1995; but a major part of that growth also stemmed from the admission of citizens from other Asian countries, recruited as trainees or as foreign students and allowed to work part-time. In addition, by 2001, there were over 250,000 foreigners in an irregular situation in Japan (Japan, Ministry of Justice, 2001).

The number of legal foreign residents in the Republic of Korea more than quadrupled between 1988 and 2001

The Republic of Korea also began to experience labour shortages in selected sectors of the economy during the 1980s, thus becoming a magnet for both legal and undocumented migrant workers. By 1988, there were 45,000 foreigners in the Republic of Korea and the number of employment-related visas issued in 1989 reached 162,000. By 2001, the number of foreign residents had more than quadrupled, reaching 230,000, of whom 129,000 were economically active (SOPEMI (Continuous Reporting System on Migration), 2004). In addition, according to authorities in the Republic of Korea, the number of migrants in an irregular situation had risen from 65,500 in 1992 to 148,000 in 1997 (Uh, 1999) and despite a reduction of unauthorized migration caused by the 1997 financial crisis, their number continued to grow after 1999 to reach an estimated 255,000 in 2002. To control undocumented migration, a regularization drive was carried out in 2002 and the Government intended to deport all those who still remained in an irregular situation in 2003 (SOPEMI (Continuous Reporting System on Migration), 2004).

In 2000, Taiwan Province of China admitted well over 300,000 foreign contract workers

Taiwan Province of China also had to resort to foreign labour to maintain its productive expansion. In 1991, it had recruited 3,000 contract workers, all destined for the construction industry. By 1993, the number of contract workers admitted had risen to 98,000, of whom 74 per cent were employed by the manufacturing industry. There was a continuous increase in the number of contract workers admitted annually, the figure reaching 316,000 in 2000 when 58 per cent were working in manufacturing, 12 per cent in construction, and 30 per cent, mostly women, in health and domestic services. In 2000, the major countries of origin of contract workers were Thailand (46 per cent), the Philippines (36 per cent) and Indonesia (17 per cent). Most of the workers in the service sector were Filipinos (Tsay, 2000; Tsay and Lin, 2001).

Malaysia has a long history of reliance on foreign workers, mostly from neighbouring Indonesia, who work as agricultural workers in the plantations of the country. The total foreign workforce in Malaysia was estimated to have been 1.2 million by 1993, constituting about 15 per cent of the total labour force in the country (Lim, 1996). During the Asian financial crisis of 1997, many undocumented Indonesian workers in Malaysia had to return home. Nevertheless, the migrant population in Malaysia is estimated to have been 1.4 million in 2000. Malaysia has also been an important source of migrant workers for neighbouring Singapore and the overseas emigration of Malaysians increased markedly in the 1980s and 1990s. One of the major destinations for Malaysian emigrants is Australia, where 87,200 persons born in Malaysia were enumerated in 2001.

Some 15 per cent of the Malaysian labour force was foreign-born in 2000

As a result of the 1997 financial crisis, several countries in Eastern and South-eastern Asia imposed restrictions on the admission of foreign workers. Yet recent data suggest that the constraining effect of the crisis on the sustained flows of migrant workers to the major receiving countries in the region was only temporary (United Nations, 2003a).

In recent years, the rapidly growing economy of China has been attracting substantial numbers of foreign workers. China has no data on the number of foreigners residing in the country, but the Ministry of Public Security granted 119,900 work visas in 2001. Foreign companies, which invested some US$ 270 billion in China during 1997-2004, are among the main employers of the expatriate labour force. Most of the foreign workers in China are in technical, professional and managerial occupations. Yet China remains mainly a country of emigration, whose citizens migrate to an increasingly varied set of destinations both within Asia and overseas.

As in other regions of the developing world, a substantial proportion of all international migration in Asia is undocumented. Authorities in several countries are frequently aware of the existence of unauthorized migrants but their presence is tolerated. In Japan, for instance, authorities track the number of persons staying beyond the expiration dates of their visas. That number stood at 224,000 in 2001. Similarly, in the Republic of Korea, there were 255,000 overstayers in 2001. More often, unauthorized migrants cross poorly patrolled borders without being controlled and merge with a country's population. By some estimates, Asia may have several million migrants in an irregular situation. The largest numbers probably involve Nepalese and Bangladeshis in India; Afghans in Pakistan and the Islamic Republic of Iran; Indonesians and Filipinos in Malaysia; and migrants from Myanmar in Thailand (International Labor Organization, 2004a).

A substantial proportion of international migration in Asia is undocumented

International migration in Africa

Migration between African countries is perhaps the least well documented migration in the developing world. The rapidity with which some movements start or reverse themselves implies that they are seldom reflected properly in censuses. Furthermore, recent censuses have not been producing as much data on the foreign-born population as earlier ones. Hence, determining recent trends in the migrant stock of African countries is often a matter of guesswork. Nevertheless, they suggest that the overall share of Africa in the international migrant stock has been declining. Thus in 1960, Africa's 9 million international migrants had constituted 12 per cent of the world's international migrants, but by 2000, with 16.3 million international migrants, Africa accounted for just 9 per cent of all international migrants in the world (table II.1). One consistent characteristic of international migration in Africa has been the high proportion of refugees among its international

The data, while not very robust, suggest that the number of international migrants in Africa increased in the 1990s, albeit slowly

migrants. Already in 1970, when the number of refugees in Africa had stood at 1 million, they constituted 10 per cent of the migrant stock in the continent (table II.7). By 1980, the 3.6 million refugees in Africa accounted for 26 per cent of all international migrants in the continent. In 1990, the share of refugees had risen to 33 per cent as their number soared to 5.4 million. By 2000, both the number and the share of refugees had declined to 3.6 million and 22 per cent, respectively, largely as a result of voluntary repatriation movements made possible during the late 1990s by the resolution of long-standing conflicts. Nevertheless, political instability and conflict still affect many African countries and the forces generating refugees and forced migration in general are not expected to subside in the region in the near future.

Although movements of refugees have been an important component of international migration in Africa, other types of migration have accounted for the bulk of international migrants in the region, amounting to 8.9 million by 1970, 10.5 million in 1980 and 10.9 million in 1990 (table II.7). By 2000, 12.7 million of the international migrants in Africa were not refugees; that is to say, the largest overall increases in non-refugee migration in the continent occurred from 1970 to 1980 and from 1990 to 2000. During this most recent decade, increases in the number of international migrants were mostly concentrated in Burkina Faso, Côte d'Ivoire, Gabon, Ghana, the Libyan Arab Jamahiriya, Mozambique, Nigeria and South Africa (United Nations, 2004c).

The leading emigration flows from Northern Africa have been to Europe and GCC countries

International migration originating in certain parts of Africa has mostly been oriented to other world regions. Thus, migrants from Northern Africa have tended to go to Europe and to the oil-producing countries of GCC in Western Asia. Within the region, Egyptians and Tunisians have worked over different periods in the Libyan Arab Jamahiriya, but there have been fluctuations in international relations among the countries involved which have been at the root of major return flows occurring at different times.

In Western Africa, migration has been largely shaped by flows of agricultural workers, including seasonal workers, from the landlocked countries bordering the Sahel to those bordering the coast. The major receiving country in Africa, Côte d'Ivoire, has attracted migrants from surrounding countries, especially Burkina Faso and Mali, to work in the cocoa and coffee plantations or as domestic workers. According to successive censuses, the foreign population in Côte d'Ivoire had increased from nearly 1.5 million in 1975 to 3 million in 1988 and further to 4 million in 1996. However, deteriorating economic conditions in the 1990s seemed to be causing significant return migration to the countries of origin (Centre d'Études et de Recherche sur la Population et le Développement (CERPOD), 1995). Furthermore, in the late 1990s, the Government of Côte d'Ivoire adopted measures to disenfranchise migrants and deport those in an irregular situation. These measures, together with the waves of violence against foreigners that occurred in the early years of the twenty-first century and the political unrest that started in 2002, have led to major return flows. It is estimated that by 2000, Burkina Faso had become a major receiver of international migrants, largely as a result of the return of its foreign-born citizens.

Other countries in Western Africa host substantial numbers of international migrants. Among them, Ghana and Nigeria had been poles of attraction in the 1960s and 1970s, respectively, but as their economic situation deteriorated, both countries resorted to the mass expulsion of international migrants in an irregular situation. Ghana did so in 1969 and Nigeria in 1983 (United Nations, 1985). Recent information on the number of international migrants in those countries is lacking; however, Ghana is estimated to have had about 600,000 foreign-born persons in 2000 and Nigeria about 750,000 (United Nations, 2004c).

In Middle Africa, Gabon, a country rich in natural resources, had hosted more than 100,000 international migrants in the early 1990s, but stringent laws enacted in 1995 requiring foreigners to pay residence fees led to the expulsion of more than half of those migrants (International Organization for Migration and United Nations, 2000).

In Southern Africa, the mining industry of South Africa used to rely heavily on migrant workers from neighbouring countries, recruiting an annual average of 300,000 in the early 1970s, a figure that dropped to about 200,000 in the 1980s and early 1990s (South Africa, Chamber of Mines, 1987 and 1993). The reduction was due both to a decision by South Africa to cut its dependency on migrant workers and to restrictions on the emigration of workers imposed by some countries of origin. South Africa also attracted white settlers from a variety of origins, yet its foreign-born population declined during the late 1980s. According to census information, the number of foreign-born residents in South Africa dropped from 1.9 million in 1985 to 1.2 million in 1991. Recent evidence suggests that the inflow of migrants may have increased after the apartheid era ended in 1994. The strictly regulated migration of workers for specific industries now coexists with substantial irregular migration of unskilled workers and the authorized inflow of skilled professionals. The number of migrants in an irregular situation is claimed to be very high. A 1997 estimate put the figure at between 3 million and 5 million (South Africa, Ministry of Home Affairs, Tax Team on International Migration, 1999).

The number of undocumented migrants in South Africa may be between 3 million and 5 million

International migration in Latin America and the Caribbean

With only 5.9 million international migrants in 2000, Latin America and the Caribbean has one of the smallest shares of the world's migrant stock (3.4 per cent). In contrast with those in Africa, most countries in Latin America and the Caribbean have a relatively long series of data on the foreign-born population derived from censuses. Hence, the finding that the number of international migrants in the region had remained practically stable during 1960-1980, increased during the 1980s and declined from 7 million in 1990 to 5.9 million in 2000 bears highlighting (table II.1). Both the increase during the 1980s and the subsequent decline are mainly attributable to the movement of refugees and displaced persons in Central America, who left their countries of origin during the conflicts that convulsed the region during the 1980s, and then returned after durable solutions to those conflicts had been found.

Latin America and the Caribbean has a comparatively small share of the world's migrants

Few countries in Latin America and the Caribbean have sizeable numbers of international migrants (table II.17). Among those that do, Argentina, Brazil and Venezuela have all had policies—sometimes dating from the nineteenth century—favouring the settlement of European migrants in their territories. During the aftermath of the Second World War, these countries attracted moderate flows of overseas migrants, but those flows had practically ceased by 1960. At least since 1970, Brazil has not been a major destination of international migrants, and Argentina and Venezuela have mostly attracted migrants from neighbouring countries. Moreover, during the 1980s, as all three countries experienced economic difficulties, many migrants of European origin and their descendants left to return to Europe. As a result of ageing and return migration, the number of migrants from overseas countries declined from close to 4 million in 1960 to some 2.5 million in 1990 (Villa and Martínez Pizarro, 2001). Whereas in 1970, Latin American migrants constituted 25 per cent of the total migrant stock in the region, by 1990, they accounted for more than half.

Migrant stocks in Latin America and the Caribbean have increasingly originated within the region; by 1990, Latin American migrants accounted for more than half of the total migrant stock

Table II.17.
International migrants in the major receiving countries of Latin America and the Caribbean, 1960-2000

Thousands					
Country	1960	1970	1980	1990	2000
Argentina	2 615	2 252	1 948	1 662	1 419
Venezuela	510	589	966	1 024	1 006
Brazil	1 404	1 270	1 214	809	546
Mexico	223	195	294	701	521
Puerto Rico	64	189	271	322	383
Costa Rica	33	25	69	418	311
Paraguay	50	73	146	183	203
Chile	106	90	82	108	153
Dominican Republic	45	34	78	103	136

Source: United Nations, *Trends in Total Migrant Stock: The 2003 Revision* (POP/DB/MIG/ Rev. 2003), data in digital form.

As of 2002, there were an estimated 800,000 undocumented migrants in Argentina

Argentina has traditionally had the largest number of international migrants in Latin America and the Caribbean but that number has been declining steadily since 1960. At that time, the country had 2.6 million international migrants, 77 per cent of whom had been born in Europe and 18 per cent of whom originated in neighbouring countries—Bolivia, Brazil, Chile, Paraguay and Uruguay. During the 1970s and early 1980s, as the economic and political situation in Argentina deteriorated, emigration and return migration began to increase but so did the inflow of workers from neighbouring countries who took the jobs that citizens did not want. By 1980, there were 1.9 million international migrants in Argentina, 57 per cent of whom had been born in Europe and 40 per cent in neighbouring countries. The share of the latter had increased to 48 per cent by 1991 when the foreign-born population in Argentina stood at 1.7 million. Although the results of the most recent census are not yet available, it seems likely that by 2000 more than half of all international migrants in Argentina would have originated in the neighbouring countries. Because most of the migrants from those countries have moved and worked without authorization, Argentina has resorted to periodic amnesties or regularization drives to grant them legal status. Amnesties were granted in 1958, 1964, 1974 and 1984 (Balán, 1992). In 1974, at least 148,000 migrants had regularized their status and an additional 142,000 did so in 1984. During the 1990s, Argentina's prosperity probably continued to act as a magnet for workers from the region, but more recently the country's economic troubles may have led to return flows. Nevertheless, one estimate puts the number of undocumented migrants in 2002, originating mainly in neighbouring countries, at 800,000 (International Labor Organization, 2004a).

In Venezuela, the oil boom of the 1970s attracted many migrants from neighbouring countries, especially Colombia. The foreign-born population in the country increased markedly, rising from 0.6 million in 1970 to 1 million in 1980. Because many Latin American migrants in Venezuela were undocumented, the Government conducted a regularization programme in 1980 in connection with the adoption of a Regulation on the Admission and Permanent Residence of Foreigners. The programme yielded 267,000 applications for regularization, 92 per cent of which were filed by Colombians. During the 1980s, the foreign-born population of Venezuela increased slightly and is estimated to have remained largely unchanged during the 1990s. According to the 1991 census, 25 per cent of the migrants in Venezuela had been born in Europe, mainly in Spain, Portugal and Italy, in order of importance. The European share of the migrant population had been declining over time, partly as a result of return migration to the countries of origin. In 1991, migrants from other Latin American and Caribbean countries accounted for 67 per cent of the foreign-born population in Venezuela and persons born in Colombia, numbering 530,000, constituted more than half of the foreign-born in the country.

Brazil had a long tradition as a country of immigration when it opened its doors to Europeans moving overseas after the Second World War; but after a relatively brief period, the inflows of European migrants to Brazil ceased. Between 1960 and 1980, immigration levels were virtually nil and emigration was also low. In the 1980s, however, instead of attracting migrants from abroad, the country began to experience significant emigration.

In the 1980s, Brazil shifted from being a country of net immigration to being one of emigration

Two other countries in South America had sizeable migrant populations in 2000: Paraguay and Chile (table II.17). Nearly half of the 203,000 migrants in Paraguay originated in Brazil. Among the rest, persons born in Argentina were the most numerous. At least some of the latter were likely to be the children of Paraguayan emigrants who had spent some of their working life in Argentina. In Chile as well, persons born in Argentina constituted an important proportion of all international migrants, but there have been increases in the number of migrants originating in other nearby countries, including Bolivia and Peru.

As table II.17 indicates, Mexico and Costa Rica were among the next tier of countries hosting significant numbers of internationals migrants in 2000. In both countries, the number of international migrants had increased markedly in the 1980s, largely as a result of the conflicts and other socio-political disruptions that affected El Salvador, Guatemala and Nicaragua during that period. For Central America and Mexico as a whole, the number of international migrants increased from 0.6 million in 1980 to 1.9 million in 1990 (United Nations, 2004c), and the number in Costa Rica, Guatemala, Honduras and Mexico rose by 1.2 million, equivalent to the estimated number of refugees and displaced persons in the region. During the 1990s, the resolution of the various conflicts made possible the voluntary repatriation of a large numbers of these refugees and displaced persons, particularly to El Salvador, Guatemala and Nicaragua. Accordingly, the number of migrants in the four major receiving countries of the region had decreased by 0.7 million in the period from 1990 to 2000. By 2000, Central America and Mexico had 1.1 million international migrants, with over half a million in Mexico and 311,000 in Costa Rica. In Costa Rica, migrants constituted 8 per cent of the population in 2000. The main countries of origin in the region remained El Salvador, Guatemala and Nicaragua (Villa and Martínez Pizarro, 2001).

As of 2000, Central America and Mexico had about 1.1 million immigrants, about half of them living in Mexico

In the Caribbean, the small size of the populations of the countries or areas in the region coupled with the long tradition of international mobility of their populations implies that international migration has had an important impact on their population composition. In half of the Caribbean countries or areas, international migrants constitute more than 10 per cent of the population, and in Aruba, the British Virgin Islands, the Cayman Islands and the United States Virgin Islands, they constitute more than a third (United Nations, 2004c). The majority of international migrants in the Caribbean originate in other Caribbean countries (Villa and Martínez Pizarro, 2001). The movement of Haitian agricultural workers to the Dominican Republic is of long-standing. Plantation owners have traditionally recruited Haitians to work during the harvesting season and an increasing number of them have settled in the country. The Dominican Republic is estimated to have had the second largest migrant stock in the Caribbean in 2000 (table II.17), outnumbered only by that of Puerto Rico. Because of its status as Associated State of the United States, Puerto Rico's immigration is governed by United States law. Given its economic prosperity and its cultural affinity to other Latin American and Caribbean countries, Puerto Rico has become an important destination for Spanish-speaking migrants admitted by the United States.

Since the 1960s, international migration in the Americas has been dominated by the flows directed to the United States and, to a lesser extent, to Canada. Migration between Latin American countries is low in comparison. Among Latin American countries, Mexico dominates the flows to the United States. In the early 1960s, when the Bracero Programme had come to an end, the United States was admitting about 40,000 Mexican immigrants annually. By the late 1980s, that number had risen to 73,000—excluding the Mexicans legalized under the Immigration Reform and Control Act (IRCA) of 1986. By the late 1990s, annual legal immigration to the United States from Mexico averaged 139,000 persons a year, excluding again Immigration Reform and Control Act legalizations. In addition, over 2 million Mexicans gained legal immigrant status in the United States from 1987 to 1997 as a result of the IRCA. Accordingly, the Mexican-born population in the United States increased from 750,000 in 1970 to 4.3 million in 1990 and to nearly 10 million in 2000 (United States Census Bureau, 2001). Despite the substantial legal immigration from Mexico, it is estimated that about half of the Mexican-born population in the United States in 2000—4.8 million—was in an irregular situation (United States Immigration and Naturalization Service, 2003). Thus, despite the hopes that the 1994 North American Free Trade Agreement might result in lower emigration from Mexico to the United States, actual flows have continued to increase.

Over the last half-century, the main flow of international migrants in Latin America and the Caribbean has been out of the region and into Northern America

The United States has also been the major destination of emigration from the Caribbean, especially that originating in Cuba, the Dominican Republic, Jamaica and Haiti. In 2000, there were 873,000 Cuban-born persons in the United States, 688,000 born in the Dominican Republic, 553,000 from Jamaica and 419,000 from Haiti. In addition, in 2000, there were nearly 2 million migrants from Central America in the United States, mainly from El Salvador (817,000) and Guatemala (481,000). Especially for these two countries, migrant remittances from the United States were a critical factor in maintaining stability during the 1990s.

International migration in the future

As already noted, international migration has become a key component of population growth for an increasing number of countries, particularly those in the developed world, where fertility levels are currently very low and are unlikely to rise again to 2 children per woman in the foreseeable future. Consequently, in the absence of international migration, the current and expected fertility and mortality levels are expected to produce population reductions at some point in the future. In that context, international migration can be instrumental in preventing or delaying population reductions and slowing population ageing. Given the inherent volatility of international migration flows, it is not possible to project with certainty the actual levels that each country may experience, but available population projections can serve to assess the likely impact that international migration might have on population growth in the future if the levels of migrant intakes experienced by most countries in the late 1990s were to be maintained in the decades to come.

Population projections to 2050 permit a comparison of two scenarios: the medium variant of the projections and a zero-migration scenario. The medium variant incorporates sustained levels of non-zero net international migration for most countries during 2000-2050, based mostly on the migration levels observed or estimated for the late 1990s. The zero-migration scenario starts with the same population as that of the medium scenario in 2000 but projects it with zero international migration until 2050 (United Nations, 2003e); that is to say, the zero-migration scenario illustrates the effect that natural population increase (in other words, that caused exclusively by the difference of births and deaths) would have on population growth. A comparison of the results of the two scenarios, in table II.18, provides an assessment of the relative impact that continued international migration is expected to have on population growth in the different world regions and in specific countries.

Overall, at the levels of net migration projected for 2000-2050, net outmigration will reduce by about 5 per cent the natural increase of the less developed regions, but the reductions will vary considerably by region, being of the order of 1 per cent for Africa, 5 per cent for Asia and 13 per cent for Latin America and the Caribbean; that is to say, without migration, the population of less developed regions would reach 7.8 billion in 2050, whereas with migration their population in 2050 would be 7.7 billion. The largest relative difference is expected for Latin America and the Caribbean, whose population would be expected to reach 286 million without migration instead of 247 million with migration.

Over the next half-century, it is projected that net emigration will reduce natural increase in the developing regions by about 5 per cent

In contrast, for the more developed regions net migration is positive, whereas the contribution of natural increase is negative; that is to say, without net migration, the population of the more developed regions would decline from 1.2 billion to 1 billion between 2000 and 2050. With migration, their population would increase very slightly.

Table II.18.
Projected population with and without international migration by region, by major area, 2000 and 2050

Millions							
		Population in 2050		Difference 2000-2050		Difference between medium and zero-migration variants	Migration as share of natural increase[a] (percentage)
Major area	Population in 2000	Medium variant	Zero-migration variant	Medium variant	Zero-migration variant		
Developed countries	1 194	1 220	1 032	26	-162	187	(116)
Developing countries	4 877	7 699	7 837	2 822	2 960	-138	-5
Africa	796	1 803	1 817	1 008	1 022	-14	-1
Asia	3 680	5 222	5 303	1 542	1 623	-81	-5
Latin America and the Caribbean	520	768	806	247	286	-38	-13
Northern America	316	448	314	132	-2	134	(6 763)
Europe	728	632	589	-96	-139	43	(30)
Oceania	31	46	40	15	9	6	67

Source: *World Population Prospects: The 2002 Revision, vol. I, Comprehensive Tables* (United Nations publications, Sales No. E.03.XIII.6).

a Figures in parentheses represent the effect of migration in reducing negative natural increase.

Over that same period, immigration will approximately offset projected population declines due to negative rates of natural increase in the developed countries

Consequently, the effect of net international migration in the more developed regions more than counterbalances the deficits brought about by negative natural increase. As with the less developed regions, the impact of net migration is not uniform at the regional level. In Northern America, the population would decline very slightly without migration (by 2 million) but with migration, it is expected to gain 134 million or more than 40 per cent of its current population. In Europe, population decline is expected to be more severe without migration, amounting to a reduction of the population by 139 million from 2000 to 2050. Even with the levels of net migration projected, Europe's population is still expected to decline, but by 96 million; that is to say, the projected levels of migration, which amount to an average annual gain of about 600,000 migrants per year, would not be sufficient to stall Europe's population decline. Lastly, in Oceania, net migration would contribute to an increase of population by 6 million over and above the 9 million gain projected to occur from natural increase alone.

At the country level, international migration has a very substantial impact on the projected population growth of many countries, particularly those in the developed world. Focusing just on the 15 countries where the difference between the population in 2050 as projected in the medium variant and that in the zero-migration scenario is largest, the list contains only 4 developing countries or areas: Afghanistan, Hong Kong SAR of China, Kuwait and Saudi Arabia. As shown in table II.19, the United States, the major receiver of international migrants, heads the list. According to the zero-migration scenario,

Table II.19.

Projected population to 2050 and dependency ratios with and without migration for selected countries or areas

Millions									
		Population in 2050		Difference between medium and zero-migration variants	Dependency ratio (per 100)		Dependency ratio in 2050 (per 100)		Difference between medium and zero-migration variants
Country or area	Population in 2000	Medium variant	Zero-migration variant		1950	2000	Medium variant	Zero migration variant	
United States of America	285	409	287	122	54	52	61	66	5
Germany	82	79	64	16	49	47	76	85	9
Canada	31	39	27	12	60	46	70	79	9
United Kingdom	59	66	54	12	49	54	65	72	7
Afghanistan	21	70	62	7	83	86	53	53	0
Australia	19	26	19	7	53	49	67	73	6
Saudi Arabia	22	55	50	4	83	73	47	49	2
Spain	41	37	33	4	52	46	93	100	7
Japan	127	110	106	4	68	47	98	101	2
France	59	64	61	4	52	53	73	73	0
Russian Federation	146	101	98	4	54	44	71	72	1
Hong Kong SAR of China	7	9	6	4	49	37	79	101	22
Italy	58	45	42	3	53	48	90	90	0
Netherlands	16	17	15	2	59	47	68	72	4
Kuwait	2	5	3	2	64	39	57	59	1

Source: *World Population Prospects: The 2002 Revision, vol. I, Comprehensive Tables* (United Nations publications, Sales No. E.03.XIII.6).

the United States population would remain virtually unchanged between 2000 and 2050, reaching 287 million. With migration, in contrast, the United States population is projected to surpass 400 million by 2050. No other country is projected to experience such high migration levels, even if it is expected that migration will have a substantial impact in preventing or slowing the decline of the populations of several other countries. Germany, for instance, would expect its population to drop from 82 million in 2000 to 64 million in 2050 were it not for migration, which would contribute an additional 15 million persons, thereby bringing up the 2050 population to 79 million. For Australia, Canada, the United Kingdom and the Netherlands, migration during 2000-2050 results in a growing population over the period rather than a declining or a stable one.

Over the next 50 years, the population of the United States is projected to increase by some 40 per cent—almost entirely due to immigration

From the viewpoint of economic sustainability, changes in the age structure and, in particular, changes in the dependency ratio (the ratio of the population aged 0-14 and 65 or over to the population aged 15-64) are probably more crucial than changes in the size of the total population. As shown in table II.19, the dependency ratio is projected to increase in most developed countries in the period from 2000 to 2050 because of population ageing, even with international migration. However, international migration at the levels projected will bring about significant reductions of the dependency ratio in countries such as Australia, Canada, Germany, Spain and the United Kingdom. Migration would reduce the projected dependency ratio in 2050 from 85 to 76 per 100 persons of working age in Germany, from 79 to 70 per 100 persons of working age in Canada, and from 72 to 65 per 100 persons of working age in the United Kingdom. In Germany, for instance, international migration would add about 11 million persons of working age to the population in the period from 2000 to 2050, while it would only add 1.5 million persons aged 65 years or over and 3.4 million aged 0-14. The case of Spain is noteworthy because it is projected to have one of the world's highest dependency ratios in 2050: 93 per 100 persons of working age with international migration or 100 persons per 100 of working age without. International migration is projected to add 2.6 million persons aged 15-64 in the period from 2000 to 2050, while adding less than 600,000 persons aged 65 years or over. The contribution of international migration to the working-age population is significant in many other developed countries. The United States, for instance, would gain 59 million persons of working age from international migration and only 8 million persons aged 65 years or over. Yet the reductions of the dependency ratio associated with international migration at the levels projected are fairly modest in the United States and in all the other developed countries included in table II.19.

These findings corroborate the main conclusion of a more detailed simulation carried out in 2000 and published in a report entitled *Replacement Migration: Is it a Solution to Declining and Ageing Populations?* (United Nations, 2001). The report presented the results of a number of scenarios that incorporated the international migration flows needed to achieve specific outcomes. These scenarios were presented for eight countries—France, Germany, Italy, Japan, the Republic of Korea, the Russian Federation, the United Kingdom and the United States—and for two regions—Europe and the European Union of 15 member States. All scenarios in that publication take off from the population in 1995 as estimated by the 1998 revision of *World Population Prospects* (United Nations, 1999). Table II.20 presents the results of selected scenarios from that report. Scenario B assumes that international migration will vary in such a way as to maintain the size of the total population at the highest level that it would have reached in the absence of migration after 1995. Scenario C assumes that international migration will vary in such a way as to maintain the size of the working-age population (15-64 years) at the highest level that it would have

Immigration is expected to mitigate demographic ageing in the developed countries

Table II.20.
Projections of net immigration for selected countries or regions, 2000-2050

Thousands				
Country or region	Scenario A	Scenario B	Scenario C	Scenario D
Total				
France	3 750	1 473	5 459	89 584
Germany	10 550	17 187	24 330	181 508
Italy	3 182	12 569	18 596	113 381
Japan	2 696	17 141	32 332	523 543
Republic of Korea	-390	1 509	6 426	5 128 147
Russian Federation	2 500	24 896	35 756	253 379
United Kingdom	6 790	2 634	6 247	59 722
United States	55 750	6 384	17 967	592 572
Europe	28 949	95 869	161 346	1 356 932
European Union	34 008	47 456	79 375	673 999
Annual average				
France	75	29	109	1 792
Germany	211	344	487	3 630
Italy	64	251	372	2 268
Japan	54	343	647	10 471
Republic of Korea	-8	30	129	102 563
Russian Federation	50	498	715	5 068
United Kingdom	136	53	125	1 194
United States	1 115	128	359	11 851
Europe	579	1 917	3 227	27 139
European Union	680	949	1 588	13 480

Sources: *Replacement Migration: Is it a Solution to Declining and Ageing Populations?* (United Nations publication, Sales No.E.01.XIII.19); *World Population Prospects: The 2002 Revision, vol. I, Comprehensive Tables* (United Nations publication, Sales No. E.03.XIII.6).

Note: Scenario A is the medium variant of *World Population Prospects: The 2002 Revision.* Scenario B shows the number of migrants required to maintain the size of the population constant. Scenario C shows the number of migrants required to maintain the size of the working population (15-64) constant. Scenario D shows the number of migrants required to maintain the potential support ratio constant.

attained after 1995 in the absence of migration and scenario D assumes that international migration will vary in such a way as to maintain the potential support ratio, that is to say, the ratio of the population aged 15-64 to the population aged 65 years or over, at the highest level that it would have reached after 1995 in the absence of migration. In addition, for comparison purposes, the results of the medium variant of the 2002 revision of *World Population Prospects* are presented as scenario A (United Nations, 2003e). As explained above, the medium variant or scenario A assumes that net international migration levels will, by and large, remain constant at about the level attained during the late 1990s.

According to scenario B, the number of migrants needed to maintain the size of the total population constant over the long run is larger than the number projected under scenario A for five of the eight countries considered—Germany, Italy, Japan, the Republic of Korea and the Russian Federation—as well as for both Europe and EU. Italy, for instance, would need 12.6 million international migrants during 2000-2050, or 251,000 annually, to maintain its population constant, whereas under scenario A, it is projected to admit an annual average of just 64,000 migrants or 3.2 million during 2000-2050. Under scenario A, France, the United Kingdom and the United States are projected to have an increasing population, implying that the net number of migrants that those countries received during the late 1990s would be sufficient, all other things being equal, to avert population reductions over the first half of the twenty-first century.

Some countries would have to increase immigration enormously to avoid population declines over the next half-century

It is expected that the number of persons of working age would decline faster than the total population in the countries selected if migration were zero. Consequently, the number of migrants needed to offset declines in the working-age population (scenario C) is substantially larger than that needed to offset overall population decline. Only in the cases of the United Kingdom and the United States does scenario A, that is to say, the medium-variant projection, result in a population of working age that increases between 2000 and 2050. For the United States, this finding means that levels of net migration need to remain at over 1 million persons a year during 2000-2050.

For France, where fertility levels are projected to remain only slightly below replacement level, net migration levels of about 100,000 a year, only slightly higher than those observed in the 1990s, could prevent a reduction of the population of working age. In contrast, countries where fertility levels are lower, such as Germany, Italy and Japan, would need higher levels of net migration, ranging from 400,000 to 600,000 migrants a year, to achieve the same goal. The 15 member States of EU in 2001 would require a net intake of 1.6 million migrants per year during 2000-2050 to avoid declines of the population of working age, instead of the 680,000 projected on the basis of levels observed during the 1990s (scenario A). Although the difference between the two projected levels of migration is high, it is conceivable that the migrant intake of EU might rise in the future and help offset the effects of low fertility to an important extent.

There is no hope, however, that acceptable levels of immigration may entirely offset the effects of population ageing. Thus, the levels of net migration needed to maintain the potential support ratio constant (scenario D) are very high and unlikely to be acceptable or sustainable for any society. For instance, the annual number of migrants necessary to keep constant the potential support ratio in the 15 member States of EU in 2001 would be of 13.5 million per year, a figure 20 times higher than recently recorded levels. By 2040-2050, EU would have to absorb about half of the world's annual population growth in the form of net migration to keep its support ratio constant. Germany alone would need to absorb 3.6 million migrants per year, or a total of 181.5 million migrants in 2000-2050

Even greater increases in immigration would be needed to offset the effects of population ageing

Therefore, whereas sustained positive levels of international migration can play a role in preventing reductions of the overall population or of that of working age, they are not a viable antidote to population ageing. The challenges posed by an ageing population require a comprehensive assessment of relevant issues, including the appropriate age at retirement, ways of increasing the labour-force participation of working-age persons, the type and level of retirement benefits, and the functioning of pension systems. International migration is likely to be fostered for the other economic benefits it brings, but its ultimate effect on slowing population ageing is unlikely to be the main driving force behind spurring its increase in the coming decades.

Increased immigration alone would not be a viable solution to the problem of population ageing

Conclusions

The global stock of international migrants more than doubled over the last 40 years, but not all regions were affected

Over the last decades of the twentieth century, population mobility increased markedly. As this chapter has shown, one measure of international mobility, the stock of international migrants, rose from 76 million in 1960 to 175 million in 2000, having more than doubled over the course of those 40 years. The data presented also show that the number of international migrants has not grown at a fast pace in every region of the world. Even without the effect of the break-up of the USSR, the pace of growth of the stock of international migrants has been more rapid in the developed regions than in the developing world. In fact, estimates for the 1990s indicate that the number of international migrants in developing countries as a whole hardly changed. This finding should have a sobering effect on the often-repeated claims about the growing pervasiveness and "globalization" of international migration.

With regard to the participation of women in international migration, current estimates show that, for as long as we can assess it, their participation has been high, especially when migration was directed to developed countries. While it is true that the participation of women in certain types of flows has risen, the main finding is that, at least since 1960, overall female migration has nearly reached parity with male migration.

Most international migrants remain concentrated in a comparatively small number of developed countries

The late twentieth century did witness some key changes in international migration trends. For one, the steady and rapid increase in the number of international migrants in the developed world has led to a greater concentration of the stock of international migrants in developed countries. The United States, in particular, now accounts for 1 out of every 5 international migrants in the world. Most international migrants remain concentrated in a few countries (28 at last count) and although that number has been growing, it has done so slowly.

International migrants do represent a high proportion (10 per cent or more) of the population of an increasing number of countries or areas, but many of them have small populations and have had high proportions of international migrants since the 1960s. There have been important changes, however, in the major poles of attraction in some regions. One of the most significant has been the transformation of a number of European countries from net sending countries into net receiving countries. In addition, flows of migrants from Eastern to Western Europe expanded as change began to take hold in the former Communist countries, and those flows became major components of the migrant intake of a number of Western countries. Concomitantly, the opening of borders between the countries of Eastern and Central Europe and the break-up of the USSR produced important migration flows between the countries of those regions, driven in part by the return of certain ethnic groups to their republics of origin.

Another important transformation was the emergence in the 1980s and 1990s of the rapidly industrializing countries of Eastern and South-eastern Asia as destinations for migrant workers, especially because a number of those countries had been important sources of emigrants just a decade before. In fact, some of them, such as Malaysia and the Republic of Korea, experienced both significant outflows of citizens and inflows of foreign workers.

International migration has never been a one-way street, although the general lack of data on emigration often leads to the false conclusion that countries receiving migrants from abroad are not themselves the origin of migrant outflows. Even the United States, the major attraction pole in the world, is estimated to lose 200,000 emigrants annually and there are significant populations of American expatriates in a number of European countries.

There have also been changes in respect of the origins of migrants, that is to say, there has been some diversification in the countries that are the main sources of migrants to the developed world, even if the migrant stock of each receiving country continues to be dominated by a handful of nationalities. In addition, the conditions under which migrants are admitted have evolved. In the 1990s, developed countries either started or redoubled efforts to attract temporary skilled workers from abroad so as to satisfy the demand in particular sectors of their economies. Consequently, temporary admissions of skilled workers increased in a number of countries.

Clearly, international migration evolves as the economic, social and political situation of countries changes. With more independent States, the possibilities for international migration increase. Furthermore, given the persistence of economic disparities between countries, population movements respond to the opportunities available, be they in the developed world or in the more prosperous developing countries. Differences in demographic dynamics also play a part, as the better-off countries tend to be those where fertility levels have been lower and where population ageing is accelerating. International migration is already contributing to preventing or slowing down the decline of a number of populations in the developed world, and it is expected to continue playing that role in the future, although it will not compensate fully the strong effect that declining fertility has had—and will continue to have—on population ageing and, particularly, on the relative size of the working-age population of many developed countries.

Notes

1 Estimates are based on census data for 210 countries or areas out of 228. The data for 156 of them relate to the number of foreign-born persons. For a further 54, the data available refer to the number of foreigners. For developing countries, the number of refugees as reported by the Office of the United Nations High Commissioner for Refugees (UNHCR) and the United Nations Relief and Works Agency for Palestine Refugees in the Near East (UNRWA) has been added to the number of international migrants derived from census data. In principle, censuses enumerate all persons present or living in a country at a particular time. Consequently, census counts do not necessarily exclude undocumented or unauthorized migrants. Evidence suggests that censuses generally include undocumented migrants in the counts they produce, thus providing a good basis for the estimation of all international migrants.

2 The estimate by the International Labour Organization (ILO) refers to the number of foreigners in the countries of the world in 1910; therefore, strictly speaking, it is not comparable with the estimates of the foreign-born population available since 1960.

3 The rate of natural increase indicates how fast a population would grow because of the difference between births and deaths in relation to population; that is to say, it does not take account of the contribution to population growth or decrease made by net international migration.

4 These numbers differ from those normally reported in United States sources because they include the number of foreign-born persons enumerated in the United States who were United States citizens by birth.

5 Other estimates had put the total of unauthorized migrants in the United States in 2000 at 8.5 million and at 9.3 million by 2002 (Passell, 2002; 2004).

Chapter III
International migration policies

Given the current high visibility of issues related to international migration, it is perhaps surprising to note that migration has not always featured so prominently in national and international agendas. When the United Nations began monitoring government views and policies on population in 1976, international migration had not been a topic of major concern for most Governments. Quinquennial inquiries and periodic assessments by the Population Division of the Department of Economic and Social Affairs of the United Nations Secretariat reveal noticeable shifts in government policies since 1976. Substantial changes in government perceptions of migration trends took place in the second half of the 1970s and the early 1980s, as Governments' concerns with the demographic, economic, social and political consequences of immigration grew. While in 1976, only 7 per cent of Governments had viewed immigration levels as too high, the proportion had risen to 20 per cent in 1986 (table III.1). In 2003, the proportion of Governments that viewed the level of immigration as too high was 21 per cent worldwide.

All Governments have the right to determine whom it admits into its jurisdiction and on what basis. While States are obligated to accept their own citizens, the admittance of non-citizens is the prerogative of individual Governments. To ensure its sovereignty, every State has introduced policies and procedures to determine who enters its territory and to monitor and control those who do enter. Some policies and procedures are more effective than others, and the extent to which these measures are implemented depends on such factors as the State's perceived need to protect its borders, financial constraints and human resources. Some countries have formulated explicit policies to vary the flow and/or composition of immigrants and emigrants. These are pursued by Governments to various degrees and are implemented in line with national objectives and political will.

During the last quarter of the twentieth century, the proportion of Governments that viewed immigration as too high increased from 7 to 21 per cent

The present chapter, which focuses on national migration policies, describes the salient features of historical and recent immigration and emigration policies. Regional and international initiatives adopted by individual countries, such as the instruments of the European Union (EU) and the North American Free Trade Agreement (NAFTA), are discussed in chapter VIII on international cooperation. A major characteristic of United Nations international population conferences during the past three decades has been the emphasis placed on the monitoring of the implementation of their goals and recommendations. Accordingly, data on migration policies are often presented for the years 1976, 1986 and 1996 in this chapter—that is to say, for the two years following the convening of the population conferences at Bucharest, Mexico City and Cairo, respectively—as well as for 2003.

Table III.1.
Government views on the level of immigration, by country's level of development and major areas, 1976, 1986, 1996 and 2003

Year	Number of countries				Percentage			
	Too low	Satisfactory	Too high	Total	Too low	Satisfactory	Too high	Total
By level of development								
World								
1976	11	129	10	150	7	86	7	100
1986	6	125	33	164	4	76	20	100
1996	4	148	41	193	2	77	21	100
2003	9	145	40	194	5	75	21	100
More developed regions								
1976	1	27	6	34	3	79	18	100
1986	0	26	8	34	0	76	24	100
1996	1	31	16	48	2	65	33	100
2003	5	32	11	48	10	67	23	100
Less developed regions								
1976	10	102	4	116	9	88	3	100
1986	6	99	25	130	5	76	19	100
1996	3	117	25	145	2	81	17	100
2003	4	113	29	146	3	77	20	100
Least developed countries								
1976	2	39	1	42	5	93	2	100
1986	1	40	7	48	2	83	15	100
1996	0	41	8	49	0	84	16	100
2003	0	44	5	49	0	90	10	100
By major Area								
Africa								
1976	5	41	2	48	10	85	4	100
1986	1	39	11	51	2	76	22	100
1996	0	46	7	53	0	87	13	100
2003	1	45	7	53	2	85	13	100
Asia								
1976	4	32	1	37	11	86	3	100
1986	1	30	7	38	3	79	18	100
1996	1	35	10	46	2	76	22	100
2003	1	31	15	46	2	66	32	100
Europe								
1976	0	24	5	29	0	83	17	100
1986	0	22	7	29	0	76	24	100
1996	0	27	16	43	0	63	37	100
2003	4	29	10	43	9	67	23	100
Latin America and the Caribbean								
1976	1	25	1	27	4	93	4	100
1986	4	23	6	33	12	70	18	100
1996	2	26	5	33	6	79	15	100
2003	1	28	4	33	3	85	12	100

Table III.1 (cont'd)

Year	Number of countries				Percentage			
	Too low	Satisfactory	Too high	Total	Too low	Satisfactory	Too high	Total
Northern America								
1976	0	2	0	2	0	100	0	100
1986	0	1	1	2	0	50	50	100
1996	0	2	0	2	0	100	0	100
2003	1	1	0	2	50	50	0	100
Oceania								
1976	1	5	1	7	14	71	14	100
1986	0	10	1	11	0	91	9	100
1996	1	12	3	16	6	75	19	100
2003	1	11	4	16	6	69	25	100

Source: *World Population Policies, 2003* (United Nations publication, Sales No. E.04.XIII.3).

Historical trends in immigration policies

Countries differ in their provisions for admitting individuals and allowing them to remain. These provisions have evolved over time, as the needs of receiving countries changed. Economic, political, social and demographic factors largely mould national immigration policies. Factors explaining migratory flows, why countries accept migrants and the consequences for countries of origin are discussed in chapter IV. Over the last three decades, the number of countries hosting migrants has grown significantly and those countries now include countries of permanent migration, labour recruitment countries and an increasing number of developing countries.

Most migrants have sought entry into developed countries where distinctive immigration regimes have been established—countries of permanent migration, labour recruitment States and those countries that have been transformed from countries of origin to those of destination (Freeman, 2003). Provisions under the 1951 Convention relating to the Status of Refugees (United Nations, 1954) for asylum and refugees constitute another legal regime discussed in chapter VIII. Significant shifts in immigration policies occurred at major historical junctions, such as the Second World War and the 1973 oil crisis (Schindlmayr, 2003).

Countries of permanent migration

In the immediate post-Second World War period, migration meant permanent settlement, or a long-term absence away from the country of origin. Travel was time-consuming and expensive. As a result, residence abroad tended to be longer-term or permanent. The traditional countries of permanent immigration - Australia, Canada, New Zealand and the United States of America - had policies that assumed as well as facilitated the long-term stay of migrants, and were largely focused on attracting European settlers. Indeed, Europe was the major source of migrants to other parts of the world after the Second World War, these often being encouraged by settlement schemes. The beginning of the decline in the number of Europeans migrating in the late 1950s, combined with criticism of their migration policies favouring Caucasians, resulted in the altering of their policies by this group of countries to allow migration from other regions. For example, Canada's immigration regulations of 1962 prohibited discrimination based on race, religion and origin. It introduced a point system based on current needs in 1967. The United States abolished its Quota System in 1965, which had given preference to migrants of European origin, and established global criteria based on skills and family ties. Australia removed a number of restrictions with respect to non-Caucasian immigrants in 1966 and abandoned its long-standing "White Australia Policy" in 1973 (Appleyard, 1977), while New Zealand liberalized its policies in 1978. Their shifting of the emphasis of their migration policies in favour of non-discriminatory practices substantially altered the composition of migrant flows to these countries, and the ethnic make-up of the population.

During the 1960s, the traditional countries of immigration dropped their European preference policies and began to welcome migrants from all countries equally

With the change in the criteria for admission, these countries began stressing family ties, language proficiency, educational qualifications, job skills and other attributes. Australia established a Numerical Assessment System in 1979 to place migrants in four groups. This was expanded to five groups in 1982—family reunification, needed labour and business skills, independent (individuals with useful skills not in demand), refugees, and special eligibility. In that same year, Australia halted its assisted immigration programme. The point system remains the basis for selecting permanent migrants in Australia, Canada and New Zealand, although the criteria for point allocation are reviewed and altered on a regular basis. Increasingly, these countries view migrant skills as a primary criterion for both permanent and temporary migration (see below). In the United States, the Immigration Act (1990) raised the number of permanent migrants allowed to enter the country. Based on criteria that emphasized family reunification, the goal was also to increase the skills and education levels of migrants The annual number of permanent migrants rose to 675,000 from 1995 onward.

Labour recruitment states

Many countries have accepted, and continue to accept, migrant workers on a largely temporary basis. In France and Switzerland, for example, the practice of recruiting workers dates back to the nineteenth century. The central premise of temporary migration policies is that workers remain while jobs are available and leave when those jobs are no longer available (Hansen, 2003). Historically, it was low-skilled workers who were sought but, increasingly, individuals with a wider range of skill levels have been recruited.

Post-Second World War labour migration into Northern and Western Europe began in the 1950s

As their economies improved in the 1950s, many European countries began to recruit migrants on a temporary basis to meet the increased demand for labour. European Governments encouraged the migration of workers from countries around the Mediterranean basin, and to this end, concluded labour agreements with Turkey and North African and Southern European States. They attracted overwhelmingly low-skilled men to perform jobs that locals increasingly disdained. As Governments were convinced that workers would return to their home countries once jobs were no longer available, these programmes were largely market-driven with minimal government involvement. France and the United Kingdom of Great Britain and Northern Ireland attracted a significant number of workers from their former colonies.

The economic turmoil that followed the oil shocks of the 1970s brought about a tightening of the previously rather relaxed immigration controls that had characterized the post-war period. The change in policy resulted in a major decline in the number of migrant workers admitted to countries with developed market economies (Appleyard, 1977) and signaled a new era in the formulation of migration policies with many European countries seeking to stabilize their foreign populations. In most of the labour-importing countries of Northern and Western Europe, the recruitment of migrant labour practically ceased. Governments unsuccessfully attempted to discourage family reunification and to promote repatriation. With a view to protecting the domestic labour market in the context of rapidly growing unemployment, Germany, for example, provided incentives for migrant workers to return to their home country. These programmes had limited success (Stalker, 2002), although the overall number of at least temporary returnees was on the order of several hundred thousand. A gradual improvement in productivity and competitiveness, along with an economic revival in the 1980s, induced most Western European countries to resume recruiting foreign labour, albeit on a smaller scale.

From the mid-1970s on, labour migration into Europe was increasingly limited

By the 1990s, labour migration to Europe had come increasingly to reflect former colonial links such as those of Latin America to Spain and Portugal. With increasing European integration, immigrant flows in the 1990s also included a mix of relatively high-income professionals from within EU, contract workers from Eastern Europe and unskilled migrant workers from Northern Africa and Asia.

In the 1990s, European labour migration increasingly reflected former colonial ties

In Asia, during the 1970s, new migration patterns emerged. Labour migration into Western Asia surged in the 1970s, then declined around 1990. In the 1970s, some countries began importing labour for the first time. Following a jump in oil prices, ambitious projects were launched to construct basic infrastructure and develop modern services in the oil-exporting countries of Western Asia. The small size of the national populations, the low rates of female participation in the labour force, the low status of manual labour and a reluctance to work in the private sector made it very difficult to meet the increased demand for labour. Therefore, the oil-producing countries of the Persian Gulf region became the main destination for migrant workers from other Arab countries and from Asia. By the late 1980s, there were some 6 million migrant workers in Western Asia. The outbreak of the Gulf war in August 1990 led to a sharp reduction in their numbers, with an ensuing harmful effect on their counties of origin. As many as 2 million migrants returned to their countries of origin immediately before and after the war.

As the demand for migrant labour in Western Asia slackened, labour recruitment shifted to the rapidly growing economies of Japan, the Republic of Korea and the newly industrialized countries of South-eastern Asia. These Governments favoured labour-import contracts with recruitment agencies, whether public or private, because of the greater ease in managing and monitoring agencies than individual migrants. Like much of Europe, Japan and the Republic of Korea legally admitted only migrants with professional skills that were in demand. By contrast, the booming economies of Brunei Darussalam, China, Hong Kong Special Administrative Region (SAR) of China, Malaysia, Singapore and Thailand in the 1990s experienced both skilled and unskilled labour shortages.

In the 1990s, labour migration demand shifted towards East Asia

The scale and patterns of international labour migration in Asia have become increasingly complex. Investments by multinational companies throughout Asia have been accompanied by significant flows of skilled labour from both Western and Asian countries (United Nations, 2003a). While a few countries can be characterized as either net labour-importing or net labour-exporting, a growing number of Asian countries—for example,

India, Malaysia, the Republic of Korea, Singapore and Thailand—are both. Although bilateral agreements exist between some countries of origin and some countries of destination in the Gulf region, these agreements have little impact on the conditions migrant workers face in the host country. Migrant workers in Western Asia are typically recruited under a guest-worker scheme that limits their rights. Recruitment and placement firms that until recently arranged most labour migration in Asia have not been responsible for dealing with the exploitative or abusive situations faced by some migrants. Usually hired on one-year contracts with the possibility of extension, migrant workers are not permitted to change employers, and only certain categories of workers are allowed to bring their families. This particularly affects women who often perform domestic tasks such as cleaning, sewing and caregiving. In some cases, the fact that their documentation is taken away by the sponsor potentially subjects them to penalties in the host countries. Legislation in some countries permits domestic workers to be transferred from one sponsor to another, subjecting migrants to different terms and conditions than those agreed upon—at times to their detriment (United Nations, 2004f).

In Africa, some countries have in the past sought to attract migrants. For example, Côte d'Ivoire encouraged migration from neighbouring countries to work on agricultural plantations well into the 1990s. Gabon recruited migrants from neighbouring countries and Europe for work mainly in the petroleum sector, while Botswana drew numerous skilled migrants after modifying immigration laws in the 1990s (International Organization for Migration and United Nations, 2000). Embracing the concept of pan-African unity, the Libyan Arab Jamahiriya admitted over 1 million migrants during the 1990s, although the policy has now largely been abandoned. As the continent's economic giant, South Africa has drawn and continues to draw many migrants, while also being a significant exporter of skilled migrants (see below). Labour migration to South Africa increased substantially with the elimination of severe penalties against undocumented migrants following the abolition of apartheid in 1994. This took place despite amendments to the Aliens Control Act in 1995 that continued to place tight controls on immigration (International Organization for Migration, 2001). South Africa now admits mostly temporary migrants, but appears to tolerate a large number of undocumented migrants. The 2002 Immigration Act sets out various provisions and conditions for labour migration to the country, creating a quota system for work permits that focuses on skilled labour and new immigration tribunals.

South Africa has a large stock of undocumented immigrants

In Latin America, several countries—most notably Argentina, Brazil, Chile, Venezuela and Uruguay—had attracted millions of migrants from Europe in the past. In recent decades, migration policies have tended to focus on improving the capacity of Governments to regulate and control their borders through bilateral and regional agreements, as discussed in chapter VIII. These agreements also enabled nationals of signatory countries to work in any of the other signatory countries. To manage migration, a number of countries (for example, Argentina, Costa, Rica and Venezuela) have also tried to cope with significant movements of undocumented migrants by implementing unilateral measures such as regularization programmes. These countries have some of the highest proportions of foreign-born population in Central and South America.

Current trends in immigration policies

Analysis of immigration policy can usefully be organized around eight leading issues: overall immigration levels, skilled workers, unskilled workers, family reunification, integration of non-nationals, the undocumented, regionalization of policies, and migration and trade.

Overall immigration levels

The first and most basic issue is the overall level of immigration. Most countries do not report policies designed to change migration from its present levels. At the same time, the overall trend during the last quarter of the twentieth century had been for a declining proportion of countries to report their immigration policy as one of "no intervention" or one of maintaining the prevailing level. However, there was an upturn in the proportion seeking to maintain/not intervene in the first years of the twenty-first century. In addition, as of 2003, some one third of countries in both the developed and developing regions wanted to lower immigration. This contrasts with 1976 when few Governments had explicit policies to modify migration flows; 7 per cent had a policy to lower immigration, while another 7 per cent had a policy to raise immigration (table III.2, fig. III.1).

More than one third of countries report policies designed to change migration from its current level

However, the proportion of more developed countries that aim to lower immigration has declined since 1986, owing in part to labour shortages in certain sectors, an expanding global economy and long-term trends in population ageing. By 2003, four developed countries had policies to raise immigration levels in line with national needs, namely, Canada, the Czech Republic, Ukraine and the United Kingdom. By comparison, in the less developed regions the proportion of countries wanting to lower immigration had risen from 3 per cent in 1976 to 34 per cent in 1996 and remained at that level in 2003. Over the same period, the proportion of countries in the less developed regions wanting to raise immigration declined from 9 per cent in 1976 to 5 per cent in 1996 and to 4 per cent in 2003.

The receptiveness of countries to new immigrants is, at least in part, a reflection of previous migration trends and the public expectation of further immigration. Disaggregating the data on migration policies by size of the migrant stock indicates that the propensity to lower immigration is greatest among countries whose proportion of this migrant stock falls into the intermediate range, that is to say, of from 1 to 4.9 per cent of the total population (fig. III.2). Among these 70 countries, some 40 per cent wish to lower immigration. On the other hand, a majority of the countries where the proportion of the migrant stock is 5 per cent or more of the total population report that they want to lower immigration or keep it at its current level.

Skilled worker migration

The second immigration policy issue is the widespread promotion of the immigration of skilled workers. Increasing restrictiveness towards overall migration in receiving countries reflects an evolution towards greater selectiveness, favouring the admission of migrants who meet specific labour needs such as those in science and technology, those with skills considered in short supply and those with capital to invest. By means either of preferential

Table III.2.

Government policies on immigration, by country's level of development and major areas, 1976, 1986, 1996 and 2003

Year	Number of countries				Percentage			
	Raise	Maintain/no intervention	Lower	Total	Raise	Maintain/no intervention	Lower	Total
By level of development								
World								
1976	11	129	10	150	7	86	7	100
1986	6	125	33	164	4	76	20	100
1996	8	107	78	193	4	55	40	100
2003	10	119	65	194	5	62	34	100
More developed regions								
1976	1	27	6	34	3	79	18	100
1986	0	21	13	34	0	62	38	100
1996	1	18	29	48	2	37	60	100
2003	4	28	16	48	8	58	33	100
Less developed regions								
1976	10	102	4	116	9	88	3	100
1986	6	104	20	130	5	80	15	100
1996	7	89	49	145	5	61	34	100
2003	6	91	49	146	4	63	34	100
Least developed countries								
1976	2	39	1	42	5	93	2	100
1986	1	43	4	48	2	90	8	100
1996	1	35	13	49	2	72	27	100
2003	1	37	11	49	2	75	22	100
By major area								
Africa								
1976	5	41	2	48	10	85	4	100
1986	1	41	9	51	2	80	18	100
1996	2	35	16	53	4	66	30	100
2003	2	38	13	53	4	72	25	100
Asia								
1976	4	32	1	37	11	86	3	100
1986	1	30	7	38	3	79	18	100
1996	2	23	21	46	4	50	46	100
2003	2	22	23	46	4	47	49	100
Europe								
1976	0	24	5	29	0	83	17	100
1986	0	16	13	29	0	55	45	100
1996	0	15	28	43	0	35	65	100
2003	3	24	16	43	7	56	37	100
Latin America and the Caribbean								
1976	1	25	1	27	4	93	4	100
1986	4	25	4	33	12	76	12	100
1996	3	20	10	33	9	60	30	100
2003	1	23	9	33	3	70	27	100

Table III.2 (cont'd)

Year	Number of countries: Raise	Maintain/no intervention	Lower	Total	Percentage: Raise	Maintain/no intervention	Lower	Total
Northern America								
1976	0	2	0	2	0	100	0	100
1986	0	2	0	2	0	100	0	100
1996	0	1	1	2	0	50	50	100
2003	1	1	0	2	50	50	0	100
Oceania								
1976	1	5	1	7	14	71	14	100
1986	0	11	0	11	0	100	0	100
1996	1	13	2	16	6	81	12	100
2003	1	11	4	16	6	69	25	100

Source: *World Population Policies, 2003* (United Nations publication, Sales No. E.04.XIII.3).

Figure III.1.
Government policies on immigration, 1976, 1986, 1996 and 2003

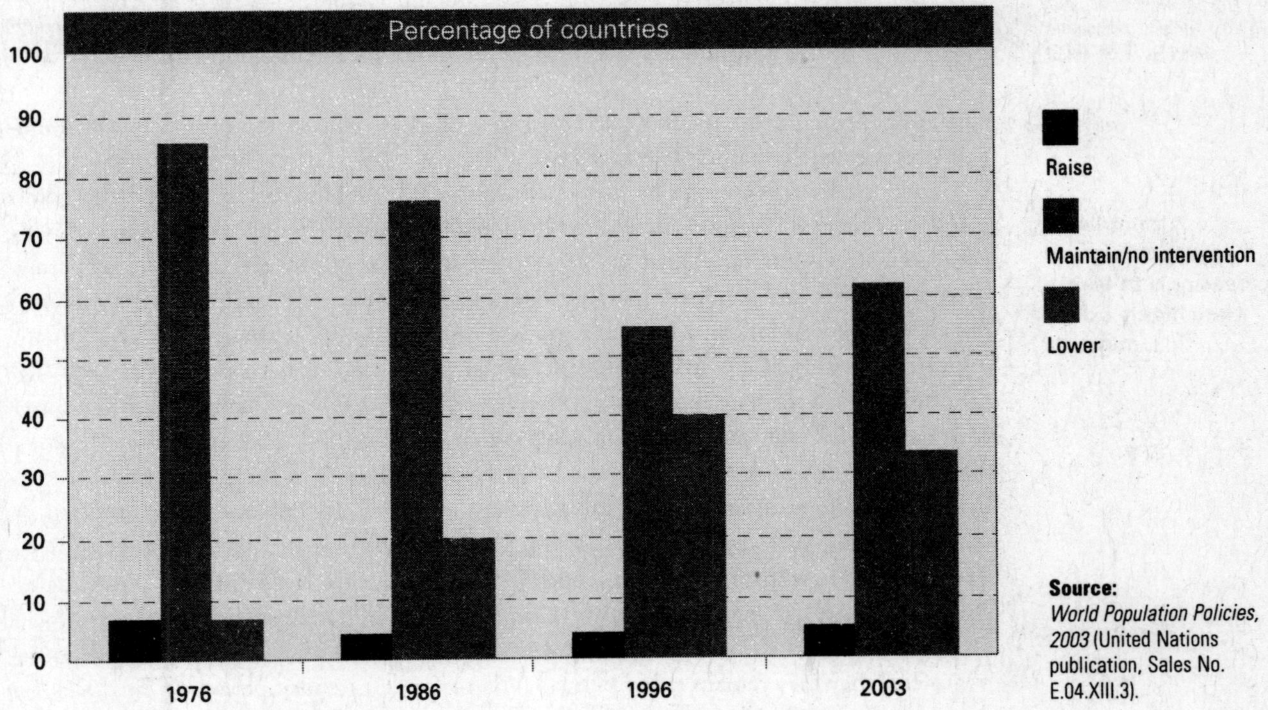

Source:
World Population Policies, 2003 (United Nations publication, Sales No. E.04.XIII.3).

categories as in the United States, or of point systems as in Australia and Canada, by the early 1990s, countries of permanent immigration had enacted legislation placing greater emphasis on migrant skills. The recruitment of foreign labour based on skills has had a significant impact on the origin and nature of overall migration flows. Under the current preference system, new immigrants to the United States are more likely to come from Asia and Europe, while in Australia and Canada, the numerical weight attached to factors such as

Figure III.2.
Government policies on immigration by size of countries' immigrant stock, 2003

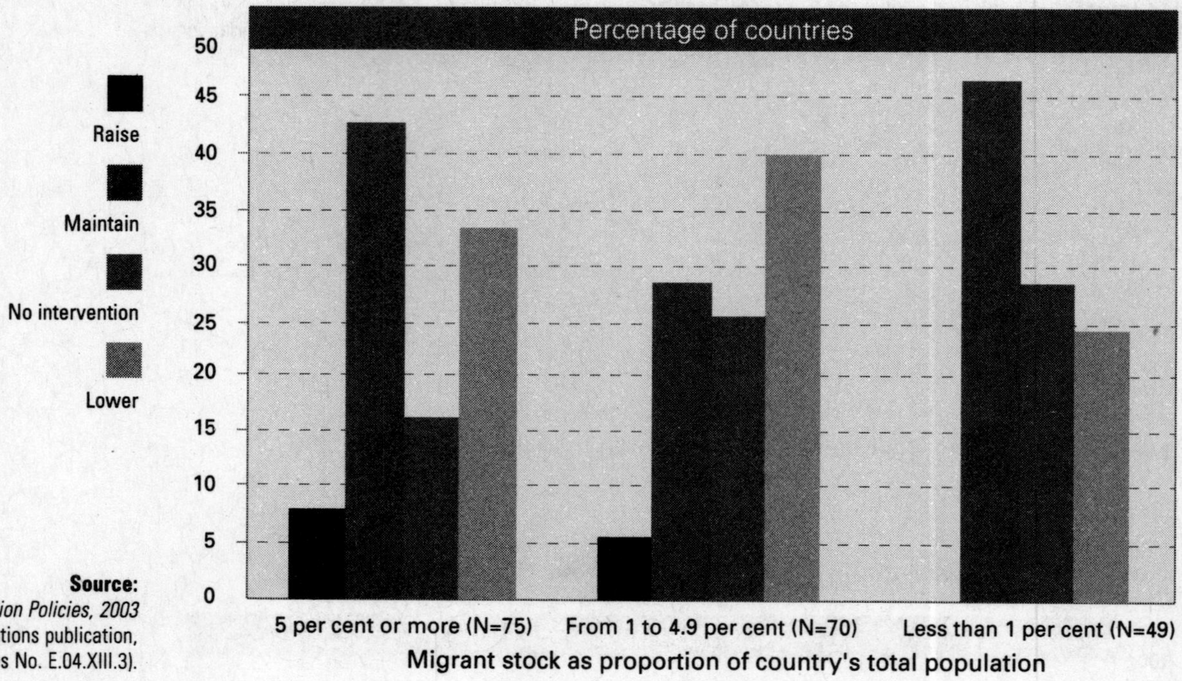

Source:
World Population Policies, 2003 (United Nations publication, Sales No. E.04.XIII.3).

education, training, occupation and language skills has reduced the proportion of immigrants dependent on family relationships.

Countries of immigration tend increasingly to favour more highly skilled migrants

Labour migration has become increasingly complex, as the skills that migrants bring with them increasingly determine the likelihood of their being admitted in receiving countries. Provisions for skilled workers differ significantly between countries of permanent settlement and labour-importing developed countries. In countries of permanent migration, skilled workers are usually granted only temporary residence, while in labour-importing developed countries, they are frequently contracted for a period that may significantly exceed the length of time granted for other types of work. Some two dozen countries have policies in place favouring the migration of skilled workers (United Nations, 2003c). Although most migrants to the United States continue to enter under family reunification provisions, a significant number of highly skilled migrants are being admitted on renewable three-year visas (H1-B visas). In 2001, nearly half of immigrants on H1-B visas were working in information technology (IT) and were from India (Martin and Midgley, 2003). In 2003, the quota for these visas was set at 195,000. Several countries also focus on attracting international students and upon their graduation, offer them preferential treatment: they may remain either permanently or for an extended period. In Australia, for example, more than 50 per cent of successful applicants under the skilled migration programme had been students in that country (Maiden, 2004).

Significant labour shortfalls in a number of sectors due to skill shortages, population ageing and population decline have fuelled an increase in the intake of migrant workers in most European countries, albeit an intake that is limited to highly skilled workers and is typically effected on a temporary basis. Examples of responses to these shortfalls include the 2000 "Green Card" initiative for IT specialists in Germany, the

2002 Highly Skilled Migrant Programme in the United Kingdom and the Czech pilot project for skilled migrants launched in December 2002. A recent report by the Commission of the European communities (2003) noted that "sustained immigration flows are increasingly likely and necessary".

Low-skilled migration

The third issue is the recruitment of low-skilled workers. Although receiving countries have emphasized the need to attract highly skilled workers, population ageing and rising job expectations are also producing labour shortages in such low-skilled fields as agriculture, construction and domestic services. The educational attainment of migrants in Western Europe and North America is lower than that of the native population, while in Southern Europe, migrants tend to be better educated (United Nations, 2003c). A Transatlantic Round-table on Low-Skilled Migration in the Twenty-first Century: Prospects and Policies, held in Brussels on 16 and 17 June 2003 and attended by Governments and international organizations, concluded that greater priority should be given to low-skilled migration (Lowell and Kemper, 2004).

Several countries have responded to these labour supply gaps by tolerating undocumented migration and visa overstayers, although this is not often widely acknowledged by Governments. Others countries, for example, those in Southern Europe, have signed bilateral agreements with Poland, Romania and Ukraine to recruit foreign workers, while Germany, Switzerland and the United States offer visas for seasonal workers (SOPEMI (Continuous Reporting System on Migration), 2004). Some countries, including Australia, Canada, New Zealand, the United Kingdom and the United States also offer working holiday schemes, giving young people from abroad the opportunity to work and travel in these countries.

At the same time, many countries continue to tolerate low-skilled—and often undocumented—immigrants to meet labour-force needs

Family reunification

The fourth issue is the promotion of family reunification. For a number of countries, family migration or family reunification is the predominant mode of legal entry. Most migrant-receiving countries have some basic provision for family reunification, which allows individuals to join family members already in the country. Not only are such provisions viewed as being consistent with the values of liberal democracy, but they are also an effective mechanism for encouraging migrants to adapt to their new society. Although no international instrument universally establishes family reunification as a right, article 16 (3) of the Universal Declaration of Human Rights (1948) (General Assembly resolution 217 A (III)) states that families are entitled to protection by society and the State. At the same time, family reunification is not universally accepted. Many contract labour arrangements preclude admission of family members. In many labour-importing countries, widespread debate has focused on the cost of providing migrants' dependants with health, education and welfare benefits.

There are many variations in the definition of the family, criteria for eligibility and rights accorded to migrants entering a country under family reunification procedures. Generally, family reunification provisions apply to spouses and unmarried dependent minors. However, there is no consensus on the age of children. Polygamous unions may be

Most countries of immigration accept some migrants on the grounds of family reunification; some countries give it strong preference

ruled out, while unmarried partners can qualify for reunification under certain conditions in an increasing number of countries. In some countries, parents, brothers, sisters and other relatives may also qualify under conditions of dependency, age and sponsorship. Patterns of family reunification often follow male-dominated migration. In some countries, it is difficult or impossible for women to bring their husbands and children (United Nations, 2004f).

Although labour migration into developed countries has been limited for over 25 years, the foreign labour force has significantly increased during this period. This apparent paradox stems from the fact that large numbers of foreign workers have been entering the host country as family members, who are now responsible for the greatest share of migration flows in countries members of the Organization for Economic Cooperation and Development (fig. III.3). Since the 1980s, family reunification has become a major reason for immigration in a significant number of countries, particularly in Europe. In OECD countries as a whole, migration for family reunification accounts for the largest share of migrant intake, in large part as a consequence of the restrictions imposed on labour migration in the mid-1970s. Along with asylum, family reunion has become the main legal justification for migration.

In recent decades, family reunification has increasingly replaced labour migration as grounds for entry

As countries experience labour shortfalls, the need for migrants grows. However, resorting to temporary migration can and often does have unintended consequences. Basing his observations on the European experience, Hansen (2003) notes that migration of young men in the 1950s and 1960s eventually led to family reunification in the host country. Thus, what had been intended as temporary migration resulted in permanent migration. A study of temporary foreign worker programmes in six countries (Ruhs, 2003) identified five unintended outcomes associated with such programmes:

Figure III.3.
Long-term immigration flows into selected OECD countries by main categories, 2001

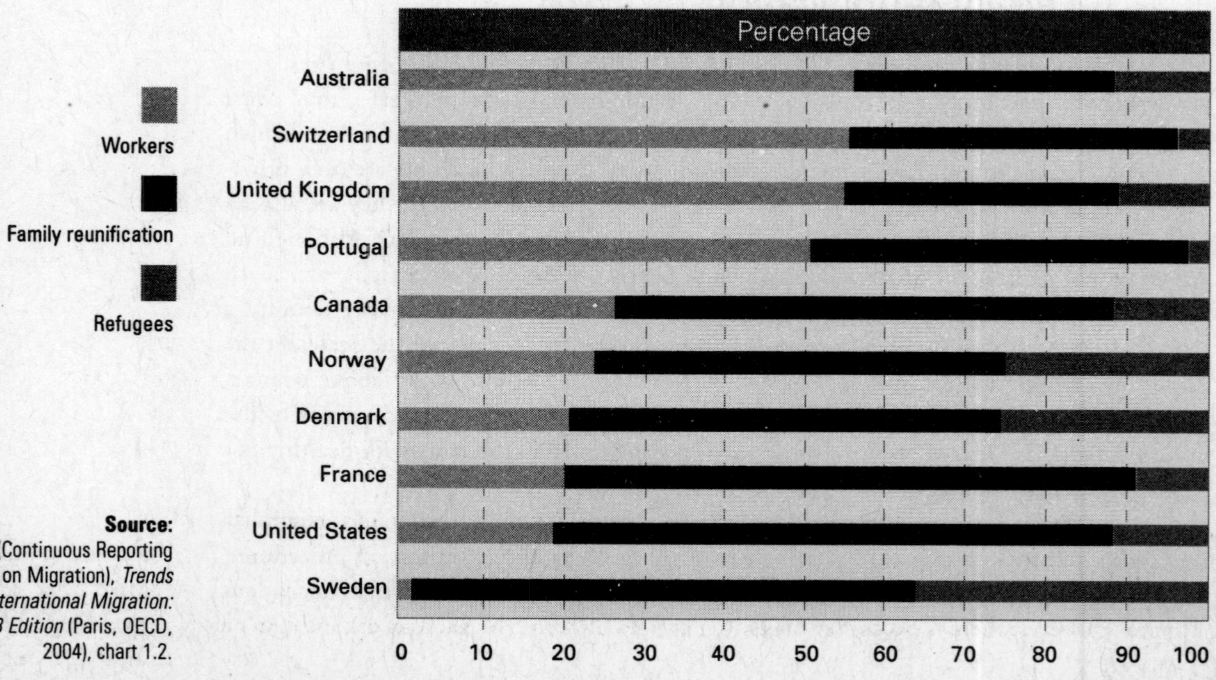

Source: SOPEMI (Continuous Reporting System on Migration), *Trends in International Migration: 2003 Edition* (Paris, OECD, 2004), chart 1.2.

(a) the establishment of "immigrant sectors" in the receiving country's labour market; (b) the vulnerability of migrant workers to exploitation in recruitment for employment; (c) an increase in immigrant numbers and a greater-than-expected length of stay; (d) the opposition to migration by native workers; and (e) an increase in undocumented migration.

Not considering themselves countries of immigration (Stalker, 2002), several countries in Western Europe had halted labour recruitment, as a means of achieving zero immigration (Kasasa, 2001; Commission for the European Communities, 2003). Thus, the surge in immigration for family reunification during the 1990s took many Governments by surprise. It was only during the second half of the 1990s that the issue of migration for family reunification was formally addressed. High levels of migration for family reunification remain a contentious issue in many European countries. Most migrants to Canada, Denmark, France, Norway, Sweden and the United States are now admitted on family reunification grounds (fig. III.3).

In some European countries, immigration for family reunification is recognized as a human right

The significance of immigration for family reunification has led several European countries to recognize family reunification as a human right. Belgium, France, Germany, Italy, the Netherlands and Spain amended their legislation in this regard in the second half of the 1990s. The Council of Europe passed six recommendations and adopted two recommendations on the right to family reunification. Within the borders of EU, the right to family reunification for European citizens has been in effect since 1998.

In all countries, family members who pose a possible threat to public order or national security are not admitted. However, the thoroughness of verification can vary among countries. A few countries require documentary evidence of the absence of a criminal record, while others check only for selected offences. There has been discussion on whether a different set of rules should apply to refugees who cannot provide the necessary documentation or may have been sentenced under criminal law.

In some countries, family members are not eligible if they have medical conditions that either endanger public health or burden the existing welfare system. At the end of the 1980s, for example, some countries denied entry to migrants with HIV/AIDS in the hope of containing the spread of the disease. Today, some 60 countries impose mandatory testing, including China, the Russian Federation and the United States. While most of these countries impose testing only on those who want to remain in the country, some countries demand testing for short-term visitors as well. Other possible grounds for exclusion include disability, previous criminal conviction, age and ill health.

While family reunification ensures the integrity of the family unit and constitutes a human right, it is a type of migration that is difficult to manage. It is open to potential abuse through sham marriages that use family reunification provisions as a means of trafficking. Such abuses have led some countries to place conditions on immigration of spouses.

Integration of non-nationals

The fifth immigration policy issue is the integration of non-nationals. To facilitate migration, receiving countries are increasingly adopting policies that focus on the integration of migrants. In 2003, 61 countries reported that they had programmes to integrate non-nationals (United Nations, 2004e). Such programmes are more commonly found in more-developed countries. While assimilation has been the accepted means of integration, many developed countries now recognize and promote the benefits that diversity brings to their society. To ensure that minimal human rights standards are respected, many countries have adopted non-discrimination provisions to protect religious freedom and the use of other languages. These protections are also applicable to migrants in most instances. Generally speaking, countries that encourage immigration have substantial integration policies including naturalization, while those that have a restrictive view of immigration are less inclusive in their approach (Lynch and Simon, 2003).

In most countries, non-citizens do not enjoy the same basic rights as are enjoyed by citizens

In most countries, non-citizens do not enjoy the same basic rights as are enjoyed by citizens; thus they are prevented from participating fully in the civil and political life of the country in which they live. In addition, they are often not able to receive social welfare benefits. Only upon becoming a citizen do migrants fully share the same responsibilities and enjoy the same privileges as nationals. Most Governments have historically not regarded themselves as receiving countries and have had long-established policies to discourage non-citizens from seeking permanent residence and eventual citizenship. To rectify this situation, Germany, Ireland, and Latvia have recently streamlined their citizenship laws to facilitate the naturalization process, thereby strengthening migrants' sense of belonging and enabling their participation in political activities.

Increasing levels of migration have induced a growing number of countries of origin to offer dual citizenship. Such provisions reflect migrants' loyalties, and enable countries to benefit from their diaspora (Martin and Aleinikoff, 2002). Most OECD countries recognize dual citizenship, allowing migrants to continue maintaining links with their country of origin as well as contribute to their adopted society. Australia, Colombia, the Dominican Republic, India, Mexico and the Philippines have adopted dual citizenship provisions, enabling their citizens to maintain their sense of identity while abroad and to foster socio-economic development in the country of origin. Some countries have changed their legal provisions with respect to granting citizenship to immigrant children so as to enable them to hold the citizenship of both their parents' country and their birth country. However, in some countries, female migrants are discriminated against in this regard, with the father's citizenship, and not the mother's, determining that of the child.

Lack of human rights protection may make migrants vulnerable in their adopted country. Women all too frequently suffer in such circumstances. Victims of domestic violence, for example, often feel that they need to remain with the abuser to avoid deportation (United Nations, 2004f).

Undocumented migration

Reducing undocumented migration (including trafficking/smuggling) is the sixth issue of immigration policy of concern to most receiving countries. Undocumented migrants are those who have either entered a country without proper authorization or stayed beyond the legal time period (for example, students, tourists, temporary workers). The upward trend in undocumented migration reflects, among other things, the increasingly restrictive admission policies in receiving countries, increasing population displacement within sending countries, and the relaxation of emigration controls in Eastern Europe and the successor States of the former Union of Soviet Socialist Republics.

Undocumented migration is increasing and is a major concern in almost all receiving countries

Developed countries have generally pursued a law-and-order approach to dealing with the inflow of undocumented migration, largely because of the transnational nature of undocumented immigration and the smuggling syndicates that support them. Undocumented migration frequently occurs through smuggling and trafficking an illegal business worth an estimated 10 billion dollars annually and serving nearly half of all undocumented migrants (International Organization for Migration, 2003c). Practitioners of trafficking range from small-scale operators who provide transport across borders to, increasingly, international criminal networks that provide an entire range of services, including bogus documentation, transportation and assistance in crossing borders, and residence and illegal employment in receiving countries. Countries are often concerned about associated criminal activities including drug trafficking, illegal arms trading and terrorism (International Migration Policy Programme, 2000).

A major development has been the criminalization of smuggling which, until recently, was not considered a crime in many countries. Trafficked women frequently find themselves trapped: forced into prostitution, marriage, domestic work, work in sweatshops and other forms of exploitation. Increasingly, sanctions also target any third person who assists undocumented migrants. A growing number of receiving countries have negotiated readmission agreements with countries of origin, obliging them to readmit their nationals who lack proper documentation in order to facilitate their expulsion. Recent examples include agreements between Germany and Albania, and between Spain and Mauritania (SOPEMI (Continuous Reporting System on Migration), 2004).

Smuggling and trafficking of international migrants are estimated to have become a 10 billion dollar-a-year industry

Efforts to counter undocumented migration have also included bilateral agreements between transit and receiving countries. Owing to their geographical location, transit countries such as those of the Maghreb, Caribbean island States, Estonia, Mexico and Turkey, which serve as a bridge between the main origin and destination countries, have had to strengthen procedures to stem the flow of undocumented migrants across their borders. The agreements between Morocco and Tunisia and some of the EU member States, for example, require these two Maghreb countries to readmit foreigners who, having transited through them, and were residing in EU without authorization (SOPEMI (Continuous Reporting System on Migration), 2004). Morocco, which had had an agreement with Spain since 1992 to readmit its own nationals and persons who had transited through Morocco before entering Spain, temporarily suspended the programme in 2003 (SOPEMI (Continuous Reporting System on Migration), 2004). The programme resumed in 2004.

Measures to combat undocumented migration include bilateral agreements between countries of origin, countries of destination and countries of transit

Since the mid-1990s, most OECD countries, as well as some developing countries, have either introduced new sanctions or increased the penalties for undocumented migrants, smugglers and those employing them. For example, the United Kingdom Asylum and Immigration Act (1996) made it an offence for employers to employ an individual without a work permit, while the United States Immigration in the National Interest Act (1995) outlined penalties for traffickers and contained provisions on carrier liability (International Organization for Migration, 1996). Similarly, the South African Immigration Act (2002) prohibits employing those without a work permit and places the onus on employers not to engage unauthorized individuals.

In recent years, large numbers of undocumented migrants are believed to have entered countries using bogus documents—counterfeit or altered documents, as well as forged unissued passports stolen from consular facilities. To combat this problem, countries have introduced counterfeit-proof visa stamps, passports with enhanced security features, and machine-readable travel documents, reflecting a technology that is believed to offer strong safeguards against tampering with official travel documents. Other innovations include microchips with which to store biometric data such as fingerprints and iris images in passports. Eurodac, the first European automated fingerprint identification system, was launched in early 2003 to register the fingerprints of asylum-seekers and certain categories of illegal immigrants arriving in the member States of EU, Iceland and Norway.

Other measures to control undocumented migration include increased penalties, the use of counterfeit-proof documents...

... and information campaigns

Information campaigns, aimed at deterring undocumented migrants, have been launched by major receiving countries in both source and transit countries. The United States, for example, conducted information campaigns to dissuade potential undocumented migrants by warning them of the dangers involved in crossing the Rio Grande and the deserts in the South-west. Similarly, in 2002 the Government of New Zealand began distributing pamphlets in Indonesian ports and towns, warning of the hazards involved in attempting to reach New Zealand by boat. Such campaigns are generally limited in their effectiveness and have largely been futile in deterring people (International Organization for Migration, Office of Programme Evaluation, 1999). Information is considered particularly important in the case of trafficking in women for sexual exploitation. In this context, there is evidence that information about the situation in the receiving countries can have a considerable impact with respect to deterring trafficking in women and also on the migration of women generally. Other measures adopted have included carrier sanctions, increased patrols of territorial waters, and heightened border controls, as well as sanctions against undocumented migrants, smugglers and employers.

Although many countries have recently enacted measures restricting the entry of undocumented migrants, other countries have largely ignored the problem, most commonly those experiencing labour shortages in sectors such as agriculture and the service industries, where both the skills required and the wages are comparatively low. Despite the fact that it contravenes official policy, undocumented migration is at times tolerated by Governments because of labour shortages. For example, significant migration to Argentina from neighbouring countries occurred throughout the second half of the twentieth century, although employing visitors was illegal (Parrado and Cerrutti, 2003). Many undocumented migrants from neighboring countries such as Malawi have found and continue to find work in the mines of South Africa.

A substantial number of Governments have offered amnesties to regularize undocumented migrants (see chap. II and table III.3). For example, in 1986, the United States granted permanent residency under the Immigration Reform and Control Act (1986) to 2.7 million undocumented migrants who had entered the country before 1982. Similarly, in early 2004, the Government of Argentina introduced a programme to regularize the status of the estimated 750,000 undocumented workers in the country. There is some evidence to suggest that regularization programmes encourage additional undocumented migration (SOPEMI (continuous Reporting System on Migration, 2003).

Regional and subregional harmonization

The seventh issue is harmonization of immigration policies among Governments. The establishment of regional and subregional processes (including bilateral agreements), which exist in virtually all regions, has facilitated information exchange and improved regional coóperation.

Consultative processes have been established at the regional and international levels to stem the flow of undocumented migrants. These include the Puebla Process covering Canada, Central America, Mexico and the United States and the consultations being carried out as a follow-up to the Bali Ministerial Conference on People Smuggling, Trafficking in Persons and Related Transnational Crime to further strengthen ties across the Asia-Pacific region. In addition, two international protocols supplementing the United Nations Convention against Transnational Organized crime (General Assembly resolution 55/25,

Table III.3.
Regularization programmes for undocumented migrants

Country	Year or period
Argentina	2004
Belgium	2000
Costa Rica	2000
France	1981-1982
	1997-1998
Greece	1997-1998
	2001
Italy	1987-1988
	1990
	1996
	1998
	2002
Malaysia	1989
	1991
	1996-1997
Portugal	1992-1993
	1996
	2001
South Africa	1996
	2000
Spain	1985-1986
	1991
	1996
	2000
	2001
Switzerland	2000
Thailand	1999-2000
United States of America	1986
	1997-1998
	2000
	2004 (proposed)
Venezuela	2004

Sources: SOPEMI (Continuous Reporting System on Migration), *Trends in International Migration: 2003 Edition* (Paris, OECD, 2004); and Population Policy Data Bank maintained by the Population Division of the Department of Economic and Social Affairs of the United Nations Secretariat.

annex I), namely, the Protocol against the Smuggling of Migrants by Land, Sea and Air (Assembly resolution 55/25, annex III), and the Protocol to Prevent, Suppress and Punish Trafficking in Persons, especially Women and Children (Assembly resolution 55/25, annex II), recently came into force. These and other initiatives are discussed further in chapter VIII.

Migration and trade

The adoption of the General Agreement on Trade in Services[1] under the General Agreement on Tariffs and Trade (1994), is the eighth issue. The agreement is discussed more fully in chapter VIII.

Changing approaches to migration since September 2001

In the wake of the events of 11 September 2001, many countries are according high priority to the monitoring of those entering their jurisdiction. Increased emphasis is placed on scrutinizing the background of visa applicants for security reasons. Concerned by the threat of international terrorism, Governments have extended their legal competencies. The Anti-terrorism, Crime and Security Act (2001) in the United Kingdom, for example, extended government provisions to cover detaining suspected terrorists and allowing fingerprints to be retained for up to 10 years so as to avoid the possibility of the assumption of multiple identities. The USA Patriot Act (2001) gave additional resources for United States border controls and inspection activities, and allows for the detainment of foreigners without charge, while the Enhanced Border Security and Visa Entry Reform Act (2002) tightens screening and allows the tracking of foreigners in the United States. In addition, there is now greater intelligence-sharing on suspected individuals among countries, as well as enhanced cooperation in the field of border control (SOPEMI (Continuous Reporting System on Migration), 2004).

National security has become a leading concern of immigration policy

Many Governments have introduced more stringent requirements for granting visas in the aftermath of 11 September, 2001, and some have (re)imposed visa requirements for nationals of countries that consistently produced undocumented migrants. The measures introduced by the United States (box III.1) are among the most stringent. Many other countries or areas are following suit. Countries that use body-recognition technology, or biometrics, to enhance security procedures, include Hong Kong Special Administrative Region (SAR) of China, Oman and Singapore. Several countries have tightened their visa-issuing procedures and enhanced their vigilance at border entry points. Electronic screening systems of airline passengers entering countries are being introduced by a number of countries, such as New Zealand and the United States. In early 2004, EU

Box III.1

United States of America: post-9/11 and immigration

In the aftermath of 11 September 2001, the United States of America has been a leader in the introduction of new measures to monitor and control those entering the country. These measures have included tightening the entry requirements for visitors; the creation of the Department of Homeland Security; and enhanced policing of the foreign-born in the United States. Visa applicants face increased background checks and interviews.

From January 2004, the United States began scanning individuals at airports under its US-VISIT Program. All foreigners entering the United States through airports and seaports would have their photograph and fingerprints taken, except for citizens from 27 "low-risk" countries (Visa Waiver Program). The Government announced in April 2004 that the US Visit Program would be extended to those remaining countries no later than 30 September 2004. Only diplomats and travellers from Canada and Mexico will be exempted.

In addition, an agreement was concluded in December 2003, whereby passenger data including credit card details of passengers departing from EU to enter the United States would be given to United States authorities. Eventually, all carriers are expected to disclose passenger records.

announced plans to require airlines to submit passenger data to the EU authorities. Further legislation designed to restrict the number of refugees, asylum-seekers and undocumented migrants is currently awaiting final approval by a number of Governments. Governments maintain that this is necessary to protect their countries, but critics argue that such legislation may do little to enhance security, while imposing undue financial costs on international trade and investment (Santangelo Group, 2004), deterring foreign students and constituting a breach of civil liberties and fundamental human rights.

Emigration Policies

Both developed and developing countries exhibit similar views and policies concerning emigration. Despite the significant increase in the number of migrants, the proportion of countries wanting to lower emigration has remained steady at about one quarter since the 1980s. In 2003, some three fourths of countries, whether developed or developing, viewed their level of emigration as satisfactory (see table III.4) and one country in four had policies aimed at lowering emigration (see table III.5). Only 6 per cent of countries aimed to raise their level of emigration. The proportion of developing countries that viewed their level of emigration as too high increased steadily from the 1970s to the mid-1990s, peaking at 30 per cent in 1996. However, since then that proportion has dropped off, to 23 per cent.

Emigration creates both opportunities and difficulties for developing countries. For most countries of origin, worker remittances are an important source of foreign exchange earnings, and for some countries, the predominate source of income. At the global level, worker remittances now exceed official development assistance (ODA). On the other hand, the loss of skilled manpower—or the brain drain—places strains in critical areas and may hinder the development process. By the 1970s, several developing countries had been grappling with the consequences of the substantial migration of their nationals to developed countries. In any case, as of 2003, more than two thirds of developing countries either did not intervene with respect to emigration or aimed to maintain the current level of emigration (table III.5).

The large majority of both developed and developing countries view their level of emigration as satisfactory

In Oceania, the number of Governments viewing emigration as too high has been moving steadily upward, reaching 38 per cent in 2003. In contrast, in Africa, Asia and Latin America and the Caribbean, concerns with respect to high emigration eased during the second half of the 1990s and the beginning of the twenty-first century. The proportion of Latin American and Caribbean countries with policies to reduce emigration, for example, declined from 45 per cent in 1986 to 21 per cent in 2003 (table III.5), in part owing to the importance of migrant remittances.

Some developed countries are similarly suffering labour shortages in critical areas because of skilled emigration. Owing to greater employment opportunities and higher salaries in Canada and the United States, scientists, engineers, information technology experts and academics from developed countries have migrated to North America. Eastern European Governments have expressed concern over the potential loss of skilled talent because of the enlargement of EU in May 2004.

While emigration is an accepted right under international law, in practice, several States discriminate against women who wish to emigrate through, for example, preventing women from leaving without their guardian's consent or setting age limits that apply only to women. The fact that measures designed to protect women from exploitation may make it more difficult for them to go abroad legally, in turn encourages them to leave

The brain drain remains a matter of concern in some countries

Table III.4.

Government views on the level of emigration, by country's level of development and major areas, 1976, 1986, 1996 and 2003

	Number of countries				Percentage			
Year	Too low	Satisfactory	Too high	Total	Too low	Satisfactory	Too high	Total
By level of development								
World								
1976	6	125	19	150	4	83	13	100
1986	9	124	31	164	5	76	19	100
1996	5	133	55	193	3	69	28	100
2003	7	142	45	194	4	73	23	100
More developed regions								
1976	1	28	5	34	3	82	15	100
1986	2	29	3	34	6	85	9	100
1996	1	35	12	48	2	73	25	100
2003	0	36	12	48	0	75	25	100
Less developed regions								
1976	5	97	14	116	4	84	12	100
1986	7	95	28	130	5	73	22	100
1996	4	98	43	145	3	68	30	100
2003	7	106	33	146	5	73	23	100
Least developed countries								
1976	0	39	3	42	0	93	7	100
1986	1	39	8	48	2	81	17	100
1996	1	37	11	49	2	76	22	100
2003	2	40	7	49	4	82	14	100
By major area								
Africa								
1976	1	44	3	48	2	92	6	100
1986	3	41	7	51	6	80	14	100
1996	2	40	11	53	4	75	21	100
2003	2	44	7	53	4	83	13	100
Asia								
1976	4	31	2	37	11	84	5	100
1986	3	28	7	38	8	74	18	100
1996	2	31	13	46	4	67	28	100
2003	5	31	11	47	11	66	23	100
Europe								
1976	1	23	5	29	3	79	17	100
1986	1	26	2	29	3	90	7	100
1996	1	31	11	43	2	72	26	100
2003	0	32	11	43	0	74	26	100
Latin America and the Caribbean								
1976	0	18	9	27	0	67	33	100
1986	2	17	14	33	6	52	42	100
1996	0	18	15	33	0	55	45	100
2003	0	23	10	33	0	70	30	100

Table III.4 (cont'd)

Year	Number of countries				Percentage			
	Too low	Satisfactory	Too high	Total	Too low	Satisfactory	Too high	Total
Northern America								
1976	0	2	0	2	0	100	0	100
1986	0	2	0	2	0	100	0	100
1996	0	2	0	2	0	100	0	100
2003	0	2	0	2	0	100	0	100
Oceania								
1976	0	7	0	7	0	100	0	100
1986	0	10	1	11	0	91	9	100
1996	0	11	5	16	0	69	31	100
2003	0	10	6	16	0	62	38	100

Source: *World Population Policies, 2003* (United Nations publication, Sales No. E.04.XIII.3).

Table III.5.

Government policies on emigration, by country's level of development and major areas, 1976, 1986, 1996 and 2003

Year	Number of countries				Percentage			
	Raise	Maintain/no intervention	Lower	Total	Raise	Maintain/no intervention	Lower	Total
By level of development								
World								
1976	6	125	19	150	4	83	13	100
1986	8	120	36	164	5	73	22	100
1996	6	142	45	193	3	74	23	100
2003	11	137	46	194	6	71	24	100
More developed regions								
1976	1	28	5	34	3	82	15	100
1986	2	28	4	34	6	82	12	100
1996	1	35	12	48	2	73	25	100
2003	1	35	12	48	2	72	25	100
Less developed regions								
1976	5	97	14	116	4	84	12	100
1986	6	92	32	130	5	71	25	100
1996	5	107	33	145	3	74	23	100
2003	10	102	34	146	7	70	23	100
Least developed countries								
1976	0	39	3	42	0	93	7	100
1986	0	39	9	48	0	81	19	100
1996	1	39	9	49	2	79	18	100
2003	2	38	9	49	4	77	18	100

Table III.5 (cont'd)

Year	Number of countries: Raise	Number of countries: Maintain/no intervention	Number of countries: Lower	Number of countries: Total	Percentage: Raise	Percentage: Maintain/no intervention	Percentage: Lower	Percentage: Total
By major area								
Africa								
1976	1	44	3	48	2	92	6	100
1986	2	41	8	51	4	80	16	100
1996	2	42	9	53	4	79	17	100
2003	1	43	9	53	2	81	17	100
Asia								
1976	4	31	2	37	11	84	5	100
1986	5	25	8	38	13	66	21	100
1996	3	32	11	46	7	70	24	100
2003	8	24	15	47	17	51	32	100
Europe								
1976	1	23	5	29	3	79	17	100
1986	1	24	4	29	3	83	14	100
1996	1	30	12	43	2	70	28	100
2003	1	30	12	43	2	70	28	100
Latin America and the Caribbean								
1976	0	18	9	27	0	67	33	100
1986	0	18	15	33	0	55	45	100
1996	0	23	10	33	0	70	30	100
2003	1	25	7	33	3	76	21	100
Northern America								
1976	0	2	0	2	0	100	0	100
1986	0	2	0	2	0	100	0	100
1996	0	2	0	2	0	100	0	100
2003	0	2	0	2	0	100	0	100
Oceania								
1976	0	7	0	7	0	100	0	100
1986	0	10	1	11	0	91	9	100
1996	0	13	3	16	0	82	19	100
2003	0	13	3	16	0	82	19	100

Source: *World Population Policies, 2003* (United Nations publication, Sales No. E.04.XIII.3).

clandestinely, thus placing them at even greater risk of abuse (Boyd and Grieco, 2003; United Nations, 2004f).

In 2003, 11 countries reported having policies to increase emigration (United Nations, 2004e). Other Governments tolerate the departure of large numbers of their citizens, although concerns are often raised about the loss of talented and highly skilled human resources. Some countries have established government units to manage emigration flows, for example, the Bureau of Manpower, Employment and Training in Bangladesh and the Indian Office of the Protector of Emigrants (Castles, 2000). Several countries of emigration, including Mexico and the Philippines, have formulated policies to assist their citizens abroad, for example, with respect to preventing abuse, and, inter alia, offer services to facilitate and reduce the costs of transferring remittances and provide assistance in cases of illness, abuse and death (box III.2). A number of countries of emigration have entered into bilateral agreements with receiving States to ensure minimum labour standards. However, the monitoring is left to consular officials who at times lack the resources to carry out all their activities. Others countries have policies to encourage migrants to remit and invest in their country of origin. These programmes have had mixed results (Waddington, 2003). Chile, Colombia, El Salvador, Mexico, Peru and Venezuela have recently initiated linkage programmes with their citizens abroad (International Organization for Migration, 2003c).

The sharp rise in emigration of skilled workers has prompted some countries to address the challenges posed by the brain drain through initiatives to encourage the return of skilled workers living abroad. Overall, 53 countries had policies and programmes in place in 2003 to encourage their nationals to return, down from 59 in 1996. Most were in the less developed regions, particularly Asia and Latin America and the Caribbean (United Nations, 2004e).

The policies were motivated by a belief in their potential positive impact on the home country through the transfer of knowledge and technology, as well as through investments and trade. In some countries, policy makers have tried to tap into these feedback effects, in particular through diaspora networks and policies to attract return migration. For instance, the South African Network of Skills Abroad (SANSA), an active network with more than 2000 members, established by the Government's National Research Foundation, has a specific human resource development focus to match South African migrants with projects. Through its web site, Thailand's Reverse Brain Drain project (RBD) provides Thai migrants who want to invest in their country with information about investment incentives, business information and business opportunities. The Government of the Republic of Korea has been actively promoting contact between scientists and engineers abroad and

Box III.2

Filipinos abroad

The Philippines is one of the world's largest exporters of labour. About 8 per cent of the Filipino population is said to live abroad, providing benefits to their country in the form of remittances. Overseas Filipino workers (OFWs) are portrayed as unsung heroes and heroines, and the Government recognizes their achievements through an annual award ceremony (O'Neil, 2004).

The Government promotes temporary migration through regulated channels and encourages the return and reintegration of migrants. The Government permits Filipinos to leave the country officially only if they are recruited by a licensed recruiter or government agency, or have a contract approved by the Philippines Overseas Employment Administration (POEA). At pre-departure seminars, the Government offers services such as life insurance and pension plans, and medical insurance, to legal emigrants. These are paid for by the recruiting agencies. Consular officials offer assistance to Filipinos once they are abroad when required; and the Government sponsors tours by entertainers to promote continued ties with the Philippines (O'Neil, 2004).

The promotion of emigration has been a successful response to high unemployment. However, it is not without its problems. The Philippines, for example, faces critical shortages of medical professionals, for example (Choo, 2003). Moreover, the many Filipinos who live abroad as undocumented migrants work mostly in vulnerable areas, such as the domestic sector.

at home. It has subsidized and supported professional associations in Canada, China, Europe, Japan and the United States. Other examples of diaspora networks are the Chinese Scholars Abroad (CHISA), the Colombian network of scientists and research professionals (Red Caldas), the Silicon Valley Indian Professionals Association, and the Digital Diaspora Network-Africa for African entrepreneurs.

A wide range of policies to encourage the return of skilled migrants have been adopted by countries in all regions

The Governments of Uruguay and Argentina have created organizations and programmes whose main goal is to relink and involve national scientists and professors abroad with groups and development projects inside these two countries. In Argentina, for example, the National Council of Scientific and Technological Research (CONICET) has created the category of "Corresponding Member of the Scientific-Technological Research Degree", through which citizens living abroad could be given honorary titles. These researchers or professors can be hired for short periods, or fully incorporated into a research career if they choose to return to Argentina.

Taiwan Province of China has induced many migrants to return with initiatives such as the creation of a venture capital industry and investments in research infrastructure. Returnees started more than half of the companies in the Hsinchu Science-based Industrial Park that now accounts for about 10 per cent of the gross national product (GNP) of Taiwan Province of China. The Government of the Republic of Korea launched a reintegration programme for return migrants. Within the first six months of the establishment of the programme, 4,000 workers were reported to be participating in the scheme. Similar programmes are also available in Mexico. In Uruguay and Argentina, the Governments have implemented policies to encourage the return of migrants through tax exemptions for the products brought back by the migrants. The Government of Uruguay, with support from the International Organization for Migration (IOM), created the National Commission for Repatriation which has supported the return of migrants, with special emphasis on scientists and professionals with ties to the academic world. In 1990, with the creation of the Sectoral Commission of Scientific Research (CSIC), several initiatives were established to reverse the brain drain, including a programme for the hiring of Uruguayan scientists and the economic support programme for returnees to facilitate their re-entry into the academic environment.

Return migration has been encouraged by several countries and the international community. For instance, since 1977, under a United Nations Development Programme (UNDP) programme entitled Transfer of Knowledge through Expatriate Nationals (TOKTEN), the work of highly skilled migrants in their country of origin is financed for a period of from 3 to 12 weeks. During this period, experts could work in the government, universities, or public and private enterprises. The programme pays for a round-trip airfare ticket and living expenses during the period of service.

To reduce the effects of the brain drain and facilitate return migration to Africa, IOM had set up the Return and Reintegration of Qualified African Nationals (RQAN) programme. From 1983 to 1999, the programme assisted in the return of more than 2,000 highly skilled migrants to 11 participating countries. An evaluation of the programme found that the return migrants contributed significantly to the financial growth of the organizations they were working with, through income-generation and cost-saving measures. Their positive contribution to the transfer of knowledge, technology and management skills was also demonstrated (African Centre for Technology Studies, 2002). In 2000, the Migration for Development in Africa (MIDA) programme was established as a follow-up to RQAN. The programme is a partnership among IOM, government authorities, the private sector and civil society in participating African home countries as well as in the host countries. Its aim is to transfer vital skills and resources from nationals in the African diaspora to their countries to support development therein.

Policies to reduce the brain drain are often ineffective

The fact that relatively few such programmes are successful probably explains the decline in the numbers of Governments with these programmes. Africa is particularly hampered by the migration of the skilled within the continent, usually to South Africa, as well as by their departure from Africa altogether. South Africa itself faces significant skill shortages owing to high emigration in areas such as academia, education, health care and information technology, as well as science and technology (SOPEMI (Continuous Reporting System on Migration), 2004; Wöcke and Klein, 2002). The United Kingdom agreed to staunch the flow of medical workers from South Africa to the United Kingdom, by halting the recruitment of such workers from South Africa. Rather than stem the flow of these workers, however, the impact of the agreement has been to redirect the outflow of these workers to Australia, the United States and other countries. The South African Government also uses the Internet to tap into the pool of skilled workers abroad. Similarly, the President of Nigeria actively exhorts skilled Nigerians to contribute to their country's development (Mutume, 2003).

In recent decades, Latin America and the Caribbean has become a significant region of emigration. The countries of the region are giving increased attention to the emigration of nationals and to their protection abroad. Some Caribbean States have in recent decades engaged in considerable efforts to encourage return migration and to ensure the rights of their citizens abroad (International Migration Policy Programme, 2003). For example, during the 1990s, Jamaica devised the Return of Talent Programme to facilitate the return of talented Jamaicans. Other Governments such as that of Grenada have implemented tax incentives to encourage nationals to return.

The Pacific island State of Niue, with a dwindling population of less than 1,600 people, has developed financial initiatives and job-creation schemes to encourage Niue nationals to return from neighbouring countries, chiefly New Zealand, with which it has a free association. The Government also recently invited Tongans and Samoans of Niue heritage to live on the island in order to bolster its population.

Conclusions

National and international issues related to migration such as brain drain and brain gain, remittances and undocumented movements have intersected with national concerns of low fertility and population ageing, unemployment, human rights and States rights, social integration, asylum, xenophobia, trafficking and national security. All together, these concerns have led to a re-examination of international migration policies and the potential benefits and disadvantages accruing therefrom to origin, destination and transit countries. As a result, over the past decades, the number of Governments adopting measures to manage migration has significantly increased. By 2003, one third of countries had policies in place to lower immigration, compared with just 7 per cent of countries in 1976. Since the mid-1970s, countries of both the more and the less developed regions have tended to pursue lower immigration; in both regions, one third of countries have policies to reduce immigration. Although countries are gradually imposing more restrictive immigration measures, a growing number of countries are simultaneously seeking to alleviate labour shortages by promoting the migration of certain categories of migrants, particularly the highly skilled. For many receiving countries, family reunification remains the foundation for accepting migrants.

In 2003, 61 countries reported that programmes were in place for the integration of non-nationals, up from 52 countries in 1996. Policies for the integration of non-nationals are more prevalent in the receiving countries of the more developed regions than in those of the developing regions. International migration is increasingly being viewed as making an important contribution to the socio-economic development of countries of origin by, among other things, providing a major source of foreign exchange through remittances. Despite the increased volume of migration, the proportion of countries that aim to lower emigration has remained at about 1 in 4 since the mid-1980s. Moreover, countries have become less inclined to encourage the return of nationals living abroad. Instead, countries of origin tend increasingly to initiate links with those citizens.

Since the adoption of the Programme of Action of the International Conference on Population and Development (United Nations, 1995, chap. I, resolution1, annex) in 1994, there has been growing recognition that international migration and development are inexorably linked and are of key relevance to the global agenda. It is becoming apparent that to reap the benefits and minimize the adverse consequences of international migration, greater international cooperation will be necessary. This requires the establishment of safe, orderly and rule-governed migration within a framework where States understand their obligations and protect the rights of migrants, and migrants recognize their rights and responsibilities, as well as respect national and international laws.

Notes

1 The full text is available from http://www.wto.org/english/tratop_e/sevv_e/gatsintr_e.htm (accessed 29 October 2004).

Chapter IV
Economic impacts of international migration

The present chapter will examine the economic impact of migration on the home and the host countries. Positive and adverse effects on migrants, labour markets and countries will be assessed in light of the magnitude, dynamics and empirical evidence of the current global migration wave.

Migration affects, first and foremost, individuals who have chosen to live abroad. Because their decisions are fundamentally personal, they involve many elements that are outside the realm of government intervention. Despite the fact that immigrants frequently face prejudice and may be working below their "capacities" owing to the lack of recognition in the receiving country for their qualifications and job experiences, they seek to improve their material well-being (including income) and to gain better opportunities for their families. The aggregate outcome of the movement of people is a complex reflection of individual attitudes and choices, and this complexity raises the question where and to whom the costs or benefits of migration accrue. Understanding national and global policies that affect the individual decisions of actual and potential migrants and the costs and benefits of immigration to individuals and the country as a whole requires delicate but critical examination.

Appropriate and effective migration policies require a careful assessment of costs and benefits to countries of both origin and destination

The migration of highly skilled labour—even though advantageous to host countries—raises concerns for origin countries, since the host economy's "brain gain" is a "brain drain" for sending economies. An immediate loss is the public investment in migrants' education and training, as well as the taxes that these skilled persons used to pay. More importantly, such loss of human capital implies that the sending country may have to rely more on semi-skilled and unskilled labour, thereby lowering the prospects of attaining higher levels of growth. The significance of brain drain for development has been highlighted in the literature on the "new growth theory", which argues that the knowledge embodied in a person has a positive effect on the productivity of another person, whose knowledge, in turn, positively affects the productivity of the first person. The departure of highly educated workers not only represents a loss of knowledge for the country, but also impairs the productivity of those left behind and, ultimately, of the country.

The migration of semi-skilled and (so-called) unskilled labour is also important for home countries. In the first place, migrants' skills and educational levels tend to be above the national average of the home country. Secondly, many of these migrants had some kind of employment before migrating and, especially if there is a large number of them, their departure represents a loss of fiscal contributions as well as of prior public investment in their education and health care.

However, the emigration of workers can also have positive consequences for development. First, the realization that skilled migrants are able to obtain well-paid jobs in developed countries may raise incentives for those left behind to pursue higher education. Second, remittances, especially remittances sent by those from poor families in their home countries, can help to reduce poverty. Based on household surveys, there is evidence that the incidence of poverty is lower in "emigrant households" and that households receiving remittances from abroad—or other regions in the same country—are more likely to send their children to school than are non-recipient households with similar incomes. The higher propensity to consume of recipient households will also have a larger impact on the economy as a whole via the multiplier effect.

This chapter will also examine the impact of migration on the host economy. One important consideration in host countries is the potential impact of migration on income distribution. Other things being equal, inflows of immigrant workers into the labour market tend to reduce the income of natives who are competing with immigrants and to increase the incomes of users of immigrant services. The size of the redistribution depends primarily on how the wages of skilled and unskilled workers respond to immigrant inflows, as well as on the share of skilled workers in the labour force.

However, even if the net effect of immigration on the host economy turns out to be small, distributional effects in certain locations or for workers with certain skills can be substantial.[1] Many studies thus examine the effects of immigration on a specific location or type of occupation so as to identify the likely channels through which the local economy or specific sectors can be affected.

There is an additional consideration that may shape immigration policy, even if the net impact of migration is marginal or non-existent. On the one hand, there is the expectation that Governments should provide social services, for example, through ensuring adequate employment and education, offering social and medical insurance and caring for the poor, to all inhabitants. On the other hand, however, there is often also a perception that immigrants are using more of these services than they are paying for. As a result, Governments often have to strike a balance between the national need for immigrants and voters' demands for more stringent immigration policies.

What is missing in these arguments, however, is recognition of the actual or potential contributions to the host economy made by immigrants or temporary workers who bring with them skills that are in short supply in the domestic labour market, for example, computer-software engineers, scientists, doctors, nurses, schoolteachers, agricultural workers and household help.

Moreover, despite public concern over immigration policy in developed countries—particularly regarding unskilled immigrants—the net overall economic impact of the migration of skilled and unskilled labour, while positive, is relatively minor in comparison with the national incomes of the host economies.

This chapter primarily addresses economically driven legal migration. In addition to such movements, some people migrate undocumented, while others are forced to migrate owing to political necessity, namely, refugees and asylum-seekers. Since the economic impact of these categories of immigrants on the economy is similar—except that undocumented immigrants make no contribution to direct taxes (although they do contribute to indirect taxes)—this chapter will not differentiate among these types of migration.

Impacts on home countries

Emigration

The primary direct effect of emigration is the reduction in the number of workers in home countries. Researchers have dealt extensively with this subject, in particular the loss of highly skilled workers—also referred to as brain drain—who are important to the home country's productivity and economic growth (see, for instance, Lowell and Findlay, 2001). Apart from the loss of skills, there may also be other costs such as lower returns from public investments in education (see table IV.1). Governments spend considerable amounts of money in educating highly skilled professionals such as medical doctors, engineers and university professionals. When these professionals emigrate, countries experience a loss of skills as well as of the corresponding investments that they made in educating their nationals to acquire those skills. The loss of urgently needed skills, especially in health and education, is incurred in addition to the financial costs. However, these potential negative effects can be offset by the favourable outcomes of migration, which include remittances, technology transfer, investments, trade and return migration.

Table IV.1.
"Balance sheet" of economic effects of migration on countries of origin

Positive effects	Negative effects
• Provides opportunities to workers not available in the home country. • May ease the effect on the domestic market of the supply of excess labour. • Inflow of remittances and foreign exchange. • Technology transfer, investments and venture capital contributed by diasporas. • Can contribute to increased trade flows between sending and receiving countries. • Stimulus to investment in domestic education and individual human capital investments. • Return of skilled workers may increase local human capital, transfer of skills and links to foreign networks.	• Loss of highly skilled workers and reduced quality of essential services. • Reduced growth and productivity because of the lower stock of highly skilled workers and its externalities. • Lower return from public investments in public education. • Selective migration may cause increasing disparities in incomes in the home country. • Loss of fiscal revenue from taxation of workers. • Remittances may diminish over time.

Source:
UN/DESA, partly based on Piyasiri Wickramasekara, "Policy responses to skilled migration: retention, return and circulation", *Perspectives on Labour Migration, 5E* (Geneva, International Labour Office, 2002).

The impact of emigration on the country of origin is complex and multifaceted

The overall balance of these potential adverse economic effects and the favourable "feedback effects" determines the economic impact of migration on the home countries. A concern is the complexity and lack of understanding of the linkages between, on the one hand, the different dynamics of migration and, on the other hand, economic growth and poverty reduction in developing countries.

Adverse economic effects

Brain drain. The impact of the migration of workers on growth in the home country depends on the skills of the emigrants and labour-market conditions. If the emigrants are low-skilled, the impact on output in the home country is likely to be insignificant. Also, if migration offers an outlet for unemployed people and/or a large proportion of the migrants

A primary effect of emigration may be a "brain drain", a loss of skilled employed workers

come from poor households, migration is unlikely to have a significant impact on the development of the country, although the standard of living of these workers and families should improve. On the other hand, if migrants are highly skilled employed workers whose contributions to output are significant, the direct effects of migration may be negative, at least in the short term (assuming no, or only modest, positive feedback effects). Given that there is likely to be "positive selection" of migrants, in other words, that above average skilled workers are more likely to emigrate from developing countries (Lowell, 2001, chap. 2)[2]—for some countries, brain drain may have an adverse impact on the economy (see box IV.1 for a discussion on migrant self-selectivity).

Box IV.1

Migrant self-selectivity

As positive selection theory would predict, immigrants tend to be better educated than those they leave behind, though they may be less well educated than the average population of the host country (Coppel, Dumont and Visco, 2001).[a] The majority of developing-country migrants to the United States of America, as well as to countries members of the Organization for Economic Cooperation and Development (OECD) as a whole, have at least secondary education and flows of migrants with only a primary education are quite small—both in absolute terms and relative to the size of the home country population in the relevant educational category (Carrington and Detragiache, 1998). Individuals with little or no education appear to have little access to migration. In 2000, 68 per cent of all immigrants to the United States and 89 per cent of those to the rest of OECD had secondary education or higher (Adams, Jr., 2003). The figure for the United States would have been even closer to the OECD average if the large number of poorly educated migrants from a single country, Mexico, which accounted for 50 per cent of immigrants, had been excluded. Mexico is a special case because of the "border effect"—the fact that it is much easier for even poor people from that country to travel to the United States than is the case for those from more distant countries. A similar border effect also applies in the case of the North African and Eastern European countries that are close to the members of the European Union (EU).

In terms of observable skills, immigrants from Mexico were drawn predominantly from the middle of the distribution, not from the bottom (Chiquiar and Hanson, 2002). The table, which reports education data for adult migrants in developed host countries by sending source and for adults

Education of home country migrants and residents, around 1990

Host region of country (number of sending countries)	Years of schooling: Migrants in host countries	Residents in home countries	Difference (migrants-residents)
Africa (4)	15.4	4.6	10.8
Mexico (1)	7.5	6.3	1.2
Caribbean and Central America (14)	11.2	5.4	5.8
South America (10)	12.5	5.9	6.6
Asia (15)	14.4	5.8	8.6
Eastern Europe, the Balkans and Turkey (3)	12.6	7.8	4.8
Average (47)	12.9	5.7	7.2

Source: Based on Hendricks (2002, table B1).

Note: All figures are unweighted averages. The stayers column is based on Barro-Lee (1996), while the migrant column is based on OECD censuses around 1990. The two columns use country observations only if they supply information on both stayers and migrants.

Box IV.1 (cont'd)

in the same sending source countries, shows that there is a general phenomenon of migrants being better educated than those who remain at home. On average, migrants in the developed countries had 7.2 more years of education than adults back in the home country, while Mexican migrants (mostly in the United States) had only 1.2 more years of education than did Mexican adults in Mexico. The data in the table do not adjust for the fact that immigrants are younger than the average adult at home, or for the fact that immigrants may have received some education in host countries after their arrival. However, it is clear that the gap between mover and stayer is much smaller for Mexicans, who are close to the United States, and for Eastern Europeans, immigrants from the Balkans and Turks, who are close to EU member countries. It appears that the revealed positive selection is weaker because, as a share of income, migration costs decrease sharply with skill level, offsetting the positive selection effects of greater inequality at the source.

The experience of the United States illustrates how high migration costs favour positive selection, and how low migration costs favour negative selection. Greater distances, lower source country inequality, weaker effect of friends and relatives and (for the poorest regions) the poverty constraint all imply that migrants coming from farther away should be more positively selected. Thus, the 1990 share of United States immigrants with tertiary schooling was more than three times higher for Asians and Africans than it was for Mexicans and Central Americans and the gap in education level between movers and stayers was greatest for Asians and Africans.

a For example, 49.3 per cent of "nationals" had a tertiary education in the United States, between 1995 and 1998, compared with 40.9 per cent of "foreigners". Conversely, 35 per cent of foreigners had only a lower secondary education (through ninth grade) compared with 15.7 per cent of nationals. A similar trend is observed in other OECD countries, Italy being one exception.

Furthermore, there are also indications that brain drain is a growing trend in the global economy. For instance, for the United States of America (the largest destination country), the stock of highly skilled migrants from a sample group of developing countries increased from 1.7 million in 1990 to 4.2 million in 2000 (calculations based on Carrington and Detragiache, 1998; Adams, Jr., 2003).

The brain drain is growing in the global economy

An analysis of the extent of the brain drain from developing countries shows that of a sample of 24 countries, 10 countries experienced brain drain (see table IV.2, report A) (Adams, Jr., 2003).[3] Results from another analysis of 61 developing countries indicate ratios higher than 10 per cent for 18 countries (see table IV.2, report B) (Carrington and Detragiache, 1998).[4]

An analysis of the magnitude of the impact of the brain drain indicates a potential negative effect on economic growth when the migration rate of the highly educated is above 20 per cent and/or the proportion of highly educated in the total population exceeds 5 per cent (Beine, Docquier and Rapoport, 2002).[5] According to this criterion, the brain drain was found to have a negative impact on the 19 countries listed in table IV.2 under report C. The analysis points out that, while there were more countries identified as "losers" (from brain drain) than "winners", the countries identified as beneficiaries included the largest countries, representing nearly 80 per cent of the population of developing countries. The winners are those countries that gain from remittances and from the encouragement to education that the possibility of migration presents. A further examination of country-level experiences provides additional confirmation that the brain drain can be a problem for some countries. It is estimated that each migrating African professional repre-

The brain drain may be costly to the country of origin, especially when it is heavy and the country is comparatively small

Table IV.2.
Countries or areas experiencing brain drain according to different reports

Report A[a]	Report B[b]	Report C[c]
Dominican Republic	Dominican Republic	Argentina
El Salvador	El Salvador	Bolivia
Guatemala	Fiji	Chile
Jamaica	Gambia	Costa Rica
Mexico	Ghana	Dominican Republic
Morocco	Guatemala	Ecuador
Philippines	Guyana	El Salvador
Sri Lanka	Honduras	Guyana
Tunisia	Iran (Islamic Republic of)	Jamaica
Turkey	Jamaica	Mexico
	Kenya	Nicaragua
	Mexico	Panama
	Nicaragua	Peru
	Panama	Philippines
	Sierra Leone	Republic of Korea
	Taiwan Province of China	Thailand
	Trinidad and Tobago	Trinidad and Tobago
	Uganda	Uruguay
		Venezuela

Source: UN/DESA, based on the studies referred to below and in the main text of the chapter.

a R. H. Adams, Jr. (2003), under the assumption that the migration of more than 10 per cent of the tertiary-educated population from a country causes brain drain.

b Carrington and Detragiache (1998), with classification based on the 10 per cent benchmark applied by R. H. Adams, Jr..

c Beine, Docquier and Rapoport (2002).

sents a loss of $184,000 to Africa (Pang, Lansang and Haines, 2002, pp. 499-500), and that South Africa has lost more than $5 billion in the migration of highly skilled labour since 1997 (McClelland, 2002, p. 793). Another study suggests that the migration of skilled labour from Eastern Europe during the 1990s slowed economic growth in some of those countries (Lowell and Findlay, 2001).

Emigration of the most highly skilled (for example, the highest-qualified among university graduates) is probably the most costly for sending countries in terms of the loss in innovation and creativity, which goes beyond the losses in economic productivity. The utilized stock of world human capital may have net gains worldwide, since the "top" level of the highly skilled migrants would likely fill positions in destination countries where their skills can be more fully exploited and developed. For instance, highly skilled immigrants working in science and technology will not only receive higher salaries but also be able to maximize their capacities through the use of the facilities of well-funded universities and corporate laboratories, as well as through their participation in, and interaction with, top-level research teams.

The brain drain of skilled professionals is often also a direct consequence of the selective immigration policies in the developed countries. Countries such as Australia, Canada, the United Kingdom of Great Britain and Northern Ireland and the United States have well organized systems through which to attract skilled migrants, ranging from English-speaking nurses from the Philippines and Jamaica, to information technology professionals from India and Pakistan (Stalker, 2001).

Fiscal effects. The fiscal losses from migration, especially of skilled workers, are a concern to developing countries. First, fiscal losses arise in terms of lower returns on public investments in education, as it is Governments (and taxpayers) who have funded the education of those workers who leave. Another possible fiscal effect of migration may be the cost of training replacement workers. For instance, the public expenditures on highly skilled graduates who subsequently emigrated to the United States were estimated at $640 million for one year alone (Stalker, 2001). Second, migration may translate into a loss in current and future income tax revenues. For example, an examination of the migration of highly skilled Indian workers to the United States showed that, although these migrants accounted for only a very small proportion of India's population, their absence had led to a potential tax revenue loss to India of $700 million, or 12 per cent of the country's personal income tax revenue (Desai, Kapur and McHale, 2000).

Emigration of skilled workers entails loss of investments in education and future tax revenues

Favourable economic effects

Migration can have positive effects on the home country (see table IV.1). First, migration may have a positive impact on employment and wages. Second, the transfer of knowledge or technology from migrants back to the home country can also contribute to economic growth. Third, migration may increase the flow of trade and investment between the home and the host country. Lastly, return migration can bring back new skills, experience and investments that may accelerate productivity. These types of positive impacts of migration are also referred to by some Governments in their argument that migration should be promoted. Indeed, Governments of countries that in fact vary considerably in size, human capital, and income per capita, such as Bangladesh, Barbados, the Dominican Republic, El Salvador, Guatemala, India, Jordan, Mexico, Morocco, Nicaragua, Pakistan, the Philippines, Tunisia, Turkey and Viet Nam, have encouraged the emigration of workers for various reasons, including its ability to provide employment opportunities not available domestically and to improve foreign currency reserves (Teitelbaum, 2002, p. 159; see also chap. III, section entitled "Emigration policies").

Migration may have a positive impact on employment and wages if it relocates workers from low-wage or labour-excess areas to areas with high wages and higher demand for labour. For international migration involving relatively large shares of the working population, this could imply that by decreasing the excess in the supply of labour in the (low-wage) home countries, migration could reduce the downward pressure on wages. This argument has been confirmed by research on mass migration flows from Ireland and Sweden in the nineteenth and early twentieth centuries (O'Rourke and Williamson, 1999, chap. I). However, in other, more recent cases, the causal link between migration and the increase in wages has been less clear. In Mexico, for example, despite the flows of migrants to the United States, real wages are still lower than 10 years ago. In this instance, factors other than migration may well have had a larger impact on wages.

Emigration my help ameliorate unemployment and low wages in the home country

Migrants are likely to maintain connections, not only with their family, but also with a broader range of people in their home country. As members of a group spread outside their country, which dispersion is also known as a diaspora, they can generate flows of knowledge, investment, goods and services to and from their home country. There are over 40 known diaspora networks around the world with the explicit purpose of connecting migrant entrepreneurs, professionals and students with each other and with the country of origin, as well as of promoting the exchange of skills and knowledge (Meyer and

Emigration may facilitate flows of knowledge, investments, goods and services to the home country

Brown, 1999). Some of these networks are directly promoted by home country Governments. Through the transmission of information, these networks facilitate technology transfer and trade, as well as promote foreign direct investment (FDI) in the home country. An examination of migrants from China and India to the United States illustrate the potential importance of diaspora networks. About 18 per cent of the migrants have invested in their own start-up businesses or in venture capital funds in their home countries. Moreover, 40 per cent have helped arrange business contacts in their home country (Institute of Public Affairs, 2002, p. 30). Approximately 70 per cent of the total FDI inflows to China have originated with the Chinese diaspora, especially from those living in South-East Asia (Rozelle, Pray and Huang, 1998; Lucas, 2001). Furthermore, migrants can increase trade flows from and to the home country. For instance, a 10 per cent increase in the number of migrants in Canada from a particular country has been associated with a 1 per cent increase in exports to, and a 3 per cent increase in imports from, that country. Chinese networks have an impact on trade through mechanisms of market information, referral services and the effect of the informal community's enforcement of proper business conduct (Trindade and Rauch, 2000).

The benefits of return migration to the home country's economy depend on various factors, such as the motives for returning (for example, retirement versus investment in a new business) and the length of the migrant's stay abroad. When workers return, they can increase their country's productivity by investing and applying the skills and experience they gained in the host country. An analysis of the impact of return migration to Egypt, Albania and Eastern Europe indicates a positive impact on labour productivity and investment, especially in urban areas, and shows that the accumulation of capital and the overseas work experience can play a useful role in development (Kule, and others, 1999; León-Ledesma and Piracha, 2001; McCormick and Wahba, 2002). Some observers believe that these rates of return are high enough to warrant dispensing with the term brain drain (Lowell and Findlay, 2001).

Remittances

Policy makers have recognized the increasing importance of remittances as a source of external financing. From a public policy perspective, it is therefore of interest to identify the factors affecting remittances.

Remittances are a major and growing source of external financing for countries of origin

At the individual level, several types of motivations have been found to explain the migrants' desire to remit. One examination indicates that migrants tend to increase remittances during periods of crisis at home, but also that they time their remittance transfers to maximize the expected returns and the recognition they receive (Hysenbegasi and Pozo, 2002). On the other hand, there are also indications that migrants are more likely to send remittances to parents or siblings as a means of providing social insurance for the future (this illustrates what are known as migrant family self-enforcement mechanisms) (Clark and Drinkwater, 2001; Stark and Lucas, 1988, pp. 465-481; Russell, 1984, pp. 595-615; Hoddinott, 1996, pp. 459-476). Furthermore, remittances may be understood as a repayment of an implicit loan taken out by migrants during their youth in order to secure a better education (Poirine, 1997, pp. 589-611).

Macroeconomic factors may have a possible impact on the amount of remittances and/or the frequency of sending them. A high rate of unemployment in the host country would discourage immigrants from sending remittances home. Interest rate differentials between home and host countries and relatively high inflation rates in the receiving country may have an impact on remittance flows (for example, high interest rates in the receiving country would encourage migrants to remit, whereas high inflation rates in the receiving country would have the opposite effect). Likewise, depreciation of the home country's currency may affect the amount of remittances positively or negatively—positively, if remitters take advantage of the higher purchasing power of the currency of the host country, and negatively, if remitters, deciding to keep the same type and quantity of goods as before the depreciation, require less of the currency of the host country (assuming a zero inflation rate in the home country).

Remittance flows are highly responsive to macroeconomic factors

Demographic factors such as age, the dependency ratio, and the marital status of the migrant are also believed to influence remittances. To illustrate, Mexican migrants are most likely to remit when they are married, are under age 40 and have strong social contacts in the host country (Duran, and others, 1996, pp. 249-264). The migrant's income, education and skill levels, as well as the number of years since migration, also affect the volume and frequency of remittances. Furthermore, the facility and cost of transferring funds, and the access to different channels of transmission have an impact on the volume and frequency of remittances. For the different types of remittances and the channels of transmission, see box IV.2.

Younger, married emigrants are more likely to remit

Box IV.2

Types of remittances and channels of transmission

Types of remittances

The present box focuses on financial remittances. Yet, remittances can also be made in kind. This latter type of remittance, however, is estimated as being of a smaller value than money remittances. It is also difficult to keep records of the magnitudes involved in remittances in kind.

Types of channels of transmission

Formal channels of transfers of remittances are represented by financial institutions recognized by the relevant authorities in both the remittance–sending and the remittance–receiving country, including commercial banks, money transfer operators (MTOs) and post offices. The 1990s witnessed growth in the share of remittances handled by non-banking financial institutions, such as money transfer operators.

Informal channels range from person-to-person transfer of remittances (either by the migrants themselves or by their relatives and friends) to informal money transfer (IMT) systems characterized by elements of trust, proximity or familiarity, such as the hawala and hundi services available in North Africa, the Middle East and South Asia. These informal systems are often connected to a currency exchange bureau, import-export business or retail shop and involve an agent in the remittance–sending country and a counterpart who will be paying out in the home country. IMT systems are thus based on very little or no (paper or electronic) documentation (Sander, 2003; Shehu, 2003; for further references, see also Buencamino and Gorbunov, 2002).

Choice of transmission method

Although there are no reliable estimates of the total value of remittances transmitted through informal arrangements, it is estimated that a significant share of the global remittances are handled by informal systems. Recent surveys of remittance recipients in different countries, however, show that the

Box IV.2 (cont'd)

shares of total remittances accounted for by formal and informal systems vary widely across countries and regions (Sander, 2003). In some countries, such as Bangladesh, informal systems account for over half the value of total remittances, whereas in other countries or regions, such as the Philippines and Latin America, formal systems are responsible for the bulk of such transactions.

The choice of transmission method is associated with several factors, notably: (a) the perceived reliability and security of the channel; (b) the legal status of the migrant (non-regularized immigrants invariably chose informal or non-banking channels); (c) the speed of transmission, and the ease of access to a specific channel in both remittance–sending and remittance–receiving countries; and (d) the transfer costs of remittances. With regard to the transfer costs, it is argued that migrants use informal sector channels in order to avoid the high costs imposed by both the formal financial sector institutions and the State financial authorities. Although the cost of remittances has lately begun to fall—primarily owing to closer supervision by central banks and the expansion of commercial banks and credit unions into the money transfer business—there are still significant cost differentials even among countries belonging to the same geographical region (see table).

These cost variations arise from different degrees of competition (or lack of competition) in the money transfer markets in different countries. There are several reasons for the lack of competition in money transfer markets, including (a) the high costs of intermediation and relatively small amounts of typical remittances (which may make them relatively more expensive to process than larger transfers); (b) the exchange-rate risk and strong foreign exchange control in some countries; and (c) the lack of reliable and efficient financial institutions in the home countries (Solimano, 2003a).[a]

Migrants tend to choose informal or non-banking channels when the financial sector at home is weak, mistrusted and/or inefficient, and when there are strong foreign exchange controls either in the home or in the host country. Conversely, it can be argued that liberalization, accompanied by measures to strengthen the domestic financial sector, encourages migrants to make greater use of formal channels of transmission (Sander, 2003). In addition, access to remittance channels in both the sending and the receiving country plays a crucial role in the choice of channels. For example, there is evidence that better-educated migrants, who usually have relatives in home countries living in urban areas, make greater use of banks and other official channels than do rural families, who tend to rely

Average cost for remitting US$ 200

Country	Percentage of remittance amount
Mozambique	1.0
Turkey	4.9
Portugal	5.0
Ecuador	5.6
Pakistan	5.7
El Salvador	6.0
Colombia	6.2
Peru	6.5
Greece	7.1
India	8.1
Philippines	8.2
Bolivia	8.4
Dominican Republic	8.4
Mexico	9.2
Venezuela	10.5
Egypt	13.8

Sources:
Manuel Orozco, *Workers Remittances: The Human Face of Globalization* (Washington, D.C., Multilateral Investment Fund, Inter-American Development Bank, 2002), pp. 23 and 31; and Andres Solimano, Economic Development Division, Economic Commission for Latin America and the Caribbean, *Remittances by Emigrants: Issues and Evidence* (United Nations publication, Sales No. E.03.G.152), p. 35.

Box IV.2 (cont'd)

more on informal channels, given that rural areas are often poorly served by the official financial sector (Amuedo-Dorantes and Pozo, 2002).

Although the modes of informal channels vary across regions, their use is often determined by long-term social traditions, relations among family and friends, and the existence of employment networks, as well as the lack or inadequate number of money transfer operators and banks that can provide the services needed, and the inability of remittance receivers to access the financial system. In general, the more difficult the access to formal channels by recipients, notably in rural areas, the more often will migrants use informal channels.

Finally, it is worth noting that informal channel services, as well as many small money transfer oeprators, do not always comply with international standards of accountability and transparency (including those covering international money laundering and tax evasion). Nonetheless, as informal channels provide essential services in cases where the formal sector is absent or inefficient, efforts to improve accountability and transparency should be "balanced with assessments of the actual risk of misuse of informal systems on the one hand, and on risk and cost of clamping down on informal services regarding the effect on flows of remittances and the cost of transfers, on the other hand ... (since they) can have strongly felt effects on livelihoods" (Sander, 2003, p. 11).

a The author also argues that commercial banks tend to be reluctant to deal with "low-income migrants who often have a non-regularized immigration status" (p. 17).

Magnitudes

Over the last decades, remittances have grown with the increase in the stock of migrants. Other contributing factors might include the liberalization in the foreign exchange controls in some developing countries (possibly shifting the use of informal networks to the formal channels), and the declining transfer costs of remittances, as well as improvements in the collection of statistical data on remittances (Kapur, 2003).

As there are no reliable estimates of the total value of remittances transmitted through informal arrangements, the present section uses only the official data on remittances.[6] Remittances are estimated to have been approximately $130 billion for the year 2002, about 60 per cent ($79 billion) of which were going to developing countries. Although comparisons of the different types of flows are imprecise, given the different economic uses of funds, for developing countries as a group, remittances have become the second largest type of financial flows: they are smaller than FDI flows but have surpassed official development assistance (ODA) flows since 1996 (see figure IV.1). Also, in comparison to FDI flows to developing countries, remittances appear to be a more stable source of external financing and to be more evenly distributed among and within countries.[7]

Global remittances in 2002 were estimated to have been some $130 billion, more than official development assistance (ODA)

In absolute terms, most remittance flows to developing countries go to Latin America and the Caribbean, and to Eastern and Southern Asia (see table IV.3). Compared with the other developing-country regions, sub-Saharan Africa has received the smallest amount of remittance flows, amounting to 1.5 per cent in 2002. Moreover, for the period 1980–2002, the regional shares for the economies in transition, Northern Africa, sub-Saharan Africa and Western Asia declined, reflecting the increase of flows to other regions rather than an absolute reduction in remittances.

Sixty per cent of global remittances flows go to countries of the developing regions

Figure IV.1.
Selected financial flows to developing countries, 1980-2003

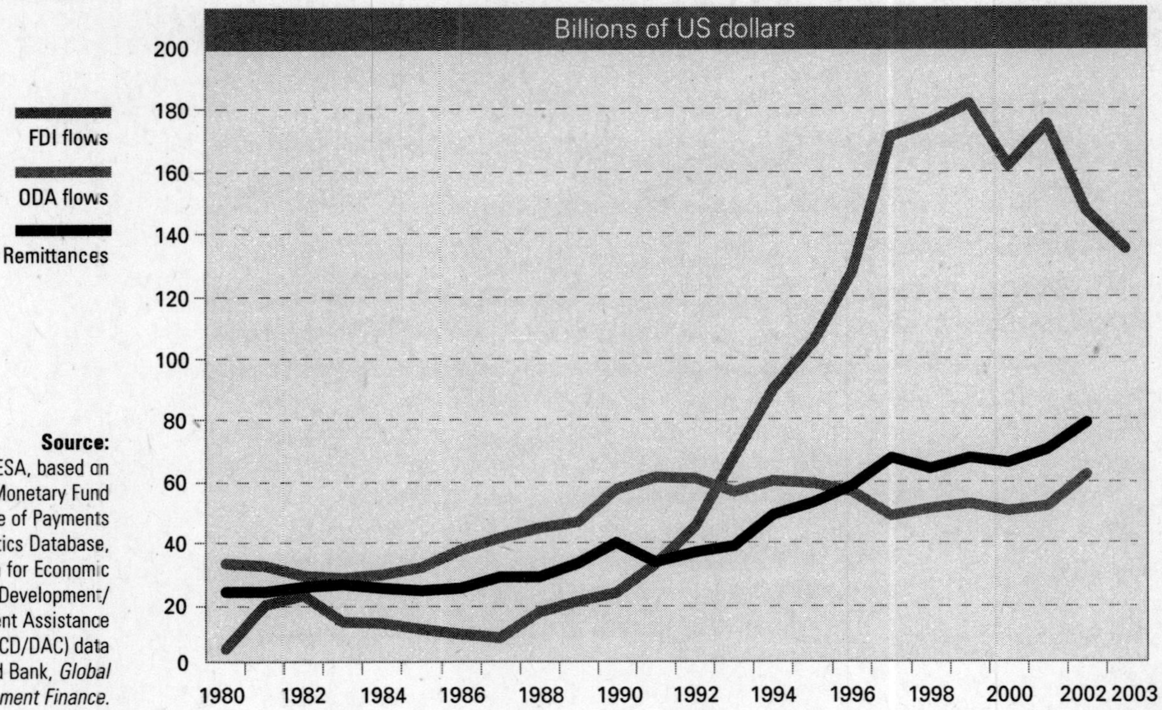

Source: UN/DESA, based on International Monetary Fund (IMF), Balance of Payments Statistics Database, Organization for Economic Cooperation and Development/ Development Assistance Committee (OECD/DAC) data and World Bank, *Global Development Finance*.

For all developing countries, remittances make up just over 1 per cent of GDP

The importance of remittances as a share of GDP for the year 2002 was highest in Northern Africa (3.1 per cent) and lowest in sub-Saharan Africa (0.6 per cent) (see table IV.3).[8] Many of the largest recipient countries of remittances in absolute terms have been large middle-income countries (see figure IV.2). As a proportion of GDP, remittances have been most significant for small low-income and lower-middle-income countries (see figure IV.3).

Especially for some smaller developing countries, remittances may constitute 5 per cent or more of GDP

For a number of developing countries, remittances have become an important source of foreign exchange and an important element in the balance of payments. For instance, during the 1980s, remittances financed 80 per cent of the current-account deficit in Botswana; they equalled almost 75 per cent of total commodity export earnings in the Sudan and accounted for more than half of Lesotho's foreign exchange earnings (Sander and Maimbo, 2003, pp. 15-16). In the Middle East, remittances helped to finance the current-account deficits, and the external debt burden, and also improved the region's debt-servicing capacity (Burney, 1987, p. 756). For El Salvador and Nicaragua, the amount of remittances was at some stage equivalent to more than 60 per cent of the total foreign currencies obtained through exports of goods and services (Inter-American Development Bank, 2001). The relative importance of remittances compared with other international inflows varies across developing countries. For instance, in Western Asia, remittances accounted for a relatively large share (50 per cent) of the total international financial inflows to the region in 2002. For other developing countries, such as those in sub-Saharan Africa, remittances have been relatively low. To illustrate, in 2002, Ethiopia received US$ 1.3 billion in ODA as compared with $33 million in official remittances. In the same year, Rwanda received $356 million in ODA and $7 million in remittances. For the United Republic of Tanzania, the

Table IV.3.
Inflows of remittances by region, 1980-2002

Billions of dollars and percentage							
		1980	1990	1995	2000	2001	2002
Latin America, Caribbean	Value	1.9	5.7	13.3	19.5	23.2	26.9
	Share of world total	4.7	7.6	14.0	17.6	19.6	20.5
	Share of GDP	0.01	0.4	0.7	1.0	1.2	1.6
North Africa	Value	4.5	7.2	5.9	5.8	7.1	6.8
	Percentage	10.9	9.5	6.2	5.2	6.0	5.2
	As percentage of GDP	3.5	4.2	3.2	2.4	3.0	3.1
Sub-Saharan Africa	Value	1.4	1.6	2.7	1.9	2.2	2.0
	Percentage	3.4	2.2	2.8	1.7	1.9	1.5
	As percentage of GDP	0.6	0.5	0.8	0.6	0.7	0.6
Eastern and scuthern Asia	Value	6.6	9.5	19.1	23.2	23.0	27.3
	Percentage	16.0	12.6	20.1	21.0	19.4	20.8
	As percentage of GDP	1.1	0.9	1.1	1.1	1.0	1.1
Western Asia	Value	5.8	6.6	7.0	8.4	6.6	5.7
	Percentage	14.1	8.7	7.4	7.5	5.6	4.4
	As percentage of GDP	1.7	1.7	1.4	1.3	1.1	..
Economies in transition	Value	4.1	9.5	5.4	7.2	8.1	10.3
	Percentage	10.0	12.5	5.7	6.5	6.8	7.9
	As percentage of GDP	--	0.9	0.7	1.0	0.9	1.1
Sub-total	Value	24.3	40.1	53.4	66.0	70.3	79.1
	Percentage	59.0	53.1	56.2	59.6	59.4	60.3
	AS percentage of GDP	--	0.9	1.0	1.1	1.1	..
Developed countries	Value	16.8	35.5	41.6	44.7	48.0	52.0
	Percentage	41.0	46.9	43.8	40.4	40.6	39.7
	As percentage of GDP	--	0.2	0.2	0.2	0.2	0.2
Total	Value	41.1	75.6	95.1	110.8	118.2	131.1

Source: UN/DESA, based on IMF, Balance of Payments Statistics Database, and World Bank, *World Development Indicators*.
Note: Two dots (..) indicate data unavailable.

data show $1.2 billion in ODA and $7 million in remittances. These numbers indicate that remittances are unlikely to be a significant factor in improving the external financial problems of some countries, and that they are not a substitute for ODA.

Regionally, EU accounts for the largest amount of remittance payments, followed by the United States and countries in the Middle East (see figure IV.4).

Migrants in EU are the largest single source of remittances

The flow of remittances has been positively correlated to growth in the host countries. Remittance payments originating in two of the largest source countries of remittances, the United States and Saudi Arabia, increased during periods of high economic growth in those economies and contracted during periods marked by recession.[9] On the other hand, remittances can be counter-cyclical with respect to the growth in the home countries, that is to say, owing to their altruistic character, they may grow in times of economic crisis (in the home countries). Moreover, in an economic downturn in a home country, emigration may rise and remittances to that country could increase. For instance, as a result of an economic crisis in Ecuador in the late 1990s, a large proportion of the population migrated within a period of two years. Remittances to Ecuador more than doubled, from US$ 643 million in 1997 to more than US$ 1.4 billion in 2001, equivalent to 10 per cent of the country's GDP (Kapur, 2003).

Figure IV.2.
Twenty largest developing-country recipients of remittances, 2002

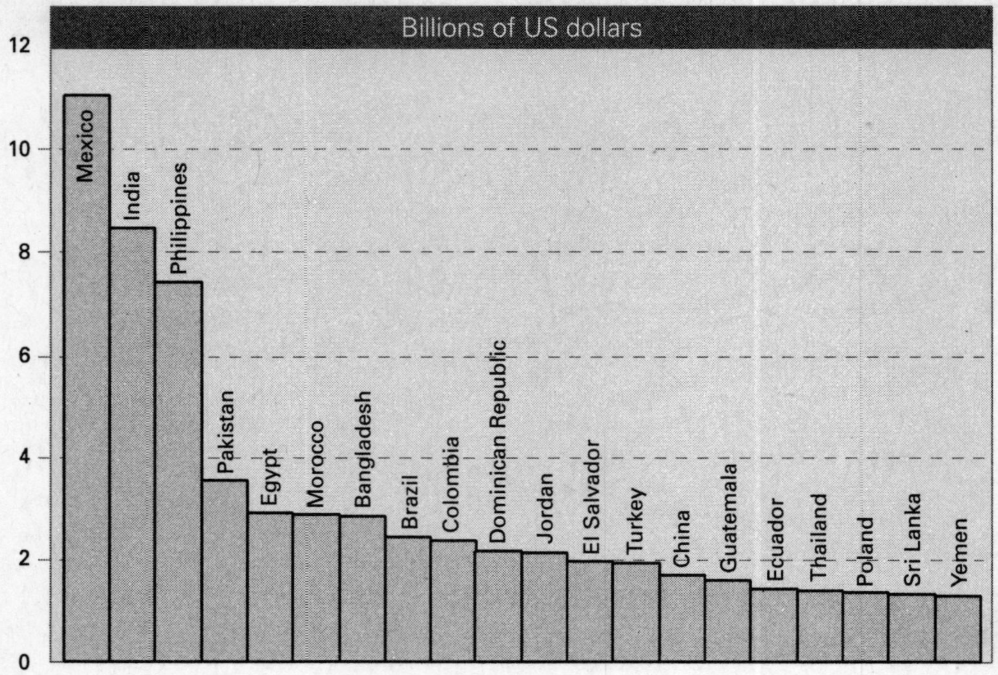

Source: UN/DESA, based on IMF, Balance of Payments Statistics Database.

Figure IV.3.
Twenty developing countries with largest ratios of remittances to GDP, 2002

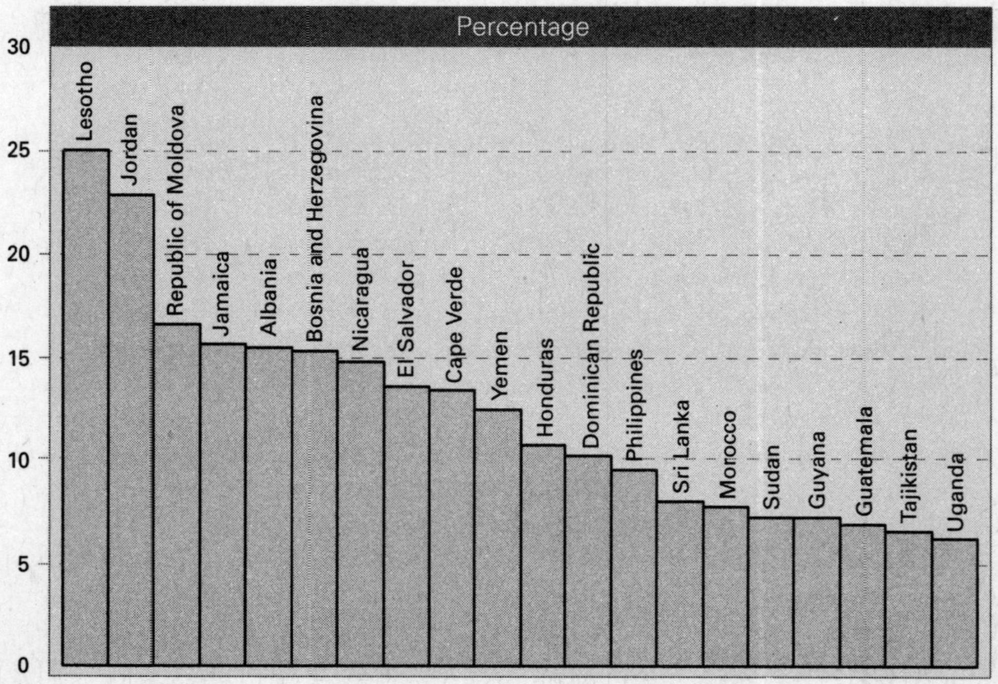

Source: UN/DESA, based on IMF, Balance of Payments Statistics Database, and World Bank, *World Development Indicators*.

Figure IV.4.
Flows of remittances by major source regions, 1980-2002

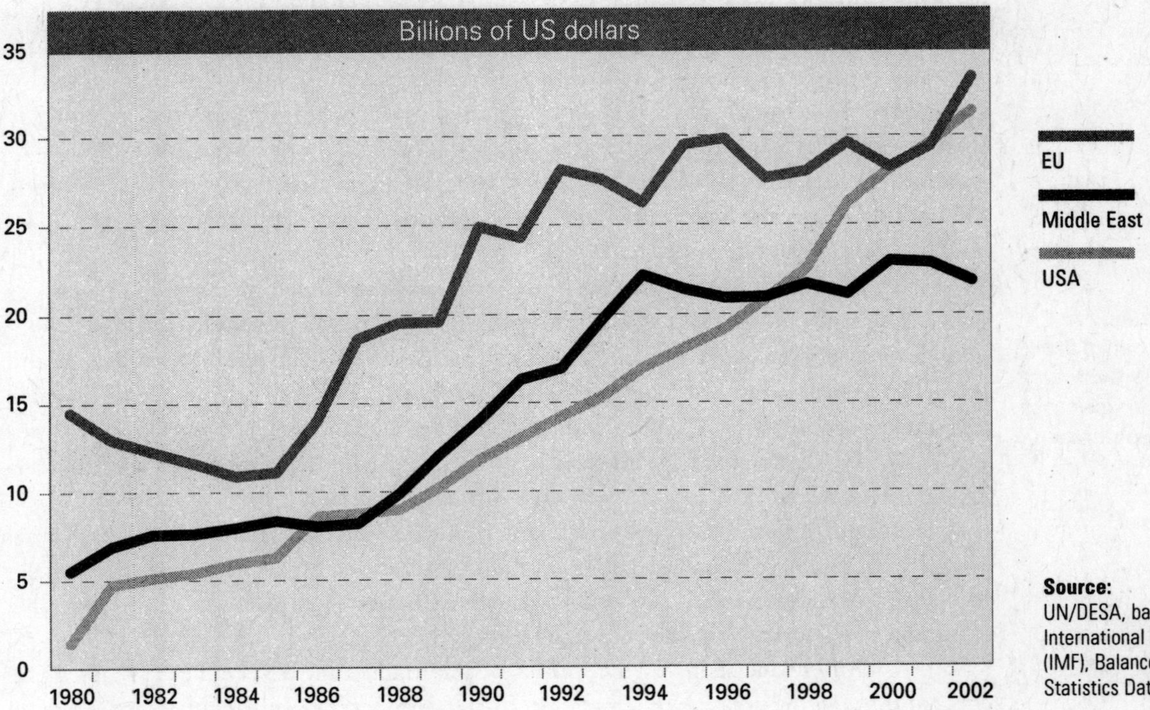

Source:
UN/DESA, based on International Monetary Fund (IMF), Balance of Payments Statistics Database.

Economic impacts of remittances

Remittances are most often used for consumption of basic subsistence needs. For example, it has been estimated that 80 per cent of receiving households in Turkey spent their remittances on daily expenses (Koc and Onan, 2001). However, remittances also encourage investments in human capital, often resulting in improved health and levels of education. To illustrate: in El Salvador's urban areas, the effect of remittances on school retention was estimated to have been 10 times the size of the effect of other household income, and in the rural areas, about 2.6 times the size of the effect of other household income (Edwards and Ureta, 2001 (revised)). Children from Mexican families in which one or several members had migrated completed between 0.7 and 1.6 more years of schooling than children who did not have family members who had migrated (*Dialogue: Dial Newsletter*, 2003). Remittances may also be turned into savings and investments (income- and employment-generating activities such as buying land, tools and machinery, starting a business, and other activities with multiplier effects) (see, for instance, Adams, Jr., 1998, p. 170; Stahl and Habib, 1989, p. 283). For example, several countries in Asia exhibited relatively high levels of savings out of remittances, ranging from 15 per cent in the Philippines to 44 per cent in Sri Lanka and 58 per cent in Thailand (Puri and Ritzema, 1999).[10]

Most remittances are used to meet basic subsistence needs; education is another major use

A noteworthy development has been the mobilization of remittances for home country investments by so-called hometown associations (HTAs). Through these associations in the host countries, migrants pool remittances to send funds to community and local development projects in their home countries. Dominican, Guatemalan, Mexican, Haitian and Salvadoran groups are among those that have started hometown associations in the United States. In one State in Mexico, the local, State and federal Governments are

Hometown associations (HTAs) are often important in mobilizing remittances

matching every dollar transferred by hometown associations to small infrastructure projects. Through this programme, more than 400 projects were completed in eight years. The total investment made by migrants on the projects amounted to approximately $4.5 million. Apart from channelling remittances through the hometown associations, migrants have also contributed their skills to these projects (Torres, 2002). Another State in Mexico works with hometown associations in the United States for the purpose of investing in small garment factories in the migrants' home towns. Under the "My Community" programme, the investments of a minimum of $60,000 are professionally managed. During the start-up phase, the State contributes three months of wages and makes low-cost loans available (Lowell and de la Garza, 2000).

Governments and commercial banks are increasingly providing transfer services to facilitate remittances

The Government of the Philippines established a programme (Lingkod sa Kapwa Pilipino) (LINKAPIL) that makes it possible for Philippine migrants abroad to support development projects at home in such areas as infrastructure, education and health care. The contributions from Philippine migrants to LINKAPIL are reported to have amounted to more than $1 billion (Addy, Wijkström and Thouez, 2003).

One example of the attainment of an increase in access to money transfer services and a lowering of the cost of receiving remittances involved the link-up of credit union cooperatives of unionized agricultural workers with a leading United States commercial bank—with extensive branch networks in the United States, Mexico and several countries in Central America (Ratha, 2003). The collaboration has contributed to a considerable reduction in the cost of transferring remittances.

An enhancement of the impact of remittances on development is also being effected through the creation of interest-bearing government bonds for emigrants as a more attractive instrument for channelling remittances, and the creation of new investment vehicles or programmes such as pension plans (see, in particular, Sander, 2003; and Solimano, 2003a). Furthermore, receiving countries have begun to recognize the benefits of refraining as much as possible from taxing remittances, given that they tend to be transfers primarily sent by low-income migrants to even lower-income relatives back home. Such taxes may contribute to reducing the total flow of remittances themselves, or encourage the expansion of illegal money transfer operations.

Remittances have significant multiplier effects on economic activity

The positive impact of remittances on economic growth comes via the effects on aggregate demand and output through consumption, as well as on savings, and investments.[11] For instance, in Mexico, remittances receipts of $2 billion are estimated to have generated $6.5 billion worth of additional economic activity, accounting for 3 per cent of its GDP (Durand, Parrado and Massey, 1996, pp. 440-441).[12] Similarly, for the Egyptian economy, it was estimated that with an increase of $10 million received from migrants abroad, the country's gross national product (GNP) would increase by $22 million (Kandil and Metwally, 1990, p. 164). In most Central American countries, remittances have increased the average per capita income by 7-14 per cent (International Organization for Migration (IOM), 2003a). A rise in employment in the origin country may well be another component of the multiplier effect.

The sustainability of remittance flows also has important implications for economic growth in the home countries. The continuity of emigration (assuming remittances from individual migrants decrease over time), as well as of remittances over time, is crucial. On the other hand, for fast-growing developing countries, wage differentials with host countries may decrease. As a result, the incentive to migrate would be reduced and the relative importance of remittances would decline.

An examination of the impact of remittances on income distribution and poverty yields several general findings. There is some evidence that the initial waves of emigration are not typically led by workers from the poorest households, but rather by the young and more highly educated, as the theory of "positive selection" would predict (see box IV.1). Consequently, remittances may have a negative impact on income distribution, as most remittances are received by upper-income families, and poor households would not directly benefit from them (see, for instance, Adams, Jr., 1989, p. 69). For instance, in Turkey, only about 5-20 per cent of the remittances-receiving households were poor families (Koc and Onan, 2001). However, there are also indications that remittances reduce income inequality in the long run, as migration by poorer persons becomes easier through the information and assistance provided by migrant networks in the host countries (Taylor, 1999). Thus, through the transfers of funds to poor family members that stay behind, remittances can function as a social safety net and contribute to alleviating poverty. An analysis of 74 developing countries has confirmed the positive impact on poverty reduction, indicating that an average 10 per cent increase in the share of remittances in a country's GDP would contribute to a 1.6 per cent decline in poverty (that is to say, a decline in the number of people living on less than US$ 1 per day).[13]

Over the longer term, remittances are likely to improve income distribution and to reduce poverty

Impacts on host countries

From the point of view of the host country, immigration raises three main issues. The first issue concerns the impact of immigration on the labour market in the host countries, where the fear of losing jobs or purchasing power because of immigrants is often widespread among the native population, particularly among those at the lower end of the labour market. The second issue concerns the impact of immigration on economic growth and the third concerns the fiscal consequences of migration, which are becoming more important in the light of the ageing of the population in the developed countries, particularly the countries of Europe, and Japan.

Impact on the labour market

Much of the popular debate in developed countries on immigration policies revolves around their effects on the labour market. It is a common concern among the native population of countries hosting migrants that immigration could lead to higher unemployment and lower wages for natives. This concern is especially evident in many European countries, where unemployment levels are high and the proportion of the long-term unemployed among the unemployed is large.

Present-day labour-market conditions

Before discussing the theoretical issues, the position of immigrants in the labour markets of the developed countries will be analysed. Immigration surged in the last decades of the twentieth century but the earnings of immigrants relative to natives declined. For example, United States immigrant males earned 4.1 per cent more than native-born men in 1960 but 16.3 per cent less in 1990 (Borjas, 1999, p. 1724). This was due in part to the gap between the educational attainment of immigrants and that of the native-born; but even when this

Earnings of immigrants have tended to fall in comparison with those of native workers

effect is controlled for, the adjusted relative wage still fell by 13.3 per cent over those 30 years. Recent immigrants always suffer an earnings disadvantage before they assimilate, but their initial relative wage deteriorated by 24 percentage points over those 30 years.

Migrant workers are a disproportionately large share of lower occupational categories

Figures for the United States illustrate how the absorption of immigrants takes place disproportionately at the lower end of the labour market. The distribution of the foreign-born and the native-born by major occupations in the United States in 2000 is presented in table IV.4. The table establishes that foreign-born men and women were consistently underrepresented in the top two categories of "Executive, administrative, and managerial" and "Professional specialty," and overrepresented at the low end of the occupational categories, encompassing "Service occupations", "Precision production, craft and repair", "Operators, fabricators and labourers" and "Farming, forestry and fishing". Moreover, while the total native-born increased their representation in the category of "Executive, administrative, and managerial" from 14.4 to 15.3 per cent between 1996 and 2000, the proportion of foreign-born employed in this category decreased from 10.6 to 9.9 per cent in the same period (Mosisa, 2002, table 8).

Trends for median usual weekly earnings (in constant dollars) for persons 25 years of age or over indicate the relatively lower earnings of the foreign-born regardless of their educational attainment (Mosisa, 2002, table 6). For example, foreign-born persons with less than a high school diploma earned $314 per week in 1996 and $322 per week in 2000, while the native-born earned $376 per week in 1996 and $389 per week in 2000. Foreign-born college graduates earned $789 per week in 1996 and $852 per week in 2000, while the native-born earned $841 per week in 1996 and $902 per week in 2000.

Migrants in the United States have lower incomes than native workers at the same educational level

In Europe, the situation facing migrants varies across countries. In Germany, "immigrants and particularly those who arrived in the framework of the guest-working schemes are marked by economic segmentation and overrepresentation at the lower part of the occupational ladder" (Kogan, 2004, p.18). In the United Kingdom, unemployment is a more serious problem for immigrants than are occupational or earnings disadvantages. However, immigrants from China, Ireland and India appear to compete on equal terms with British-born whites of similar social background and educational characteristics,

Table IV.4.
Distribution of foreign-born and native-born employees by major occupation in the United States, 2000

	Percentage of respective labour force			
	Men		Women	
Selected occupations	Foreign-born	Native-born	Foreign-born	Native-born
Executive, administrative and managerial	9.8	15.8	10.0	14.8
Professional specialty	12.9	13.6	14.5	18.5
Service occupations	13.4	9.5	26.9	16.4
Precision production, craft and repair	12.2	6.5	22.2	14.8
Operators, fabricators and labourers	22.7	18.8	13.5	6.1
Farming, forestry and fishing	6.3	3.3	1.6	1.1

Source:
Abraham T. Mosisa, "The role of foreign-born workers in the U.S. economy", *Monthly Labor Review*, vol. 125, no. 5 (May), table 5.

whereas others, such as blacks from the Caribbean and Pakistanis, seem disadvantaged in the salaried labour market but less so in the manual labour market.

In the second half of the 1990s, immigrants entering the United Kingdom and immigrants entering Germany followed different occupational paths. In the United Kingdom, immigrants have occupational careers similar to those of the native-born. This could be partly due to the fact that many immigrants come from Commonwealth countries, speak English and have formal qualifications or licences that are recognized by the United Kingdom authorities. In Germany, the occupational careers for immigrants are rather segmented in manual, mostly unskilled blue-collar jobs. Immigrants in Germany have less stable employment and occupational careers, with more frequent employment transitions than the native-born. In the United Kingdom, the distributions of occupations held by immigrants and the native-born seem to converge, although there are other factors that account for the disadvantaged occupational position of immigrants. For example, immigrant doctors concentrate in medical specialties that are unpopular among native-born white doctors and have had to accept placements in less popular geographical locations of the United Kingdom (Kogan, 2004).

In Germany, migrant workers are concentrated in the lower-skilled occupations

Occupational segregation in Germany can be explained only partly by the inadequate educational qualifications of immigrants, because the formal qualifications of immigrants seem to be of little relevance in the German labour market. In the United Kingdom, formal qualifications seem to have more importance for the occupations of immigrants, as noted above. While in the United Kingdom the risks immigrants incur of losing their employment are similar to those incurred by the native-born, in Germany, the risk of losing their employment is higher among immigrants, which is attributed to their placement in vulnerable occupations and industries. Likewise, in the German labour market, white-collar jobs are almost closed to all unemployed immigrants, irrespective of their educational levels; whereas in the United Kingdom immigrants seem to compete with the native-born on more similar terms (Kogan, 2004).

In the United Kingdom, some migrant groups compete effectively with the native-born

Migration and the labour market: analytical and empirical considerations

The above analysis of present-day migration patterns points to the varied impact of migrants on local labour markets and the way in which their participation changes over time. However, much theoretical analysis has started with a static analysis which fails to capture many of the elements of the immigrants' adaptation to local labour markets over time. As a very first approximation, this static analysis indicated that immigration has the effect of increasing the labour supply in economic terms, shifting the curve outward by the quantity of labour supplied by immigrants.[14] If the total demand for labour is unaffected—an assumption that is not tenable, as will be seen below—a new equilibrium is established in a competitive labour market, at a higher level of employment and a lower wage rate than before immigration. If only a small number of natives were willing to work at lower wages, the effect of immigration would be to reduce the number of employed natives. The number of jobs lost by natives, however, will be less than the number of jobs taken by immigrants because, at lower wages, the labour market would generate more jobs. Immigration will lower wages even more if immigrants are prepared to work for lower wages than natives. This seems plausible in the case of undocumented immigrants, for example, because an influx of such immigrants not only shifts the labour supply, but makes it more

The effect of labour immigration is not limited to an increase in the number of workers and a fall in wages

elastic (Friedberg and Hunt, 1995). The assumption that labour markets are competitive might not hold if, for example, wages are made rigid by such institutional arrangements as collective bargaining agreements. In such a case, migration will have an impact on the level of employment of natives rather than on wages.

However, immigrants are not homogeneous in terms of skills and thus they participate in a variety of segments of the labour market. To reflect this fact, the above reasoning should be repeated for any occupational group with a more pronounced labour supply shift for occupations that require skills more frequent in immigrants. Thus, the effect of immigration on different occupations depends on the skill content of migrants and how it compares with the skill content of natives. In addition, immigrants, in filling both cyclical and structural labour supply shortages, do not compete with natives. (For an analysis of the educational attainments and skills of today's immigrants, see box IV.3.).

Box IV.3

Skills and educational attainments of immigrants in developed countries

The most developed areas of the North are the great magnet to which are drawn the many highly skilled professionals from all corners of the world who would like to be exposed to the latest technology or ideas, a key characteristic in jobs in the service sector in areas such as computer engineering, law, finance and marketing management, and health care. It is expected that a labour supply gap in some key sectors such as medical services will continue. A more acute gap in the United States of America is predicted for the next 25 years because the physician pipeline is at its narrowest in regions with the highest expected rates of population growth, whereas capacity will exceed demand in regions of declining or minimal population growth (Hallock, Seeling and Norcini, 2003). Increasingly, medical doctors move from India to the United Kingdom of Great Britain and Northern Ireland, the United States or Canada; from Pakistan to the United States or Canada; and from South Africa to Canada.

It is less often noted, however, that medium- and low-skilled labour, like nurses and babysitters, is also demanded in the developed countries and jobs requiring such labour are being filled by migrants from developing countries.[a] For instance, Australia is expecting a shortfall of 31,000 nurses by 2006 and, given the policy of the Government of the Philippines to encourage the emigration of nurses, Australia is recruiting Filipino nurses (Armstrong, 1998; Glaessel-Brown, 1998; Xu, 2003). The United States had passed the Immigration Nursing Relief Act of 1989 to respond to the nursing shortage of the late 1980s. In the year 2000, the United States had nearly 100,000 overseas-trained nurses. Chinese nurses are migrating to the United States, adding to the more permanent flow thereto of Filipino nurses. Similarly, in Europe, labour shortages are frequently reported in firms operating in the service sector and in education (Doudeijns and Dumond, 2003, pp. 4-5).

Some manufacturing and agricultural work also represents a niche for migrants in the labour market of the developed countries. In this sense, some developed countries' labour shortages include semi- and low-skilled labour, particularly in seasonal or cyclical economic activities. For instance, not less than 85 per cent of all employers in the French construction industry recently reported recruitment difficulties. In Belgium, employer organizations confirm that the most urgent needs are for low-skilled and unskilled jobs. In the Netherlands, 50 per cent of all hard-to-fill vacancies were in the category of low-skilled personnel. In Norway, increasing tightness is expected in low-skilled occupations in agriculture, fisheries, hotels and restaurants. In Canada, 50 per cent of all hard-to-fill vacan-

Box IV.3 (cont'd)

cies were found outside the high-technology sectors, mainly in retail trade and consumer services (Doudeijns and Dumond, 2003).

The level of education of migrants is highly diverse. Contrary to widespread perceptions, the proportion of immigrants to the United States with at least a college education has been steadily increasing. Whereas before 1970 this segment had represented 19.3 per cent of total immigrants, the proportion rose to 23.6 per cent for the period 1970-1979 and to 28.9 per cent for the period 1990-1996. However, the proportion of immigrants into the United States who have no high school diploma also increased, from 30.7 per cent before 1970, to 35.8 per cent, 38.5 per cent and 36.8 per cent for the periods 1970-1979, 1980-1989, and 1990-1996, respectively (United States Department of Commerce, Economics and Statistics Administration, Bureau of the Census, 1997). Increasingly, then, there have been two extremes in immigrants' educational attainment, at the top and at the bottom, rather than only at the bottom (Williamson, 2004). The foreign-born are disproportionately overrepresented with respect to the native-born at the lowest end of the educational spectrum (those who have not completed secondary school) but are roughly represented as proportionately as the native-born, both men and women, at the top level (those with at least a college degree) (United Nations, 2003d).

Data for the European Union (EU) in 2001 indicate similar patterns to those of the United States, although with slightly higher proportions of native-born than foreign-born men and women with at least a college degree. Thus, 17.9 and 14.2 per cent of native-born men and women, respectively, had at least a college degree, as against 15.1 and 14.1 per cent, respectively, of foreign-born men and women. At the other end of the education spectrum, 38.1 and 44.1 per cent of native-born men and women, respectively, had not completed high school or less, while the comparable figures for foreign-born were 45.1 and 48.1 per cent (United Nations, 2003d). Figures for Germany, Sweden and the United Kingdom are given below (see table) and illustrate that, in general, the rates of higher education among immigrants are rather similar across these three countries, and that, except for Germany, higher education is more common among immigrants than among native-born nationals of the same gender (Kesler, 2004). As in the case of the United States, there is also a concentration of immigrants, as compared with the native-born, at the other end of the spectrum of educational attainment (non-high school graduates) in Germany and the United Kingdom, but not in Sweden.

Level of education among the native- and foreign-born in Germany, Sweden and the United Kingdom, 1995

Percentage

	Lowest level of education		Highest level of education	
	Native-born	Foreign-born	Native-born	Foreign-born
Germany				
Men	8.4	22.8	35.0	22.9
Women	13.7	34.7	21.8	21.7
United Kingdom				
Men	22.7	47.5	26.7	28.9
Women	27.6	54.7	24.0	24.2
Sweden				
Men	13.0	13.5	23.5	24.1
Women	10.2	11.3	31.9	34.3

Source: Christel Kesler, "Defining migrant status and assessing employment outcomes in Europe", May 2004, unpublished paper.

Box IV.3 (cont'd)

After arrival, many immigrants continue to advance their careers and specialize and have made a major contribution in scientific and highly specialized domains. For example, in 1995, 40 per cent of all recipients of doctorates in science and engineering from United States universities were citizens of foreign countries, compared with only 27 per cent in 1985. Even more striking, 56 per cent of all recipients of doctorates in engineering in the United States in 1995 were foreigners who had received their undergraduate degrees in foreign countries. Foreigners have been steadily gaining in respect of their share of recipients of doctorates in highly specialized disciplines such as physics, computer science, biology, mathematics and chemistry (for a full report, see National Science Foundation, 1996). Educated foreigners find work easily: the unemployment rate for foreign-born men with a college degree or more was only 2.1 per cent in the United States in 2000, about half the national overall unemployment rate.

a It is noteworthy that in the case of the United States, the members of the largest group of immigrants, numbering about 3.7 million, have finished secondary school and work in low-skilled jobs (Carrington, 1999, p.165).

Several factors contribute to the comparative skills of migrants and natives, including migration policies in host countries, and the skill content of the native labour force, as well as the countries of origin of migrants, for the reasons reviewed in chapters I and III. In respect of the contribution of host countries' migration policies to determining the skill content of migrants, countries like Australia, Canada, Germany, the United Kingdom and the United States have selectively opened their labour markets to highly skilled immigrants. Second, the skill content of the native labour force, both in absolute terms and relative to that of immigrants, has increased over time in host countries. The United States has hosted migrants since its formation and the skill content of its labour force has increased steadily over time. Nowadays, a low-skilled United States labourer is, for statistical purposes, someone with between 9-11 years of education. This was not the case in the beginning of the twentieth century. In that period, the skill content of immigrants, generally from Europe, compared well with the skill content of the native labour force. In New Zealand, for example, the wages of migrants from the United Kingdom were higher that those of natives. The shift in the source of immigrants from Europe to Asia and the Pacific islands, involving individuals with little knowledge of the language and less ability to integrate, has modified the balance, and immigrants now earn less than natives (Winkelmann, 2000). Third, the countries of origin of migrants influence the skill content of migrants through the self-selection process (see box IV.1). On the one hand, evidence suggests that migrants from countries where skill does not receive a high premium tend to be skilled and that migrants from countries where skill does receive a high premium tend to be less skilled. On the other hand, since migrants have to bear an up-front out-of-pocket cost to migrate, skilled individuals are more likely to have the resources required to leave. These two facts help explain the fact that current migrants are both highly skilled and low-skilled, but not from the poorest segment of society in the home countries.

Migrants increase the size of the labour force, but also increase the demand for goods and services

Whatever their skills, the fact that migrants not only increase the labour force and thus aggregate supply, but also demand goods and services in turn increases labour demand. Moreover, some immigrants use their entrepreneurial abilities to set up businesses using capital they brought with them or raised locally and, as a result, raise the demand for labour (see box IV.4). Immigrants also enlarge the variety of goods and services at the

Box IV.4

Self-employed foreign workers

Self-employment is one of the options available to immigrants. Indeed, in a number of receiving countries, setting up a company or building upon an individual activity is a usual way for foreign workers to enter the labour market. Self-employed workers are numerous in countries like Canada, Denmark, Finland, Spain, Ireland, the United Kingdom and the United States but less so in Austria, Greece, Italy and Switzerland.

One of the explanations for the relatively large numbers of foreigner entrepreneurs is based on the selective nature of migration, the suggestion being that immigrants are more dynamic and less reluctant to take risks than natives. There is, however, little empirical evidence to confirm this argument in those terms. Another argument, the converse of the first, emphasizes the case of foreigners who experience specific difficulties in securing salaried jobs -- not on account of their intrinsic qualities, however, but rather because of discrimination, language barriers or inadequate access to information. In such cases, foreigners are more likely than nationals to establish their own business.

The development of economic activities aimed at immigrants' communities of origin (ethnic businesses) is a third explanation for self-employment among foreign workers. Such activities can include the provision of services, notably in the field of health, education and catering, or they can involve strengthening merchandise trade with countries of origin. Community-type activities often extend beyond the ethnic community and sometimes foster integration in the host society. For example, the Asian, Indian, Italian and Turkish culinary specialties were largely introduced by immigrants and are now an integral part of eating habits all over the world.

In contrast, the complexity of legislation in host countries, coupled with the difficulty of obtaining credit, can sometimes curb the ability of foreigners to set up businesses. Also, it may be hard for foreigners to enter some professions because of the institutional provisions involved (certification procedures, for example, in the medical profession) or the specificity of the knowledge required (in the legal profession).

Some receiving countries have specific immigration programmes to attract foreign investors, but they usually involve limited numbers because of the scale of the financial guarantees required. In 2000, for example, Canada received 1,390 foreign investors, each with at least 800,000 Canadian dollars, and over 1,600 entrepreneurs. In the case of Australia, 7,250 people, each with at least 250,000 Australian dollars to invest, entered the country in 2000-2001.

Source: SOPEMI (Continuous Reporting System on Migration) *Trends in International Migration: Annual Report - 2002 Edition* (Paris, OECD, 2003).

disposal of consumers, and contribute to the smooth functioning of the labour market by supplying services that natives are no longer willing to provide at existing market prices. They thus help to expand the production frontier, to remove the constraints on economic activity and to make possible a faster rate of economic growth.

These considerations show that a static approach may not fully reflect the realities of international migration. The impact of migration on the labour market is likely to vary over time as immigrants acquire new skills and experience in the local labour market. Moreover, as relative wages change, investment in education and training by both natives and immigrants is also likely to adjust. In addition, the skills of migrants tend to be underemployed for a period of time after arrival in the host countries, in other words, they take jobs that require skills lower than those they possess. As they assimilate into the labour market and obtain jobs more closely related to their skills, the impact on low-skill jobs may dissipate. Once they have established themselves in jobs more suited to their skills, they will be competing with natives for these higher-skilled jobs.

Empirical findings show that immigrants have only a modest impact on wages and employment in host countries

In any case, empirical results show that immigrants have only a modest impact both on wages and on employment. This impact is the same whether the immigrant workers are documented or undocumented, temporary or permanent. The evidence on this subject can be divided into two types: evidence that assesses the impact on the host country's labour market of a sudden increase in the labour supply, and evidence that estimates the impact of migration flows over several decades.

Several episodes in recent history have provided useful "natural experiments" for the first group of case studies, the majority of which found that immigration did not have any significant impact. For example, in 1962, 900,000 people of European origin living in Algeria had moved to France, increasing the French labour force by 1.6 per cent. An empirical analysis found that a 1 percentage point increase in the labour force reduced the wage of a region by at most 0.8 per cent and raised the unemployment rate of natives by 0.2 percentage points (Hunt, 1992, pp. 556-572). In 1974, 600,000 colonists returned to Portugal from the African colonies of Angola and Mozambique. Empirical analysis was unable to detect any impact on the labour market (Carrington and deLima, 1994). Between April and September 1980, about 125,000 Cubans had entered Miami, increasing the local labour force by 7 per cent. When the impact of this on unskilled labour from different ethnicities was assessed, only Cubans appeared to have been negatively affected. It is possible, however, that the new migrants were earning less and were subject to higher unemployment, thus lowering the average figures for Cubans (Card, 1990, pp. 245-257). Between 1989 and 1995, over 600,000 highly educated migrants moved from the former Soviet Union to Israel, increasing the size of the Israeli population by 13.6 per cent, with no sizable impact on the labour market (Friedberg, 1997).

Analyses that have focused on migration flows also conclude that immigration does not affect natives' wages and employment, even in cases where the share of migrants in the labour force is large (see table IV.5). Several methodologies have been used to estimate the impact of migration on the host country's labour market, but all point to the same conclusions: (a) there is no significant reduction in employment of natives; and (b) a 1 per cent increase in the fraction of immigrants in the population reduces native wages by at most 0.1 per cent. Even those natives who should be the closest substitutes for immigrant labour have not been found to suffer significantly as a result of increased immigration (Borjas, 2003).[15]

Table IV.5.
Foreign-born labour force in selected OECD countries, 2000

Country	Foreign labour force (thousands)	Share of total labour force (percentage)
Australia	2 364.5	24.5
Canada[a]	2 839.1	19.2
France	1 577.6	6.0
Germany	3 546.0	8.8
New Zealand[a]	--	18.9
Sweden	222.0	5.0
United Kingdom	1 229.0	4.4
United States	17 400.0	12.4

Sources: OECD database for all countries except New Zealand; Winkelmann (2001), for New Zealand.

a Data refer to 1996.

Besides the evidence regarding the direct effect of migration on wages and employment, there is empirical evidence from the United States that suggests that immigrants may play an important role in removing rigidities in the labour market. By choosing to move to those States that offer the highest wages for the skills they possess, immigrants make up a disproportionately large fraction of the marginal workers whose decisions on where to live reduce wage differences across labour markets; that is to say, immigration improves labour-market efficiency. An estimate for the United States indicates that the gain from improved efficiency in the labour market would amount to $10 billion. Moreover, part of this gain would accrue to natives, suggesting that the benefits from immigration may be underestimated (Borjas, 2001).

Immigrants have improved overall labour-market efficiency in the United States, ...

Immigration can improve efficiency of the labour market when that market is competitive, but may accentuate the market's failures when it is not competitive. Analyses tend to find that immigration has a larger impact in Europe, where the labour market is less flexible, than in the United States. It appears that reduced flexibility in the labour market makes absorption of immigrants more difficult. Such an effect may be explained, however, by the fact that there has been little employment-creation in most of Western Europe in the last two decades, while immigrants' employment has grown considerably, so that their jobs may have come at the expense of those of natives (Angrist and Kugler, 2001).

...but not in Europe

The enlargement of the European Union (EU) from 15 to 25 members, and the potential influx of immigrants from Eastern Europe, could provide the opportunity to reduce existing rigidities in European labour markets (see also chap. VIII). Absent restrictions on migration, it is estimated that, on average, 220,000 to 350,000 people will migrate from Eastern to Western Europe each year: Germany is expected to attract more than 60 per cent of this inflow. This would mean a net impact on annual population growth for the EU-15 of about 0.1 percentage point and 0.2 percentage points for Germany. The direct impact on the labour market would thus be small. However, migration could provide an opportunity for the EU-15 to lift their own growth potential, by allowing more rapid growth of their labour force at a time of population ageing and diminishing growth of the natural population. While unemployment is high across the EU-15, there are still shortages in some sectors that can be filled with foreign labour. The indirect impacts of migration from the new EU members could prove beneficial in the long term by adding flexibility to wage settlements, as well as by lowering the average age of the working population. Nevertheless, the social frictions created by immigration require active policies to address the adjustment costs (Zimmerman, 1995).

Migration, income inequality and growth in host countries

One criticism of immigration is based upon trends in income inequality over time. The past three decades have seen an increase in income inequality in developed countries and migration has been viewed as one of the causes. However, skill-biased technological progress and trade with labour-abundant countries are also likely to generate downward pressures on wages, and it is argued that the former rather than the latter is likely to have been the key explanatory element in the changes in the wage structure of recent years (Adams, 1997). While recognizing the contribution of technological progress, a study found that the rise in inequality was largely explained by other factors such as the fall in the real minimum wage and declining unionization (Card, 1990).[16] It can be argued that both trade and international migration have an impact on both the minimum wage and

Labour immigration probably has less to do with growing income inequality than do technology change and trade with low-wage countries

unions' bargaining power. With increasing trade and immigration flows, workers can be more easily replaced by workers from other countries, to the extent that it has been suggested that the wages of low-skill workers are set in Beijing, but those of highly educated workers, in New York (de Ferranti and others, 2003). For those who lack the skills to make themselves hard to replace, the result is greater economic insecurity (Rodrik, 2001).

Assessing the effects of immigration on growth very much depends on the assumptions made. One survey of the evidence concluded that "while recent theoretical work has made strides toward explaining the possible links between immigration and growth, only a few empirical studies have been conducted, and no clear picture has emerged from these" (Borjas, 1995, p. 39). A more recent survey concluded that "in general these models indicate that migration should increase growth, in terms of both endogenous and short-run growth. This is particularly the case if the inflow of workers consists mainly of the highly skilled" (Drinkwater and others, 2002, p. 39). It is necessary to take into account the human capital of the migrants, but at the same time it is difficult to measure the contribution to growth of dynamic immigrant entrepreneurs such as James Watt, Nathan Mayer Rothschild and the Indian and Chinese entrepreneurs of Silicon Valley. Nevertheless, most evidence suggests that the effects of immigrants on growth are positive.

Empirical evidence indicates that immigration is positively related to economic growth

One estimate for the United States was that a 1 percentage point increase in the net migration rate is associated with a 0.1 per cent increase in the growth rate (Borjas, 1995, p. 41). The British Government estimated that net migration contributes about 0.4 percentage points of its forecast long-term growth trend of about 2.75 per cent a year. A 1 per cent increase in population through immigration could lead to a 1.15 per cent increase in gross domestic product (GDP) (*Financial Times*, 2004, p. 6). Another analysis, for the western Länder (States) of Germany, estimated that GDP in 1992 had been 6 per cent higher than it would have been without migration, that 30,000 jobs had been created, and that migration had created a surplus of 14 billion deutsche mark (DM) in the public sector compared with the baseline (Gieseck, Heilemann and von Loeffelholz, 1995).

Fiscal effects of immigration

Another concern that determines policy towards immigration is the effect on the fiscal situation, especially in the light of demographic trends. Without immigration, the populations of many European countries would begin to shrink (see also chap. II). In 2001, over three quarters of the increase in the population of EU was due to immigration, and 80 per cent in the case of Spain, the country with the lowest rate of fertility in EU (Collado, Iturbe-Ormaetxe and Valera, 2003, p. 2). Given the fact that, within the shrinking populations of many European countries and Japan, there is a proportion that is rapidly ageing, the ratio of those of working age to those retired will rise sharply in coming decades. In these circumstances, an argument in favour of immigration is that it would provide the labour force required to support the older population.

Immigration has particular importance in countries with ageing populations

An infusion of immigrants will have an effect on the fiscal position of the host countries that is partially related to the effects on the labour market and on growth. Over their lifetime, immigrants will contribute to government revenues through their taxes and social security contributions, but they will also increase government expenditure on health, education and welfare, as well as on the provision of public goods such as defence, maintenance of law and order, and infrastructure, if a larger population requires increased expenditure on these goods.

Generational accounting calls for the present value of all future net tax payments by current and future generations to be sufficient to cover the present value of future government expenditure, as well as to service the Government's initial net indebtedness. Calculating these flows over time for a situation without migrants and for one with migrants provides the net present value of the immigrants' net fiscal contribution to the country. In these calculations, much depends upon the assumed future direction of fiscal policy—in particular, whether an expected future deficit will give rise to an immediate rise in taxes or whether policy will change only when that deficit arises. Also, the age and skills of the immigrant entering the country are important, because an educated immigrant will not absorb the educational resources of the host country and because skilled workers are more likely than unskilled workers to find well-paid jobs. However, the immigrant's children will require education in the host country and can be expected to enter the labour force. Finally, an assessment has to be made of how much government expenditure on public goods will increase with immigration—whether, for instance, new roads, hospitals and schools would have to be built.[17]

Immigrants make a substantial contribution to relieving the fiscal burden on future generations in low-fertility countries

In general, such exercises tend to show that immigrants make a substantial contribution to relieving the fiscal burden on future generations in the low-fertility countries of Europe (see, for instance, Collado, Iturbe-Ormaetxe and Valera, 2003; and Bonin, 2002). Calculations for Germany showed that natives' fiscal gain from admitting labour migration was potentially large, and that if the aggregate net payments made by the immigrant population were evenly distributed among future-born natives, their net tax burden would fall by approximately 30 per cent, assuming a constant annual immigration inflow of 0.25 per cent of the initial resident population (Bonin, Raffelhüschen and Walliser, 2000). This positive impact would come from two sources. First, owing to the immigrants' favourable age composition, their average payment to the public sector would be positive, even when taking into account the additional government expenditure that they gave rise to. Second, immigration would raise the size of future-born native generations who would share in the additional tax burden required to meet the intertemporal budget constraint.

The United States does not face as acute a problem of an ageing population as that faced by Europe and Japan, and studies of the fiscal impact of immigration have less clearly positive results. One study found a positive impact but that "the impact of immigration on fiscal balance is extremely small relative to the size of the overall imbalance itself. Thus, immigration should be viewed neither as a major source of the existing imbalance nor as a potential solution to it" (Auerbach and Oreopoulos, 1999, p. 180).

Other studies of the fiscal effects of immigration on traditional settler countries have also shown a positive impact. A study of New Zealand that calculated the contribution of migrants to central government revenue less government expenditure attributable to the migrant population also came up with a positive contribution, of 1.7 billion New Zealand dollars (NZ$) per annum, compared with the New Zealand-born contribution of NZ$ 5.3 billion (New Zealand Department of Labour, 2003, p. 34, table 6.1). On an age-adjusted per head basis, each migrant made a net annual fiscal contribution of NZ$ 3,240, compared with NZ$ 2,980 for a New Zealand-born. Only new migrants from Asia and the Pacific islands did not make a positive fiscal contribution. However, once they had been in the country longer than five years, these migrants also exerted a positive impact.

While immigrants can make a positive contribution to government revenues, they cannot provide a long-term solution to the financial problems of an ageing population. To expect the net contribution to government revenue of new immigrants to be used

However, the positive contribution of immigrants to fiscal problems of countries with ageing populations is not a permanent solution

for the health and pension expenditures of the existing elderly population would be to set off an explosive chain of immigration, whereby fresh immigrants, in ever-larger numbers, would be needed to supply the needs of each generation (see also chap. II). A country whose inhabitants, including first- and later-generation immigrants, are not reproducing at the replacement rate should not rely on immigration to keep the population young (Rowthorn, 2004, p. 11).

Conclusions

In the analysis of the economic impact of migration on developing countries, brain drain and remittances are the most important factors. The extent to which remittances may offset some of the output losses that developing countries can experience from the migration of workers, especially the highly skilled, ultimately depends on the particular circumstances in each country.

For countries where the balance between brain drain and remittances is negative, the challenge is to create domestic opportunities for those workers who feel motivated to migrate for financial and/or professional reasons. Initiatives to improve the economic environment should be developed in those sectors where the brain drain experienced by countries entails high economic and social costs, including, in particular, investments by host countries in the educational sector of the countries of origin of skilled migration. Brain drain with respect to workers in the health-care sector, as well as academics and teachers, appears to require special attention. These initiatives should be supported by development partners.

Whether through direct contact or through the so-called home town associations, the migrant diaspora can be a significant source of, and facilitator in, technology, knowledge, skill and financial transfers, as well as a facilitator of FDI in the home countries. The leveraging of diaspora contacts and resources by policy makers, as well as by the private sector in developing countries, should be encouraged, as in the collaboration, for example, between the United Nations Information and Communication Technologies (ICT) Task Force and its partners in the Digital Diaspora Network of African entrepreneurs. Other specific policies and initiatives focusing on the strengthening of diaspora networks and home town associations should be developed with a view to increasing their development impact.

Return migration can be beneficial to the home countries and may result in new investments and new skill transfers. Some countries have developed innovative approaches to encouraging return migration, such as the creation of a venture capital industry and greater investments in research infrastructure. At the international level, the International Organization for Migration (IOM) and the United Nations Development Programme (UNDP) have undertaken initiatives to promote return migration. These types of initiatives at the country and the international level should be further explored and encouraged.

An increasing number of Governments have recognized the development impact of remittances (see also chap. VIII). Policies to reduce the transfer costs of remittances and to increase their positive economic effects can be implemented in both remittances-sending and remittances-receiving countries. In remittances-sending countries, policies aimed at increasing the efficiency of formal channels include: (a) measures to reduce barriers to entry by new money transfer operators and other operators, notably by expediting and reducing the costs of certification of new remittance operators; (b) incentives for commercial banks to lower the cost of remittances and develop new product lines specifically targeted at migrants; and (c) measures to expedite the formalization of migrants' legal status so as to enhance their access to formal banking services (Solimano, 2003a, pp. 20-22).

Some developing countries have encouraged the migration of workers and supported their nationals abroad with specific policies. Further analysis of these policies and their impacts should be encouraged. In general, remittances can contribute to short-term poverty reduction in developing countries. The volume of remittances, their stable growth over time, and their counter-cyclical nature make them a valuable source of external funds. For home countries, the challenge is to link remittances more effectively to productive investments and development, not to reduce dependence on remittances by restricting emigration opportunities. On the other hand, the international community should be aware that the relatively low level of remittances to a number of poor countries is an indication that remittances cannot be a substitute for ODA, especially for the least developed countries. More generally, remittances should not be a distraction from the ODA commitments of the Monterrey Consensus of the International Conference on Financing for Development (United Nations, 2002b, chap. I, resolution 1, annex) and the United Nations Millennium Declaration (see General Assembly resolution 55/2).

There is a need to further encourage banks—both private and State-owned—that have broad domestic networks to increase their presence in transferring remittances and to facilitate and lower the cost of sending remittances. The development of closer alliances between banks in remittances-receiving and remittances-sending countries and closer bilateral cooperation between Governments of receiving and sending countries are to be welcomed.[18]

The relatively small portion of remittances that are used for investment reflects not only the immediate consumption needs of poor receiving families, but also the possible lack of access to financial services and enterprise development facilities. Consistent government policies to promote the use of remittances in productive activities would be to the benefit of home countries. Some countries have developed specific programmes, such as matching funds for projects financed with remittances. Further analysis of these types of initiatives, as well as new mechanisms, including those from the international donor community, to stimulate the productive use and development impact of remittances, should be encouraged.

This chapter has also argued that, despite sometimes intense public concern or outcry over immigration—particularly over the inflow of unskilled immigrants—in developed countries, the net overall economic impacts of migration—skilled and unskilled—are positive albeit modest in relation to the size of the national income of a receiving country. In general, immigrants contribute positively to economic entrepreneurship, to growth and to fiscal revenues in receiving countries. Skilled or unskilled immigrants fill many positions that the native labour market cannot or will not fill in sufficient volume at the prevailing wage. They contribute to the economic growth of the host country by increasing effective demand and by supplying labour needed to reach, and perhaps expand, the production frontier. This must be set against the fact that inflows of unskilled immigrants might have a small adverse effect on the wages of native unskilled workers or crowd them out of the labour market. Furthermore, in contrast with what some people in receiving countries may perceive to be the case, immigrants are generally net contributors to government revenues. Young or working-age immigrants can also help to reduce the dependency ratio in developed countries faced with an ageing population in the short and medium terms. Yet, immigration cannot be expected to be a solution to the long-term challenges posed by the ageing population.

Any adverse impacts of immigration can be minimized in host countries if handled within the framework of national labour and social policies. For example, when the labour market is inflexible, the negative impact of immigration on the employment of native workers is more pronounced. A national programme for lifetime job training, with some monetary incentives for participants, should make the labour market more flexible by increasing the employability of low-skilled workers and providing the latest managerial and technological knowledge to skilled workers. The same programme would help immigrants raise their human capital. This would entail costs to the public during the period in which the immigrant has not been assimilated in the new country, but after the completion of the programme, the immigrant with higher skills is likely to contribute to fiscal revenues and productivity, thereby covering the costs previously invested.

To maximize the benefits from migration, policy makers are required to devise innovative approaches. As long as there is an incentive, owing to the large disparity in living standards between developing and developed countries, people will try to migrate. Restrictive immigration policies will reduce the flow, but cannot stop it completely. Moreover, such policies are likely to substitute undocumented for documented immigrants (Bhagwati, 2004, chap. 14).

For the past 50 years, Governments all over the world have undertaken various liberalization measures in the area of goods, services and capital, multilaterally and unilaterally. The basic premise of such policies is to maximize economic efficiency at the national and global levels. Yet, the current international movement of people is largely shaped by restrictive migration laws and policies enacted by the Governments of developed countries, resulting in a high efficiency loss (Rodrik, 2001). While efficiency considerations should not constitute the sole basis for the formulation of immigration policies at the national and international levels, it should be recognized in this regard that immigrants make a positive contribution to the growth and development of their new countries and help generate external financial resources for the sending countries. To consolidate these benefits, the world is in need of an international architecture that ensures orderly and predictable migration flows across borders.

Notes

1 For example, inflows of immigrants into a large city can have a negative impact on employment opportunities, as well as on the wages of natives, particularly in construction and service industries which attract migrant labour.

2 Measuring the degree to which migrants from selected regions tend to be highly educated, the study indicates that about 75 per cent of all migrants from Africa are highly educated, followed by more than 50 per cent of those from Asia and the Pacific and close to 50 per cent of those from South America. An additional indicator, the number of highly educated (tertiary) workers who are abroad as compared with those who have stayed behind in the home country, shows the proportion of lost highly skilled labour to be highest for Africa (7 per cent), followed by Asia (5 per cent) and South America (3 per cent).

3 Using the 2000 United States Population Census and estimates from the 2001 OECD Continuous Reporting System on Migration, the study estimated the level of brain drain from 24 labour exporting countries. The data set of the study included those developing countries that had received more than US$ 500 million in official worker remittances in the year 2000. Using data from the United States Population Census and the Barro-Lee Data Set (2000) on educational attainment in developing countries, the study defined brain drain as the migration of more than 10 per cent of the tertiary-educated population from a country. The data set is available from http://www.cid.harvard.edu/ciddata/ciddata.html (accessed 25 October 2004).

4 The study itself did not apply the 10 per cent benchmark.

5 Using a sample containing 50 developing countries, this study measured the effect of brain drain on the incentive to acquire education in the home countries, as well as its impact on GDP. The analysis points out that the growth in GDP of those countries combining low levels of human capital and low migration rates of skilled workers may be positively affected by brain drain. From the sample of 50 developing countries, the following countries were identified as having gained from brain drain: Brazil, China, Colombia, Guatemala, Honduras, Indonesia, India, Pakistan and Paraguay.

6 International data on official remittances are recorded by the International Monetary Fund (IMF) in the *Balance of Payments Statistics Yearbook*. IMF separates remittances into three categories: (a) workers' remittances recorded under the heading "current transfers" in the current account of the balance of payments; (b) compensation of employees which includes wages, salaries, and other benefits of border, seasonal and other non-resident workers (such as local staff of embassies) and is recorded under the "income" subcategory of the current account; and (c) migrants' transfers which are reported under "capital transfers" in the capital account of the IMF *Balance of Payments Statistics Yearbook* (item codes 2391, 2310 and 2431, respectively). The data used for this section cover all three categories but do not include informal remittance transfers. The numbers for most countries therefore appear to be underestimated (from a study by D. Ratha (2003) which also provides a more detailed discussion and analysis of remittances flows (chap. 7, p. 171).

7 The relative stability of remittances as a source of foreign exchange was witnessed in the late 1990s when, as a result of the Asian financial crisis, the other sources of financial flows to developing countries declined (see also figure IV.1 and Gammeltoft, 2002).

8 For a detailed analysis of migrant remittances in Africa, see Sander and Maimbo (2003).

9 For instance, the downward trend in remittances from the Middle East in the mid-1980s has generally been explained by the recession during the decade following the collapse of oil prices, triggering a return of workers to their home countries (see Wahba, 1991, p. 42).

10 An explanation provided by the study for the high savings rates is that, unlike the migrants in Europe who often stay in the host countries for a long period of time, the Asian migrants tend to be "target savers" who go abroad on short contracts. As a result, Asian migrant families may consider remittances as only a transitory income, and therefore tend to save as much as possible.

11 For a detailed discussion of both channels and multiplier effects, see Solimano (2003b).

12 See also Dilip Ratha (2003), in which findings from another study indicated that for each dollar received from migrants abroad, Mexico's gross national product (GNP) had increased by $2.69 to $3.17.

13 Moreover, a 10 per cent increase in the share of migrants in a country's population would lead to a 1.9 per cent decline in poverty.

14 For a detailed analysis see G. J. Borjas, (1999) pp. 1697-1760.

15 However, a stronger impact has been recently estimated for the United States, whereby a 1 per cent increase in labour supply would reduce wages by from 0.3 to 0.4 per cent (Borjas, 2003).

16 Friedberg and Hunt (1995) found that, for the United States, immigration is able to explain at most one quarter of the increase in wage inequality across workers on the basis of skills.

17 See Borjas (1994, p. 1706-1707), which shows that the way in which expenditure on non-means tested entitlement programmes is assumed to be distributed between immigrants and natives can make a profound difference to the calculation as to the fiscal contribution of immigrants.

18 For example, the Governments of Mexico and the United States have recently begun to collaborate to provide better financial services to Mexican migrants (including undocumented ones) with a view to increasing their access to, and use of, commercial banking services, particularly those for wiring funds to families in Mexico at cheaper rates than those of current services (see World Bank, 2003, pp. 165-166).

Chapter V
Temporary migration and its relation to trade in services

Temporary labour migration presents some potential advantages over longer-term migration. Migration policies and programmes have therefore been giving increasing attention to temporary labour migration, and flows of temporary labour have been increasing.

Temporary labour migration has potential advantages over longer-term migration

The main categories of temporary migrants are highly skilled professionals, seasonal workers in the agricultural, construction and tourism sectors, and trainees.[1] The temporary worker has a fixed-term contract that specifies the *authorized* occupation, the employer and the geographical area in which the occupation may be carried out. For unskilled workers, the approved duration of stay is often less than one year. Temporary migrants may not be entitled to job-related benefits nor may they have the right to reunite with their family in the host country.[2]

Temporary labour migrants come on a fixed-term contract to fill an authorized post

For receiving (host) countries, temporary migration can fill demand-supply gaps that are observed in a particular period or location. The additional benefit of the temporary element is that the turnover of immigrants reduces some of the negative attitudes and reactions of parts of the native population to permanent migration and reduces the difficulties of social integration in the receiving countries. Concerns may be expressed, however, that temporary migrants could acquire a more permanent status.

In host countries, temporary labour migration can help meet specific labour-force needs while not adding to the stock of long-term immigrants

For origin (home) countries, temporary work has the usual beneficial effects of reducing domestic unemployment and contributing to financial inflows through remittances (see chap. IV). The additional benefit of temporary migration is that it not only reduces the extent of the brain drain (because the migrant returns after an interval) but can also involve a "brain gain" in the form of additional skills (and possibly also a capital gain in the form of repatriated assets) when the migrant returns.

In origin countries, temporary migration can reduce unemployment and contribute remittances, and may diminish brain drain losses

Gains from more extensive use of temporary movements of workers are especially large for unskilled workers, as it is at low levels of skill that the gap in compensations between developed and developing countries is widest (Winters and others 2002; Stiglitz and Charlton, with the Initiative for Policy Dialogue, 2004).

Gains may be greatest to low-skilled temporary migrants

In addition to its benefits, temporary migration has been made more feasible by the development of faster and less expensive means of transportation. Temporary migrants can work in one country and reside, along with their family, in their country of origin. Such transnational communities are increasingly common; apart from seasonal agricultural workers, they tend to comprise mostly highly skilled and highly paid professionals.

The present chapter will first illustrate the magnitude of the temporary movement of workers. Second, it will look at a promising avenue within the trade domain that contemplates trade in services whereby the person who actually provides the service moves, exemplifying so-called Mode 4 under the General Agreement on Trade in Services.[3] Third, a brief digression will take up outsourcing as another area of export potential for developing countries. Finally, conclusions and policy recommendations will be provided.

Trends in temporary migration

The United States of America now hosts the largest number of temporary labour migrants

There have been steady increases in the flow of temporary migrants to the developed countries in the past decade and a change in the legislation of the most important host countries (see table V.1). In the early 1990s, Germany was host to the largest number of temporary workers and the flow into that country has remained roughly constant. In the meantime, the inflow of temporary workers into the United States has approximately quadrupled since the early 1990s, increasing by some 50 per cent between 1998 and 2001 alone. This increase included the distribution of more than 163,000 temporary visas for highly qualified workers in 2001, an increase of more than 40 per cent from the previous year. Flows of temporary workers into all other developed countries for which there are data, other than Switzerland, also rose, although less dramatically.

Skill shortages in many developed countries have led to relaxation of entry conditions for migrant workers

Because of the need to meet the tight skill shortages in many developed countries, there has been an increasing trend towards the relaxation of entry conditions for certain categories of foreign workers in these countries. The United Kingdom of Great Britain and Northern Ireland, for example, increased its work permit approvals from 58,200 in 1999 to 85,600 in 2000 and to 115,700 in 2001. Sectors that registered the highest increase were education (100 per cent), health care (over 40 per cent) and computer technology (roughly 25 per cent). In Japan, the number of foreigners (mostly entertainers) obtaining temporary residence for employment reasons in 2001 was 142,000, an increase of almost 10 per cent over 2000 and of almost 40 per cent over 1998. Germany's "green card" programme, instituted in August 2000, has resulted in the tripling of the employment of foreigners in the health-care sector and the granting of more than 13,000 green cards to foreign computer engineers. In the United States of America, the quota of highly qualified temporary visas was raised substantially in 2001. The trend is even apparent in some of the more advanced developing countries. In the Republic of Korea, for example, the number of documented skilled foreign workers rose from 17,700 in 2000 to nearly 28,200 in 2001.

Many developed countries are making substantially increased use of unskilled migrant labour, especially in agriculture

Several developed countries have made considerable use of unskilled foreign labour, particularly in the agricultural sector and on a seasonal basis. In most of the countries for which data are available, there has been a generally steady upward trend in inflows of seasonal workers since the beginning of the 1990s. At present, the agricultural sector of the European Union (EU) employs almost 500,000 seasonal workers from countries outside the EU-15 every year. In Germany, 260,000 seasonal workers obtained work permits

Table V.1.
Entry of temporary workers into selected developed countries, 1992-2001

	Thousands				
	1992	1998	1999	2000	2001
Australia	40.5	92.9	99.7	115.7	128.5
Canada	70.4	79.4	85.4	93.7	93.1
France	18.1	11.8	13.4	15.4	20.4
Germany	332.6	244.0	274.1	331.6	..
Japan	..	151.7	156.0	183.9	201.1
New Zealand	..	29.5	32.5	43.1	54.6
Switzerland	127.8	40.3	46.1	50.3	56.2
United Kingdom	63.8	98.4	109.0	115.4	132.0
United States	143.0	342.7	422.5	505.1	536.3

Source: SOPEMI (Continuous Reporting System on Migration) (2004).
Note: Two dots (..) signify data unavailable.

in 2001; most of them were from Poland and 95 per cent were employed in agriculture. The increase in seasonal workers with temporary work permits has become particularly pronounced in more recent years, even in countries, such as Switzerland, where there was previously a downward trend (see table V.1). One possible exception is the United States where official data show a steep rise in the inflow of seasonal agricultural workers at the end of the 1990s, but a fall, possibly temporary, in 2001 (SOPEMI (Continuous Reporting System on Migration), 2004).[4]

There has also been increasing use of temporary low-skilled migrant workers in the service sector

Although less numerous, there are also temporary unskilled migrants outside the agricultural sector. In the United States, such immigration had increased by 50 per cent in 2000 and reached 72,400 in 2001. The admission of temporary workers in the service sector has also increased in other developed countries, particularly in business and household services. Given the ageing populations of those countries, foreign workers are likely to play an increasing role in household services in numerous developed countries in the future. Some developed countries, such as Japan, also grant a significant number of temporary work visas to trainees[5] in industry. In Japan, this category has been increasing and reached 59,100 in 2001. Similarly, in the Republic of Korea there were more than 100,000 trainees in 2000 and 2001.

Most temporary labour migrant flows are from developing to developed countries, but they are also found between developing countries

While most temporary movements are from developing to developed countries, there are considerable flows of temporary workers between developing countries. Most oil-producing countries in Western Asia, for example, rely heavily on temporary foreign labour for low-paid services that are not supplied by the native labour force. Data specifically on these temporary flows are not available, but most legal immigrants in the oil-producing countries in Western Asia are considered to be temporary workers, so that data on total inflows provide an approximation of the number of temporary migrants. Such data suggest that there were about 1 million temporary migrants from Eastern and Southern Asia working in Western Asia in the first half of the 1990s (see table V.2). This figure is large when compared with that for the temporary migrant workers in all developed countries, numbering about 1.5 million. Anecdotal evidence suggests that there has been increasing feminization of these temporary flows in the past decade.

Temporary labour migration flows are sometimes managed by means of bilateral or multilateral agreements

Several existing bilateral and multilateral agreements that encompass not only movements of people but also various economic activities, have proved to be useful in managing temporary migration. For example, a number of countries maintain bilateral labour agreements covering mainly lower-skilled or seasonal workers, especially geographically proximate countries. With the increasing needs for health-care providers, some countries have also

Table V.2.
Flows of temporary migrants from selected countries in Eastern and Southern Asia to Western Asia, 1980-1999

Thousands

Sending country	1980-1984	1985-1989	1990-1994	1995-1999
Bangladesh	48.8	74.8	145.4	..
China	30.1	29.5	5.0	..
India	206.5	133.9	285.3	..
Indonesia	15.8	49.5	47.9	123.7
Pakistan	121.0	76.7	142.4	..
Philippines	232.4	254.1	290.1	237.2
Sri Lanka	..	17.9	49.9	154.5
Thailand	49.1	64.9	21.2	17.2

Source:
SOPEMI (Continuous Reporting System on Migration) (2004).

Note:
Two dots (..) signify data unavailable.

entered into special recruitment agreements for the movement of nurses and other health professionals. The Recruitment Agreement between the Government of the Republic of the Philippines and the Government of the United Kingdom of Great Britain and Northern Ireland aims to facilitate the recruitment of Filipino health-care professionals in response to the need for professionals in the health-care sector of the United Kingdom. It provides details of procedure of recruitment (pre-advertising, advertising, actual selection procedure, work permit and visa arrangements, travel arrangements) and outlines the rights and privileges (fees and terms of payment and compliance with United Kingdom law and immigration rules) relating to the employment of Filipino nurses. The contract is valid for three years and is automatically renewed unless revoked by either one of the parties.

A good example of such an arrangement is the Canada and the Caribbean and Mexican Seasonal Agricultural Worker Programme

The Canada and the Caribbean and Mexican Seasonal Agricultural Worker Programme, which involves Canada and Jamaica, Mexico, Trinidad and Tobago, Barbados, Antigua and Barbuda, Dominica, Grenada, Montserrat, Saint Kitts and Nevis, Saint Lucia, Saint Vincent and the Grenadines and operates in Alberta, Manitoba, Ontario, Quebec and Nova Scotia, was introduced in response to shortages of available Canadian agricultural workers; thus, some needs test has to be fulfilled before employers are allowed to hire foreign workers. In cases where Canadians are unavailable, employers submit an application specifying the number of workers required, the length and location of the work, and the working and living conditions. The employer can either accept individual applications from specific workers or leave it to the participating Governments to recruit and select the workers in the countries of origin. Work permit applications are then processed by the local Canadian embassy or consulate. The programme is strictly seasonal and allows for a stay in Canada of a maximum of eight months. It does not open any right of access to more permanent status but allows for the possibility of recirculation or re-entry through the programme if the workers demonstrate good behaviour, in other words, if they comply with the requirements. This partly explains the lower number of overstayers compared with those in other similar programmes. While in Canada, workers cannot seek alternative or additional employment or transfer to another farm without government approval.

The North American Free Trade Agreement includes provisions on facilitating the temporary movement of citizens of the parties to the Agreement

Among the regional trade agreements, the North American Free Trade Agreement (NAFTA) includes provisions on facilitating the temporary movement of the citizens of the parties to the Agreement. Access is limited to four higher-skill categories: traders and investors, intra-company transferees, business visitors, and specific categories of professionals. These groups are not limited to those engaged in services and may include persons in activities related to agriculture or manufacturing. Labour certification or labour-market assessment/tests are waived but work permits are required, except for business visitors. Visas and other general immigration requirements apply, and entry may be refused if authorities believe it may adversely affect settlement of a labour dispute in progress at the intended place of employment, or the employment of any person who is involved in such a dispute. Under the North American Free Trade Agreement, the United States provides "Trade NAFTA" (TN) visas for professionals, which are valid for one year and renewable. Canadians can be granted TN status at the port of entry upon presentation of a letter from a United States employer. Mexicans must arrange for their employer to file a labour condition application, and then must apply for a visa at the United States Embassy in Mexico.

The Asia-Pacific Economic Cooperation group's Business Travel Card Scheme facilitates short-term business travel

The Asia-Pacific Economic Cooperation (APEC) grouping provides another example of an arrangement to facilitate the entry of business visitors. APEC does not grant any right of entry but has established a scheme to facilitate the entry of business visitors under the APEC Business Travel Card Scheme. The Card has a validity of three years and permits multiple short-term business visits for a period of two or three months on each arrival. Card holders are required to present their passports but receive expedited airport processing and are not required to submit separate applications for business visitor visas. Participating economies commit to implementing the Scheme on a best-endeavour basis and are allowed to apply existing visa requirements for business visitors. All economies also retain the right to refuse an individual without providing reasons which includes refusing entry to APEC Business Travel Card holders at the border.

The World Trade Organization, through the General Agreement on Trade in Services, includes provisions for the supply of services through the presence of natural persons of one member of the World Trade Organisation in the territory of another member. The next section elaborates on this particular means of facilitating trade in services, known as Mode 4.

The World Trade Organization General Agreement on Trade in Services provides for temporary labour migration through its Mode 4

International regime for the temporary movement of natural persons in the services sector or the temporary movement of service suppliers

Mode 4 under the General Agreement on Trade in Services

A gain in efficiency is the result of both migration and trade. The difference between them lies in the fact that in the case of migration, a factor of production, labour, moves, while in the case of trade, the output that embodies factors of production moves. More recently, however, an additional link has been established between migration and trade through the arrangement on trade in services. That arrangement had been foreseen as constituting one of the main Agreements within the World Trade Organization when that organization was established and when it was agreed that the World Trade Organization, in contrast with its predecessor, the General Agreement on Tariffs and Trade (GATT), should include trade in services as part of its overall mandate.

To this end, the General Agreement on Trade in Services entered into force on 1 January 1995. The Agreement provides for four modes by which services may be traded. Of relevance in the context of this chapter is Mode 4 (movement of natural persons) which regulates the supply of a service by a supplier in one member country, through the presence of natural persons of that member in the territory of any other member.[6]

The General Agreement on Trade in Services entered into force on 1 January 1995

The coverage of the General Agreement on Trade in Services is very specific: it refers only to service suppliers as natural persons or as employees of service suppliers who enter a country to provide a particular service. The stay is temporary, although the Agreement does not specify what counts as temporary. The period of stay of temporary service suppliers can range from two months to several years, with renewal of permits allowed, depending on the member's schedule of commitments. However, neither Mode 4, nor any other part of the Agreement, covers individuals seeking general access to a foreign employment market, nor does it contain measures regarding citizenship, residence or employment on a permanent basis.

Mode 4 of the General Agreement on Trade in Services refers specifically to temporary international movement of individuals ("natural persons") or employees of service suppliers

Paragraph 1 of the Annex on the Movement of Natural Persons Supplying Services under the Agreement (hereinafter referred to as the annex) specifies Mode 4 as covering the movements of two categories of natural persons: (a) natural persons who are *service suppliers* of a member (self-employed contractual service suppliers) and (b) natural

The Annex on the Movement of Natural Persons Supplying Services under the Agreement details precisely the terms and conditions in respect of Mode 4 workers

persons who are *employees of a service supplier* of a member. The latter may be employed either by (a) a foreign company that has a commercial presence in the host country (intra-corporate transferees); or by (b) a company outside the territory of a member[7] whose employee is sent to the other member to supply a service. It must be emphasized that there is no a priori exclusion of any occupation or skill level from the General Agreement on Trade in Services.

The Annex further provides that the General Agreement on Trade in Services does not cover natural persons seeking access to the employment market of a member, nor does it cover measures regarding citizenship, residence or employment on a permanent basis. The Agreement is not an instrument enabling foreign nationals to cross borders in active search of employment. Rather, it aims to create a multilateral framework for the predictable temporary exchange of skills and expertise. Governments are free to regulate entry and temporary stay, provided these measures do not nullify or impair the commitments. Footnote 1 to the Annex further indicates that differential visa requirements should not be regarded as nullifying or impairing benefits under a specific commitment.

Mode 4 trade comprises a very small proportion of all trade in services

Available statistics show that Mode 4 trade is characterized by very limited bindings under the General Agreement on Trade in Services and accounts for a very small fraction of total trade in services. According to the World Trade Organization, Mode 4-related trade in services accounts for just over 1 per cent of world services trade, whereas Mode 3 trade accounts for more than half of world trade in services, Mode 1 for about one fourth and Mode 2 for less than one fifth (WTO, 2002).[8]

Measuring the economic value of Mode 4 trade is difficult

Measuring the economic value of Mode 4 trade is challenging. The proxies used are data on compensation of employees and data on workers' remittances, both of which have their limitations and may overestimate or underestimate the value generated by Mode 4. Mode 4 covers the movement of service providers but not all kinds of worker movements (for example, it excludes workers in the goods sector and the foreign employees of domestic firms) and refers to temporary movements (which could involve a period of anywhere from two months to five years, depending on countries' schedule of specific commitments). On the one hand, data on compensation of employees and workers' remittances may overestimate the economic value of Mode 4, as they do not distinguish between goods-related and services-related activities. On the other hand, these measures may also underestimate Mode 4 movements in that compensation of employees cover only movements of less than a year and exclude business visitors while workers' remittances capture only movements of more than a year and record only remittances that go through official channels.

The Manual on Statistics of International Trade in Services is designed to improve knowledge of comparability and coverage

Efforts at improving the collection and monitoring of data on trade in services has resulted in the joint publication by the World Trade Organisation, the European Commission, the International Monetary Fund, OECD, the United Nations Conference on Trade and Development (UNCTAD) and the United Nations of the *Manual on Statistics of International Trade in Services* (United Nations, European Commission, International Monetary Fund, Organisation for Economic Co-operation and Development, United Nations Conference on Trade and Development and World Trade Organisation, 2002). The Manual sets out an internationally agreed framework to meet the need for more comparable and comprehensive statistics on trade in services. The recommendations in the *Manual* will enable countries to progressively expand and structure information on trade in services in an internationally comparable way.

Current utilization of the channel provided by Mode 4

In spite of the gains that could be derived from the utilization of Mode 4, countries have made fewer commitments under the General Agreement on Trade in Services to Mode 4 than to the other three Modes. Overall, Mode 4 commitments under the Agreement remain restrictive: commitments refer mainly to a limited set of categories of service providers, mostly high-skilled and linked to a commercial presence. In addition to this limitation, countries also maintain pre-employment requirements, nationality and residency requirements, qualification and registration requirements, and economic needs tests (ENTs), among other restrictions.

Countries have made less use of Mode 4 than of the other three Modes

The movement of foreign natural persons to another country is limited by a number of barriers in the Schedules of Commitments maintained by each country. The *limited number of categories of workers* for which countries have made commitments and a bias towards movement linked to Mode 3 (which have shaped the "template" for scheduling Mode 4 commitments) are a constraint on expanding countries' Mode 4 commitments (see table V.3). Currently, countries have commitments on the following: (a) intra-corpo-

Countries have tended to impose limitations on the sets of worker categories for which they make Mode 4 commitments

Table V.3.
Types of natural persons supplying services (horizontal commitments), 2003[a,b]

Category	Percentage	Number of countries
Intra-corporate transferees	57	62
Other executive, managerial, specialist[c]	21	23
Business visitors to set up commercial presence	18	19
Business visitors to negotiate the sale of a service	26	28
Other types of business visitors	12	13
Contractual service suppliers (employees of juridical persons)	14	15
Contractual service suppliers (independent providers)	6	7
No categories specified[d]	14	15

Source: World Trade Organization (2002).

a World Trade Organization members may schedule their specific commitments under the General Agreement on Trade in Services in two ways: (a) horizontally, whereby limitations/commitments apply to all of the sectors/subsectors on which a particular Member made commitments; and (b) sector-specifically, whereby limitations/commitments apply only to a specific sector/subsector. Most World Trade Organisation members' Mode 4 commitments have been made on a horizontal basis, and as positive undertaking, that is to say, indicating only the extent of its bindingness with respect to specific categories of persons, the duration of stay, other requirements for entry, etc. Consequently, their sector-specific commitments with respect to Mode 4 normally read as follows: "Unbound, except as provided for in the horizontal section of this schedule".

b For a total number of 108 countries that have included commitments on Mode 4 in the horizontal section of their schedules. The percentages refer to the proportion of countries that have made entries for the above categories in their schedule of commitments. The percentages do not add up to 100 because of multiple entries.

c Involving commitments on executive and managerial positions; however, respondents did not specify the category to be that of ICTs.

d This being the case for countries that had horizontal commitments on Mode 4 but did not specify any category of personnel. Instead, the commitments refered to regulations and conditions relating to entry, namely, requirements to be fulfilled, economic needs tests (ENTs), administrative procedures, etc.

rate transferees (ICTs), mostly executives, managers and other specialists; (b) other executive and managerial positions (not necessarily specified as ICTs); (c) business visitors; and (d) contractual service suppliers (either as independent professionals or as employees of juridical persons). Close to 60 per cent of the 108 countries with Mode 4 commitments have entries referring to movement of ICTs linked to commercial presence, while only 14 per cent have commitments on contractual service suppliers.

Another barrier to Mode 4 trade is the lack of generally agreed-upon definitions of natural persons

The *absence of generally agreed-upon definitions* or precise descriptions of the types of natural persons to whom access is to be granted under Mode 4 is also a barrier, as the entry of persons is thereby subject to administrative discretion which detracts from the predictability of entry conditions. Subjecting the movement of temporary workers to the general immigration procedures of host countries, that is to say, to a situation where there is *no separation between temporary and permanent movement,* also hampers the processing of entry visas for temporary foreign service providers. Considering that some services are urgently required and have to be provided immediately, any delays caused by visa procedures become barriers to the delivery of services through Mode 4.

Lack of clarity about economic needs tests (ENTs) can also hinder wider use of Mode 4

Some of the more specific limitations contained in countries' schedule include requirements for economic needs tests or labour-market tests (ENTs/LMTs), as conditions for the provision of access to foreign service suppliers. Economic needs test requirements, together with the presence of numerical quotas, monopolies and exclusive service suppliers, are among the limitations that countries are allowed to maintain, if specifically listed in the market access limitation column of their schedule. Paragraph 9 of the Guidelines for the Scheduling of Specific Commitments under the General Agreement on Trade in Services (GATS) (document S/L/92) of 28 March 2001 states that entries with regard to the economic needs tests "should indicate the main criteria on which the test is based". Countries, however, often list compliance with an economic needs test as a requirement, but do not clearly indicate the criteria for these tests. In the absence of specific criteria, entry conditions become vulnerable to discretionary application and may serve as market access barriers (see box V.1 for a more detailed discussion of economic needs tests).

Other obstacles in respect of Mode 4 commitments can be government procedures to assess professional qualifications, to set pre-employment requirements and to regulate wage parity and social security arrangements

Countries also have the freedom to assess whether a foreign natural person satisfies some educational and professional qualifications before giving that person a licence or permit to work (as part of the *Government's regulatory function*). These procedures for assessing qualifications, skills and experience can be used as a barrier to entry, especially in the area of professional services, as they may either deny market access to service providers from other countries or force service providers to accept job conditions that are below their level of qualification and training. Requirements for *accreditation (or authorization)* by local professional bodies before a practice of profession is allowed also disadvantage foreign workers and impose an undue burden on them.

There are also *pre-employment requirements*, for example, for a person to have been employed by the firm for a specified number of years immediately preceding the transfer, as may be the case for intra-corporate transferees and, to some extent, contractual service suppliers. While the intention is to ensure that the employment with the firm is not being used as an excuse to facilitate access to another country's territory, this requirement may also serve as a barrier to entry. In addition, there are *quota or numerical caps*, through which the entry of foreign natural persons is limited to a specified number or, in some instances, to some percentage of the number of local employees. *Nationality and residency requirements* are also set, specifically regarding the composition of high-level management personnel, such as the membership of a board of directors, or in some speciality occupations (for example, that of chef or ski instructor).

Box V.1

Economic needs tests (ENTs)

Economic needs tests (ENTs) (which, as the name implies, are requirements based on a country's economic needs) are used by World Trade Organization members as a means of restricting market access. For Mode 4, a certain kind of a labour-market test is applied, that is to say, companies have to demonstrate that local skills are not available after an extensive search and publication of need have been undertaken The General Agreement on Trade in Services sanctions the use of ENTs but requires that the specific criteria for their application be laid out by countries using such measures. That most countries' commitments have failed to do this, opens up possibilities for their discriminatory application and affects the predictability and certainty of market access conditions. For Mode 4, ENTs as a requirement have been attached to some category of movements but not to others, with countries being more lenient on intra-corporate transferees, in general. Experts as well as negotiators acknowledge the need to eliminate or reduce the application of ENTs or, if this is not possible, to provide details for their application. Some have also suggested the use of numerical ceilings as an alternative.

It might be difficult for countries to agree on the elimination of ENTs altogether as they may serve legitimate objectives, especially in view of the economic cycles that countries go through. In this regard, countries may as a first priority seek to ensure that no rollback in policies related to Mode 4 trade is allowed in the negotiations and that the binding of existing conditions should be pursued. ENTs may be a means to undertake commitments that would not otherwise be made; they may not always be discriminatory in nature and may be applied on a national treatment basis.

Exchange of information with a view to enhancing transparency in this area could identify best national practices and further enlighten the debate on how to minimize the burden on service suppliers facing such tests. Transparency could become part of the negotiations on specific commitments as a means of obtaining clear information on all requirements related to Mode 4. Best practices and examples of the removal of ENTs by some developed countries, like Norway, members of the European Union (EU), Canada and Japan, need to be broadened, deepened and replicated in categories of interest to developing countries.

Source: United Nations Conference on Trade and Development (UNCTAD) (2003).

Wage parity requirements, or the application of domestic wage legislation[9], disadvantages foreign natural persons relative to nationals, as such measures nullify the cost advantage that foreign suppliers have. *Social security contributions,* in the absence of their portability, is an additional cost to foreign service providers and serves as a de facto discriminatory measure.

The terrorist attacks of 11 September 2001 in the United States have contributed to a further tightening of border entry measures, which were already very restrictive for some countries. In general, receiving countries maintain entry barriers because of fear that easy access would result in an unregulated flow of, and permanent stay by, foreigners. This gives rise to concerns regarding security, the use of infrastructural services, cultural sensitivities, conditions in the labour market, the impact on the wages of natives and other enforcement-related concerns.

Maintaining bilateral labour arrangements has become more convenient for some countries, as this provides for greater flexibility than does binding commitments multilaterally. Some countries also consider paramount their long-standing historical and cultural ties that resulted in, among others, common linguistic and religious practices and are more relaxed in their policies relating to the movement of people from countries with which they share a common historical heritage. Other countries facilitate the movement of service providers at the regional level. Nevertheless, in order to ensure predictability and security of market access conditions and to benefit from the progressive liberalization of the movement of natural persons, developing countries still encourage major importing countries to broaden their commitments on Mode 4 at the multilateral level during this round of negotiations.

Enhancing temporary movement under Mode 4

A strong case can be made for liberalizing Mode 4 trade

There are both political and economic justifications for substantially liberalizing Mode 4 trade. There is already an increasing global movement of workers, mainly from developing to developed countries, and evidence suggests that specific needs remain unmet in key skilled occupations in developed countries, notably in the health and computer-related fields. One means of meeting such needs is to take advantage of the present opportunity to liberalize Mode 4 as part of the Doha trade negotiations. Existing bilateral schemes work well for some countries, but the security and predictability offered by the General Agreement on Trade in Services justify seeking binding commitments multilaterally.

The current Doha negotiations offer a useful opportunity to liberalize Mode 4; several issues need clarification

Several issues relating to the coverage of Mode 4 need clarification during the negotiations. The first is employment by foreign nationals in domestically owned firms in the host country. From the practical national policy perspective, there may be no distinction as to whether a person engaged to work for a firm enters under a service contract or an employment contract. This is important for developing countries because most of the current movements are made possible through employment contracts (for example, with respect to the Philippines, it was found that close to 99 per cent of their current outward flows have been effected through employment contracts). It would be useful to clarify this issue, as developing countries have a strong interest in a wide coverage of Mode 4, particularly in respect of contractual service suppliers. Second, there is the related issue of what constitutes a service for this impact on the coverage of the General Agreement on Trade in Services. The case of temporary agricultural labourers and manufacturing workers providing services incidental to agriculture or manufactures is also relevant to Mode 4. Consequently, one suggestion is to expand Mode 4 coverage beyond service suppliers to include workers related to agriculture and manufacturing. The language of the General Agreement on Trade in Services and its Annex on Mode 4 allows the above-mentioned categories. Such broad coverage would also cater to the commercial reality of trade in services through Mode 4 and migration regimes.

Some initiatives to liberalize Mode 4 have been undertaken, but more are desirable in order to broaden the scope of commitments and to reduce national treatment limitations

In the negotiations in the World Trade Organization, initial offers in respect of liberalizing Mode 4 have not been very promising (see annex to the present chapter). However, some countries have already made offers on categories that are delinked from commercial presence and that can be of benefit to developing countries (see annex for the main issues under negotiation). Some countries have also eliminated nationality requirements and clarified the application of economic needs tests. This suggests there is room for further progress. To this end, the ongoing negotiations should address the following issues:

Broadening the scope of commitments by: *(a) Expanding the scope and coverage of commitments* beyond those linked to commercial presence, so as to include commitment on contractual services suppliers (for both employees of juridical persons and independent service providers) covering all levels of skills;[10] (b) *expanding the sectors* to which such commitments apply. There is a need as well to agree on *common categories* (preferably based on the International Labour Organization (ILO) International Standard Classification of Occupations) and, to incorporate movements involving the less skilled. In cases where the commitment is confined to specific sectors/subsectors, those sectors that would benefit developing countries most (for example, tourism, construction, maintenance work and cleaning services, among others) should be taken into account. *Common definitions* for each category are also desirable, as this contributes to the predictability of commitments and would better facilitate cross references to national legislation and administrative procedures.

National treatment limitations. Current schedules also contain additional requirements on nationality and residency, wage parity and social security contributions. The requirements on the latter two, as they are aimed at cost equalization, undermine the comparative advantage of developing-country service providers and should also be addressed. The portability of social security insurance or the refund of payments has been suggested.

Schemes to facilitate entry. This includes such suggestions as a model schedule for members' Mode 4 commitments, adopting a General Agreement on Trade in Services or service provider visa,[11] elimination of ENTs, formulating multilateral guidelines on the application of economic needs tests and rationalizing and facilitating developing countries' participation in mutual recognition arrangements (MRAs). Suggestions have also been made relating to deriving lessons from bilateral labour arrangements, particularly on the aspect of extracting obligations/commitments from source (sending) countries to cooperate with regard to assessing and vouching for the character and qualification of the service supplier and ensuring his or her temporary stay in the host country.

Measures are needed to facilitate entry under Mode 4, possibly in the form of a General Agreement on Trade in Services Visa or the elimination of economic needs tests

Improving transparency. To improve transparency, existing regulations, including barriers and limitations relating to the movement of natural persons, should be reflected in countries' commitments, either as a part of market access/national treatment or, if appropriate, as an additional commitment column or in the form of a reference paper. With regard to better operationalizing Mode 4 commitments, suggestions have been made for countries to provide detailed information to the World Trade Organization, in a consolidated form, of all measures (particularly administrative measures) pertaining to the temporary admission of natural persons covered by commitments. The consolidated form could include information on the material or evidence required for an applicant seeking temporary admission as well as a description of the complete process for its submission, consideration and approval, as well as a full description of the manner in which any limitations to market access and national treatment in respect of the temporary entry of natural persons are administered by the country's authorities.

In addition to the above, the following could help lay the groundwork for negotiations on Mode 4 (UNCTAD, 2003):

Concerned bodies and organizations need to continue their dialogue on Mode 4, and relevant statistics need to be strengthened and harmonized

- Continuing the dialogue on conceptual, policy, legal, institutional and administrative frameworks facilitating movement of natural persons to supply services as a means of regularly exchanging information including research, updating experiences, and sharing best practices. This could involve multiple organizations dealing directly or indirectly with the movement of people or those interested in the issue such as UNCTAD, the International Organization for Migration (IOM), ILO and the World Trade Organization and stakeholders: government representatives (relevant ministries as well as regulators), the private sector, non-governmental organizations, the service providers and, to some extent, academia;

- Contributing to the improvement of statistics on Mode 4 to ensure that negotiations proceed in an informed manner and based on a common set of measurements. The compilation of the *Manual on Statistics of International Trade in Services* should serve as an initial step in compiling and harmonizing data that are necessary for a meaningful assessment of the liberalization of trade in services;
- Contributing to the strengthening of capacities of developing-country Governments in managing the trade agenda surrounding the issues of Mode 4, including providing support for the following:
    - Sequencing of the implementation of domestic policy reforms, and ensuring a steady supply of healthy members of the population and an educated and skilled workforce by investing in human capital including ensuring access to education, sanitation, clean water and basic health care.
    - Formulation of innovative employment policies and training programmes, including upgrading human resources aimed at strengthening competitiveness and boosting export opportunities that could be realized only with more liberal Mode 4 commitments.
    - Establishment of appropriate structures and framework to properly manage the movement of natural persons, including addressing issues of return migration, brain drain, maximization of the gains from remittances, and cushioning the social and economic effects of such movements on the service provider and his family.
    - Creation of institutional capacities to allow recognition of qualifications at all levels in those services with export potential through this Mode.

Much work needs to be done at the national level as well

- Analyzing national and existing regional experiences in the treatment and liberalization of Mode 4 in schemes relating to integration, free trade areas and bilateral agreements in order to draw lessons for the treatment of the movement of natural persons at the multilateral level.

Outsourcing: an alternative way of taking advantage of wage differentials

Business practice outsourcing (BPO) is a leading alternative to Mode 4 trade

Increase in the scope of operations and the interest in maximizing gains have led some large companies to outsource entire business functions, a practice sometimes called offshoring. Studies have shown that taking advantage of the low-cost quality service offered by skilled and specialized workers can reduce operation costs by up to 60 per cent for some companies. Some developing countries (India, China, the Philippines and some Caribbean States) have taken advantage of this opportunity to emerge as major players in business process outsourcing (BPO), providing services such as software application and development, and finance and account management services. It is estimated that global outsourcing expenditures, currently amounting to $320 billion (2003) will grow to $827 in 2008. Expenditure for global outsourcing of computer software and services is expected to increase from $10 billion in 2003 to $31 billion in 2008, representing a 26 per cent annual growth rate.

One major concern raised with regard to outsourcing relates to employment dislocation and job migration from home countries to host countries, and the increasing wage differential between low-skill and high-skill labour in the home countries. Forrester Research (2002) estimates that offshore outsourcing will displace 3.3 million jobs from the United States to developing countries by 2015 and of these, 2.31 million jobs are expected to go to India. This is equivalent to US$ 136 billion in wages, a staggering figure compared with that of only US$ 4 billion in 2000.

There are major concerns that outsourcing can lead to permanent loss of jobs in countries that outsource

However, some other studies have shown that demand for United States services remains high and actually increased between 1997 and 2003. The United States runs a trade surplus in high-value services including financial, legal, engineering and software development. Companies likewise still undertake much at their headquarters, as there are intrinsic limits to the number and types of jobs that can be moved offshore. This means that job growth in white-collar occupations deemed to be at risk from outsourcing (which growth is at present actually expanding) will continue to expand (for example, the number of computer and mathematics-related occupations was up by 6 per cent and the number of business and financial occupations was up by 9 per cent in the period 1999-2003).

However, countries that have come to depend heavily on business process outsourcing continue to enjoy high domestic demand for services

Amid concerns on the negative impact of offshoring, studies show that countries could actually benefit from its impact on increasing productivity, reducing inflation and increasing the purchasing power of consumers. Estimates indicate that for every dollar of outsourcing by United States companies to India, the United States gains 67 cents in savings and direct returns and an additional 45 cents in new value from redeploying United States labour (that is to say, $1.12 or 79 per cent of the total gains), while India gains 33 cents per dollar in terms of increased employment and investment. Moreover, it is estimated that the boost in economic activity arising from improved productivity generated 90,000 net additional jobs in the United States in 2003; this figure is forecast to rise to 317,000 in 2008.

Some analyse projects that countries that use business process outsourcing will gain in terms of economic growth and also in terms of job creation

Some sectors of the economy will have to bear losses but gains, on the whole, will be greater, especially for developing countries that are able to take advantage of the opportunities provided by offshoring. Financial and technology transfer gains feed into investments and other productive activities, generating employment and improving developing-country Governments' overall capacity to fulfil their development goals.

Conclusions

It is widely recognized that a liberalization of the movement of people (workers and services providers) that is not for resettlement purposes would result in gains to the world economy and especially to most developing countries. Some observers have argued that such gains would be greater than the total gains expected from all of the other initiatives under discussion in the Doha work programme.

Improving the way temporary migrant flows are managed is a promising option. A step forward would be to implement such arrangements for the less skilled. This is already being achieved to a certain degree with seasonal workers, mostly in agriculture, who are brought in annually to perform specific tasks that last only a few months. The movement of unskilled workers from developing to developed countries promises to yield the greatest gains because this is where the difference between factor prices is largest and where there is considerable scope for movement. For example, one study computed gains of some $200 billion annually if a temporary work visa scheme was designed and adopted multilaterally so that skilled and unskilled workers from developing countries (with a quota

There are great unrealized potential gains to the world economy in the further liberalization of temporary labour migration

set at 3 per cent of a developed country's labour force) would be allowed employment in developed countries for from three to five years and replaced by a new wave of inflows at the end of their assignment (Rodrik, 2002).

One important deterrent to such liberalization is the concern that temporary labour migrants may become permanent immigrants

Nevertheless, segments of the native population remain cautious as to the effectiveness of existing domestic migration policies and mechanisms to properly manage temporary migration. Indeed, the fear that temporary movements are just the first step towards permanent resettlement in the host country remains. This sentiment tends to be correlated with the vicissitudes of the business cycle; and during downturns, pressures for reducing the entry of foreign workers/service providers increase. However, reducing or shutting down temporary movement of services suppliers would reduce a country's growth potential and is not likely to be the best way forward; furthermore, such an approach is also unlikely to succeed in deterring people from moving (except at considerable cost in terms of enforcement). It may, on the contrary, act as an incentive to illegal migration (which also gives rise to negative reactions but is more difficult to manage).

Participants in temporary labour migration programmes (employers and migrant workers) have strong incentives with respect to a worker's converting to permanent status

Concerns regarding the duration of stay of workers/service providers are partly legitimate. Foreign workers/service providers often have an incentive to shift from a temporary to a permanent status, and employers have an incentive for them to do so. For their part, the employers become dependent on these workers/service providers, who often accept lower wages than natives and are less likely to leave for better alternatives. For their part, with weak enforcement of policies and the existence of a labour market for illegal entrants, these workers/service providers are able to stay beyond the expiration of their permit to obtain maximum benefit from their move. Temporary work programmes must recognize that some immigrants will move from being temporary to becoming more permanent and thus must provide for such an eventuality by channelling otherwise unauthorized migrants into legal status. They have to act, at the same time, in response to the above-mentioned incentives of employers and immigrants.

A crucial issue is how well temporary labour migration programmes are managed

In considering how to improve the management of migration, three principles should be kept in mind. First, government policies make a difference in respect of how migrants arrive and in what numbers, how they are treated within the country, and whether they return or stay. Second, the overall economic benefits of moving workers over borders are positive, since individual migrants and their employers become better off and world gross domestic product (GDP) rises as more workers obtain higher-wage jobs. Third, legal and orderly labour migration is best for all parties.

Both improved enforcement immigration regulations and economic incentives may be used in temporary labour migration programme management

Policy can create incentives for the different parties—employers and migrants in particular—to respect temporary migration programmes. Such mechanisms could either involve improved enforcement or be economic in nature. For example, the bilateral agreement between Canada and Mexico on the provision of seasonal agricultural workers provides an example of how enforcement can be used effectively; most likely neither the Government of Mexico nor the seasonal migrants are willing to take the risk of jeopardizing the future of the programme. In many cases, however, enforcement may be difficult or costly and economic incentives may be preferable.

Economic incentives can apply to either the employer or the migrant. For example, many existing programmes require that the employer provide a justification for why he/she is recruiting abroad rather than domestically, for example, by requesting that the employer prove the non-availability of natives suitable for the job. However, as long as there is an economic advantage for the employer to recruit abroad, he/she will find ways to do so. Alternatively, one could think of measures that reduce such an advantage, for example, a tax on the recruitment of migrants—one that is small enough not to discourage recruitment abroad if absolutely necessary but high enough to discourage firms from recruiting only from abroad. A caveat is that such a measure would work only if illegal recruitment of migrants was not an option.

Other incentives could be designed to encourage migrants to return to their home country at the end of the contract; for example, certain taxes and other, similar payments levied during their stay (notably those levied for social security and pension purposes) could be wholly or partially refunded or forced savings could be accumulated and held, either in the host country or in the country of origin. Such arrangements would both promote the voluntary return of migrants and provide financial capital for use in the home country. However, such schemes also provide an incentive for immigrants wishing to remain in the host country on a long-term basis to switch to illegal employment early in their stay in order that a smaller amount of savings might be forfeited. As an alternative, the onus of ensuring that workers return could be put on employers, who could also have to show that they are not recruiting illegal workers.[12]

There is a range of economic incentives available to encourage migrants to return to their country of origin

Another approach is to select private contractors to provide the migrant workforce in order to ensure better adherence to the rules of the game and to protect migrants from being exploited.[13] In the Persian Gulf States, for example, more than 1 million workers stayed for short periods of employment during the two decades of the construction boom that followed the oil price increase of 1973.

An alternative way of exploiting gains from trade is through Mode 4 of the General Agreement on Trade in Services which entails the movement of natural persons for the purpose of providing a service. Significant potential gains from relaxing the conditions for movement of persons, especially the less skilled, have been established. Developing countries have also indicated this to be among their key export interests and it is in this regard that realizing a commercially meaningful liberalization of the conditions for movement of natural persons under the General Agreement on Trade in Services would constitute "a litmus test for the development content of the Doha Work Programmme" (United Nations Conference on Trade and Development, 2003).

Another way of exploiting gains from trade is through General Agreement on Trade in Services Mode 4

To date, however, exploiting trade gains through Mode 4 remains among the more neglected aspects of globalization. Progress in the negotiations on Mode 4 is moving at a very slow pace. However, small and positive developments are being observed as reflected, for example, by the offers being made related to contractual service suppliers and the continuous engagement in discussions on how best to reconcile domestic immigration concerns and the pressure to liberalize the movement of people. The growing involvement of immigration officials in discussions relating to the movement of natural persons is a positive step and contributes significantly to building confidence and assuaging fears relating to domestic pressures and concerns associated with migration (especially permanent migration).

Progress in negotiations on Mode 4 has moved slowly

Moreover, there is interest among both developed and developing countries in easing some administrative hurdles relating to the entry of foreign service providers through greater transparency of rules and regulations. There are also exchanges pertaining to adopting within the framework of the General Agreement on Trade in Services some elements of bilateral and regional arrangements on facilitating movement of people. Key to the success of these arrangements is the sharing of responsibility by both the sending and the receiving countries with respect to the orderly movement of people (which would include pre-deployment screening and ensuring return). If such sharing of responsibility could be effected within the context of the General Agreement on Trade in Services (and if, at the same time, issues related to most favoured nation status could be satisfactorily tackled), more significant progress with regard to extracting more liberal Mode 4 commitments would be foreseeable.

The potential of Mode 4 remains very great

Ultimately, the goal is to create an international framework for trade in services that is fair, equitable, balanced, more open, more predictable and more transparent. With the liberalization of temporary movement of service workers, especially movements of semi- and less-skilled personnel, globalization could claim to have been a "force for good" (Department of Trade and Industry, United Kingdom, 2004) for both developing and developed countries.

Notes

1 Students are also considered temporary migrants, but this category will not be analysed. Another category, which includes working holidaymakers, permits partial access to the labour market and generally does not require a minimum level of education. Several countries members of the Organisation for Economic Cooperation and Development (OECD) have bilateral agreements relating to this type of temporary entry in order to increase mobility among member countries (see SOPEMI (Continuous Reporting System on Migration), 2004).

2 Unauthorized international migrants who stay in a host country for a short duration of time are not considered here.

3 The full text of the General Agreement on Trade in Services is available from http://www.wto.org/english/tratop_e/serv_e/gatsintr_e.htm (accessed 15 November 2004).

4 These data record only documented migrants; there are also unskilled workers who cross national boundaries to work for temporary periods without going through formal channels. In some countries, these flows probably exceed the number of officially recorded temporary unskilled migrants.

5 Anecdotal evidence from sending countries reveals, however, that some receiving countries use the "trainee" category as a backdoor through which to take in more foreign workers who are then made to perform menial tasks, or work as "entertainers". This constitutes a violation of their contract but the foreign workers remain silent because they have an interest in working in the foreign territory.

6 The other modes are: Mode 1 (cross-border supply), covering the flow of a service from the territory of one member into the territory of any other member; Mode 2 (consumption abroad), covering the situation where a service consumer of one member moves into the territory of another member to obtain a service; and Mode 3 (commercial presence), covering the establishment by the service supplier of one member of a commercial presence in the territory of another member (see World Trade Organization (1999), pp. 286-287).

7 The contract is between the home country company and a host country consumer (juridical contractual service supplier).

8 However, services delivered through Mode 3, by their very nature, generate more economic value because of the sheer bulk of upstream and downstream activities involved in setting up a commercial presence.

9 Some countries' schedule of commitments makes access of foreign suppliers conditional on the employer's paying the same level of wage he would give to locals/residents. Analysts have contended that this erodes the comparative advantage of developing countries in providing low-cost but high-quality service and thus diminishes the motivation of employers to seek for alternative sources of service providers (unless there is clearly an absence of any local who could provide the same service).

10 Commitments on contract service suppliers (CSS) can actually be made to apply horizontally, as services provided by service suppliers on the basis of a contract can cut across activities (including those incidental to agriculture and manufacturing) and sectors. This category can also be genuinely temporary, as the contract is tied to specific duration.

11 Driven by regulatory and security concerns associated with the freer mobility of service providers, such a scheme would seek to differentiate between permanent and temporary movement and would relax entry conditions for the latter. Some countries have been undertaking reforms in facilitating the processing of work permits. The United Kingdom is a good example and, lately, Switzerland has announced that the canton of Zürich is now implementing an e-permit system that allows the processing of work permits within 48 hours, provided that the required documentation is complete.

12 As is the case, for example, in Greece and Israel (ILO, 2004).

13 As this channel of recruitment has allowed exploitation of migrants, the selectivity of organizations is recommended.

Annex
Status of negotiations in the World Trade Organization on Mode 4 of the General Agreement on Trade in Services

Current negotiating proposals: a brief overview[a]

Seven negotiating proposals relating to Mode 4 have been discussed in the negotiations in the World Trade Organization. A summary of the major points raised in these submissions are presented below.

In current negotiations on Mode 4, the United States of America, the European Communities and Canada all call for strengthening regulatory disciplines and greater transparency

The papers from the United States of America (World Trade Organization, 2000b), the European Communities (World Trade Organization, 2001a) and Canada (World Trade Organization, 2001b) all recognize the sensitive nature of the movement of natural persons and thus call for strengthening regulatory disciplines and enhancing transparency to ensure the implementation of market access commitments. The United States proposal stresses the need for improved access to information and ensuring procedural transparency which it believes could affect the ability of natural persons to compete as service suppliers in the potential host-country market. The United States also suggests the adoption of a "tailored approach" to the horizontal restrictions on the movement of natural persons which is a highly regulated area of trade in services.

The European Communities has focused on intra-corporate transferees and contract suppliers

In various communications, the European Communities has established parameters for discussions on Mode 4 liberalization, that is to say, it would limit discussions to only those that relate to the temporary movement of intra-corporate transferees, as well as contract suppliers.[b] It equally stresses that discussions on the temporary movement of service suppliers is a sensitive subject because of the importance countries attach to regulating the presence of foreigners in their territory (World Trade Organization, 2001a). The European Communities paper also suggests the following: harmonization of definitions and/or description of the Mode 4 categories specifically in the context of intra-corporate transferees; specification of unspecified labour-market tests from future commitments to ensure effective application of Mode 4 liberalization; and rendering economic needs tests more specific, transparent and non-discriminatory.

Canada suggested a broad improvement in Mode 4 commitments

Canada's proposal expresses the need to strengthen the transparency obligations of the General Agreement on Trade in Services which it perceives would benefit, in particular, individual service suppliers and small and medium-sized enterprises (SMEs). It suggests that countries should improve their Mode 4 commitments, both horizontal and sectoral, and that countries should make commitments on general business visitors and on professionals including those entering on a contractual basis and not linked to commercial presence. Specifically to improve transparency and predictability of existing and new Mode 4 commitments, countries should look into: immigration laws and regulations, including procedural information related to temporary movement; available foreign worker programmes and their entry criteria; applicable conditions for economic needs tests; and maximum duration of stay and market access limitations as cited in commitments (World Trade Organization, 2001b).

Japan focused on intra-corporate transferees

The Japanese proposal, which focuses on the reduction of limitations on intra-corporate transferees, calls for greater transparency and better facilitation of immigration procedures relating to the movement of temporary workers. It also calls upon countries to endeavour to limit the use of economic needs tests or, if this is unavoidable, to specify clear criteria for their application (World Trade Organization, 2001c).

Among other things, India proposed the introduction of a special General Agreement on Trade in Services visa

The communication from India (World Trade Organization, 2000a) proposes the inclusion of a separate category on individual professionals and delinking their movements to Mode 3. India also suggests the introduction of a special General Agreement on Trade in Services visa to cover the movements of temporary service providers and to differentiate them from permanent flows which should be the only ones that go through the normal immigration procedures. The Indian proposal has also recommended the following: developing more specific, finer classifications and wider coverage of personnel categories; using the International Standard Classification of Occupations as a basis for expanding the coverage of foreign worker movement (in other world, for including mid- and lower-level professionals); and establishing disciplines relating to economic needs tests as well as multilateral norms on recognition of academic and work-related qualifications to ensure transparency, minimize discretion and maintain a greater degree of certainty. India also reiterated the need for an assessment of Mode 4 liberalization to determine the extent to which the objectives of article IV of the General Agreement on Trade in Services have been met.

These negotiating proposals all seek to address certain aspects of liberalizing Mode 4 trade. Some specifically address issues relating to the broadening and deepening of Mode 4 commitments, while others suggest means by which movements could be better facilitated including through delinking Mode 4 from commercial presence (Mode 3). In the offers stage of the services negotiations,[c] countries are expected to address these concerns, including requests put forward by developing countries in particular.

Offers

As of September 2004, 12 members of the World Trade Organization had made public offers on liberalizing trade in services

As of September 2004, 48 members of the World Trade Organization (62 countries if members of the European Communities are counted individually) had submitted initial offers relating to the liberalization of trade in services. Of the 47, only 12 had made their offers public. Some preliminary analysis of the publicly available offers indicate improvements of the following nature: inclusion of additional categories of natural persons or provision of detailed definitions for each category; extension of the duration of stay; providing criteria for the application of economic needs test requirements; and eliminating previously existing limitations (for example, those relating to work permit, qualification, educational requirements, nationality requirements, etc.).

Some countries made new or improved commitments on contractual service suppliers

Some countries have made new commitments or improved existing commitments on contractual service suppliers (CSS), both for independent providers and for employees of service suppliers, by providing extensions for their length of stay, allowing for the renewal of permits or including more subsectors where CSS commitments apply. Commitments on CSS are of interest, especially to some developing countries, as CSS movements are delinked from Mode 3 and movements of semi- and low-skilled workers may be negotiated under CSS (depending on the sectors/subsectors that countries are willing to commit on). Criteria for the application of economic needs tests have also been indicated in some of the offers.

In an initial assessment of offers, a group of 18 developing countries argue that current offers do not present significant improvements over existing Mode 4 commitments. Only a few of the offers presented new categories delinked from commercial presence, whereas developing countries have consistently reiterated that they could benefit more if countries opened up their markets to categories such as contractual service suppliers and independent service providers. In addition, a significant number of horizontal and sectoral limitations that countries maintain have not been removed. The issuance of work permits and visa procedures have not been addressed in any of the offers, even amid requests from some developing countries that this concern be addressed through improved transparency in countries' regulations (which could be scheduled under the Additional Commitments column) or the introduction of a General Agreement on Trade in Services visa or a service provider visa.

In general, developing countries have viewed the new offers as affording little improvement

The outlook for Mode 4

Discussions in the Council for Trade in Services

In July 2003, 15 developing country countries circulated to the Council for Trade in Services a paper on "Proposed liberalization of Mode 4 under GATS negotiations". The paper highlighted the bias in current commitments in favour of movements linked to commercial presence and the need for countries to remedy this imbalance by making meaningful commitments on other categories of service providers delinked from commercial presence (for example, independent professionals and other contractual service suppliers). The paper also stressed the need to complement countries' horizontal commitments with specific sectoral commitments for deeper liberalization or the inclusion of categories of persons not covered in the horizontal section. Other elements included:

In the Council for Trade in Services, 15 developing countries have called for greater liberalization of Mode 4, beyond services linked to a commercial presence

- Addressing administrative procedures relating to visas and work permits, transparency of regulations and economic needs tests, with the aim of facilitating rather than impeding the entry of foreign service providers.
- Dealing with the recognition of qualifications through any of the following: (a) the development of disciplines under article VI, paragraph 4, of the General Agreement on Trade in Services; (b) undertaking additional commitments under article XVIII; (c) strengthening the framework for recognition agreements under article VII of the Agreement; and (d) considering a model schedule to provide a framework for uniformity in commitments.

In addition to this formal venue, there is also a group organized by some countries called Friends of Mode 4 where Mode 4-related issues are discussed.

Where can progress be made?

Both developed and developing countries in the World Trade Organization recognize the importance of facilitating Mode 4 trade and the interest on both sides in moving the negotiations forward.

Additional commitments on categories of persons covered

Most developed countries wish to broaden commitments on employees of service suppliers, whereas developing countries seek more meaningful commitments on movements that are not linked to commercial presence for example, those of contractual service suppliers (especially independent service suppliers), and on the inclusion of semi- or low-skilled persons. However, demand for such lower-skilled services as construction services, caregiving and household help from both developed and developing countries is currently met through bilateral or regional arrangements. One reason for not binding such commitments under the General Agreement on Trade in Services is flexibility: bilateral arrangements are easier to manage and negotiate and countries do not face the danger of being subjected to the Dispute Settlement Body of the World Trade Organization. Some countries are also more open to making binding commitments on professionals or highly skilled persons because there is a higher probability that they will return to their home country rather than become permanent immigrants.

There is need to broaden the categories of persons covered under Mode 4 trade, and to reach common agreement on the definitions of categories of persons covered

It has been suggested that there should be a template for the categories of persons covered and the International Labour Organization (ILO) International Standard Classification of Occupations has been suggested as providing a means of broadening those categories and skill levels that could be negotiated. A concern was expressed that using the classification would complicate matters, given the lack of concordance with existing national classification systems. A common understanding needs to be developed in establishing clear definitions of categories of persons covered, including those covered in the horizontal commitments (for example, business visitors, intra-corporate transferees and contractual service suppliers), and establishing their correspondence with national immigration regimes.

Movements towards meaningful commitments for contractual service suppliers is possible[d] but there is a need for a unified stance and further concrete requests by developing countries in respect of seeking real and effective market access.

Eliminating/reducing other forms of limitations

In their offers, countries have made limited progress in reducing such barriers to Mode 4 trade as citizenship requirements and use of economic needs tests

Countries in their offers had, to some limited extent, responded to the call to reduce other Mode 4 trade barriers (including nationality and citizenship requirements, application of economic needs tests, compulsory hiring of local staff, and quotas). Other areas where countries could seek improvements include: pre-employment requirements and the duration of stay for each category of service providers; discriminatory taxes; wage parity conditions; and compulsory social security contributions.

Mutual recognition arrangements (MRAs)

The assessment of qualifications and skills may facilitate or impede entry. Depending on the approach used, the service provider may obtain a job commensurate with his/her qualifications or end up in a less desirable position.

It would be highly beneficial to enhance arrangements for the mutual recognition of educational qualifications

Article VII of the General Agreement on Trade in Services permits countries to enter into bilateral or plurilateral mutual recognition arrangements and to deviate from the most-favoured-nation (MFN) principle in this matter. However, article VII also obliges countries to notify of existing mutual recognition arrangements and those under negotiation and to provide an opportunity for other countries to negotiate their accession or negotiate comparable agreements. So far, there have only been 39 notifications by 19 countries of the World Trade Organization, but this number does not reflect the total number of mutual recognition arrangements negotiated. The overall objective of notifications is to increase transparency in this area; and achieving timely and comprehensive notifications is in the interest of developing countries. The development of disciplines under article VI, paragraph 4, of the Agreement to determine the discriminatory nature of a domestic regulation would also enhance the possibilities for the recognition of qualifications, but only when basic definitions had been agreed upon.

Mutual recognition arrangements are most often concluded between countries with relatively similar training systems and regulatory regimes and to date have been forged mainly by developed-country partners. The fact that acceding to an existing mutual recognition arrangement could be difficult for countries that lack national recognition systems, professional bodies and/or industry associations, explains the call by developing countries for multilateral guidelines on mutual recognition arrangements. While the current issue relates to the recognition of earned degrees (or diplomas), it would benefit developing countries if the recognition of experience and other non-educational aspects, as well as qualifications for groups other than those of highly skilled professionals, was tackled at the multilateral level. In line with this, developing countries could benefit from obtaining information at the multilateral level on qualification requirements and procedures and information specifying the hierarchy of measures required to obtain such recognition, and the ways to expedite the processing of licences, authorizations and the recognition of qualifications, and associated fees.

Transparency

Some countries have highlighted (in their proposals relating to Mode 4, or in separate papers) the need to provide for full transparency regarding the domestic regulatory framework in order to facilitate the movement of service providers. Canada has suggested that countries provide footnotes in their commitments on where to obtain information for each category of person with commitments in the schedule in order to make the regulatory context of a particular commitment transparent and to clarify its relationship with the corresponding parts of the national administrative rules and regulations (Government of Canada, 2003).[e] This would be the same information that a country could expect to receive from the official inquiry point of another country if a request was lodged under paragraph 4 of article III of the General Agreement on Trade in Services (Transparency).

Other possible approaches

Other approaches proposed include specific arrangements for short-term visits for trade in services, a General Agreement on Trade in Services visa and standardization of transparency commitments

A model schedule for adoption by countries making Mode 4 commitments has been suggested, one that might embody the following key elements (Mattoo Chauduri and self, 2003):

(a) Full market access and national treatment commitments for: (i) short-term intra-company visits; (ii) short-term visits to fulfil contracts as an employee and; (iii) short-term visits to fulfil contracts independently;

(b) A General Agreement on Trade in Services visa[f] with the following key elements: (i) limited to persons with demonstrated qualifications; (ii) proof of contract and citizenship; (iii) fees that reflect costs; (iv) three-year validity, for no more than one year at a time; (v) no wage parity conditions; (vi) stays under categories (ii) and (iii) above may be subject to renewal, but upon proof of terms and conditions, value or invitation; (vii) no change of status to another non-immigrant visa category; (viii) issuance of visa under categories (i) and (ii) without unreasonable delay; (ix) special safeguards against fraudulent use by companies; and (x) a penalty (for example, a one-year suspension for abuse under categories (i) and (ii)).

(c) An annex or additional commitments on transparency and regulation with the following elements: (i) publication in consolidated form of all pertinent measures; (ii) opportunity for prior comment on proposed changes in regimes; (iii) use of international standards for qualifications, as available, unless departure is justified, or alternatively, some tests of competence; (iv) training and experience, where necessary, to make up objectively verifiable deficiencies in education.

The model schedule addresses concerns relating to existing barriers to the movement of natural persons and suggests ways of facilitating such movement. Since the model schedule is intended for acceptance by the entire World Trade Organization membership, it is expected to be "balanced" in terms of its expectations or requirements from countries. For instance, in terms of categories, full market access and national treatment are limited to three sets of service providers (and these do not directly pertain to low-skilled movements as well). The General Agreement on Trade in Services visa to facilitate entry and transparency were also included as key elements. It remains to be seen how countries will respond to the suggested model when it is formally proposed.

Linkages between Mode 4 and other Modes

Mode 4 trade is important not only in its own right but also because of the interlinkages with other Modes (Chanda, 2003).

An increase in trade under Mode 4 tends to bring about increases in trade under Mode 1 and in foreign direct investment (FDI)

A study of the relationship between trade in services under Mode 4 and under the other modes (World Trade Organization, 2004)[g] found that a 10 per cent increase in the temporary movement of people increased imports of services under Mode 1[h] by 3.1 per cent and increased exports by 2.9 per cent, and was correlated with an increase of 8 per cent in inflows and 3.5 per cent in outflows of foreign direct investment (FDI) (a proxy for trade in services under Mode 3). The magnitude of the estimated impact of the movement of persons on FDI flows can be explained in part by the fact that the relationship between FDI and Mode 4 runs in two directions: larger temporary movements of persons lead to larger flows of FDI and vice versa. No significant relationship was found between services trade under Mode 2 and that under Mode 4.

FDI may be viewed as a proxy for Mode 3 trade

The linkage between Mode 4 and Mode 3 is well-documented, with increasing intra-corporate movements serving as proof that countries wish to encourage FDI flows into their economies and thus want to facilitate corporate transfers and entry of business visitors to establish commercial presence. Mode 3 trade has limited value for developing countries given that, generally, they do not have the financial strength to set up commercial presence. As to the Mode 2-Mode 4 connection, the circulation of a country's nationals in other countries is a marketing opportunity that could lead to increased tourism and consumption of health services, for instance.

The growing trend towards outsourcing of services and the current and projected shortage of workers in most developed countries (10 million in the United States in 2001) provide opportunities for the expansion of both Mode 4 and Mode 1 trade, while outsourcing has given rise to increased interest in the linkages between the two Modes, since developing countries host most of the services that are currently outsourced by developed countries. Host economies benefit from outsourcing in a number of ways including, among others, employment creation and diversification, higher wage rates, and increased possibilities for strategic investments (including local subsidiaries, joint ventures and the establishment of research and development (R&D) centres), and there are other spillover benefits from the transfer and upgrading of skills and technology and gains from consumption by outsourcing firms.

Growth in outsourcing provides opportunities for expansion of Mode 4 trade

Countries that outsource activities also benefit, mostly through reduced costs, estimated to range from 40 to 60 per cent for developed-country firms. Banking and financial services in the United States are reported to have benefited by about $8 billion in 2001-2003 from outsourcing in India. Outsourcing activities lead to increased productivity, for example, increased average speed of response at call centres, reduction in the number of errors in data processing, and better quality of transcription.

There are also concerns about job displacement resulting from outsourcing. The validity of such concerns, however, is not borne out by employment data which show that the highest job losses are still in manufacturing and "management occupations".

Linkages between Mode 4 and Mode 1 should be viewed in the context of whether the two modes are substitutable or complementary (Chanda, 2003). Substitutability or complementarity depends in large part on the activity that is being outsourced and the level of the service provider that is involved. As one moves up the value chain in Mode 1 supply of services, the relationship between Modes 1 and 4 becomes more complementary.

Higher-value outsourced activities are more complementary to Mode 4 trade

Low-value outsourcing activities (involving call centres, billing, processing, and transcription typing services) are expected to substitute (but not completely) for local jobs in the outsourcing country; this therefore indirectly affects the movement of natural persons, if there are shortages in the latter. Some personnel movement is still expected, with companies sending some staff, usually at the managerial and technical levels, to the client site for familiarization with client procedures and work processes.

As countries move up to higher-value outsourcing and business process outsourcing activities, their need for cross-border mobility of labour will not diminish, but rather shift towards higher-level service providers (for example, business visitors and intra-company transferees). Countries engaged in outsourcing activities may strive to move towards higher-end services, as they are likely to face fewer restrictions on the movement of such service providers. They are also less likely to face opposition in terms of their perceived threat to local jobs in the outsourcing economy, as the volumes involved will be smaller and will concern only specialized and niche services. The threat of unemployment arising from both Modes 1 and 4 is likely to be greatest for low-value outsourcing, where the volumes are larger and job relocation to low-cost centres is directly visible.

In a broader context, it was recognized that liberalization of Mode 4 would be beneficial to all trading partners and, under certain conditions, would also be beneficial because of its linkages with Modes 1, 2 and 3. Consequently, market access barriers to Mode 4 affect the development of Mode 1 trade and the execution of some types of outsourcing contracts (those with higher value added). Limitations across Modes include

In the broader context, liberalization of Mode 4 would benefit all trading partners

recognition requirements, licensing, nationality and residency requirements, commercial presence requirements and other requirements related to security (data protection, liability, privacy).

In order to facilitate trade related to Modes 1 and 4, it has been suggested that developing countries should seek unrestricted Mode 1 commitments on a formula basis or a positive sectoral list basis. They should prevent efforts to ban outsourcing through government and industry-level discussions, clarify categories and requirements for different visas, seek liberal market access conditions for intra-corporate transferees (in addition to independent professional and contractual service suppliers), delink Modes 1 and 4 from commercial presence, and seek transparency in the recognition and facilitation of mutual recognition arrangements.

Notes

a The countries included in this discussion are those that had submitted proposals specifically on the movement of natural persons. Kenya and Colombia, had also submitted proposals but they were very limited in scope and mostly focused on reiterating those countries' support for the broadening of Mode 4 commitments by members.

b Defined as employees of a company not established in the member's territory who supply services on the basis of a contract.

c The members of the World Trade Organization have adopted the request-offer process for this round of services negotiations where members are to submit confidential requests for liberalization to their choice of bilateral partner(s), after which offers will then be tabled. The indicative deadlines for requests and offers were June 2002 and July 2003, respectively, but members could still submit requests/offers as the negotiations continued.

d Most commitments on CSS apply only to a limited category of persons or subsectors, mostly under professional services (engineering, architectural services, urban planning) and computer-related services.

e The Mode 4 paper submitted by 15 members of the World Trade Organization to the Council for Trade in Services also mentioned transparency as one of the elements needed to facilitate the movement of natural persons.

f This idea originated in a suggestion by Mark Hatcher of the European Service Forum but was later picked up by other authors, including Aaditya Mattoo, Richard Self and Sumantha Chauduri. Because there is no differentiation with regard to the requirements for permanent and temporary movements, applications for short-term/temporary service providers become cumbersome and costly, especially for service providers who are entering only for short business visits. A General Agreement on Trade in Services visa is meant to tackle this problem.

g Bilateral trade in services under the various modes is modelled on the basis of the traditional gravity equation augmented by a measure of temporary movement of workers. Due to the lack of data, this study only refers to the United States and the United Kingdom.

h The value of commercial services imports under Mode 1 is calculated by subtracting the value of imports of travel services (Mode 2) from the value of total commercial services imports.

Chapter VI
Social dimensions of international mobility

Existing policy frameworks and ongoing public discussions focus on certain aspects of international migration such as the orderly management of international flows of migrants, the curtailment of undocumented migration, the discrimination against migrants, the benefits of remittances and the human capital effects of migration on countries of origin. By offering a social perspective on international mobility, the present chapter attempts to bring both the human and social dimensions into the discussion of migration. The key components of the complex dynamics of the social relationships among immigrants, and home and host societies are: the social networks of migration (see, for example, Woolcock and Narayan, 2000),[1] the integration of migrants in host societies, the effects of migration on the social fabric of societies, and the public perceptions of migration.

Social networks of migration

Kin and kith networks

The family plays a central role in the support of migrants

The family is the first link in the chain of entities that will likely support migrants in their journey to their projected destinations. In their home countries, the information, advice and economic and emotional support received by potential migrants from family members makes their trip possible. In countries of destination, migrants are hosted, receive job information, and are introduced to other migrants by family members. Nuclear and extended family members are usually the first to know when a family member has decided to migrate overseas; they can then be ready to provide any help for the migration journey. More importantly, migration is often organized as a family enterprise, in which support and responsibilities are allocated between the migrant and family members (Stark, 1991).

Members of the migrants' local community may strongly complement the family

However, potential migrants may also have the support of neighbourhood friends and friends from their jobs, particularly when family members do not always have all the available resources needed for the migration project. In general, and although there is not an overarching rule, immigrants coming from urban areas, and particularly the most educated ones, are more likely to use kith (friends and neighbours) networks than kin networks. Typically, however, a labour migrant uses all available networks to secure a place to live and a job at the destination. The support of kith networks, though perhaps more anonymous than that of family members, is key to reaching wider networks in host countries, particularly when destinations are large cities. Getting a better job by establishing contacts is linked to achieving greater possibilities of residing in a better neighbourhood, and goes hand in hand with reaching additional contacts key to making the immigrant's life easier by enabling him or her to set up a base for personal development in the host country (Tilly, 1988).

Networks of friends only complement family networks. Notwithstanding the limited reach of contacts through family members, family support involves strong social and economic responsibilities that migrants will honour as a sign of reciprocity and commitment to the family's future. Migrants become a form of social insurance for family members in home countries by repaying family loans gathered to fund migration costs, as well as by sending remittances for undertakings such as supporting the elderly, educating children, procuring health care, constructing a house and establishing a small business (Braw, Taylor and Rozelle, 2003).

Thus, if the general reason for migration lies in the differential in income levels between home and host countries, kin and kith networks are the key institutions that make migration flows possible. They facilitate migration by providing the resources necessary to make the migration project possible. They also sustain migration flows by engaging in social and economic projects at home (made possible, for example, through remittances sent for various purposes) and in host countries (for example, by bringing over more migrants); these projects may include the setting up of businesses in the former and/or the latter.

In general, kin play a more important role early in the migration process; networks of friends become increasingly important as the length of time spent in the host country increases

Migrants who are of urban origin and have higher education tend to rely relatively more on the support of friends than on family members; however, the duration of residence in the host country is also an important factor. The longer the migrant's stay at a destination, the more developed the network of friends and people. Family networks are crucial on arrival, but as time goes on, networks of friends assume higher importance. At the destination, friends from work and people coming from the same hometown get together to celebrate parties, to share information about jobs and housing, and to provide and to plan for providing economic support to each other.

Hometown associations

Migrant's social networks often take the form of hometown associations

It is in this context that migrants set up hometown associations in host countries. These help migrants not only to maintain and celebrate features of their original cultures but also to facilitate their institutional integration into the social milieu of host countries. Moreover, hometown associations organize social events for the purpose of collecting funds to send to hometowns for such undertakings as building a bridge, a school or a clinic, or helping in case of natural disasters.[2] These associations are crucial for understanding the transnational development of vibrant communities in home and host countries, while the synergy generated regarding community development goes beyond the individual efforts of migrants to send remittances to their families. A mixture of solidarity with their homeland and an eagerness to gain prestige in their place of origin motivates migrants to become engaged in the transnational activities of these associations (Guarnizo, 2003). On the other hand, migrant associations could have different objectives in different contexts. For example, Indian nationals who migrate to Gulf countries for temporary work have been able to establish associations of migrant workers even though many of these countries prohibit this type of organization. These associations are useful in preventing abuses, as exemplified by excessive costs charged by agencies processing documents for would-be migrants, wages lower than were promised before departure, sexual abuse of domestic workers and so on (D'Sami, 2000).

Hometown associations can strengthen migrants' social links both to their country of origin and in the host country

Hometown association networks are thus embedded in the exchange and flows of information, money, goods and people between home and host countries that are generated by migrants, migrants' families, home villagers and friends. Information about job situations, income levels, education and social mobility possibilities is shuttled back and forth between origins and destinations. Money is sent as remittances to families and hometowns from immigrants, associations and diasporas (see chap. IV) to improve social and economic development, and includes the funding of the immigration of other network members. Cars and electrical appliances are some of the goods that flow from host to home countries, while traditional ethnic food typically flows from home to host countries.

In sum, social networks are often the key link between migrants and the institutional milieu at destinations. They help migrants become familiar with labour markets and legal systems in host countries. Such social capital is the means by which immigrants can cope with the gyrations and ease the uncertainties of present-day flexible labour markets, ensuring a steadier flow of income for immigrants and families in home and/or at host countries. Thus, networks help to decrease the unemployment of their members, as well as offer socio-economic protection during times of financial stress to some of their members.

However, as much as social networks can be extremely useful for migrants' livelihoods, they may also have shortcomings and limitations. Migration of a family member means that, at least temporarily, there will be a break in the normal relations with the rest of the family, sometimes in respect of children and spouses. Family members will inevitably try to preserve from a distance the social interactions that they enjoyed before migration: they will attempt to maintain the strength of social ties, and exert the same control over economic projects, and the management and magnitude of resources after migration that they exerted before migration. This may now involve, for example, the question whether to use remittances in dollars or euros. Close attachments to ethnic networks, in particular, may inhibit immigrants from learning the language and contacting more resourceful networks at their destinations. Moreover, an immigrant may want to extend her/his networks and reach local citizens rather than remain in his or her original network, because being part of more established networks may open up the possibility of faster upward social mobility (Cordero-Guzman, Smith, Grosfoguel, 2002). The following section will extend the analysis of these processes by examining the integration of migrants in host countries, through, for example, language learning, job and legal issues, access to social services, etc.

In some situations, hometown networks may impede the development of migrants' links to the host society

Integration of migrants in host societies

The degree of integration of migrants into host societies largely depends on their command of the language of host countries, the availability of work generating a sufficient income, their legal status, their participation in civil and political life, their access to social services, and the possibilities for family reunification.

Education and language skills

Education is the basic social service that is the most widely available to all categories of migrants and migrants' children. Education is also the sector that has made the most effort to address migrants' special language and cultural needs.

Often, lack of skills in the host country's official language, for example, English, may not prevent immigrants from finding a job or a residence at their destination, but it greatly reduces possibilities for promotion in their jobs and compromises possibilities of social mobility in the future. Restriction to temporary jobs, a feature of current labour markets, is more likely when migrants do not have command of the language spoken by mainstream residents in host countries. Language skills can help the migrant to reach a wide range of information resources, extending beyond those avail-

Education, and especially the ability to speak the language of the host country, improves the outlook for migrants

able from newspapers written in, and social communication dependent on, the original language of the migrant.

In general, immigrants' children may have a better chance of achieving a command of the language of the host country than their parents. However, some studies point out that immigration, educational and labour policies are crucial for improving such chances. The degrees of successful assimilation vary across main destination countries. While the United States of America has historically been cited as a country that has fostered successful immigrant assimilation, the increase in economic inequality in the past 35 years has made the success of the last migration wave more controversial. Similarly, it is argued that the age of school initiation and the type of job found by migrants in Germany play determining roles with respect to the risks incurred by migrants of being segregated. The experience of this country has shown mixed results.[3]

Jobs and sufficient income

The desire for work that is more remunerative is what generally motivates emigration. Evidence of the fact that many migrant workers manage to obtain better-remunerated work is provided by the magnitude of the sums of money sent home by emigrants: official remittances are estimated at some $130 billion for the year 2002, of which some $80 billion went to developing countries (see chap. IV). The magnitude of this amount, however, should not obscure the problems faced by people seeking to make a living in a foreign country.

In the recent past, policy attention has been devoted mostly to the immigration of highly skilled workers who met specific labour needs, but a very large majority of migrant workers are concentrated in the lowest socio-occupational categories of their host countries (see table VI.1) are off the wage scale and are subjected to the harshest working conditions. They also tend to occupy temporary jobs and are the first victims of unemployment during periods of economic recession (see below and figure VI.1).

Less-skilled migrant workers often work under exploitative conditions

Deception, discrimination, exploitation and sometimes abuse are employment-related indignities commonly and increasingly faced by poorly skilled migrant workers (Taran and Geronimi, 2003). While this situation is partly explained by the xenophobia that currently permeates many societies, it is also due to migrants' position in the labour market and the lack of application and enforcement of labour standards in host countries.

Migrants' employment under substandard working conditions offers a low-cost and flexible manpower alternative for those small and medium-sized companies that do not have the option of relocating their operations abroad. The presence of large numbers of undocumented migrants—an unintended consequence of restrictive immigration policies—has been a significant contributing factor to this trend. On the other hand, the intense economic competition associated with the various forms of liberalization of the world economy has increased the propensity of entrepreneurs to hire legal and undocumented immigrants at below-standard salaries and under below-standard working conditions.

Migrants, especially those recruited as guest workers, find their access to labour markets seriously restricted

In most countries, migrants' access to labour markets and their engagement in professions and trade are restricted. These restrictions may apply for a limited period of time, as in those cases where migrants are forbidden to change employers or jobs during their first year of residence. However, this restriction usually applies permanently to migrants recruited under guest-worker contracts. In this case, migrant workers remain confined to one sector of activity without being entitled to occupational mobility and have no

Table VI.1.
Employment of foreign workers by sector, 2001-2002 average

	Percentage of total foreign employment								
	Agriculture and fishing	Mining, manufacturing and energy	Construction	Wholesale and retail trade	Hotels and restaurants	Education	Health and other community services	Households	Other services
Austria	1	24	13	15	11	2	6	<1	25
Belgium	<1	21	9	16	8	4	8	<1	32
Czech Republic	3	31	11	19	7	3	5	-	18
Finland	-	15	8	14	11	11	11	-	27
France	3	17	17	11	7	3	5	7	28
Germany	1	33	8	13	11	3	7	<1	24
Greece	3	18	28	11	10	2	2	17	9
Ireland	3	17	7	10	14	5	10	-	30
Japan	<1	62	2	9	-	-	-	-	27
Luxembourg	<1	10	16	14	8	2	6	3	38
Netherlands	4	21	5	15	8	4	12	-	31
Norway	-	16	6	12	7	9	21	-	23
Spain	9	11	16	11	16	3	2	15	17
Sweden	-	19	3	11	6	8	19	-	32
Switzerland	<1	23	10	18	7	5	12	1	23
United Kingdom	-	12	4	12	11	8	14	1	37
Australia	2	17	7	17	5	6	10	3	31
Canada[a]	2	19	5	14	7	6	9	<1	37
United States	3	17	8	20	10	6	11	1	23

Source:
SOPEMI (Continuous Reporting System on Migration), *Trends in International Migration: Annual Report, 2003 Edition* (Paris, Organization for Economic Cooperation and Development (OECD), 2004), table I.12.

a 2001.

option in case of loss of employment.[4] In the absence of official certification of skills standards, proper recognition of a migrant's qualifications is often left open to interpretation by private parties, which remains a potential basis for exploitation.

Migrants' economic and employment rights are often circumscribed

While immigration laws dictate migrants' economic rights, they rarely contain provisions for the enforcement of migrants' rights. Therefore, there often is no easy resource to due process for the enforcement of those rights. This creates a problem for migrants who are expelled or for those who have left the host country upon termination of employment, as they usually face enormous difficulties in recovering any outstanding employment-related payments.

Furthermore, there is some evidence that immigrants tend to be among the first to be laid off during times of economic difficulties, while they are the last to be rehired when economic prospects are better. As a result, high rates of unemployment have been observed among immigrant workers in many Western European and other countries members of the Organization for Economic Cooperation and Development (OECD) (see table VI.2). In the United States, negative change in overall employment has been found to have a greater-than-proportional impact on migrants' welfare-related caseloads.

Figure VI.1.
Proportion of temporary jobs occupied by nationals and by foreigners, selected host countries, March-April 2003

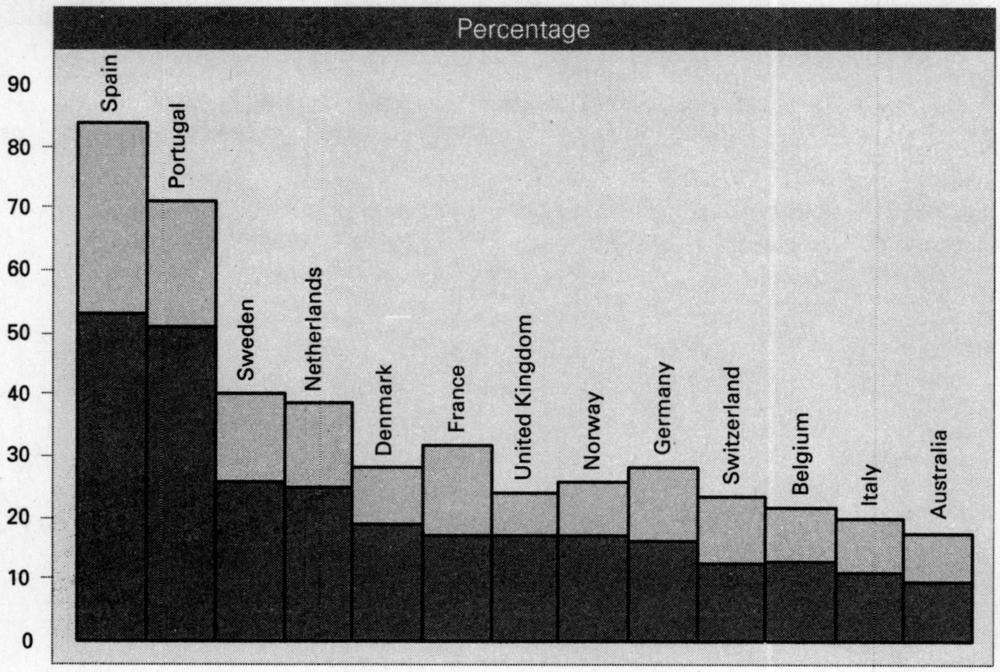

Source: SOPEMI (Continuous Reporting System on Migration), *Trends in International Migration: Annual Report, 2002 Edition* (Paris, OECD, 2003), chart I.14.

Table VI.2.
Unemployment rates of nationals and foreigners by sex, in selected OECD countries, 2000-2001 average

Percentage

Country	Male		Female	
	Nationals	Foreigners[a]	Nationals	Foreigners[a]
Austria	3.9	8.4	3.9	8.6
Belgium	4.6	14.2	7.0	16.5
Denmark	3.6	12.2	4.9	7.2
Finland	10.0	24.2	11.2	29.9
France	7.1	17.1	10.7	23.9
Germany	7.2	13.4	7.8	11.7
Greece	7.2	7.6	16.2	17.6
Ireland	4.1	5.1	3.8	6.2
Italy	8.0	7.4	13.9	21.3
Netherlands	1.9	4.7	2.9	7.0
Norway	3.7	5.3	3.4	4.5
Portugal	3.1	8.4	5.1	9.6
Spain	9.3	12.9	19.8	17.2
Sweden	5.5	16.1	4.6	13.0
Switzerland	1.3	4.3	2.6	6.4
United Kingdom	5.5	9.8	4.4	7.9
Australia	6.7	6.6	5.8	6.9
Canada	10.3	9.9	9.5	11.6
United States	4.9	4.4	4.1	5.6

Source: SOPEMI (Continuous Reporting System on Migration), *Trends in International Migration: Annual Report, 2003 Edition* (Paris, OECD, 2004), table I.14.

a Non-nationals (Europe) or foreign-born (Australia, Canada, United States).

Nonetheless, labour-market deregulation, both de jure and de facto, has allowed a large number of undocumented migrants to find jobs despite relatively high levels of unemployment in developed countries. In contrast, employment-related discrimination has made it more difficult for legitimate migrants to find or change jobs. The sparse evidence available suggests that discrimination against migrants, as well as against ethnic minorities, is a worldwide phenomenon: studies carried out by the International Labour Organization (ILO) in Belgium, Germany, the Netherlands and Spain found that more than one in three job applications by immigrants and members of minorities were rejected or not given consideration (Zegers de Beijl, 2000).

Legal status and participation in civil and political life

Together with a decent job and a decent income, a clearly defined and secure legal status is a critical component of the social condition of the international migrant. A temporary residence permit or work contract is normally sufficient to give a sense of security to short-term immigrants. Many receiving countries, while attempting to control immigration movements, have taken measures to clarify and simplify their rules and procedures regarding conditions for residence and employment. This is also taking place with respect to asylum applications, as the blurring of the distinction between migrant workers and asylum-seekers has raised acute problems for the individuals and families concerned. Nevertheless, apart from their great diversity among countries, conditions for residence are often unclear and applied inconsistently within individual countries. For long-term immigrants seeking citizenship in their new country, difficulties, delays and conditions have generally not eased in recent years.

Both documented and undocumented migrants face a seriously disadvantaged legal status

As a great number of countries, including most developed countries, have tightened controls over the entry of foreigners into their territories, and as an increasing number of people have felt the need—or have been forced—to emigrate, the flow of undocumented immigrants may have increased in recent years. Lacking legal status in the receiving country, many of these immigrants become the victims of traffickers, who often deprive them of their passports or other papers establishing their identity and nationality. Cases of women in particular who have been forced into this situation of complete vulnerability and dependence, abound and the possible forms of discrimination specifically directed against female migrants are many: wage discrimination, unpaid work (as family/ethnic co-workers), prohibition against marrying a host-country citizen, denial of residential status, termination of contract and deportation in case of pregnancy, loss of child custody in case of divorce, and physical, sexual and verbal abuse (Plant, 2002).

Female migrants commonly face especially disadvantaged legal conditions

In most countries, immigration regulations are not gender-specific. Yet, until very recently, immigration laws and policies tended to assume that female migrants were secondary migrants joining other migrants rather than initiators themselves of migration, a view that has been increasingly challenged by the facts and a growing body of research. This assumption, which reflects the widespread traditional views of the status and role of women within the family and in society, has had far-reaching consequences for both the admission of migrant women and their status after arrival (Zlotnik, 2004).[5]

The decision regarding who enters and resides in national territories, and which rights are to be granted to non-citizens in national territories, is the sovereign prerogative of States. It is therefore not surprising that international law provides little regulation of international migration: international migration is largely a matter of national legislation. Yet, the issue of discriminatory and sometimes abusive treatment of migrant workers has long been in the international agenda. As discussed more fully in chap. VIII, three principal instruments have been adopted that address this concern: two are conventions that were developed under the auspices of ILO and the third is a convention developed by the United Nations. However, ratification of the three instruments has been notably slow and sparse.

Complementary and pursuant to the three conventions, there has been a continuing process of codification of the human rights of migrants, as discussed in chapter VIII. However, it is rights enforcement at the national level, rather than legal standards, that is the central issue. In many parts of the world, there is greater governmental awareness of problems in enforcement of migrants' rights than there are reported measures to address the issue.

A growing number of countries permit migrants to vote in local elections and to hold local office

On the other hand, the idea that immigrants should have certain political rights, such as that of participating in local elections, has gained ground in recent decades in several developed countries. To a significant extent, this development is the result of a growing awareness that long-term residence of large numbers of foreign citizens on national territory has become a persistent condition. The rationale for granting political rights to legally resident non-citizens is threefold. First, some proponents of such rights argue that participation in the political process of one's community of residence is a basic human right. Second, granting political rights to migrants can symbolize recognition of the contribution that migrants make to the host country's prosperity. Third, promoting migrants' integration in the economic, social and cultural spheres without facilitating their political participation could lead to social tension and conflict.

In a few European countries (including Denmark, Finland, Ireland, the Netherlands, Norway and Sweden), foreign residents from third countries are allowed, under condition of a minimum residence requirement, to vote and run for office in local elections, although only nationals may take part in national elections. Other countries (such as Finland, Portugal, Spain and the United Kingdom of Great Britain and Northern Ireland) have granted voting rights to certain nationalities or on the basis of reciprocity agreements with selected countries.

The Council of Europe has adopted a Convention on the Participation of Foreigners in Public Life at Local Level

On 5 February 1992, the Council of Europe opened for signature a Convention on the Participation of Foreigners in Public Life at Local Level whose main objective was to foster the integration of foreign residents into local communities by, inter alia, granting them voting rights. The Convention, which came into force on 1 May 1997, has been ratified by only seven countries: Denmark, Finland, Iceland, Italy, the Netherlands, Norway and Sweden (Council of Europe, 2004).

Several Governments have argued that the participation of immigrants in the civil and political life of host countries should be achieved through naturalization. However, in many countries, the scope for naturalization is limited, as general conditions for acquiring citizenship remain restrictive and do not apply equally to all family members. In addition, many migrants would have to give up their citizenship of origin, as many countries do not allow their nationals to have dual citizenship.

Many developed countries have set up consultative bodies where migrant communities can be represented

From the late 1960s onward, many developed countries, particularly European countries, have set up consultative assemblies or councils, at the national or the local level, aimed at making representations to public authorities on behalf of migrant communities. However, given migrants' lack of voting rights, these bodies have not raised much interest in migrant communities and have led to mixed outcomes.

Provisions for absentee voting rights are limited in most countries of the world. Consequently, most nationals living abroad have little voice in the public debate. However, in some developing countries to which large numbers of nationals have been expatriated, the issue of absentee voting rights has gained political significance and salience, although few changes have been recorded.

Migrants from the many countries that do not provide for absentee voting are effectively disenfranchised

Access to social protection and health care

Access to social protection has become a major issue, both for the immigrants themselves and for the receiving countries. The social protection of migrants is a question that often lies at the core of the migration debate. Extending the existing social protection regime to migrants is viewed by many as undermining the economic benefits of migration for the host countries. In developing countries that offer only very elementary social services and welfare systems to their nationals, the question of welfare costs for migrants sometimes becomes even more contentious.

The cost of welfare services for migrants is a major point of contention in many host countries

At a basic level, migrants' entitlement to social protection depends on whether they meet criteria of either employment or residence: whether they live in a country (such as one of the former labour-importing countries of Western Europe) where welfare benefits depend primarily on being employed and having contributed to the social insurance system, or in a country where benefits are granted on the basis of residence—such as one of the traditional resettlement countries, one of the Scandinavian countries or the United Kingdom. In the latter group of countries, the provision of social benefits is largely contingent on a migrant's specific status—for example, whether he or she is a primary visa holder, dependant or refugee—and on time requirements. Differences in benefits may also depend on the migrant's country of origin, as welfare provisions are sometimes contained in bilateral treaties. In federal States, social assistance programmes may differ from one subnational authority to the next. In general, social provisions for migrants can be unequal both within and among host countries.

Welfare entitlements vary among countries in terms of level of support and criteria

The non-portability of retirement benefits is among the various issues of equity that have been raised in relation to the social protection of migrants, and it is increasingly attracting attention. Few countries allow portability of pension benefits. Although many bilateral agreements have been signed, a large number of migrants, in particular from developing countries, fall outside the purview of these agreements and cannot receive pension benefits if they decide to leave the host country. The issue of the non-portability of benefits has gained additional momentum following the surge in the international recruitment and mobility of skilled workers.

Non-exportability of migrants' acquired pensions benefits is widespread and a matter of growing concern

While health care is in general available to all migrants, including undocumented migrants on an emergency basis, the scope and quality of health services accessible to migrants vary greatly. Furthermore, there is evidence that migrants may sometimes be reluctant to assert their rights and stop short of availing themselves of the health services they are entitled to for reasons that are not totally clear but may range from language problems and lack of information to cultural gaps and various forms of discrimination.

In principle, health care is available to all migrants, but its scope and quality vary greatly

The health risks faced by migrants are compounded by more limited access to health information, health promotion, health services and health insurance. In addition, migrants as a group suffer disproportionately from high exposure to occupational and environmental hazards, and are at greater risk because some of their specific health needs are routinely ignored or not well understood and therefore not adequately addressed (International Labour Organization, 2004).

Concerns with migrants' pre-existing and untreated conditions, such as infectious and communicable diseases, have long been the priority of health authorities. A few years ago, considerable public and media attention was devoted to the association between migrants and HIV/AIDS. While this debate has faded in most countries, the focus has now switched to the perceived or real health threats posed by undocumented migrants. There is also speculation about whether the health-care entitlements in host countries, in particular access to treatment that is either not available or not affordable in the migrant's country of origin, might be a motivating factor in migration. It is argued that the provision of health care to migrants puts additional financial stress on already overstretched and underperforming public-health systems. In general, courts have not accepted challenges to an expulsion order based on the state of the migrant's health.

Concentration of migrant workers in more dangerous occupations exposes them to greater risk of accidents

Migrant health poses a triple challenge by raising fundamental questions of social equity, public health and human rights. The current controversial context makes it difficult to confront these challenges despite ample evidence of the plight of migrants. For example, in Europe, occupational accident rates are, on average, twice as high for migrant workers as for native workers. A particularly dramatic case is that of seasonal farm workers (Bollini and Siem, 1995). In both developed and developing countries, many migrant workers employed in agriculture display pathologies related to exposure to toxic pesticides. The large majority of these migrants do not have medical coverage or access to health services.

Work carried out by the World Health Organization (WHO) on mental health has found that immigrants and refugees are among the groups that are disproportionately affected (Grondin, 2004). Although knowledge of the mental health of migrant populations remains limited, there is evidence to suggest that severe psychological stress due to uprooting, disruption of family life and a hostile social environment is common. A large number of migrants have little or no access to mental health care, either because they are excluded from existing service arrangements or because such services do not exist in more than 40 per cent of countries.

Family reunification

The very great weight attached by net immigration countries to family reunification as grounds for entry for long-term residence strongly reinforces the importance of kin groups in the migration process. The topic is discussed in detail in chapter III.

Effects on the social fabric of societies and public perceptions

Effects on home countries

In home countries, migration may be perceived as helping to reduce population pressures. However, for most large emigration countries such as China and India, the effects are necessarily slight. Even in the case of Mexico, a country with a large emigration flow towards the United States, studies estimate that the annual population growth is reduced only from 1.8 to 1.5 per cent. Likewise, the impact of emigration on unemployment/underemployment may be modest. The unemployment problems of countries such as Kuwait or Senegal may be too deep-rooted to be eased, even barely, by large emigration flows (International Labour Organization, 2004a).

Where emigration flows include large numbers of highly skilled workers, the various problems and prospects associated with the "brain drain" may also arise. This issue is discussed in some detail in chapter IV.

In addition to facilitating migration (see above), kin and kith relationships in the home country are themselves affected by migration. Migration often transforms the kin structure and creates new relationships. From the family perspective, even though the family may eventually reunify, in many cases it will face temporary, possibly lengthy separation. It takes time for migrants to obtain a secure job, save money and fund the legal and economic costs needed to sponsor the immigration of a family member. In the case of undocumented migrants, the separation from close family members may last longer and be less certain.

Emigration may lead to changes in kinship relationships in the migrants' country of origin

Although the members of the immediate family may join the migrant in host countries, members of the extended family may stay in the home country and thus may be permanently separated from, and even lose contact with, the emigrant. This distant relationship between nuclear and extended family members may introduce changes in family ties. Likewise, new friends from work and neighbours are likely to fill the social space created as a result of former friends' having stayed in the home country. From a social point of view, remittances sent to family members change the relations between senders and receivers: the sender gains prestige, while recipients gain economic resources. Finally, family relations in the home country without the emigrant may involve a new assignment of roles and ties among those remaining. This may also be the case in host countries, where, in addition, family relationships are now embedded in a new milieu of social and cultural relations.

Effects on host countries

Researchers, policy makers and immigrants hold a variety of views on the forces that shape the interaction between immigrants and the host society. Interpretative frameworks that place various emphases on economic, social, cultural, legal or political factors have been proposed. Three developments have had a bearing on this interaction during the 1980s and 1990s: changes in the public perception of immigration, accentuated patterns of settlement, and a rise of ethnic identities.

In Europe, spatial concentration of immigrants has increasingly been perceived as challenging the social cohesion of host communities, as well as the immigrants' sense of citizenship. It is unclear to what extent the concentration of immigrants is the result of spatial and social discrimination or the outcome of a strategy of adaptation that takes advantage of ethnic resources. Equally unclear is the impact of spatial and ethnic concentration on the ability of immigrants to become socially and economically integrated in the medium term. Analysis of past immigration provides examples that lead to opposite conclusions.

Research conducted in the United States suggests that the presence of large, geographically concentrated and economically diverse migrant communities tends to facilitate the integration of new immigrants, while communities that are small, scattered or predominantly composed of manual workers do not. However, the development of either type of communities seems to depend, to a significant extent, on whether public authorities are receptive, indifferent or unreceptive and whether public opinion is prejudiced or not (Portes, 1995). Some of these findings seem to be supported by European studies on comparative achievements of selected ethnic groups in different countries. For instance, while in some countries, second-generation Turks' were responsible for educational and voca-

In some countries, the concentration of immigrants in residential enclaves has become a matter of concern

tional achievements that were conducive to their social integration, in other countries, they were at risk of becoming an underclass (Crul and Vermeulen, 2002). In any case, most historical and contemporary research shows that assimilation is a generational process (Smith and Edmonston, 1997).

Up until the 1970s, policy approaches to the integration of immigrants ranged from assimilation to integration and had cultural homogenization as a primary objective. Immigration was perceived as desirable to the extent that it had no impact on the social fabric of receiving societies (Castles, 2002). The rise of ethnic identities led to the introduction of policies of multiculturalism, first in Canada, then in Australia and the United States, and finally in several European countries. In contrast, in countries that consider migration from a labour-importing perspective, migrants are regarded as temporary residents and are therefore not encouraged to integrate.

In many countries of immigration, there has been a broad shift in overall orientation from assimilation to multiculturalism

The adoption of multicultural approaches shifted the focus of policy frameworks of social integration from facilitating the adaptation of individual migrants to their new living environment to comprehending the social interaction between immigrants and the host society. During the last two decades of the twentieth century, the policy model of integration that relied on a single approach and an exclusive focus on paid work and education was further challenged, as mounting evidence showed that integration varied among the different groups of migrants and that not all migrants had similar opportunities for social integration and mobility.

The means of integration—or exclusion—are mediated and experienced at the local and community levels. For example, in Sweden, immigrants are legally included but socially excluded, mainly because their limited use of the language causes them to be rejected by employers. In contrast, illegal immigrants in Italy are legally excluded but the informal sector provides a means for them to be socially included (European Commission, 2003).

The impact of migration on the poverty status of the migrants themselves depends largely on how successful they are in the labour market at their destination and, if they decide to stay, on how quickly they escape from low-paid and unstable employment, and how successful their children are in achieving social mobility through education. Experiences suggest that initial skill endowment among migrants and their commitment to building their own human capital through the acquisition of language and other skills have been critical to rapid social and economic upward mobility. There is ample evidence, however, that skill endowment among recent cohorts of migrants has been lower than in the past. This raises questions about their eventual upward mobility.

Public perceptions

Public perceptions of immigration tend to vary considerably over time

Notwithstanding the positive effects that migration may have for home and host countries, whether in temporary labour-importing countries or countries that have traditionally attracted permanent immigrants, migration and migrants have increasingly developed a controversial image. Media attention focuses on uncontrolled "flows" of people seeking work or asylum, on undocumented immigration, on the criminal activities of traffickers and smugglers, and on problems of integration of immigrants with the local population.

These perceptions reflect prevailing economic conditions, and many other factors as well

Public perceptions may reflect real issues and real problems, but they also reflect ignorance, prejudices and fear. Moreover, public opinion fluctuates with events and is subject to a great variety of influences. The majority tend to change their views with the ups and downs of the economy, but are also responsive to the information and political messages coming from public authorities. It has been argued, for example, that political regimes and economic cycles have affected the migration waves to Argentina throughout the twentieth century (Solimano, 2003). Similarly, during the reconstruction of Europe (1945-1973), strong economic growth prompted employment-related internal and international migration to core European countries, as well as the signing of bilateral agreements between home and host countries, which nurtured a positive view of immigration. This also reflects the historical experience of the United States, where public attitudes towards immigration have long been ambivalent: considerable public support and welcome during periods of large-scale immigration have alternated with great distrust and antagonism towards immigrants during other periods.[6] Similarly, public authorities and their political parties are watchful of trends in perceptions and public opinion, especially when seeking to retain electoral support.

Prior to the 1970s, international migration had not been a topic of major concern for most Governments (see chap. III). However, in the context of the global recession that followed the first oil shock, in the mid-1970s, Governments' concerns with the economic and social consequences of immigration grew. Several developed countries adopted policies aimed at lowering immigration, thereby setting a trend that, by the 1990s, had spread to many regions of the world. As of 2003, one third of both developed and developing countries had policies aimed at lowering their immigration levels (see chap. III, sect. C).

The surge in the number of refugees during the 1980s and early 1990s, a development prompted by rising restrictive immigration policies, triggered another change in Governments' perspectives. Whereas asylum and migration had been previously viewed as separate issues by Governments, asylum policies now became core to the discussions on migration in many parts of the world. The end of the cold war brought about another development: restrictions on emigration were lifted in Eastern and Central Europe so that some Governments from European Union (EU) countries in particular had additional reasons for aiming towards more restrictive immigration policies. These have now been extended with the accession of the new EU country members in 2004 (Wallace, 2000).[7]

In some countries, public attitudes about immigrants have become highly politicized

In many countries, particularly in Europe (Lloyd, 2003), violence against migrants is on the rise and migration has become extremely politicized. Migrants and foreigners have typically been scapegoats for existing or perceived social and economic problems ranging from unemployment to criminality. For example, the Eurobarometer reported in 1997 that 63 per cent of those interviewed believed that the presence of minority groups had increased unemployment (Eurobarometer, 1997). Migrants are also met with hostile attitudes in other parts of the world: according to an Associated Press poll, 40 per cent of Mexican respondents believed that immigrants took jobs away from natives. However, economic and labour dynamics, while prevalent in influencing perceptions of both the costs and benefits of migration, are not the only basis for general concerns. Less tangible fears about the impact of migration on the social and cultural fabric seem to play a role. Attitudes towards immigration are predicated on the existence of competition from immigrants, whether real or perceived, sometimes even when there is evidence that immigration has a positive economic impact.

Following the events of 11 September 2001, there has been some increase in hostility directed at migrants thought to be from Muslim countries

Furthermore, the terrorist attacks of 11 September 2001 in the United States have fostered the perception of migrants, in particular those of Muslim and/or Arab origin, as a threat to social stability. In a report dated 3 January 2003 on the situation of Muslim and Arab peoples in various parts of the world in the wake of the events of 11 September 2001 (E/CN.4/2003/23), the United Nations Special Rapporteur on contemporary forms of racism, racial discrimination, xenophobia and related intolerance found that, in most non-Muslim countries, but primarily in North America and Europe, violence and discrimination towards people originating from the Near East, the Middle East and South-East Asia had became more frequent. They may have been facilitated by the climate of suspicion and mistrust "openly fostered not only by certain politicians and parts of the media, but also, and perhaps more so, by a school of thought through which certain intellectuals are not afraid to lend legitimacy to a form of intolerance thought to belong to a bygone age" (E/CN.4/2003/23, para. 30).

Many Governments of countries of immigration lack clear and convincing policies regarding their migrant populations

The lack of readily available and reliable information also tends to reinforce the perception that current migration trends are beyond the control of State authorities, as well as to undermine the credibility of policy statements. Moreover, in many countries, the discourse on international migration is not perceived to be the reflection of a clear, coherent and committed policy, a fact that further undermines its credibility. The formulation of such a policy, while increasingly difficult owing to the changing nature of migration flows as well as to the fact that many countries are at the same time countries of emigration, immigration and transit, has the potential to steer public opinion away from the temptation of adopting simplistic and erroneous views.

The media may have a powerful impact on how the public views migration

The media has an impact on how the public views migration. While the media does have a propensity for concentrating on bad news which tends to reinforce prejudice, at the same time it also exposes problems that need to be addressed, such as the poor living conditions of many migrants and the violence and discrimination to which they are exposed. Paradoxically, although the 1997 Eurobarometer poll revealed strongly negative views on migration, it also found that the majority of those surveyed (71 per cent) believed that the authorities should make efforts to improve the situation of those belonging to minority groups. Support for the hypothesis that exposure breeds tolerance was also found in Southern Africa, where a large majority reported that it had a positive interaction with foreigners (Crush and Pendleton, 2004). Similarly, it could be assumed that, in receiving countries, public opinion would benefit greatly from more information on the contribution that migrant workers are making to the economy and the society.

The importance of promoting mutual awareness of cultures, civilizations and religions and the interaction and cross-fertilization between them has long been recognized. Nevertheless, the need to take action concretely aimed at promoting respect for diversity and cultural, religious and ethnic pluralism has become even more critical in a world of globalization and increased mobility, as noted by the Special Rapporteur on contemporary forms of racism, racial discrimination, xenophobia and related intolerance in the above-cited report (UNDP, 2004). To this end, the Special Rapporteur called for special consideration to be given to intercultural education, as well as to the way in which history was written and taught.

Conclusions

Kin and kith relations, as well as hometown associations, are the most basic enabling and permeating mechanisms of migration. They help migrants to gather all kinds of resources necessary to initiate and sustain migration. Through a mixture of individual entrepreneurship and social help and reciprocity, these relations facilitate transnational exchanges of information, economic resources and people, while also making possible personal enhancement of immigrants' and the development of their communities in home countries. The challenge for these types of relations is to develop links with more established networks in host societies and thus contribute to the social, political and economic integration of immigrants.

The integration of immigrants in host societies is the result of various factors, such as the process of learning the language of the host country, the opportunities for obtaining a steady income, the chances for higher education, the extent of civil and political participation, and the access to social services. Although most countries have the legal instruments to facilitate and protect the integration of immigrants in host societies, this process has required significant resources and has presented cultural challenges to both immigrants and host societies. Programmes to facilitate the integration of immigrants have had varying degrees of success. In general, restrictive immigration policies have coincided with a reduction in the programmes and social services offered to immigrants, which may have accentuated social segregation.

Migration has both positive and negative effects on home and host societies. Family separation and brain drain are offset by the positive effects of remittances, the acquisition of new skills, and the opportunities for community development that immigrants provide to their families and hometowns. Although economic opportunities and social programmes for immigrants have often faltered, partly owing to budget cuts in cities with large immigrant populations, various degrees of cultural adaptation have been achieved. Immigrants have helped to create more diverse and open societies in home countries.

Notes

1 These are also known as migrants' social capital.

2 For different public works funded by hometown associations, see Alarcón (2002).

3 For the case in the United States, see Massey, Durand and Malone (2002). For the case in Germany, see Pries (2003).

4 For migration under guest-worker contracts in Gulf States, see International Organization for Migration (2003d).

5 A counter-argument on sex differentials in migration is given by Zachariah and Rajan (2001).

6 For the case of Europe, see Garson and Loizillon (2003). For the case of the United States, see Smith and Edmonston (1997).

7 Estonia, Hungary, Slovenia, Malta, Cyprus, Poland, Czech Republic, Latvia, Lithuania and Slovakia.

Chapter VII
Levels and trends in international displacement

Most transnational movements of people are the result of voluntary decisions taken by the individuals themselves and are usually motivated by the prospect of economic gain. In some cases, however, fear of persecution or death compels individuals to leave their home country to seek safety and security elsewhere. Displacement because of war or political, religious or social persecution has always been a part of history and may involve only small numbers of people moving independently. Sometimes, however, there is mass displacement and the creation of large refugee communities in the receiving countries. Such mass movements of refugees tend to be the result of specific developments, such as the outbreak of conflict or a change in regime, and are therefore sporadic. In cases of mass displacement, the refugees usually face difficulties in integrating into their country of destination or even sustaining their well-being.

Given the above-mentioned reasons for such movements, their precise magnitudes, particularly in the case of refugee groups, have often been difficult to document. However, with the establishment of the United Nations Relief and Works Agency for Palestine Refugees in the Near East (UNRWA) and the Office of the United Nations High Commissioner for Refugees (UNHCR) as the international organizations responsible for addressing such displacements, more systematic data have become available. By the end of 2003, UNRWA was providing support to 4.1 million people and UNHCR was responsible for some 17.1 million individuals (see box VII.1), of whom 9.7 million were refugees.

The present chapter relies upon the data that have become available to provide an overview of the extent of international displacement and discusses some recent policy aspects. The first section provides an historical overview of institutional developments and trends in the number of refugees. The second section documents global and regional refugee trends over the past decade, as well as progress towards achieving durable global solutions for the challenge presented by new refugee flows. The scope and direction of recent asylum flows to the industrialized countries are analysed in the third section. Section four addresses various policy issues, including international cooperation, the impact of refugees on host countries and data considerations.

Historical background

The Second World War and its aftermath had witnessed a displacement of more than 40 million persons in Europe, excluding millions of forced labourers living in Germany, ethnic Germans expelled from Eastern Europe and those fleeing communist domination (United Nations High Commissioner for Refugees, 2000b). The international community responded to these unprecedented levels of displacement by creating the United Nations Relief and Rehabilitation Administration (UNRRA) in 1943, which was replaced by the International Refugee Organization (IRO) in 1947. Although limited to European refugees, IRO was the first international body mandated to protect and assist refugees and to find durable solutions.

Box VII.1

Populations of concern to the Office of the United Nations High Commissioner for Refugees (UNHCR)

Refugees: Persons recognized as refugees under the 1951 Convention relating to the Status of Refugees[a] and the 1967 Protocol thereto,[b] under the 1969 Organization of African Unity Convention governing the specific aspects of refugee problems in Africa,[c] or in accordance with the Statute of the UNHCR,[d] persons granted a humanitarian status and those granted temporary protection. These numbered 9.7 million at the end of 2003.

Asylum-seekers: Persons who applied for asylum or refugee status but have not yet received a final decision on their claim (985,000 at the end of 2003).

Returned refugees: Refugees who have returned to their place of origin (1.1 million in 2003).

Internally displaced persons (IDPs): Persons who have been displaced within their country and to whom UNHCR extends protection and/or assistance pursuant to a special request by a competent organ of the United Nations IDPs are often in a more precarious situation than refugees owing to the absence of international protection and assistance. The 4.2 million IDPs under UNHCR care in 2003 constituted only a small proportion of all IDPs.

Returned IDPs: IDPs who have returned to their place of origin (232,000 in 2003).

Others of concern: Persons of concern to UNHCR who are not included in the previous categories, including "forced migrants" (Russian Federation), stateless persons (Belarus, Kuwait, Kazakhstan, Ukraine), local residents at risk (Kosovo, Serbia and Montenegro), Sahrawis (Mauritania), Afghan asylum-seekers (Russian Federation, UNHCR estimate), rejected Eritreans following cessation (Sudan), Muslims from the Philippines (Malaysia), Colombians (Venezuela), etc. (912,000 at the end of 2003).

a United Nations, Treaty Series, vol. 189, No. 2545.
b Ibid., vol. 606, No. 8791.
c Ibid., vol. 1001, No. 14691.
d General Assembly resolution 428 (V), annex.

The world's existing refugee regime emerged in the late 1940s and early 1950s

Following the Arab/Israeli conflict of 1948 and the mass exodus of Palestinian refugees from what had become Israel into neighbouring areas, the General Assembly, in its resolution 194 (III) of 11 December 1948, created the United Nations Conciliation Commission for Palestine (UNCCP). Its mandate was to mediate a solution to the conflict and "to facilitate the repatriation, resettlement and economic and social rehabilitation of the refugees and the payment of compensation" (para.11). "At the time, observers considered the refugees' return to be imminent. UNRWA had been established by Assembly resolution 302 (IV) of 8 December 1949 (para. 7) to complement the protection mandate of UNCCP by providing direct relief and works programmes for Palestine refugees and to prepare local governments for an end to international assistance. The Agency began operations on 1 May 1950. In the absence of a solution to the Palestine refugee problem, the Assembly has repeatedly renewed the UNRWA mandate, most recently extending it until 30 June 2005. Governments now contribute to UNRWA to enable it to provide long-term support, rather than short-term assistance.

Also in December 1949, the General Assembly, in resolution 319 (IV) of 3 December, decided to establish, for an initial period of three years, the Office of the United Nations High Commissioner for Refugees (UNHCR) as the international agency with a comprehensive mandate to provide refugees with legal protection. In parallel with the creation of UNHCR, the 1951 Convention relating to the Status of Refugees was adopted by the United Nations Conference of Plenipotentiaries on the Status of Refugees and Stateless Persons convened under Assembly resolution 429 (V) of 14 December 1950. It was the 1951 Convention that, for the first time, applied the term "refugee" universally (in that it was no longer limited to a particular nationality) and the range of the concept, as covering situations of mass displacement, was extended to encompass cases of individual persecution. The Convention set forth the rights of refugees in general and provided a legal framework for their international protection. However, article 1.D of the Convention does stipulate that "this convention shall not apply to persons who are at present receiving from organs or agencies of the United Nations other than the United Nations High Commissioner for Refugees protection or assistance". The statute of UNHCR, adopted by the Assembly on 14 December 1950, contains similar language. Because Palestinians receiving support from UNRWA are already benefiting from the protection or assistance of an existing United Nations agency, the activities of UNHCR and the protection of the Convention relating to the Status of Refugees do not apply to them. In 1967, a Protocol to the 1951 Convention came into force. The Protocol removed the geographical and time limitations; thereby making the Convention truly universal in its application. More than 140 countries had acceded to the 1951 Convention and the 1967 Protocol thereto as of October 2004.

The Provisional Intergovernmental Committee for the Movements of Migrants from Europe (PICMME) was established at an international conference held in Brussels in 1951 and in 1952, was transformed into the Intergovernmental Committee for European Migration (ICEM). This subsequently became the International Organization for Migration (IOM) which was initially set up as a temporary agency. IOM was created outside the United Nations system and membership was open only to States having a demonstrated interest in the principle of free movement of persons.

At that time, the main concern of IOM was the surplus population in Europe, following the displacements of the Second World War. The highest priority of IOM in terms of activities and resources was to transport 800,000 emigrants—be they refugees, displaced persons or national migrants—out of Europe in five years. Permanent resettlement of refugees was also a task of IOM.

The mandate of IOM was extended as migration flows kept occurring. Its first emergency operation had been in response to the mass exodus following the Soviet invasion of Hungary in 1956. In 1979, a Council resolution affirmed the need for the Organization to provide migration services on a global basis. In 1984, it was decided to review the IOM Constitution with a view to bringing it in line with the realities of its work. The amended Constitution that entered into force on 14 November 1989 abolished the geographical limitation and the focus on European migration was superseded by a worldwide mandate. Since then, IOM has grown from a body with 35 member States and 22 observer States to one whose membership comprises 105 member States and 27 observer States, and it now has over 160 field offices.

Reflecting the lack of progress in Israeli-Palestinian negotiations, UNRWA has gradually adjusted its programmes to meet the needs of its refugee population on a long-term basis. It is now the main provider of basic services—education, health, relief and social services—to registered Palestine refugees in the Middle East. The total number of Palestine refugees cared for by UNRWA rose from 914,000 in 1950 to almost 4.1 million in 2003 (see figure VII.1). Of these, 1.7 million were in Jordan, almost 1.5 million in the Occupied Palestinian Territory, 400,000 in the Syrian Arab Republic and 390,000 in

During the 1950s, there were about 1 million refugees receiving UNRWA assistance and some 2 million under UNHCR care, mostly in Europe

Figure VII.1.
Refugee population by region of asylum, 1953-2003

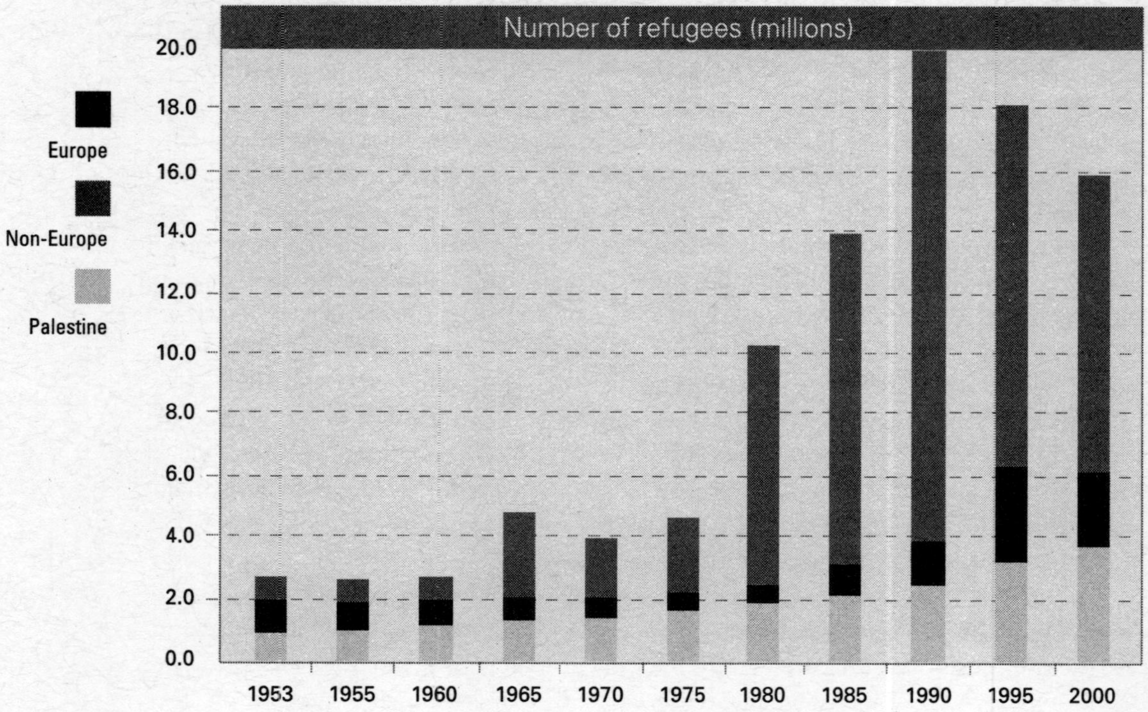

Lebanon. Refugees under the care of UNRWA are not included in the UNHCR statistics and are therefore, unless otherwise indicated, not referred to in the analysis of recent trends and patterns in the composition of global refugee flows.

The total number of refugees under the mandate of UNHCR in the 1950s was estimated at about 2 million or less, the majority of whom were living in Europe (see figure VII.1). With the exception of the period 1964-1966, when more than 1 million Chinese refugees were reported in Hong Kong Special Administrative Region (SAR) of China, which was then under British rule, the global number of refugees did not exceed 3 million until the mid-1970s. During the second part of the 1970s, the global refugee figure almost tripled, from 3.0 million in 1975 to 8.4 million in 1980. During this period, large numbers of Ethiopian refugees fled to Somalia and the Sudan, reaching a peak in 1980 (2.6 million). The late 1970s also witnessed the beginning of large refugee movements from Afghanistan to the Islamic Republic of Iran and Pakistan, reaching a peak of more than 6 million in the early 1990s. The Vietnamese refugee crisis was the third major refugee situation during this period. The number of Vietnamese refugees swelled to 400,000 during 1978-1979.

The global number of refugees began to surge in the later 1970s, mainly in the developing regions

During the 1980s, refugee levels had continued to increase, reaching almost 18 million in the early 1990s. In addition to the refugee crises in Afghanistan (5 million refugees), Ethiopia (1.5 million) and Viet Nam (350,000-400,000), a number of new, large situations erupted. The Mozambican crisis produced more than 1 million refugees in the late 1980s. Angola continued to be a major source of refugees during the 1980s (about 400,000), although the number was slightly below the levels of the late 1970s. By 1990, UNHCR reported more than 500,000 Sudanese refugees, up from 30,000 in 1983. Another major emerging refugee situation was that of Somalia. Following a peak of 800,000 Somali refugees in 1992, their numbers fell steadily to reach some 400,000 by the end of 2003. During the second part of the 1980s, the number of Iraqi refugees, primarily hosted by the Islamic Republic of Iran, rose sharply to reach more than 1 million in the early 1990s. Countries of origin producing an increasing number of refugees during the 1980s also included Burundi, Chad, the Lao People's Democratic Republic (since 1975), Liberia, Chad, El Salvador, Nicaragua, Rwanda, Uganda and the Territory of Western Sahara.

Having risen from 4.1 million in 1976-80 to over 12 million in 1986-90, the number of refugees in developing countries stabilized during 1991-1995 and fell to some 8 million during 1996-2000. In the more developed countries, however, the refugee population doubled from some 1.7 million in the 1980s to about 3.4 million during much of the 1990s as a result of the collapse of the Soviet Union, the break-up of the former Yugoslavia, and the rise in asylum-seekers and refugee resettlement from first-asylum countries. Countries producing important new refugee outflows during the 1990s included Armenia, Azerbaijan, Bosnia and Herzegovina, Croatia, the Russian Federation and the Federal Republic of Yugoslavia. In Africa, more than 1 million Mozambican refugees returned home, whereas the number of Ethiopian refugees fell sharply. However, new conflicts in Africa produced large new waves of refugees from the Democratic Republic of the Congo, Eritrea, Liberia and Sierra Leone. More than 2 million Rwandan refugees fled their country following the 1994 genocide. In Asia, countries of origin producing large numbers of refugees during the 1990s included Bhutan, China (Tibet), the Islamic Republic of Iran, Sri Lanka and Myanmar. The global number of refugees fell steadily during the 1990s to reach less than 10 million in 2003.

By the 1990s, the numbers of refugees in the developing regions had begun to decline, but there were new surges in the developed regions

Trends in refugee flows over the past decade

Refugee population

The average annual refugee population under the mandate of UNHCR was 17 per cent lower in 1999-2003 than in 1994-1998. The number of refugees declined in all regions, but Africa recorded the largest absolute decrease, from 4.8 million in 1994-1998 to 3.4 million refugees in 1999-2003. The second largest absolute decrease was reported for Europe, which hosted 600,000 fewer refugees in 1999-2003 than during 1994-1998. The average annual refugee population in Asia and North America fell by some 100,000 refugees.

The largest relative decline in the UNHCR refugee population in 1999-2003 compared with 1994-1998 was registered in Latin America and the Caribbean (-51 per cent), followed by Africa (-29 per cent), Europe (-20 per cent) and North America (-15 per cent). The refugee population in Asia, the largest asylum region since 1996, dropped sharply in 2002 and 2003 owing to the voluntary repatriation of more than 2.6 million Afghan refugees (see figure VII.2).

The total number of refugees in the world has tended to fall since the later 1990s

Because most refugees seek asylum in neighbouring countries, these trends in refugee populations in host countries are generally mirrored when the origins of refugees are considered. During 1999-2003, the average annual number of refugees from Latin America and the Caribbean fell by 37 per cent compared with the period 1994-1998, the number of African refugees decreased by 24 per cent, whereas the number of refugees from Europe dropped by 21 per cent. The average annual number of refugees originating from Asia during the past 10 years remained quite stable, however (-1 per cent).

Figure VII.2.
Refugee population under the mandate of UNHCR, by main asylum region, 1994-2003

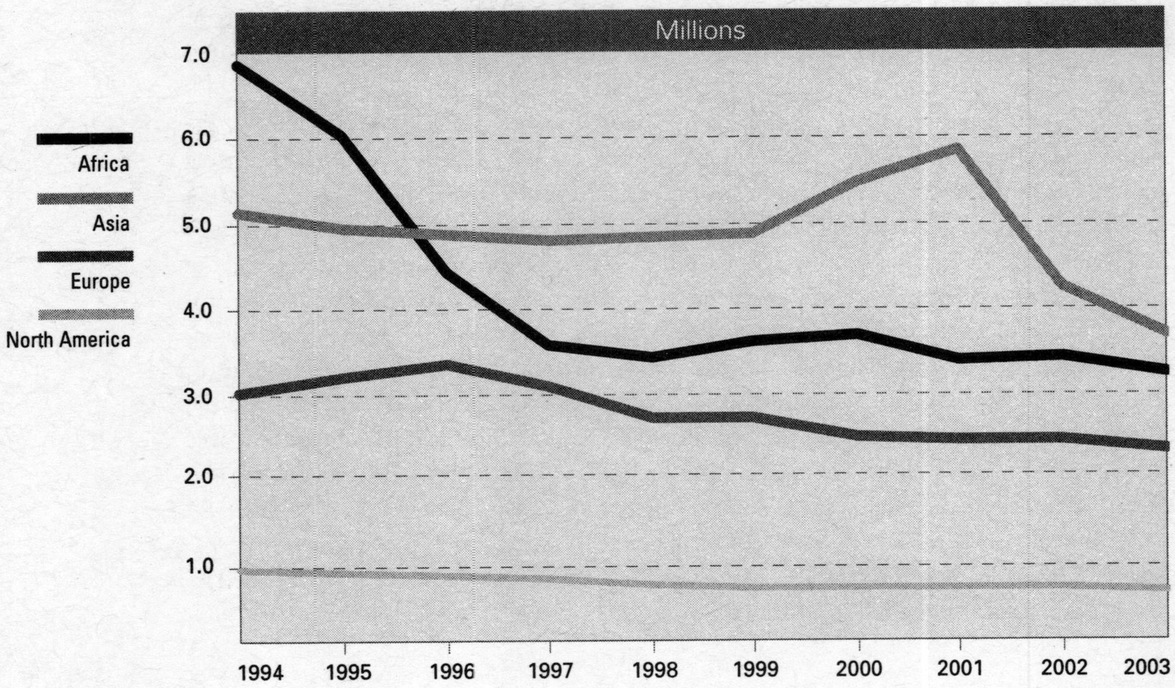

Not only are changes in the refugee population under the mandate of UNHCR caused by the demographic events of births, deaths and international movements, but they also result from legal circumstances, such as the granting of refugee status and naturalization. Owing to the many possible reasons, it is often difficult to attribute a change in the refugee population to one particular factor. Since refugee populations are highly mobile compared with other groups of international migrants, new inflows and return movements are generally the key determinants of size of the refugee population and are therefore considered in more detail below.

Although refugee trends by region of asylum and by origin are similar, they are not identical. If the global number of refugees originating from a region, regardless of their country of asylum, is greater than the number of refugees hosted by that region, regardless of their country of origin, the region can be considered to have a negative "refugee migration balance". Conversely, regions that receive more refugees than they "generate" can be considered to have a positive refugee migration balance.

Over the past 10 years, Europe has been the region where the largest proportion of refugees were from outside the region

During 1994-2003, Europe recorded the largest positive refugee migration balance. During this period, the average annual refugee population in Europe was 2.7 million, whereas only 1.3 million refugees had originated from this region. Although North America and Oceania hosted significantly fewer refugees than Europe, there were also very few refugees originating from these regions. As a result, these two regions also recorded a positive refugee migration balance, although one that was much smaller than that of Europe. Conversely, for Latin America and the Caribbean, Africa and Asia, the number of refugees originating from these regions is greater than the number of refugees that they host. A breakdown by five-year period suggests that the net refugee migration balance has narrowed for the developed regions, but widened for the developing regions (see figure VII.3).

Figure VII.3.
Migration balance of refugees under the mandate of UNHCR, 1994-2003

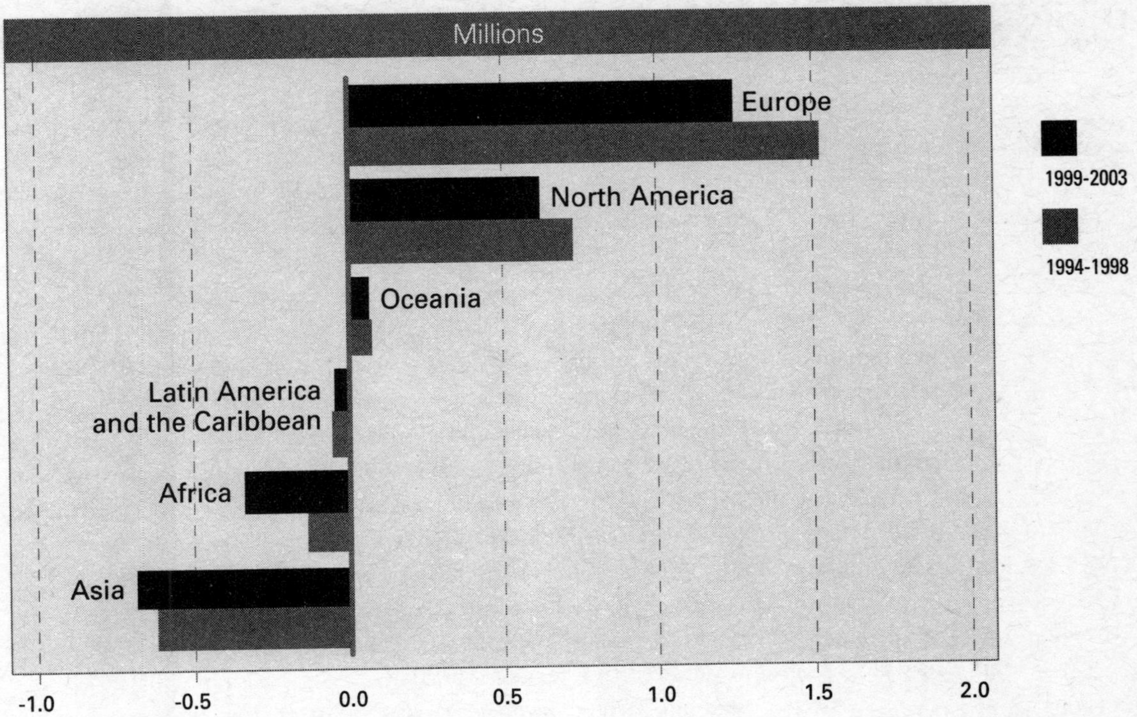

These refugee migration balances suggest that developing regions tend to generate more refugees than they receive, whereas the developed regions are in the opposite situation. The size of the refugee flow from developing to developed countries should not be overemphasized, however. As was noted earlier, the large majority of refugees find asylum in the region of origin. Considering that most refugee-producing countries are located in the developing regions, most refugees are also hosted by these regions. The large majority of the world's refugees thus not only originate from, but are also hosted by the developing regions. By the end of 2003, Africa, Asia and Latin America and the Caribbean were the origin of some 8.2 million of the world's refugees but these three regions together also hosted 6.8 million refugees, about two thirds of the world total. Some 2.5 million refugees, one quarter of all refugees, are hosted by least developed countries. Sub-Saharan countries host 2.9 million refugees, about 30 per cent of the world total. This contrasts with the situation 50 years ago when refugee flows were primarily a European phenomenon.

The large majority of the world's refugees originate in and are hosted by the developing regions

The decrease in the global refugee population during 1994-2003 is also reflected in the number of countries producing large refugee populations. The number of countries from which more than 25,000 refugees had originated fell from 43 in 1994 to 36 in 2003. The total number of refugees originating from these major source countries decreased even more, from 13.7 million in 1994 to 8.9 million in 2003 (-35 per cent).

In contrast with the decrease in the number of refugees, it is estimated that the average duration of major refugee situations in developing countries almost doubled, from 9 years in 1993 to 17 years in 2003 (United Nations High Commissioner for Refugees, 2004b). The number of long-standing or protracted refugee situations, involving more than 25,000 refugees and lasting five years or more, increased from 27 in 1993 to 38 at the end of 2003. However, in line with the global decline in the refugee population, the num-

The average duration of stay in a refugee status increased markedly during the past decade

ber of refugees living in protracted situations fell from 7.9 million in 1993 to 6.2 million in 2003. The recent increase in the duration of refugee situations can be largely attributed to two factors. First, a significant number of new refugee situations arose in the early 1990s, few of which had been fully resolved by 2003. Second, the number of new refugee emergencies that occurred during the period 1994-2003 was relatively small.

An important principle of international refugee protection is the sharing of responsibilities among countries. The contribution to the international refugee cause is expressed in two main ways: by providing asylum to refugees and by providing international assistance to poor countries hosting large refugee populations. For developing countries that, owing to their proximity to conflict zones, host large groups of refugees, caring for refugees implies a significant additional burden imposed on an already fragile economy. To alleviate these pressures, high-income countries provide international assistance through UNHCR, other international organizations or bilaterally. Industrialized countries also admit refugees, either through planned resettlement programmes or by accepting asylum-seekers.

Burden-sharing for refugees involves issues ranging from international assistance and national asylum policies to the impact on the environment, access to land and the labour market and the use of services. Two possibilities for quantifying of the burden on refugee-hosting countries in relation to their capacity are to compare the refugee population with gross domestic product (GDP) per capita and with national population.

However, analysis using these two variables, such as that presented below, does not include the positive contribution of refugees to the host economy, which can be significant when refugees are allowed to integrate locally.

Pakistan hosted the largest number of refugees in relation to its per capita national income: 3,800 refugees per United States dollar of per capita GDP in 1999-2003. The Democratic Republic of the Congo carried the second largest burden by this measure—2,800 refugees per United States dollar of per capita GDP, followed by the United Republic of Tanzania (2,500), Ethiopia (2,000) and the Islamic Republic of Iran (1,000).

The longer refugees stay, the more their impact is felt by host societies. Four out of the five countries with the highest burden in relation to per capita GDP in 1999-2003 had also been among the top five countries in 1994-1998. Thirteen of the 20 countries with the highest number of refugees per United States dollar of per capita GDP in 1999-2003 were on the African continent. In brief, the same developing countries have shouldered most of the refugee burden in recent years.

Armenia hosts more refugees per national inhabitant than any other country

Comparing the number of refugees in a country to the size of the national population reveals that Armenia hosted the largest number of refugees per 1,000 inhabitants (87) during 1999-2003, followed by Serbia and Montenegro (39), Guinea (35), Djibouti (34) and the Congo (27). Countries with a high refugee burden in relation to population size are geographically dispersed. Of the 20 countries bearing the heaviest burden, half are in Africa, eight are in Europe and two in Asia. There has been little change over time in the countries with the highest number of refugees in relation to national population size (UNHCR, 2002b). If the 4 million Palestinian refugees under the mandate of UNRWA are included in this analysis, Jordan, Lebanon and the Occupied Palestinian Territory would all rank among the four main host territories for refugees in relation to the size of their national population.

In 2003, UNHCR received a demographic breakdown for more than 10 million persons. Although the global data coverage has markedly improved in recent years, most industrialized countries continue to be unable to provide UNHCR with gender- and age-disaggregated refugee statistics owing to a lack of adequate refugee registration.

Almost half (48 per cent) of the population of concern to UNHCR are women of all ages. The proportion of females is very close to the average in age groups 0 to 4 (49 per cent) and 5 to 17 (48 per cent). Women are overrepresented in the oldest group of those aged 60 years or over (53 per cent), a reflection of the higher life expectancy of women generally.

Almost half of all refugees of concern to UNHCR are women

The age distribution of refugees and other persons of concern to UNHCR reflects global demographic patterns (see table VII.1). The proportion of refugees who are children under age 5 is the highest in Africa (19 per cent), a function of the high fertility levels in this region. The low proportion of older refugees in Africa mirrors the low life expectancy in many African countries.

Table VII.1.
Age distribution of refugees and other persons of concern to UNHCR, by region, 2003

	Percentage			
Region	0-4	5-17	18-59	60+
Africa	19	36	42	4
Asia	12	34	48	6
Europe	3	23	57	18
Latin America and the Caribbean	3	17	75	5
Oceania	12	36	48	4
Total	13	33	47	7

Europe shows the opposite demographic structure. Almost 20 per cent of the refugees are aged 60 years or over, whereas less than 5 per cent are children under age 5. Again, the demographic structure of the refugee population is not unlike that of the resident population, characterized by low birth rates and significant population ageing. Most information on the age of refugees in Europe is from Commonwealth of Independent States (CIS) countries and the Balkans, where population ageing is particularly advanced.

Durable solutions

The role of UNHCR is both to protect and assist refugees and to find permanent solutions to their plight. These solutions include the voluntary repatriation of refugees to their country of origin, their full integration in the country of asylum, and resettlement to third countries.

Voluntary repatriation

Voluntary repatriation is the durable solution that is generally preferred and by far the most important solution numerically speaking. During the period 1994-2003, an estimated 14.6 million refugees were able to repatriate to their country of origin, either with the assistance of UNHCR or spontaneously (see table VII.2). While most refugee returns took place in Africa (53 per cent) and Asia (36 per cent), there was a sizeable number of refugees who repatriated in Europe (12 per cent).

During the past decade, nearly 15 million refugees were able to repatriate to their country of origin

Table VII.2.
Voluntary repatriation of refugees by region of origin, 1994-2003

Thousands			
Region	1994-1998	1999-2003	Total
Africa	6 169.6	1 502.7	7 672.3
Asia	1 608.4	3 565.4	5 173.8
Europe	398.8	1 277.9	1 676.7
Latin America and the Caribbean	36.3	3.5	39.8
Total	8 213.1	6 349.5	14 562.6

It is estimated that some 6.3 million refugees repatriated to their home country during 1999-2003, 23 per cent fewer than during 1994-1998. During the five-year period 1994-1998, Africa was the main focus of voluntary repatriation, accounting for 75 per cent of the global return flows. The main countries receiving back their citizens during this period were Rwanda (3.1 million), Afghanistan (1.0 million), Mozambique (965,000) and Burundi (500,000).

During 1999-2003, the focus of durable solutions shifted from Africa, with most refugees repatriating in Asia (56 per cent). Almost as many refugees returned to their country of origin in Europe (20 per cent) as in Africa (24 per cent). The largest number of refugees repatriated to Afghanistan (3.2 million), Serbia and Montenegro (981,000), Angola (262,000), Sierra Leone (246,000) and Timor-Leste (226,000).

Resettlement

Resettlement in third countries makes a limited but crucial contribution to managing the global refugee situation

Although the quantitative contribution of resettlement to finding durable solutions is limited, it plays an important role in the sharing of refugee burdens by the developed countries. Resettlement concerns the transfer of refugees from countries of temporary or first asylum to third countries, where they are admitted on a permanent basis. Although UNHCR seeks to widen the number of countries accepting resettled refugees, the large majority of refugees are resettled in a limited number of industrialized immigration countries, most notably Australia, Canada and the United States of America. While many refugees are resettled under the auspices of UNHCR, resettlement may also take place bilaterally, that is to say, by agreement between the country of settlement and the refugee, or with the help of other organizations.

The leading countries of resettlement are Australia, Canada and the United States

The selection process for resettlement under the auspices of UNHCR involves a number of steps. First, refugees are interviewed on an individual basis to ensure that they meet the criteria for refugee status. Second, resettlement candidates should meet one of the resettlement criteria (women at risk, family reunification, children and adolescents, medical needs, legal or physical protection needs, older refugees, lack of local integration prospects, survivors of violence or torture). Third, arrangements for departure of refugees are assigned a priority ranging from normal to emergency. The resettlement quota of the receiving countries may also include criteria or preferences, based, inter alia, on region of origin or a particular type of vulnerability (for example, that of women at risk).

During 1994-2003, almost 267,000 refugees were resettled under UNHCR auspices. Refugees originating in Asia accounted for the largest proportion of those who benefited from this form of durable solution (46 per cent), followed by refugees from

Africa (38 per cent) and Europe (16 per cent). The resettlement of African refugees has been generally on the rise since 1994, whereas resettlement from Asia and, in particular, from Europe has declined.

While voluntary repatriation often reflects a comprehensive solution, resettlement is more selective. Individual refugees may be resettled from refugee camps in the absence of a clear solution for the majority of those at the same facility. Resettlement trends reflect both the protection needs of refugees as well as the preferences of resettlement countries.

The decrease in resettlement from Europe has been closely linked to the end of the conflict in former Yugoslavia. During 1995-1997, some 20,000 refugees from Bosnia and Herzegovina had been resettled through UNHCR. The high level of departures from Asia in 1994 reflected resettlement under the Central Plan of Action for refugees in South-East Asia. In 1994 alone, 12,200 refugees from Viet Nam and the Lao People's Democratic Republic were resettled under UNHCR auspices. The fall in resettlement from Africa in 2001 and 2002 was largely the result of increased screening procedures by the United States, following the events of 11 September 2001.

The United States has been the main country receiving resettled refugees. In 2003, about half of all refugees who were resettled under UNHCR auspices settled in the United States. Canada was the second largest recipient of resettled refugees (16 per cent), followed by Australia (15 per cent), Norway (6 per cent), Sweden (3 per cent), Denmark (2 per cent) and Finland (2 per cent).

Local integration

Local integration, the third durable solution for refugees, may take many different forms. In some asylum countries, prospects for local integration are limited, requiring that the international community sustain refugees living in camps on a daily basis. In other countries, refugees may have freedom of movement, allowing them to settle among the local population, while access to land or the labour market may allow refugees to become economically self-sufficient. Access to naturalization can be considered the final and decisive step towards the local integration of refugees. By obtaining the citizenship of the host country, refugees enjoy the full protection of their new country of nationality. While the extent of economic or social integration is difficult to measure, some countries provide statistics on naturalization.

Despite the paucity of data, it is evident that tens of thousands of refugees benefit from naturalization each year. Some sizeable refugee groups that were granted citizenship of the host country in recent years include Armenian refugees in Azerbaijan (188,000 in 2000), Azerbaijani refugees in Armenia (48,000 in 1999-2002), refugees from Bosnia and Herzegovina and Croatia in Serbia and Montenegro (42,000 in 1998) and refugees from Guatemala in Mexico (17,000 during 1998-2002). In developed countries, most refugees are locally integrated. After having received long-term residence status, they eventually obtain the citizenship of the host country.

Although complete data are lacking, tens of thousands of refugees are able to naturalize and integrate into their host country population each year

Refugee outflows

While hundreds of thousands of refugees find a durable solution to their difficulties each year, new displacements do continue. From 1994 to 2003, an estimated 8.7 million persons had fled their country of origin as part of various mass outflows (see sect. entitled "Asylum trends in industrialized countries" for an overview of individual asylum-seekers applying for refugee status). Nevertheless, the number of refugees becoming displaced has dropped significantly since 1999. In 2002 and 2003, less than 300,000 refugees fled their country of origin, the lowest level of the past 10 years. As noted earlier, the low level of new displacement, combined with ongoing durable solutions, had a favourable impact on the size of the global refugee population. The high refugee outflow in 1994 had been caused by the Rwandan crisis, whereas the peak in 1999 reflected the crises in Kosovo (900,000 refugees) and Timor-Leste (300,000 refugees) (see figure VII.4).

In 2002 and 2003, less than 300,000 refugees fled their country of origin each year, the lowest number for several years

Although the total number of new refugee displacements during 1999-2003 was less than in the previous five years, the number of countries producing major flows increased from 8 to 10. During 1994-1998, Rwanda had been the main source of new refugee outflows (2.4 million refugees), followed by Burundi (424,000) and Sierra Leone (365,000). Only five other countries (Liberia, the Democratic Republic of the Congo, Croatia, Somalia and the Sudan) had outflows exceeding 100,000. During the period 1999-2003, the countries from which most refugees fled were more dispersed geographically, with the largest flows originating in Serbia and Montenegro (871,000 from Kosovo), Afghanistan (641,000), the Democratic Republic of the Congo (365,000), Timor-Leste (280,000), Sudan (249,000), and Liberia (220,000). There were outflows of 100,000-200,000 refugees from four countries (Angola, Burundi, Eritrea and Somalia).

Figure VII.4.
Outflows of refugees under the mandate of UNHCR, 1994-2003

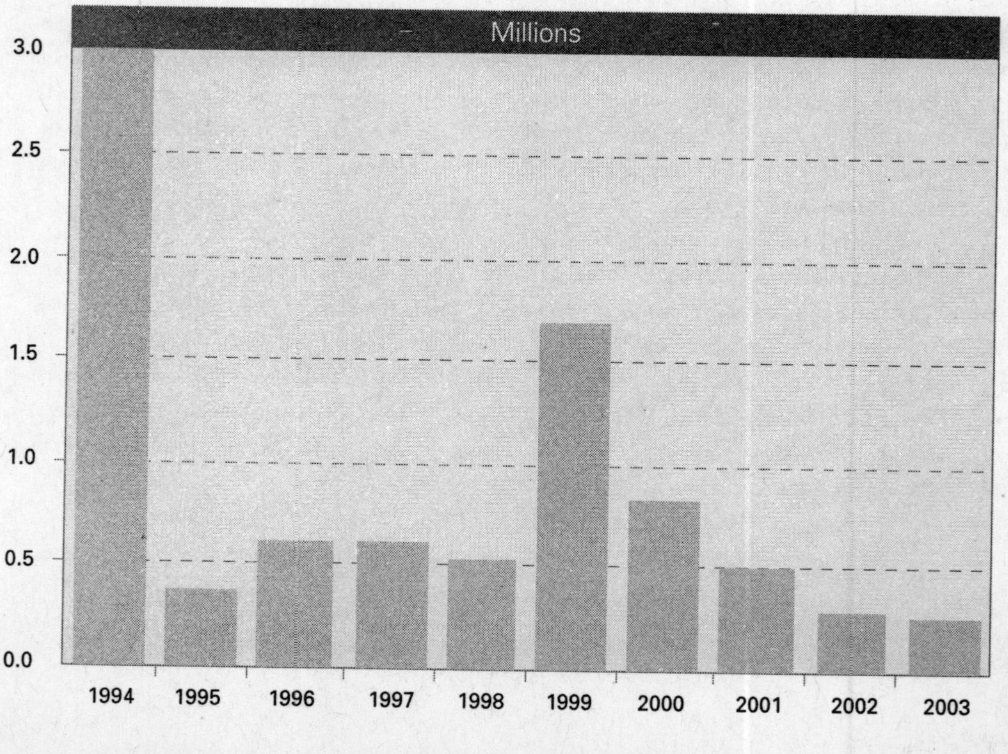

Some countries (Burundi, the Democratic Republic of the Congo, Somalia and the Sudan) were a source of refugees during much of the period, whereas other countries (Sierra Leone, Croatia, Kosovo (Serbia and Montenegro), Afghanistan, Timor-Leste, Angola and Eritrea) had outflows of a shorter duration.

Conclusions

Trends in the refugee population during the 10-year period 1994-2003 suggest that the global refugee situation has improved. The total refugee population fell from an estimated 15.7 million persons in 1994 to 9.7 million in 2003, a decrease of 40 per cent. The largest decrease in the number of refugees was in Latin America and the Caribbean, followed by Africa, Asia, North America and Europe. Oceania was the only region where the number of refugees remained stable.

The analysis of refugee movements confirms this generally positive image. A combination of high levels of refugees returning coupled with the prevention of new refugee situations caused an unprecedented fall in the global refugee population. During 1994-2003, the number of refugees who were able to repatriate to their country of origin far exceeded the number of refugees who became displaced.[1] The number of refugees who returned to their country of origin during 2002 in relation to the global refugee population (1 in 5) was the highest for at least 10 years.

Progress in finding durable solutions and in preventing new mass outflows has been uneven across regions. During 1994-1998, all regions had recorded a net return flow. Whereas Africa recorded the highest net return flow in 1994-1998, Asia was the centre of durable solutions during 1999-2003. In Europe, the number of refugees who returned home was greater than the number who became displaced during the period 1994-2003, although the difference was small (see figure VII.5).

Figure VII.5.
Net flows of refugees under the mandate of UNHCR, by region, 1994-2003

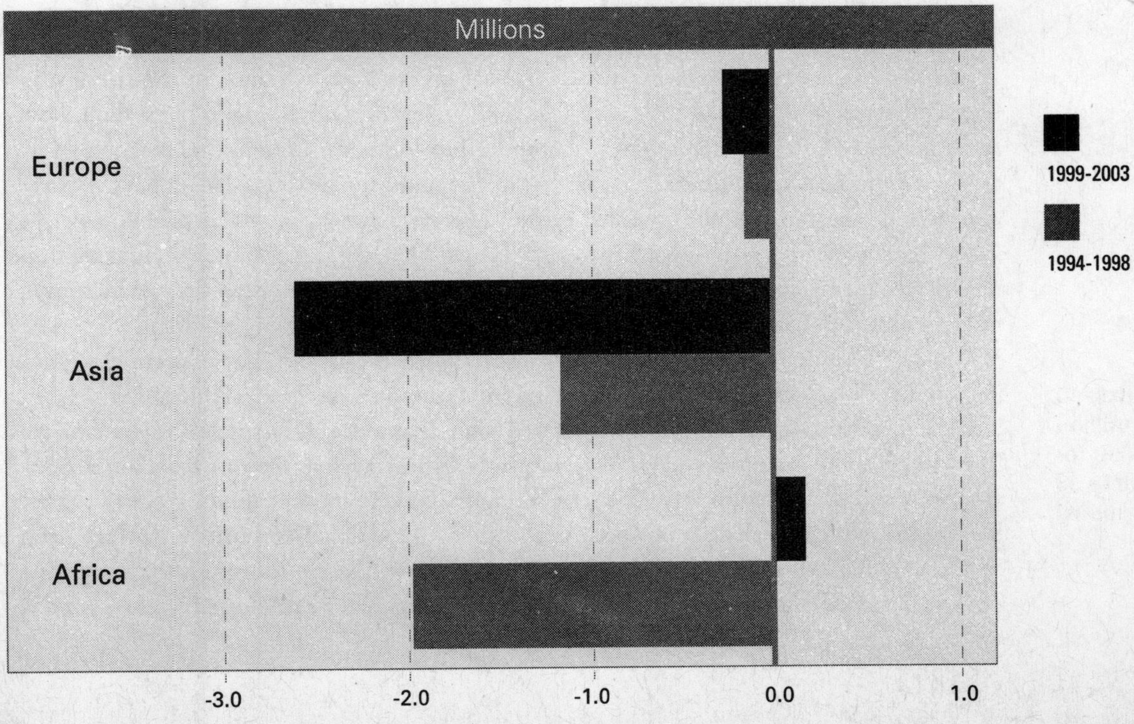

Voluntary repatriation on the African continent had exceeded new outflows by 2 million during 1994-1998, but the most recent five years show slightly more refugees becoming displaced than finding a durable solution. To reverse this worrying trend, UNHCR launched a *Dialogue on Voluntary Repatriation and Sustainable Reintegration in Africa* in March 2004.[2]

The number and duration of protracted situations have increased markedly since the early 1990s. At the same time, the absolute number of refugees in protracted situations has declined, reflecting the fall in the global refugee population. The growing importance of protracted situations is due partly to success in averting new refugee flows.

The experiences of refugees in protracted situations differ widely. Many refugees have been able to integrate locally and to become self-sufficient. Such refugees impose less of a burden on host countries, as they contribute to the economy as workers and consumers. However, such contributions can be fully realized, only if refugees are allowed to integrate locally.

Nevertheless, millions of refugees do continue to linger in camps, where they depend on international aid for their survival. Each protracted refugee situation is unique, requiring its own solution, based on the conditions in the countries of origin and asylum. Since many refugees in protracted situations come from countries that have been affected by conflict for many years, it is unlikely that large-scale voluntary repatriation is a solution in the short run. For these refugees, local integration seems the most logical option, although it may not necessarily be available to them in the country where they currently reside.

Although the available evidence suggests that the plight of refugees has improved during the 10-year period under review, this may not be case for those who have been displaced by conflict, but do not conform to the official definition of a refugee. In many cases, internally displaced persons (IDPs) substantially outnumber refugees as such. In terms of human suffering, their plight may be just as painful as that of refugees. However, IDPs fall outside the purview of this publication, whose focus is on international population movements.

Asylum trends in industrialized countries

In addition to the mass movements discussed in the previous section, there are thousands who seek asylum on an individual basis each year. The present section examines the asylum flows to 38 mostly industrialized countries in Europe, North America, Oceania and Asia. Not only are these countries the recipients of, by far, the largest number of asylum-seekers, but they have also become the focus of the so-called asylum-migration nexus, in which asylum becomes intertwined with migration flows. Between 1994 and 2003, some 5.3 million asylum applications were submitted in these 38 countries. However, it should be noted that an increasing number of individual asylum claims are also being lodged in developing countries.

During the past 10 years, 5.3 million persons applied for asylum in 38 developed countries

This section uses mostly official government statistics. They concern the number of "new" applications: second or appeal applications have been excluded, as persons lodging these appeal claims would be counted more than once. Nevertheless, these data are likely to overstate the actual arrival of asylum-seekers inasmuch as they are based on national sources and double-counting of persons seeking asylum in more than one country cannot be avoided if such cases have not been detected by the national authorities. Asylum data, although indicative of actual movements, differ from immigration statistics. Although most claims are lodged upon arrival, an asylum application may also be submitted after lawful residence has been established, for instance, to avoid return to the country of origin. In addition, asylum claims are sometimes filed at embassies in the region of origin.

Most asylum countries report the number of persons applying for asylum. In the United Kingdom of Great Britain and Northern Ireland and the United States, the statistics are based on the number of applications ("cases"), not persons. In some instances, UNHCR has made adjustments, based on estimates from the competent authorities. Most data are reported by calendar year, except the United States figures, which are based on the United States fiscal year. The French data exclude children under age 16.

Asylum flows by country of asylum

During 1994-2003, some 5.3 million asylum applications were submitted in the 38 countries considered. Europe was the main destination of asylum-seekers (73 per cent), North America was the second largest receiving region (25 per cent), whereas relatively few claims were submitted in Australia and New Zealand (2 per cent). The highest level of claims had been reached in 2001, when 619,000 asylum applications were registered. In 2003, the 38 countries received some 468,000 new asylum claims, the lowest figure since 1997 (see figure VII.6).

Whereas asylum levels in Europe and those in the other countries were comparable in 1994-1996, trends started to diverge in 1997. While the number of asylum applications in the non-European countries had dropped since the mid-1990s, Europe experienced a strong rise in the arrival of asylum-seekers. In both regions, the number of asylum claims has dropped since 2001.

Nearly three quarters of all requests for asylum during the past 10 years were submitted in European countries

Figure VII.6.
Asylum applications lodged in 38 industrialized countries, 1994-2003

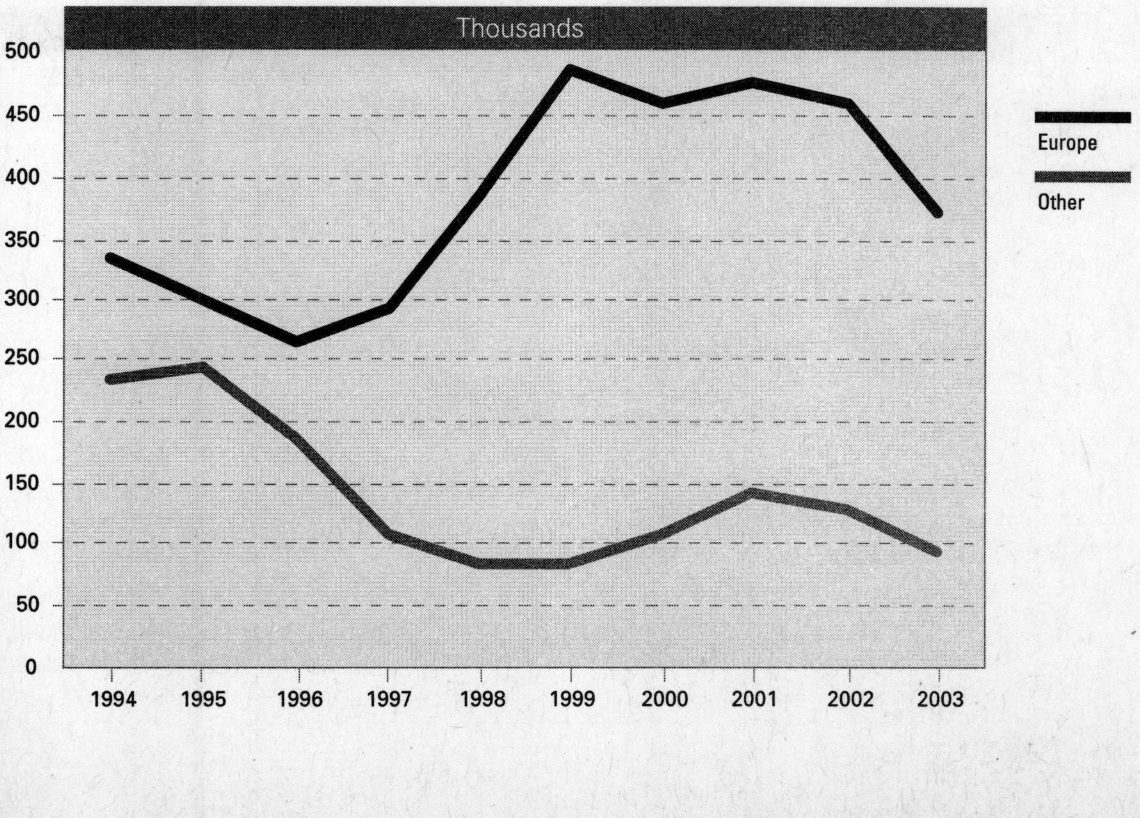

The number of new requests for asylum has been falling in all regions since 2001

During the period 1999-2003, 2.8 million asylum claims were lodged in the industrialized countries, 16 per cent more than in the previous five-year period. While the total inflow of asylum-seekers increased, important shifts took place in their destination. Major asylum countries that were able to significantly reduce the inflow of asylum-seekers included the United States (-52 per cent), Germany (-33 per cent) and the Netherlands (-18 per cent). Conversely, the number of new asylum claims rose in Austria (264 per cent), Sweden (106 per cent), France (105 per cent), Belgium (93 per cent), the United Kingdom (90 per cent) and Canada (48 per cent).

A major diversification took place in the receiving countries. The number of countries receiving 90 per cent of all asylum claims increased from 10 in 1994-1998 to 15 in 1999-2003. In can be concluded that the "asylum space" has widened notably, with an increasing number of countries shouldering the responsibility for receiving asylum claims and admitting refugees.

The number of countries receiving substantial numbers of requests for asylum has increased in recent years

Further insight into this diversification is provided by comparing the number of asylum-seekers in European countries with the size of the national populations. On average, Europe received almost 7 asylum-seekers per 1,000 inhabitants during 1994-2003. Switzerland received five times more asylum-seekers (35 per 1,000 inhabitants) than the European average. A number of small countries were among those that received a significant number of asylum claims in relation to their national population size (see table VII.3).

Germany and the United Kingdom are the only two of the more populous countries that receive more asylum-seekers than the European average. All other countries with larger populations receive fewer asylum-seekers than the European average, including France, Italy Poland and Spain. Southern Europe (Greece, Italy, Spain and Portugal) is the

Table VII.3.
Top 20 asylum-seeker receiving countries in Europe, 1994-2003

	Number of asylum-seekers per thousand inhabitants		
Country of asylum	1994-1998	1999-2003	1994-2003
Switzerland	16.2	18.3	34.5
Liechtenstein	6.9	22.2	29.1
Austria	4.7	17.3	22.0
Luxembourg	6.2	15.2	21.5
Netherlands	11.4	9.4	20.8
Belgium	7.0	13.5	20.5
Sweden	6.3	13.0	19.3
Norway	3.8	15.3	19.2
Ireland	2.7	12.4	15.1
Denmark	6.0	8.9	14.9
Germany	7.0	4.7	11.6
United Kingdom	4.0	7.5	11.5
Cyprus	0.7	10.8	11.4
Average	2.8	4.0	6.8
Slovenia	0.3	6.8	7.1
Czech Republic	1.1	5.3	6.3
Slovakia	0.4	5.8	6.1
France	1.8	3.7	5.5
Hungary	0.8	3.8	4.6
Malta	1.2	3.1	4.3
Finland	0.9	2.8	3.7

destination of very few asylum-seekers in Europe on a per capita basis. These data indicate that, although the "asylum space" has widened, the geographical distribution of asylum-seekers remains unbalanced.

Origin of asylum-seekers

Outflows of asylum-seekers are often an indication of conflict. During 1994-2003, Asia had been the main region of origin of asylum-seekers in industrialized countries, accounting for 41 per cent of the total inflow. The leading source countries of asylum-seekers in this period were Iraq (354,000), Turkey (300,000) and Afghanistan (229,000). In 2001 and 2002, almost half of all asylum-seekers came from countries in Asia (see figure VII.7).

One quarter of the more than 5 million asylum applicants in 1994-2003 originated from Europe. Serbia and Montenegro, including Kosovo, was the main European country of origin (552,000), followed by the Russian Federation (134,000, mostly from Chechnya), Bosnia and Herzegovina (110,000) and Romania (107,000). In 1998 and 1999, more than one third of all asylum claims lodged in the industrialized countries originated from Europe owing to the Kosovo crisis.

Asia accounted for over 40 per cent of asylum-seekers in developed countries in 1994-2003

Some 935,000 African citizens sought asylum in industrialized countries during 1994-2003, constituting 19 per cent of the total asylum influx. The proportion of African asylum-seekers increased from 16 per cent in 1999 to 25 per cent in 2003. Somali asylum-seekers were the most numerous (140,000), followed by nationals from the Democratic Republic of the Congo (98,000), Algeria (87,000) and Nigeria (87,000).

In Europe, the Kosovo crisis was the one most important event leading to a flow of asylum-seekers in recent years

Figure VII.7.
Proportion of asylum claims lodged in 38 countries by region of origin, 1994-2003

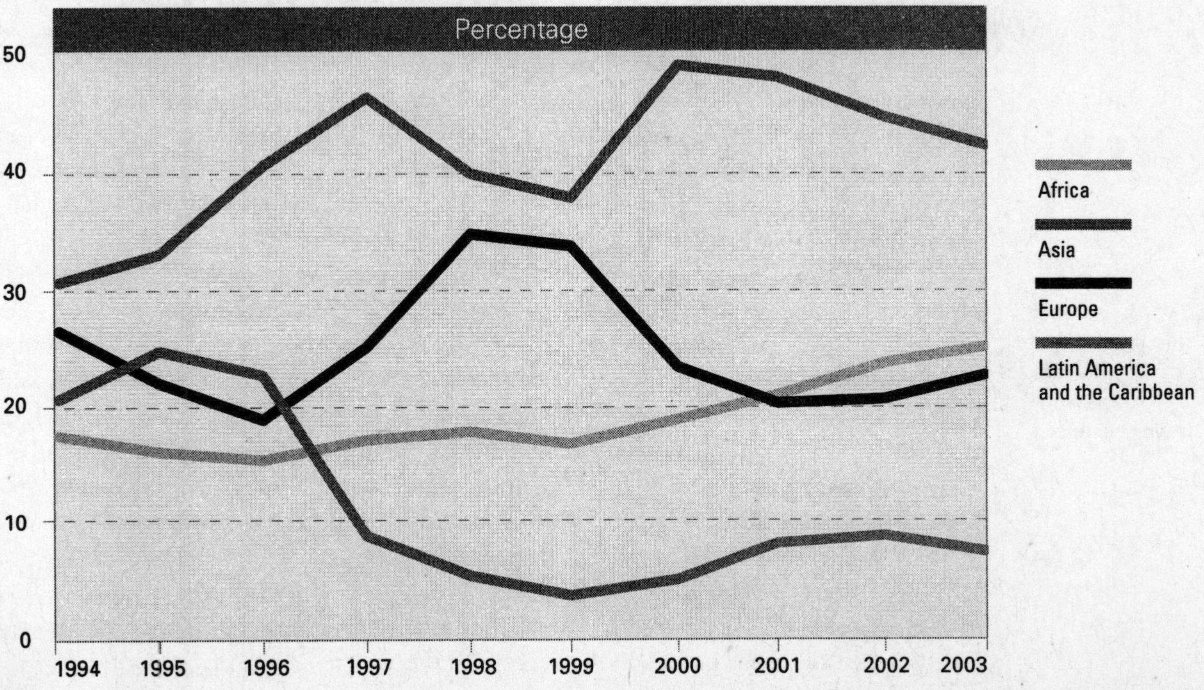

Nineteen per cent of all those who requested asylum in a developed country during 1994-2003 had originated in Africa

In general, people tend to seek asylum in a country that is comparatively close to their country of origin

The number of asylum-seekers from Latin America and the Caribbean has fallen drastically since the mid-1990s, reflecting in particular the ending of conflict in Central America. Most asylum-seekers from this region came from El Salvador (175,000), Mexico (85,000) and Guatemala (79,000).

As is the case with other types of movement, proximity is an important determinant of asylum-seeker flows. In Europe, Asia is the main source region of asylum-seekers (44 per cent), followed by Europe (30 per cent) and Africa (21 per cent). Only 2 per cent of all persons seeking asylum in Europe are from Latin America and the Caribbean. In North America, however, half the asylum-seekers originate from Latin America and the Caribbean. Asia is the source of 27 per cent of the asylum-seekers, whereas only 14 per cent of asylum-seekers come from Africa and 7 per cent from Europe. In Australia and New Zealand, 60 per cent of those who applied for asylum during 1994-2003 came from Asia.

The decrease in asylum claims of citizens from Bosnia and Herzegovina, El Salvador and Guatemala mirror the end of the large-scale conflicts in those countries. Asylum claims from Serbia and Montenegro fell by only 14 per cent in 1999-2003 compared with 1994-1998, mostly because of the Kosovo crisis which had erupted in 1999. The decline in asylum-seekers from Sri Lanka also coincides with recent peace-building activities. More recent conflicts in Afghanistan, Iraq and the Russian Federation (Chechnya) have caused a rise in applications from these countries.

Another group of countries of origin of asylum-seekers are those characterized by protracted conflict and instability (for example, the Democratic Republic of the Congo and Somalia) or internal displacement (for example, Algeria and Turkey). Lastly, there are countries of origin without large-scale conflict (for example, China and India) whose asylum-seekers are likely to claim to have suffered individual persecution.

Admission of refugees

Of those who seek asylum, only a minority are granted refugee status or allowed to remain on humanitarian grounds. The return of asylum-seekers who are deemed not to be in need of international protection is therefore one of the main preoccupations of Governments that consider granting asylum. Unfortunately, the compilation and international analysis of statistics on the return of rejected asylum-seekers are fraught with pitfalls. Some data on returnees fail to make a distinction between undocumented migrants in general and rejected asylum-seekers. Furthermore, the definition of return may range from requesting the unsuccessful applicant to leave the country to effecting his or her physical removal from the territory.

During the past decade, about one quarter of all requests for asylum were granted

During the period 1994-2003, it is estimated that the industrialized countries granted refugee status according to the 1951 Convention relating to the Status of Refugees to some 901,000 asylum-seekers in first instance or on appeal, and that another 492,000 asylum-seekers were allowed to remain for humanitarian reasons. In total, almost 1.4 million asylum-seekers, constituting 28 per cent of the total number of those who had lodged new asylum claims during the period, were thus granted residence rights. The United Kingdom granted refugee or humanitarian status to the largest number of asylum-seekers (264,000), followed by Germany (190,000), the United States (188,000), Germany (178,000), the Netherlands (138,000), Canada (130,000) and Switzerland (118,500).

Europe granted temporary protection on a group basis to more than 500,000 refugees during 1994-2003. Some 350,000 of these refugees had come from Bosnia and Herzegovina and were hosted by Germany. By the end of 2003, the majority of these refugees had returned to their country of origin.

Whereas Convention and resettled refugees are generally granted long-term residence and are thus unlikely to be subject to refoulement, the protection accorded to asylum-seekers who are admitted on humanitarian grounds, as well as persons granted temporary protection, is of a shorter duration and may not amount to full and adequate protection under the Convention. A substantial number of refugees or persons in a refugee-like situation granted temporary residence status may be required to return to their home countries once the host State determines that conditions in the country of origin have improved, even if the safety and security of returnees may not have been adequately established.

While trends and levels in asylum and refugee migration are generally well documented, it is almost impossible to determine the contribution of asylum-seekers and refugees to total immigration. Even when data by immigrant category are available, the sources, definitions and frequency of reporting differ so widely that the resulting statistics are difficult to compare between countries. The main exceptions are the countries of permanent settlement (Australia, Canada, New Zealand and the United States), where humanitarian inflows are generally well distinguished from other inflows. The Agenda for Protection, adopted by UNHCR and States in 2002, advocates better data collection and research on the nexus between asylum and migration.[3] In particular, it calls upon States to tabulate data according to the revised *United Nations Recommendations on Statistics of International Migration* (United Nations, 1998a).

Individual asylum-seekers who are in need of protection, but who are not granted Convention refugee status, may be subject to greater likelihood of refoulement

International cooperation

Recent developments

International cooperation and genuine burden-sharing can strengthen respect by all States for their international protection responsibilities towards refugees. This theme was examined at length during the UNHCR Global Consultations on International Protection process held from 2000-2002 and is central to the Agenda for Protection which was endorsed by States in the Executive Committee of the Programme of the United Nations High Commissioner for Refugees. The Agenda identifies the following six objectives, with accompanying activities that are designed to achieve a more equitable sharing of burdens and responsibilities, to build capacities to receive and protect refugees and to find durable solutions to their displacement:

The UNHCR Global Consultation process has set forth an Agenda for Protection calling for increased international cooperation in the protection of refugees

(a) Better responsibility-sharing arrangements through which the burdens of first-asylum countries may be shouldered;
(b) More effective cooperation to strengthen protection capacities in refugee-receiving countries;
(c) Strengthened partnerships for protection with civil society including non-governmental organizations;
(d) Refugee communities empowered to meet their own protection needs;
(e) Refugee issues anchored within national, regional and multilateral development agendas;
(f) Resettlement used more effectively as a tool of burden-sharing.

Examples of enhanced cooperation can be found in the development by UNHCR of a Framework for Durable Solutions for Refugees and Persons of Concern, which consists of three tools: development assistance for refugees; repatriation, reintegration, rehabilitation, and reconstruction; and development through local integration. Closely linked to this Framework are the efforts to initiate "Convention Plus" agreements, aiming to build upon the 1951 Convention and its 1967 Protocol relating to the Status of Refugees. These agreements aim to clarify responsibilities and to promote better burden-sharing among States, notably in the context of mass influxes, and mixed migratory flows, and in implementing durable solutions. Through close cooperation among host Governments, donors and other United Nations organizations, durable solutions programmes have been initiated in many regions including Afghanistan, Eritrea, Sierra Leone, Sri Lanka, Uganda and Zambia.

International cooperation is also necessary in efforts to protect refugees within broader migration movements. In this area, the Agenda for Protection identifies a number of objectives and activities that include:

(a) Better identification of and proper response to the needs of asylum-seekers and refugees, including access to protection within the broader context of migration management;
(b) Strengthened international efforts to combat smuggling and trafficking;
(c) Better data collection and research on the nexus between asylum and migration;
(d) Reduction of irregular or secondary movements;
(e) Closer dialogue between UNHCR and IOM;
(f) Information campaigns to ensure that potential migrants are aware of the prospects for legal migration and the dangers of human smuggling and trafficking;
(g) Return of persons found not to be in need of international protection.

In this area, UNHCR works in close cooperation with a number of actors, such as participants in the Berne Initiative. UNHCR is also a participant in a number of regional processes where the linkages among refugee protection, asylum and migration are frequently explored.

Improving data collection

Solid data on gender and age of refugees are essential for planning, implementing, monitoring and evaluating refugee programmes. In particular, the UNHCR policy priorities in respect of gender equity, children and adolescents and older refugees require the establishment of accurate gender and age profiles.

Under the 1951 Convention, countries have an obligation to provide statistics to UNHCR. In the past 10 years, much progress has been made in collecting and disseminating refugee statistics. The first UNHCR *Statistical Yearbook*, (United Nations High Commissioner for Refugee, 2001), issued in October 2002, is one of the most tangible results of these advances. Yet a number of important data gaps still need to be filled, while existing statistics should be improved in a number of ways.

An important gap in global refugee statistics is caused by the absence of official government estimates of the number of refugees in industrialized countries. Despite the fact that refugees are an increasingly important segment of the foreign population in developed countries, basic data on their presence and characteristics remain scarce. Without a register, it is difficult to estimate the size of the refugee population with any degree of accuracy.

Thus, one of the priority areas for UNHCR with respect to strengthening refugee protection is registration: individual registration is a prerequisite for refugees as regards their obtaining adequate protection and support. To this end, the Executive Committee of the Programme of the United Nations High Commissioner for Refugees adopted a conclusion on registration of refugees and asylum-seekers in 2001.[4]

One may also note that it was individual registration that constituted the basis for collecting most of the statistics presented in this chapter.

Notes

1 The number of refugees who register for repatriation or upon arrival in their home country is sometimes higher than the number of refugees who registered in the country of asylum. It is, therefore, likely that refugee outflows are underestimated, whereas the number of returning refugees may be overstated.

2 Launched at the High-level forum organized by UNHCR on 8 and 9 March 2004 in Geneva. For further information, see http://www.unhcr.ch/Path: Special events (accessed 10 November 2004).

3 The Agenda for Protection was originally issued in document A/AC.96/965/Add.1 of 26 June 2002, and endorsed by the fifty-third session of the Executive Committee of the Programme of the United Nations High Commissioner for Refugees.

4 See the report of the Executive Committee of the Programme of the United Nations High Commissioner for Refugees, fifty-second session (1-5 October 2001) (Official Records of the General Assembly, Fifty-second Session, Supplement No. 12A (A/56/12/Add.1), chap. III.B - Executive Committee Conclusion No. 91 (L11).

Chapter VIII
International cooperation for migration management

Efforts to seek viable mechanisms of cooperation for the better management of international migration are not new. The mass population displacements that occurred during and just after the Second World War made the cooperative management of international migration desirable. That belief gave birth to international organizations such as the Office of the United Nations High Commissioner for Refugees (UNHCR) and the Intergovernmental Committee for European Migration (ICEM).[1] Similarly, during the period of rapid growth of worker migration to countries of Europe, the International Labour Organization (ILO) adopted several international conventions and recommendations to set standards for the employment and treatment of migrant workers. In addition, many Governments cooperated in the management of labour migration through bilateral agreements or programmes, mostly regulating the mechanisms for the legal recruitment of migrant workers and their rotation.

Calls for international cooperation to manage international migration are increasing

The 1990s witnessed not only a rise of international migration flows directed to developed countries, but also a resurgence of calls to strengthen international cooperation in the field of international migration. These calls were prompted by the realization that because of growing disparities in economic development, the international mobility of people was unlikely to lessen in the foreseeable future. In addition, conflict and political instability in some areas of the world continued to produce flows of involuntary migrants. Moreover, growing security concerns arising from the expansion of international terrorism have added urgency to the need to improve border management. All these considerations have increased the saliency of international migration in the global agenda. The impact of international migration both on domestic politics and on international relations has led to a growing realization of the limitations of unilateralism in this field and has strengthened the conviction that cooperative management is an effective way to establish the basis for orderly migration.

The present chapter examines existing cooperative mechanisms and recent developments in the orderly management of international migration at the bilateral, regional and multilateral levels. Bilateral agreements have been a traditional means to manage the international flows joining countries. The 1990s witnessed an upsurge in the use of such an approach. At the regional level, regional economic integration agreements have as yet made little progress towards ensuring the free movement of persons or workers, with the exception of agreements reached by the European Union (EU); but regional consultative processes have emerged in virtually all world regions, and have become viable mechanisms of cooperation through which to enhance the management of migration. Furthermore, international migration has been increasingly identified as a priority issue for the international community. There has been a wide array of multilateral activities undertaken by international institutions within and outside the United Nations system. They have contributed to the formulation of global norms on migration management through adoption of legal instruments and provision of forums for intergovernmental dialogue on international migration issues.

Bilateral approach

There has been a notable upsurge in bilateral migration agreements

Bilateral arrangements on international migration, which are often formalized through agreements signed by Governments, are a useful means of responding rapidly to changing migration trends, or characteristics, or to specific issues on a case-by-case basis. The agreements formalize commitments by both countries to ensure that international migration takes place in accordance with established rules and conditions that are mutually beneficial. Bilateral agreements are normally concluded between countries of origin and countries of destination of international migrants, but sometimes between countries sharing borders and countries that are members of the same regional economies. The present section reviews the role of bilateral agreements in cooperative action taken by two countries to ensure that international migration occurs in an orderly fashion.

Unlike regional or multilateral agreements, bilateral agreements on international migration have long existed. Arrangements regulating the international mobility of people date back to the late eighteenth and the nineteenth century (International Organization for Migration, 2003b). At that time, the United States signed consular agreements or treaties of friendship, commerce and navigation with a number of countries. These treaties were mostly concerned with trade but also provided to citizens of States parties the right to enter the ports of the parties and a limited right of establishment or residence in each other's territories. Just after the Second World War, the promotion of free movement of people dominated bilateral agreements in Latin America (Mármora, 2003). In the 1960s, several countries in Western Europe facing serious shortages of labour entered into bilateral agreements with countries in the Mediterranean region for the temporary recruitment of migrant workers. However, with the economic downturn that followed, a large number of these agreements have been replaced by a much looser framework of agreements, memorandums of understanding and declarations of mutual cooperation on the contracting and protection of foreign workers (International Labour Organization, 2004a). By the early 1970s, the peak demand for labour had shifted from Western Europe to the oil-producing countries in Western Asia. The oil-producing countries of that region concluded agreements or statements of mutual cooperation with countries of origin regarding the recruitment and protection of their workers, although the recruitment of workers was normally left to private recruitment agents operating under State supervision (Abella, 1997).

Many countries entered into bilateral agreements during the 1990s

The 1990s saw many countries entering into bilateral migration agreements. The opening of borders in Eastern Europe and the dissolution of the former Union of Soviet Socialist Republics (USSR) led to an upsurge in such agreements between countries in Eastern Europe and members of the Commonwealth of Independent Sates (CIS), and between Eastern European countries and members of the EU or countries outside Europe (International Labour Organization, 2004a). By 2000, there were 173 bilateral agreements involving member States of the Organization for Economic Cooperation and Development (OECD), a fivefold increase since 1990 (ibid.). In Latin America, 84 bilateral agreements on international migration were signed between 1991 and 2000 (Mármora, 2003), 42 per cent of which were between countries in Latin America and 58 per cent with countries in other regions.

Bilateral agreements on migration aim at managing a wide range of issues. In recent years, Governments typically rely on bilateral agreements to address issues related to temporary labour migration, control of irregular migration, border management, the return of migrants, and remittance management. Agreements between developed and developing countries sometimes include provisions on foreign aid or technical assistance.

Bilateral cooperation is common with regard to temporary labour migration. Malaysia, for instance, has concluded bilateral agreements with Bangladesh, Indonesia, Pakistan, the Philippines and Thailand to recruit temporary migrant workers. Workers from these countries are primarily engaged in manufacturing, and plantation and construction work, as well as in the service sector (United Nations, 2003a). South Africa has a well-established temporary migration programme through which more than 100,000 foreign workers are recruited annually to work in the gold and coal mines of the country (Adepoju, 2000). Labour contracts are regulated by South Africa's bilateral treaties with Botswana, Lesotho, Malawi, Mozambique and Swaziland. Similarly, Germany has bilateral arrangements with a number of countries in Eastern Europe to obtain temporary migrant labour (Stalker, 1994). Quotas on foreign worker admissions from specific countries have been set through bilateral agreements concluded by Algeria, the Czech Republic, Guatemala, the Republic of Korea, Singapore, Slovakia, Spain and Switzerland (International Labour Organization, 2004a).

In recent years, bilateral agreements on labour migration have become more far-reaching, aiming to control the process from the point of origin to the point of destination. Since 1999, Spain has concluded bilateral agreements with eight countries, namely, Bulgaria, Colombia, the Dominican Republic, Ecuador, Guinea-Bissau, Morocco, Poland and Romania (Internal Labour Organization, 2004a), all of which go so far as to cover the preselection of workers and the conditions under which family reunification is possible.

Bilateral cooperation can also be useful in ensuring the welfare of migrants abroad. The Philippines, a major country of origin of migrant workers, has been actively involved in securing the best possible terms for Filipino workers abroad. It has concluded 15 bilateral agreements concerning the protection of the rights of its migrant workers, 13 of which are with countries in Western Asia (United Nations, 2003a).

Some bilateral agreements are explicitly designed to benefit countries of origin as well as countries of destination

Strategies to ensure the positive effects of international migration for both the country of origin and the country of destination have been promoted through, for instance, the French "co-development" model which promotes the circulation of international migrants between countries of origin and countries of destination, and provides technical and financial assistance for migrants who decide to return to their countries of origin (Weil, 2002). In this scheme, the country of origin benefits from the return of skilled persons, retirees or seasonal workers, while the labour needs of the country of destination are met. Since 2000, the annual Mali-France Consultation on Migration has dealt with the integration of Malians who want to stay in France, the co-management of migration flows, and the cooperative development of areas of emigration in Mali (Martin, Martin and Weil, 2002).

The Working Holiday Scheme is a unique programme that allows young people to combine work with tourism under a bilateral agreement. It has been implemented by a growing number of countries, including Australia, Canada, France, Germany, Spain and the United Kingdom of Great Britain and Northern Ireland. As of early 2000, Australia had such an arrangement with eight countries[2] (Organization for Economic Cooperation and Development, 2001). In 2000 alone, the Australian Government issued about 71,500 visas under this programme.

Bilateral agreements have increasingly focused on control of trafficking in undocumented migrants

In recent years, the prevention and control of undocumented migration, especially when it involves trafficking in migrants, have also become one of the major priorities for bilateral cooperation. In 2000, Colombia and Ecuador signed the Permanent Statute on Migration and a Memorandum of Understanding aiming to combat irregular migration, and illegal drug trafficking, and to ensure common action on all aspects of the problem (Mármora, 2003). Similarly, Costa Rica and Nicaragua have signed an agreement to curb irregular migration.

In 1993, Mexico and the United States of America entered into an arrangement referred to as the Border Liaison Mechanism (BLM) (International Organization for Migration, 2003b) which has become a useful tool with which to manage cases related to the smuggling of migrants and border violations. More recently, the two countries adopted the Border Partnership Action Plan which reaffirms and revitalizes existing bilateral coordination mechanisms at the local, State and federal levels, with a specific focus on operations at border crossing points. Similarly, Canada and the United States have reaffirmed their commitment to enhancing collaboration between their respective border agencies in the Canada-United States Smart Border Declaration of 2001 (ibid.).

Under international law, States have the obligation to readmit their own citizens. Several bilateral arrangements aim at facilitating the orderly return of migrants, including those in an irregular situation, to their country of origin. In 1998, for instance, Italy and Tunisia signed a readmission agreement whereby Tunisia accepts the return of Tunisians in an irregular situation who have been apprehended in Italy (Migration News, 1998). In return, Italy promises to invest in Tunisia so as to create jobs and discourage emigration. Since 1990, there has been an increase in the number of readmission and assisted-return agreements in Latin America (Mármora, 2003).

Another leading focus of bilateral agreements has been to enhance remittances

Migrant remittances continue to be a major source of foreign exchange and an important addition to the gross national income (GNI) of many countries. An increasing number of countries try to foster the inflow of remittances from their citizens abroad. Bilateral cooperation to ensure stable exchange rates and to promote the safe and timely transfer of remittances has developed slowly. The programme developed by Mexico and the United States represents a pioneering effort. In 2001, the Government of Mexico concluded agreements with banks and wire transfer agencies in the United States to facilitate and reduce the costs of transferring money from the United States to Mexico (International Organization for Migration, 2003b). According to this arrangement, about 15 banks would allow Mexicans in the United States to open bank accounts upon presentation of identification cards provided by Mexican consulates, thus facilitating the sending of remittances more quickly and safely.

Bilateral approaches, although geographically limited, provide an effective means of seeking mutually beneficial arrangements for the management of international migration. Bilateral agreements have been a valuable tool for advancing the interests of the two Governments involved, often in a relatively short period of time. Since 1990, the number of bilateral agreements has been increasing and the range in respect of the nature of the issues covered has been expanding.

Regional approach

European Union

Regional intergovernmental agreements for economic cooperation often include provisions to facilitate migration

The better management of cross-border movements of people has also moved high in the agenda of regional and subregional bodies. In particular, the drive towards economic and, in some cases, political integration has resulted in formal agreements among member States of various regional groups concerning the free movement of their citizens and other types of cooperation regarding the harmonization of measures to manage migration.

EU has made the greatest progress in this regard. The free movement of workers within its borders is one of the fundamental principles of a common market. Already, the 1957 Treaty of Rome (United Nations, 1958), the founding document of EU (then the

European Economic Community (EEC)), had established the right to free movement of workers within the community. It was introduced by progressive stages in the six original member States of the European Community and was fully achieved by 1968 (European Commission, 2001). Thereafter, EU added new member States, although fears of uncontrolled migration flows obliged some accession countries such as Greece, Portugal and Spain to go through relatively lengthy transition periods before the entry into full force of the migration provisions. EU also gradually established the principle of the free movement of all persons, not only workers. Since 1993, freedom of movement has been extended to all citizens of member States of EU as a right inherent in European citizenship. In a parallel development, a process to remove controls on all persons, irrespective of their nationality, who crossed borders between EU member States was started in 1985 with the Schengen Agreement on the Gradual Abolition of Checks at Their Common Borders, signed by Belgium, France, Germany, Luxembourg and the Netherlands. The 1999 Treaty of Amsterdam incorporated the Schengen Agreement into the EU founding treaties, and by 2001, all member States at that time (15), except Ireland and the United Kingdom, were applying its provisions.

The European Union has gone farthest in this direction

In May 2004, an additional 10 countries, mostly Eastern European, joined the 15 member States of EU. While EU guarantees the citizens of newly admitted States the right to live and work within the Union borders, old member States have again raised concerns about the impacts that an influx of workers from the accession countries may have on the existing labour market. Thus, under the enlargement agreement, for the first two years following the accession, the old 15 member States are limiting the influx of workers from the accession countries by various measures. Only two countries, Cyprus and Malta, are exempted from restrictions on free movement of workers. At present, access to the labour markets of the old member States depends on national measures and policies, as well as on bilateral agreements that they may have with the new member States. At the end of the first two years, in 2006, the functioning of such transitional arrangements will be reviewed. It is expected that the free movement of workers from the new member States will be fully achieved by 2011, seven years after their accession.

The free movement of people as well as of workers within EU borders has been envisaged in parallel with tougher controls at EU external borders. In 1999, at a special summit meeting in Tampere, Finland, EU Governments pledged to work towards a common policy on asylum and immigration, focusing efforts on the more efficient management of international migration flows, a more effective control of external borders to combat illegal migration, trafficking and smuggling, and issues of migrant integration. Since then, EU has been forging partnerships with countries of origin, developing a common European asylum system, and fostering the equitable treatment of third-country nationals in EU member States. Most recently, the draft EU constitution has defined the respective responsibilities in the field of international migration and migrant integration of the EU governing bodies and of member States.

The European Union is strengthening and harmonizing policies on migration from non-Union countries

Regional initiatives in the context of economic integration

Outside Europe, agreements to facilitate the movement of persons or workers under specific conditions have also been part of the regulatory framework for common market or free trade group agreements. However, none of these arrangements has advanced as yet to the level of economic integration of EU. Migration between member States of each of the

Outside Europe, prospects for regional migration agreements are less favourable

various agreements continues to be restricted. In fact, because of continued economic disparities between the member States of the various groups, prospects for a fuller integration of their respective labour markets and free movement of persons remain dim.

In Africa, for example, there have been the Protocol on the Free Movement of Persons, the Right of Residence and Establishment (in West Africa) adopted by the Economic Community of West African States (ECOWAS) in 1979; and the Protocol on the Free Movement of Persons, Labour, Services and the Right of Establishment in the States of the Common Market for Eastern and Southern Africa (COMESA) adopted by COMESA in 1994. However, neither of these instruments has been fully implemented. In 2003, the Central African Economic and Monetary Community (CEMAC) agreed to establish new measures to put into effect its accord on free circulation of labour, replacing the older measures that had never been implemented effectively (International Labour Organization, 2004a).

In Western Asia, the primary document concerned with migration is the Agreement of the Council of Arab Economic Unity (the Council was established by the Arab Economic Council of the Arab League), adopted in 1965. The Council aimed to achieve economic integration of the region through the framework of economic and social development. The Agreement provided for freedom of movement, employment and residence and abolishes certain restrictions upon movement within the region (International Organization for Migration, 2003b). In 1984, the Arab Declaration of Principles on the Movement of Manpower was adopted. It underlined the need to give preference to Arab nationals and calls for intraregional cooperation. Elsewhere in Asia, countries have not yet established formal regional agreements dealing specifically with the free movement of workers. The only exception has been provided by Asia-Pacific Economic Cooperation (APEC) which has introduced a business travel card that aims to facilitate short-term visits of business persons in the region by eliminating the need for a visa.

In the Americas, the Andean Community, a subregional group made up of Bolivia, Colombia, Ecuador, Peru and Venezuela, adopted in 1977 the Andean Instrument for Labour Migration. Revised in 2003, the instrument seeks to facilitate the free movement of persons in the Andean region (International Labour Organization, 2004a). Similarly, the Southern Common Market (MERCOSUR) pact countries approved in 2002 an agreement on residence of their nationals, in order to strengthen the integration process of the group (ibid.). The North American Free Trade Agreement (NAFTA) between Canada, Mexico and the United States went into effect in 1994. It has provisions to facilitate the cross-border movement of business persons who are citizens of member countries. However, free movements of persons between the member States are not allowed.

Regional intergovernmental organizations

Regional intergovernmental institutions for political cooperation often have migration high in their agendas

A number of intergovernmental institutions have been active in the field of international migration and have contributed much to the understanding of the phenomenon on the regional level. Some of the most prominent initiatives merit attention.

The Council of Europe, with 45 member States, has the goal of promoting human rights and working to consolidate European cooperation in the area of international migration. The main body responsible for migration activities in the Council of Europe is the European Committee on Migration, whose terms of reference are, inter alia, to develop European cooperation on migration, on the situation and social integration of populations of migrant origin and refugees, and on community relations. The Council has issued recommendations, guidelines and principles to promote the protection of long-term migrants, persons admitted for family reunification and migrant workers. A major achievement in setting European standards was the adoption of the European Convention on the Legal Status of Migrant Workers (United Nations, 1997b, sect. B.26), which was adopted at Strasbourg on 24 November 1977 and entered into force in 1983. More recent activities have focused on the integration of immigrants and persons of immigrant origin into host societies and the building of good community relations in multi-ethnic societies.

The International Centre for Migration Policy Development (ICMPD) is an inter-governmental organization with a European focus and global interests. It was created in 1993 to promote comprehensive and sustainable migration policies, and to foster exchanges among Governments concerned with European migration issues. ICMPD acts as secretariat for the Budapest Process, whose goal is the harmonization of control mechanisms for the entry of foreigners. This Process involves more than 40 States and 10 international organizations. ICMPD has organized 70 inter-governmental meetings since 1995 under the aegis of the Budapest Process.

The Organization for Security and Cooperation in Europe (OSCE), with participating States in Europe, Central Asia and North America, provides training for border guards, assists in the development of migration legislation and coordinates activities among various government agencies involved in the management of international migration.

In Africa, the African Union, previously known as the Organization of African Unity (OAU), was established in 2000. The protection of people forced to flee their country had been a widespread concern of the OAU member States in the 1960s. Recognizing the need to take account of special characteristics of the refugee situation in Africa, OAU adopted in 1969 the Convention Governing the Specific Aspects of Refugee Problems in Africa (United Nations, 1983) which expanded the definition of "refugee". Within the new mandate of the African Union, the issues of migration have been discussed by various departments of the secretariat under the existing portfolios for implementation, monitoring and follow-up.

In Asia, the Association of Southeast Asian Nations (ASEAN) adopted the Plan of Action on Immigration Matters in 2000. The Plan serves as the institutional framework for ASEAN cooperation in international migration. ASEAN also adopted in 2002 a comprehensive work programme detailing practical initiatives and measures to be carried out by all member States. The Directors-General of Immigration Departments and Heads of Consular Divisions of the ASEAN Ministries of Foreign Affairs, which comprises representatives of member countries, is the highest policy-making body within ASEAN on migration matters. Increasingly, the South Asian Association for Regional Cooperation (SAARC) has become concerned with the trafficking of women and children within and between countries of the subregion. Member States signed, in 2002, a regional Convention on Preventing and Combating the Crime of Trafficking in Women and Children for Prostitution at their eleventh Summit in Kathmandu, Nepal.

In the Americas, the Organization of American States (OAS) acts as a legal framework that brings together Government leaders from member States to cooperate at the regional level on education, justice, security and other, related issues, including migration. In 2000, the Inter-American Commission on Human Rights, an autonomous organ of OAS, signed an institutional cooperation agreement with IOM and consolidated hemispheric efforts to improve the promotion and protection of the rights of migrants in general, and especially those of migrant workers and their family members. To this end, the Commission established the Special Rapporteurship on Migrant Workers and Members of Their Families.

Regional consultative processes

Governments have established consultative processes on international migration ...

On the premise that common understanding among Governments is often easier to achieve at the regional level, a number of regional and subregional consultative processes have emerged during the last decade. These processes were often spawned by regional conferences or seminars focused on specific migration issues of regional concern. The consultative process typically revolves around a particular issue such as undocumented migration, asylum or trafficking in persons. Each process brings together representatives of States in the region in addition to international organizations and, in some cases, non-governmental organizations as well. Organizations such as ICMPD, IOM, the United Nations Institute for Training and Research (UNITAR) and UNHCR have provided substantive and logistic support to establishing and maintaining such consultative processes. Table VIII.1 presents the number of members by region of the major consultative processes on international migration.

... in Europe ...

The Intergovernmental Consultations on Asylum, Refugee and Migration Policies in Europe, North America and Australia (IGC) is the oldest consultative process listed in the table. It emerged from a meeting held in 1985 to discuss the management of asylum-seekers and refugees in Europe. IGC has provided a forum for the exchange of information and the discussion of policy direction among participating Governments. It has currently six working groups dealing with various issues related to the management of international migration and asylum.

In the Commonwealth of Independent States (CIS) and neighbouring countries, the 1996 Regional Conference to Address the Problems of Refugees, Displaced Persons, Other Forms of Involuntary Displacement and Returnees in the Countries of the Commonwealth of Independent States and Relevant Neighbouring States, which was organized to address concerns about population displacement after the disintegration of the Soviet Union, led to a comprehensive technical cooperation programme aimed at establishing, improving and harmonizing national migration legislation, policies and administrative structures in CIS. Therefore, it established a regional consultative process to manage the follow-up to the Conference. One of the distinctive features of the CIS Conference process has been its emphasis on non-governmental organization participation and the development of local non-governmental organization capacity (International Organization for Migration, 2003b).

The Budapest Process was born out of the concern raised by irregular migration from Eastern and Central Europe towards Western Europe after the fall of the Berlin Wall and liberalization of emigration regulations in Eastern and Central Europe (Klekowski von Koppenfels, 2001). Since its first meeting in 1991, the Budapest Process has expanded both its membership and its focus. It now functions as a consultative forum for more than 40 Governments and has developed closer ties with EU. The 1997 Prague Ministerial Conference of the Budapest Process adopted a set of recommendations, many of which addressed the issue of trafficking (International Organization for Migration, 2003b).

The Berne Initiative is a consultative process that has been expanding to include countries not only in Europe but also in other regions. The Initiative was launched by the Government of Switzerland at the International Symposium on Migration held in June 2001. The Symposium identified interests common to all States as well as the benefits that could be derived from enhanced cooperation (Omelaniuk, 2003). The Berne Initiative enables Governments from all the world's regions to discuss their policy priori-

Table VIII.1.
Number of Governments participating in regional consultative processes on international migration

	Europe				Africa		Asia			Americas	
Region and subregion	IGC[a]	Budapest Process	Conference process[b]	Five plus Five[c]	MIDSA[d]	MIDWA[e]	APC[f]	Manila Process	Bali Process	Puebla Process[g]	Lima Process[h]
Africa											
Eastern Africa					6						
Middle Africa					2						
Northern Africa				4							
Southern Africa					5						
Western Africa				1		15					
Asia											
Eastern Asia							5[i]	4[i]	5[i]		
South-central Asia			5				6		7		
South-eastern Asia							10	10	9		
Western Asia		3	3								
Europe											
Eastern Europe		10	4								
Northern Europe	6	10									
Southern Europe	2	10		4							
Western Europe	5	7		1							
Americas											
Caribbean										1	
Central America										8	
South America											10
North America	2	2								2	
Oceania											
Australia/ New Zealand	1	1					2	2	2		
Melanesia							4	1	4		
Micronesia							3		2		
Polynesia							1		1		
Total	16	43	12	10	13	15	31[i]	17[i]	32[i]	11	10

a Intergovernmental Consultations on Asylum, Refugee and Migration Policies in Europe, North America and Australia (IGC).
b Commonwealth of Independent States (CIS) and Relevant Neighbouring States Conference process.
c Conference on Migration in the Western Mediterranean.
d Migration Dialogue for Southern Africa (MIDSA).
e Migration Dialogue for Western Africa (MIDWA).
f Intergovernmental Asia-Pacific Consultations on Refugees, Displaced Persons and Migrants (APC).
g Regional Conference on Migration (RCM).
h South American Migration Dialogue.
i Including the Governent of Hong Kong Special Administrative Region (SAR) of China as a participant.

ties and identify long-term interests in the area of international migration, and offers the opportunity to develop a common orientation towards the management of international migration. The Berne Initiative aims at developing a broad policy framework to facilitate cooperation among Governments in managing the movement of people in a humane and orderly fashion.

More recently, the consultative process known as "Five plus Five" provides a forum for dialogue among countries of origin, countries of transit and countries of destination in the Mediterranean region. It originated at the First Ministerial Conference on Migration in the Western Mediterranean held in Tunis in 2002. It aims to improve understanding of international migration dynamics by sharing information and best practices, so as to address issues relating to international migration and development (International Organization for Migration, 2003b).

... in Africa,...

In Africa, two consultative processes have been set in motion since 2000, one involving countries of Eastern, Middle and Southern Africa (MIDSA) and the other involving those of Western Africa (MIDWA). MIDSA, created from a technical cooperation workshop for senior government officials, explores ways of improving the management of border control and labour migration by means of technical cooperation, training and information-sharing among Governments. The Migration Dialogue for Western Africa (MIDWA) was established in 2002 as a follow-up process to the Dakar Declaration adopted in 2000 at the West African Regional Ministerial Meeting on the Participation of Migrants in the Development of their Country of Origin. The MIDWA seeks regional approaches to combating trafficking in persons, to addressing issues linked to labour migration, and to promoting peace and stability in Western Africa (International Organization for Migration, 2003b).

... in Asia, ...

In Asia, the intergovernmental Asia-Pacific Consultations on Refugees, Displaced Persons and Migrants (APC), established in 1996, consist of a series of meetings involving countries from both Asia and Oceania. It discusses a broad range of international migration issues, including those related to refugees and displaced persons. The Manila Process, developed as a result of a conference held in 1996, brings together countries of Eastern and South-eastern Asia for the exchange of information, primarily on irregular migration and trafficking. The two processes have been strengthened by the ministerial-level International Symposium on Migration, which led to the adoption of the Bangkok Declaration on Irregular Migration in 1999.

More recently, the Bali Ministerial Conference on People Smuggling, Trafficking in Persons and Related Transnational Crime, held in 2002, involved a more extended regional coverage. As a follow-up to the Conference, consultations will be carried out to enhance the implementation of the recommendations adopted and to coordinate actions to combat people smuggling, trafficking in persons and related transnational crime in the region.[3] In 2003, ministerial-level consultations among major labour sending countries in Asia took place in Colombo, Sri Lanka. It became a forum within which to share experiences and identify challenges of labour migration management. The participating States have agreed to a regular follow-up of the issue.

... and in the Americas

Since 1996, the Governments of Central and Northern American countries have been holding consultations at regular intervals in what has come to be known as the "Puebla Process". Launched at a time when the debate on the implementation of the North American Free Trade Agreement (NAFTA) was at its peak, the Puebla Process originally focused on reducing irregular migration, especially the transit of irregular migrants though Central America and Mexico to the United States and Canada. In 1997, a Plan of Action was drawn up to address the main issues of concern. Since then, the scope of the Puebla Process has expanded to include technical cooperation (International Organization for Migration, 2003b).

Representatives of the countries of South America met in Lima in 1999 and started a tradition of annual meetings to share views on international migration and to seek regional cooperation. The meeting's Lima Declaration sets forth their decision to closely monitor international migration in the region. Its commitment to promoting safe international migration and to strengthening the mechanisms to combat trafficking in persons was reaffirmed in 2002 (International Organization for Migration, 2003b).

Most consultative processes provide a level of informality that facilitates wider participation, the free flow of information and unhampered dialogue among participants. The conclusions and recommendations of such processes are non-binding, unlike those of other, more formal forums. The consultative processes focus on cooperative dialogue and seek common understandings on international migration issues. Goals are identified and often recommendations or a plan of action is adopted. Because full agreement on all issues is not required, various options can be explored openly, thus increasing the number of possible solutions to issues (Klekowski von Koppenfels, 2001). Although a consultative process is not a formal institution, but rather a continuing arrangement involving a minimum of administration, direct communication among high-level officials is possible and fostered. Often, consultative processes bring together countries of origin, countries of transit and countries of destination, as well as delegates from different governmental departments, thus fostering communication and coordination even within countries.

Some regional consultation processes are evolving from forums to action-oriented approached

Though regional consultative processes were initially intended to provide a forum for dialogue and exchange of information among participating Governments, over the years, as participants gained confidence and a common understanding, some processes have moved towards more comprehensive, action-oriented approaches. The Puebla Process, for example, has advanced on a wide range of issues. It has contributed to mobilizing resources and developing regional strategies. The success of the Puebla Process has inspired other regional processes to devise concrete action plans based on the relationships and understandings forged through these informal consultations (International Organization for Migration, 2003b).

Given the relatively short history of regional consultative processes, it is probably too early to assess the contributions that they have made in strengthening international cooperation on international migration. While the impact of informal dialogue and information-sharing remains intangible, there seems to be a consensus that the processes, by providing a venue for repeated personal contact among decision makers in a region, contribute usefully to the international cooperative management of international migration.

International approach

Role of the United Nations system

The search for a new world order after the end of the cold war in the early 1990s coupled with the accelerating globalization of markets and economies helped underscore the global nature of international migration and the importance of managing it effectively so as to maximize its benefits for all actors concerned. Thus, in the 9 September 2002 report of the Secretary-General entitled "Strengthening of the United Nations: an agenda for further change" (A/57/387 and Corr.1), the Secretary-General identified international migration as one of the main issues on which the organization had to deepen its knowledge, sharpen its focus and act more effectively.

The United Nations has pursued international cooperation in the field of international migration in three ways: (a) through the adoption of legal instruments on international migration; (b) through regular activities of offices within their respective mandates; and (c) through the establishment of international norms adopted by global conferences.

Establishment of international legal norms and instruments related to international migration

At the global level, the human rights of migrants are progressively being codified by bodies of the United Nations system

While States exert a sovereign right to protect their own national interests, they may voluntarily limit their sovereignty by entering into binding international commitments. The United Nations system has long contributed to the formulation of global legal norms and instruments relevant to the management of international migration.

Table VIII.2 lists the key human rights instruments of the United Nations, indicating the date when each was adopted, and the date when each entered into force, as well as the number of countries that have ratified each. As these instruments primarily address fundamental rights of individuals and freedoms for all without distinctions, they have been ratified by a large number of countries. While these instruments have played a limited role in the debates on international migration, they do include a number of provisions relating to

Table VIII.2.
Major United Nations legal instruments that make reference to international migration

Instrument	Year adopted	Year entered into force	Number of countries ratified[a]
Universal Declaration of Human Rights[b]	1948	-	-
International Covenant on Civil and Political Rights[c]	1966	1976	152
International Covenant on Economic, Social and Cultural Rights	1966	1976	149
International Convention on the Elimination of All Forms of Racial Discrimination[d]	1965	1969	169
Convention on the Elimination of All Forms of Discrimination against Women[e]	1979	1981	177
Convention on the Rights of the Child[f]	1989	1990	192

a As of 1 May 2004. The number includes non-member States of the United Nations and the Governments of Cook Islands and Niue.
b Article 13 provides the right to the freedom of movement, and the right to leave and the right to return to one's country. Article 14 provides the right to seek asylum and article 15 provides the right to a nationality.
c Article 12 provides the right to freedom of movement, and the right to emigrate from and the right to return to one's country.
d Article 5 provides the right to emigrate from and return to one's country.
e Article 9 provides the right to a nationality.
f Article 7 provides the right to a nationality. Article 10 refers to entering or leaving a State party for the purpose of family reunification.

population movements. For instance, the Universal Declaration of Human Rights (General Assembly resolution 217 A (III)), adopted in 1948, proclaimed the right to freedom of movement and residence within the borders of each State and the right to leave any country including one's own and to return to that country (article 13), the right to seek and to enjoy in other countries asylum from persecution (article 14) and the right to a nationality (article 15). The right to leave any country, including one's own, was reaffirmed in article 12 of the 1966 International Covenant on Civil and Political Rights (see Assembly resolution 2200 (XXI), annex) and in article 5 of the 1965 International Convention on the Elimination of All Forms of Racial Discrimination (Assembly resolution 2106 A (XX), annex). It is also cited in article 10 of the 1989 Convention on the Rights of the Child (Assembly resolution 44/25, annex) in relation to the movement of children and parents.

Table VIII.3 lists international instruments specifically concerning international migration. Of these, there are three principal international instruments dealing

Table VIII.3.
Legal instruments relevant to international migration

		Countries ratified[a]		*Of which:* Countries with net immigration at the time of ratification	
Instrument	Year adopted	Number	Percentage[b]	Number	Percentage[c]
Migrant workers					
ILO Convention concerning Migration for Employment (Revised 1949) (No. 97)	1949	42	21.5	12	28.6
ILO Convention concerning Migrations in Abusive Conditions and the Promotion of Equality of Opportunity and Treatment of Migrant Workers (Supplementary Provisions) (No. 143)	1975	18	9.2	8	44.4
International Convention on the Protection of the Rights of All Migrant Workers and Members of Their Families	1990	26	13.3	2	7.7
Smuggling and trafficking					
Protocol to Prevent, Suppress and Punish Trafficking in Persons, Especially Women and Children[d]	2000	54	27.7	16	29.6
Protocol Against the Smuggling of Migrants by Land, Air and Sea[d]	2000	48	24.6	14	29.2
Refugees					
1951 Convention relating to the Status of Refugees	1951	142	72.8	39	27.5
1967 Protocol relating to the Status of Refugees	1967	141	72.3	47	33.3

a As of 1 September 2004. The number includes non-member States of the United Nations and the Governments of Cook Islands and Niue.
b Of States Members of the United Nations.
c Of countries that have ratified.
d Supplementing the United Nations Convention against Transnational Organized Crime.

Three principal international instruments deal specifically with the rights of migrant workers

with the protection and treatment of international migrant workers: two conventions elaborated by the International Labour Organization (ILO) and the International Convention on the Protection of the Rights of All Migrant Workers and Members of Their Families adopted by the General Assembly (Assembly resolution 45/158, annex). As may be seen from the table, for each of the three Conventions, there has been an exceedingly low number of ratifications, indicating the lack of broad consensual support for the issue.

Two of the three are ILO conventions ...

The ILO Convention concerning Migration for Employment (Revised 1949) (No. 97) contains provisions designed to proscribe the inequalities of treatment of international migrants compared with nationals with respect to employment that may result from legal or other measures taken by public authorities. It applies only to legal migrants. Although 55 years have passed since the adoption of this Convention, it has been ratified by only 42 countries. Furthermore, the Convention has gained limited support among countries that experience net immigration. As shown in the last columns of table VIII.3, out of all the countries that ratified Convention No. 97, only 12 were net immigration countries at the time of ratification. The migration experience of a country, however, may change after ratification, thus compelling Governments to look at the issue of the protection of migrants from a different perspective. This has been the case for Italy, Kenya, the Netherlands, Norway and Spain which were countries of net emigration at the time of ratification, but are currently net recipients of migrants.

The adoption of ILO Convention No. 97 of 1949 was prompted by the interest in facilitating the movement of surplus labour from Europe to other parts of the world (International Labour Organization, 2004a). Since then, the international economic and social context has undergone significant changes. By 1975, when the International Labour Conference of ILO adopted Convention No. 143, Governments had become increasingly concerned about unemployment and the increase in irregular migration; thus their focus had shifted towards bringing migration flows under control (International Labour Organization, 2004a). ILO Convention No. 143 provides that migrant workers should be entitled not only to equal treatment, but also to equality, regarding access to employment, trade union rights, cultural rights and individual and collective freedoms. The number of countries that have ratified this Convention has been extremely low: only 18 have done so.

... and one Convention was adopted by the United Nations General Assembly

In 1990, the General Assembly of the United Nations adopted and opened for signature and ratification the International Convention on the Protection of the Rights of All Migrant Workers and Members of Their Families. This Convention was the first instrument relating to the rights of migrant workers that had been elaborated by the United Nations. As an outgrowth of the ILO migration conventions, it establishes the basic human rights and fundamental freedoms that all migrant workers and members of their families should enjoy, whether they are in a regular or in an irregular situation in the receiving country. It officially entered into force on 1 July 2003, 13 years after its adoption, and there are now 25 States parties to this Convention. Among these, only two, namely, Bosnia and Herzegovina and Timor-Leste, were net immigration countries at the time of ratification.

The three Conventions have entered into force, but ratification has been slow and sparse

The slow ratification of the International Convention on the Protection of the Rights of All Migrant Workers and Members of Their Families has been due in some countries to lack of understanding of its value and relevance to countries of origin and countries of destination. To many countries of origin, the ratification and the implementation processes are expensive undertakings and the budgets and human resources assigned to such matters tend to be limited (Iredale and Piper, 2003). Such countries are also afraid that if they ratify the Convention, they may lose labour markets abroad and remittances. In receiving countries, migrant workers are seen as well protected in their capacity as workers under national legislation. Inconsistencies with national laws and regulations or duplication of existing rights are also among the obstacles that prevent receiving countries from signing and ratifying the Convention. However, further progress was made at the ninety-second session of the International Labour Conference in June 2004 when a plan of action was adopted that called for the development of a non-binding multilateral framework for a rights-based approach to labour migration (International Labour Organization, 2004b).

However, two protocols, on international trafficking in persons and smuggling of migrants, were quickly and widely ratified

In contrast to the instruments concerning migrant workers which have been ratified by relatively few countries, the two Protocols to the United Nations Convention Against Transnational Organized Crime adopted in 2000 (General Assembly resolution 55/25 of 15 November 2000, annex I), namely, the Protocol to Prevent, Suppress and Punish Trafficking in Persons, Especially Women and Children, supplementing the United Nations Convention against Transnational Organized Crime (Assembly resolution 55/25, annex II), and the Protocol against the Smuggling of Migrants by Land, Sea and Air, supplementing the United Nations Convention against Transnational Organized Crime (Assembly resolution 55/25, annex III), have already been ratified by 54 and 48 countries, respectively, and both have already entered into force. The first Protocol defines trafficking in such a way as to ensure that all forms are covered. The second Protocol criminalizes the smuggling of migrants, and establishes which State has the obligation to investigate and prosecute offenders who facilitate the smuggling of migrants. The fact that a large number of countries have become parties to these instruments affirms the importance that Member States attach to the issue of irregular migration and to the need for cooperation through a well-defined framework within which to combat trafficking and smuggling.

Two key instruments on refugees have been in force for more than a third of a century

Finally, there are two key international instruments on refugees that seek to protect people who have been forced to flee their home country, and whose own Governments are unwilling or unable to protect them. The need to provide international protection to millions of refugees in the aftermath of the Second World War helped shape the 1951 Convention relating to the Status of Refugees (United Nations, 1954) and led to the establishment of UNHCR. The 1951 Convention defines the term "refugee" and establishes the principle of non-refoulement, according to which no person may be returned against his or her will to a territory where he or she may be exposed to persecution. It regulates the conduct of States in matters relating to the treatment of refugees, including their legal status, employment and welfare. Initially, the terms of the Convention had been applicable only to countries affected by the Second World War in Europe. The 1967 Protocol relating to the Status of Refugees (United Nations, 1967) removed that restriction. Unlike the other instruments listed in table VIII.3, these two humanitarian instruments relating to refugees have been ratified by the majority of countries. Approximately, one third of countries that ratified these instruments were experiencing the net immigration of population at that time of ratification. Yet, given the changes in the migration experience of countries over time, the net immigration countries now represent nearly 40 per cent of the countries that ratified these two conventions.

Regular activities on international migration

No single United Nations office or organization is charged with international migration

Although the United Nations has a long history of addressing international migration issues, under the present institutional architecture, no single office in the United Nations system has a mandate to work systematically on the full spectrum of international migration issues. The absence of a leading office for international migration is sometimes considered to have weakened the role of the United Nations in the international migration debate. Recently, there have been calls for the establishment of a new body, consolidating the responsibilities of offices that heretofore have had different mandates (Bhagwati, 2003). However, this type of proposal has failed to garner widespread support.

Within the United Nations Secretariat, DESA provides data and analysis, ...

In the United Nations Secretariat, the Department of Economic and Social Affairs (DESA) has contributed to the gaining of a better understanding of various complex facets of international migration through the collection, analysis and dissemination of information. The Population Division of DESA monitors levels and trends of international migration as well as migration policies, and studies the interrelations between international migration and socio-economic development and political change. The United Nations Statistics Division of DESA guides efforts to increase the accuracy and cross-country comparability of statistics on international migration. In addition to these regular activities, there is increasing consideration of international migration issues by various functional commissions and forums. The sub-item entitled "International migration and development" was included in the agenda of the General Assembly every two years until 2003 and allocated to the Second Committee for consideration. The sub-item was also included in the agenda of the fifty-ninth session of the Assembly to be held in September–December 2004.

... supplemented by the regional commissions

The work of the Secretariat is also complemented by that of the regional commissions of the United Nations, such as the Economic Commission for Europe (ECE), the Economic Commission for Latin America and the Caribbean (ECLAC), the Economic and Social Commission for Asia and the Pacific (ESCAP) and the Economic and Social Commission for Western Asia (ESCWA), which consider the regional aspects of international migration.

Several United Nations entities are responsible for various aspects of international migration

The Office of the United Nations High Commissioner for Human Rights is responsible for ensuring the implementation of universally recognized human rights and of key human rights instruments relating to international migration, including the International Convention on the Protection of the Rights of All Migrant Workers and Members of Their Families. The Special Rapporteur on the human rights of migrants, appointed by the Commission on Human Rights, examines ways and means of overcoming existing obstacles to the full and effective protection of the human rights of international migrants.

The United Nations Office on Drugs and Crime, being responsible for crime prevention, carries out technical cooperation projects to combat the trafficking of human beings and raises awareness of the pervasiveness of this crime. The international response to the problems caused by the trafficking of persons has been swift. Several United Nations organizations have collaborated in combating human trafficking, including the United Nations Children's Fund (UNICEF), which focuses its efforts on the prevention of trafficking in children.

Since 1998, the United Nations Institute for Training and Research (UNITAR) has been executing the International Migration Policy Programme (IMP), an inter-agency programme co-sponsored by ILO, IOM, the United Nations Population Fund (UNFPA) and UNITAR. The aim has been to strengthen the capacity of Governments to manage migration and to reach a shared understanding of migration policy issues. The programme organizes regional conferences, seminars and training workshops for concerned senior government officials.

The Office of the United Nations High Commissioner for Refugees (UNHCR) leads and coordinates international action for the protection of refugees, and seeks solutions for problems of refugees. UNHCR provides essential services to refugees and promotes their self-reliance in countries of asylum. It also facilitates the return of refugees to their home country and their sustainable reintegration therein. Its protection activities have been extended to people who are stateless or whose nationality is disputed and, under certain circumstances, to internally displaced persons as well. Further information on the extent of UNHCR's activities and on recent initiatives under UNHCR's Global Consultation process are reported in Chapter VII. The United Nations Relief and Works Agency for Palestine Refugees in the Near East (UNRWA), which was established before UNHCR, provides basic services to Palestinian refugees and their descendants in the Middle East.

Specialized agencies and other autonomous bodies are also dealing with international migration

Among the specialized agencies and related organizations, the activities of ILO, the World Bank and the World Trade Organization are of particular concern. ILO has the responsibility of promoting the equality of opportunity and treatment of migrant workers in relation to natives. As noted above, a number of conventions, recommendations and labour standards adopted by ILO set international standards for the treatment of migrant workers employed in a country other than their own and protect them from discrimination and exploitation. ILO encourages adherence to these standards by monitoring laws, regulations and practices concerning the treatment of migrant workers; by providing advisory services to its tripartite constituents on the effective management of labour migration; and by building a knowledge base on labour migration and its impact through research activities, meetings and seminars.

The World Bank has undertaken a number of studies on the interplay between international migration and development, especially on remittances and labour migration. Its policy dialogue addresses the issues arising from significant population movements and their impacts on the economies of developing countries.

Within the framework of the World Trade Organization, the General Agreement on Trade in Services[4] sets legally enforceable rules for the international trade in services. The Agreement identifies the temporary movement of skilled professionals as Mode 4, which is one of the four ways in which services can be supplied. Hence, the World Trade Organization facilitates negotiations among member States on the temporary movement of labour under specific circumstances and on the individual's right to stay temporarily in a country other than his or her own to provide a specific service. However, negotiations concerning the movement of persons under Mode 4 have been slow and difficult, reflecting the concern of countries of destination about the likelihood that temporary migration may become long-term or permanent (International Labour Organization, 2004a).

This review indicates that a substantial number of offices, programmes and agencies of the United Nations system and related organizations have addressed a variety of issues posed by international migration. The expanding scope of activities has demanded better coordination among the concerned organizations. In order to further the exchange of information on international migration and to coordinate activities in the field, the Population Division of DESA has been organizing annual Coordination Meetings on International Migration since 2002. The Meetings bring together representatives of major actors within the United Nations system as well as of concerned institutions outside the system.

International conferences and meetings

The United Nations has played a key role in fostering inter-governmental dialogue on international migration issues at international conferences and meetings, the results of which have contributed to the development of norms and guidelines for policy formulation and migration management. The international conferences, in particular, have established a platform for cooperative action at the regional and global levels. The outcome documents adopted by international conferences, albeit non-binding, can help shape the normative framework within which country activities develop.

The International Conference on Population and Development (Cairo, 1994) gave prominence to international migration

All inter-governmental conferences on population convened by the United Nations have dealt with international migration issues; moreover the attention given to this subject has been increasing over time. In particular, the Programme of Action of the International Conference on Population and Development (United Nations, 1995, chap. I, resolution 1, annex), held in 1994 in Cairo, devotes a whole chapter to the topic (chap. X) and provides a comprehensive set of objectives in relation to international migration and development (sect. A); documented migrants (sect. B); undocumented migrants (sect. C); and refugees, asylum-seekers and displaced persons (sect. D). The Programme of Action emphasizes the basic rights of migrants, irrespective of their legal status, and recognizes the benefits of international migration to the host country. It also invites Governments to cooperate by exchanging information, providing technical cooperation and engaging in bilateral or multilateral negotiations. A major objective of the Programme of Action is to encourage cooperation and dialogue between countries of origin and countries of destination so as to maximize the benefits of migration and increase the likelihood that migration will have positive consequences for development. It thus provides a rationale for the regional consultative processes that have been evolving since its adoption (Klekowski von Koppenfels, 2001).

The discussions on international migration issues that started at the International Conference on Population and Development gave rise to a call for the convening of an international conference on international migration and development, an issue that the Second Committee of the General Assembly had been considering every two years since 1995. The results of inquiries among Governments regarding their views on the possibility of convening an international conference have shown that there is as yet no consensus on moving ahead with such a proposal. In the interim, in its resolution 58/208 of 23 December 2003, the Assembly decided that in 2006 it would devote a high-level dialogue to international migration and development.

Other recent international conferences have also considered international migration

Since 1994, there have been other international conferences and meetings organized by bodies of the United Nations system that have addressed international migration issues. Thus, the former Administrative Committee on Coordination (ACC) Task Force on Basic Social Services for All organized a Technical Symposium on International Migration and Development that took place in The Hague in June-July 1998. The Symposium reviewed the state of the art in research on international migration and development and evaluated the merits of various policy options (Castles, 1999). The World Summit for Social Development held in Copenhagen in 1995, as well as its follow-up at the twenty-fourth special session of the General Assembly, entitled "World Summit for Social Development and beyond: achieving social development for all in a globalizing world", held at Geneva from 26 June to 1 July 2000, considered the challenges posed by the social integration of international migrants. Both the Fourth World Conference on Women, held in Beijing in 1995, and the twenty-third special session of the Assembly, entitled "Women 2000: gender equality, development and peace for the twenty-first century", held from 5 to 10 June 2000, focused attention on the particular needs of migrant women and children, especially those who were victims of trafficking. Lastly, the World Conference against Racism, Racial Discrimination, Xenophobia and Related Intolerance, held in Durban, South Africa, in 2001, reaffirmed the urgent need to prevent, combat and eliminate all forms of discriminatory practices against migrants.

The United Nations Millenium Assembly of September 2000 presented an opportunity to review the role of the United Nations in relation to the challenges facing humanity at the dawn of the twenty-first century. Although the issues posed by international migration were not directly reflected in the goals set for the implementation of the United Nations Millenium Declaration (see General Assembly resolution 55/2), the Declaration did call for the respect and protection of the human rights of migrants, migrant workers and their families, for the elimination of acts of racism and xenophobia, and for the promotion of greater harmony and tolerance in all societies (para. 25).

Role of intergovernmental organizations outside the United Nations system

Outside the United Nations system, there are also a number of international organizations whose activities on international migration facilitate international cooperation. The present section describes the role and activities of the key international organizations that have an active interest in areas related to international migration.

Leading international organizations outside the United Nations that deal with migration include IOM,...

The International Organization for Migration (IOM) established in 1951, plays an increasing role in migration management worldwide. Comprising 105 member States and 27 States with observer status, the guiding principle of IOM is that humane and orderly migration can benefit migrants as well as the countries they come from and the societies that host them. IOM undertakes a variety of operational activities, including capacity-building; assisting returning migrants; working on effective counter-trafficking measures; facilitating labour migration; and disseminating timely and credible information on international migration via the mass media. The organization also undertakes research, and its publications include a biennial *World Migration Report.* Since 2000, IOM has organized annually an International Dialogue on Migration where the international community can discuss and share experiences and good practices in migration management. Between annual Dialogues, IOM works with partner organizations to mount workshops on emerging themes such as migration and trade. IOM has also been instrumental in supporting the establishment and development of many regional migration consultative processes among Governments.

... OECD,...

Through its Working Party on Migration, the Organization for Economic Cooperation and Development (OECD) is active in debates, studies and the production of information on various aspects of international migration. The work of OECD on international migration is based on continued monitoring of international migration movements and policies in member countries and in selected countries outside the OECD area, as well as on the in-depth analysis of the economic and social aspects of migration. Issues dealt with include the role of international migration in alleviating labour shortages; links among international migration, demographic dynamics and economic growth; and the fiscal impact of international migration.

... the International Federation of Red Cross and Red Crescent Societies...

The International Federation of Red Cross and Red Crescent Societies, specializing in disaster response, disaster preparedness, health and community care, provides direct assistance to refugees, internally displaced persons and migrants who are victims of natural disasters, socio-economic crises and health emergencies.

... and the Global Commission on International Migration

The Global Commission on International Migration, established in December 2003 in response to a call by the Secretary-General of the United Nations, is an independent body comprising 12 eminent persons from all regions of the world. The Commission's objectives are: (a) to place international migration in the global agenda, (b) to analyse gaps in current migration policy and examine its linkages to other issues and (c) to present recommendations to the Secretary-General and other stakeholders on how best to address international migration issues at the international level. The Commission will organize a series of regional hearings and present a report to the Secretary-General in mid-2005.

Conclusions

International migration issues have been high in the political agenda of an increasing number of countries since 1990. The complexity of international migration flows and their growing scale have pressed governments to look beyond traditional unilateral or bilateral mechanisms used to manage international migration. In response, Governments have been exploring new ways of collaboration and cooperation in migration management.

This chapter has reviewed a variety of cooperative activities whose aim is to enhance the management of international migration. The bilateral approach is being used by a growing number of countries. In the absence of an international regime for international migration, regional consultative processes of an informal nature have become a key component of migration management and they now exist in virtually all areas of the world. While some international legal instruments concerning international migration still lack worldwide support, various inter-governmental bodies and organizations have become increasingly active in this area.

Given the complexity of international migration, Governments are resorting to a growing range of cooperative measures in order to manage it in an orderly fashion that, to the extent possible, benefits all concerned. Each approach has strengths and limitations. Given that international migration is not likely to decrease in volume or importance in the foreseeable future, it is in the best interest of the various stakeholders—Governments, international and intergovernmental organizations, and non-governmental organizations—to continue to utilize existing mechanisms that are beneficial while seeking new and more effective forms of international cooperation.

Notes

1 The Intergovernmental Committee for European Migration (ICEM) had changed its name to the Intergovernmental Committee for Migration (ICM) in 1980, and became the International Organization for Migration (IOM) in 1989.

2 Canada, Germany, Ireland, Japan, Malta, the Netherlands, the Republic of Korea and the United Kingdom.

3 See http://www.baliprocess.net (accessed 15 March 2004).

4 The full text is available from http://www.wto.org/english/tratop_e/serv_e/gatsintr_e.htm (accessed 19 October 2004).

Annex

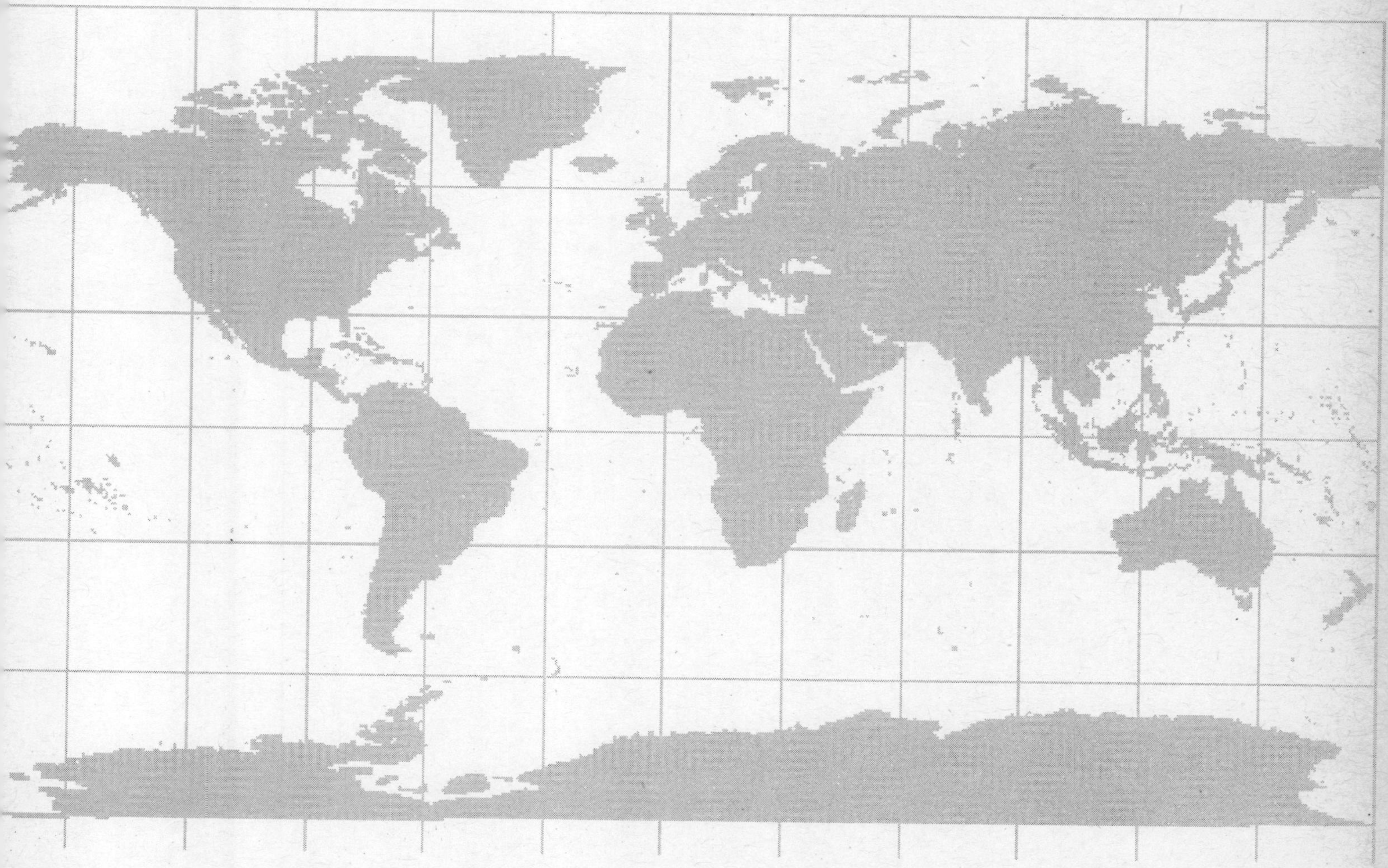

Annex
Current status of the collection of international migration statistics

The Statistics Division of the Department of Economic and Social Affairs of the United Nations (United Nations Statistics Division) has been collecting statistics on international migration for more than 50 years. The lack of uniformity among countries in determining who is an international migrant has long been recognized by national authorities as well as by the international communities. Efforts towards creating uniform definitions and methods in producing comparable international migration statistics had been initiated in the early 1920s by the International Labour Conference. In the late 1940s, the Population Commission and the Statistical Commission of the United Nations had addressed the issue of producing recommendations on international migration statistics. As a result, the first set of United Nations recommendations was adopted in 1953 (United Nations, 1953). The recommendations were then revised in 1976 (United Nations, 1979). Subsequently, revised recommendations were produced and published as *Recommendations on Statistics of International Migration, Revision 1,* in 1998 (United Nations, 1998c).

Facilitated by reliable and inexpensive modes of transportation and communication, there was a steady climb in the number of migrants during the latter half of the twentieth century, an era of increasing globalization and continuing disparities between countries. Despite the growing importance of international migration and the concerns it often raises, the statistics needed to characterize migration flows, monitor changes over time and provide Governments with a solid basis for the formulation and implementation of policy are very often lacking. For the developing world in particular, there is evidence suggesting that the availability of statistics of international migration flows has declined since 1976 (Bilsborrow, 1997; United Nations, 2004a).

Recognizing the need to improve international migration statistics, the Statistical Commission requested at its twenty-seventh session that the 1976 recommendations on statistics of international migration be reviewed.[1] Revision 1 of the *Recommendations* was a result of collaborative work between the United Nations Statistics Division and the Statistical Office of the European Communities (Eurostat), in cooperation with the Population Division of the United Nations Secretariat, the regional commissions and other interested organizations.

In addition to the compilation of revision 1 of the *Recommendations* on international migration statistics and its implementation, the United Nations Statistics Division has also been involved in the development of other standards and methods that are relevant to international migration statistics, as well as in more than 50 years of migration data collection. The present annex aims to provide an overview of the current status of the data collection on international migration statistics by the Statistics Division. The first part of the annex highlights the activities in developing standards and methods undertaken by the Statistics Division in the area of international migration. The second part examines the information collected related to migrant stocks. It analyses the availability of data from countries and exhibits the level of reporting of the last two census decades (1985-1994 and 1995-2004) to the United Nations *Demographic Yearbook*.[2] The last part of the annex identifies challenges in the collection of international migration statistics on flows and illustrates the continuing efforts that have been taken by the Statistics Division in improving the availability and comparability of international migration data on flows.

Development of standards and methods

The United Nations Statistics Division has issued guidelines and recommendations on concepts and methods to help countries in the collection and dissemination of their data. The recommendations were developed with a view to improving the quality of data on international migration and promoting the application of common definitions and concepts by countries so as to enhance the comparability of data at the international level. Two of the most recent sets of United Nations *recommendations* are related to the data collection on international migration: the aforementioned *Recommendations on Statistics of International Migration, Revision 1* and *Principles and Recommendations for Population and Housing Censuses, Revision 1* (United Nations, 1998d).

The latest revision of the set of recommendations on international migration, *Recommendations on Statistics of International Migration, Revision 1*, was published (in 1998) pursuant to the request of the Statistical Commission. That publication reviews new internationally agreed definitions and relevant data sources and proposes a revised taxonomy of inflows and outflows of international travellers (table 1 and box 2).[3] The *Recommendations* also present a framework for the compilation of statistics on flows, giving particular attention to the compilation of policy-oriented statistics from existing data. In addition, the *Recommendations* give emphasis to the topics of asylum-seekers and refugees, and provide definitions of relevant concepts and present recommended tabulations.

Principles and Recommendations for Population and Housing Censuses, Revision 1 was published to assist countries in planning and conducting population and housing censuses. That publication examines the operational aspects of population and housing cen-

Countries and areas that provided statistics on foreign-born or foreign population to the United Nations *Demographic Yearbook* at least once, 1985-2004

Region	Data provided on						Total number of countries
	Foreign-born population			Population by citizenship			
	1985-1994	1995-2004	1985-2004	1985-1994	1995-2004	1985-2004	
Africa	12	4	15	19	6	22	56
America, North	14	6	17	11	2	11	37
America, South	7	3	7	3	1	3	14
Asia	13	7	15	15	13	20	50
Europe	16	13	25	17	10	23	48
Oceania	7	5	11	5	2	6	25
Total	69	38	90	70	34	85	230

suses, and the topics for the censuses, as well as census products and data utilization. International migration, as a census topic, is considered in the publication. *Principles and Recommendations* offers a list of sub-topics that could be used in the census to identify immigrant stock and its characteristics, and also provides selected tabulations related to international migration for census data dissemination purposes.

Data collection on migrant stocks

Data on international migration are commonly referred as data on stocks and data on flows. According to both sets of *Recommendations*, the stock of international migrants present in a country encompasses the set of persons who have ever changed their country of usual residence. However, for the study of the impact of international migration, two sub-populations are the focus of interest: (a) that of foreigners (non-citizens) living in a country; and (b) that of persons born in a country other than the one in which they live (the foreign-born). Population censuses are underscored as being the best source for collecting data on the immigrant stock and its characteristics.

The United Nations Statistics Division collects most of its data from national statistical authorities through a set of *Demographic Yearbook* questionnaires. The development of the data collection is primarily in the area of migration stocks. Migrant stocks data are collected through two population census questionnaires, which are sent to countries when it is known that a census has been conducted; they are sent every year until most of the data have been received. The Population Census Questionnaire on General Characteristics collects the following information:

- Native and foreign-born population by age, sex and urban/rural residence
- Foreign-born population by country of birth, age and sex
- Foreign-born population in the country for less than five years by country of birth, age and sex
- Population by country of citizenship and sex.

The Population Census Questionnaire on Economic Characteristics collects information on economically active foreign-born population by occupation, age, sex and urban/rural residence.

Since migrant stocks are mostly expressed in terms of foreign-born population and foreigners (non-citizens), the level of response from countries and areas is illustrated using the availability of data on foreign-born or population classified by citizenship collected for the latest two rounds of population censuses (1985-1994 and 1995-2004). Since many of the *Demographic Yearbook* questionnaires also request data disaggregated by sex, the number of countries that have been able to provide data on foreign-born population or population by citizenship disaggregated by sex is also examined. Further elaboration will not be provided here, although it is known that the more detailed the information requested by the questionnaire, the lower the response level.

Thus far, the number of countries and areas that have ever provided any information on native and foreign-born population since 1985 is 90 out of 230. The number of countries that reported those data in the 1990 census round (1985-1994) is higher than that in the 2000 round (1995-2004) at this point in time. The lower level of reporting on native and foreign-born population for the 2000 census decade is due to the fact that some countries have not yet conducted their censuses in the 2000 round and that some others, although they have conducted their censuses, did not submit data to the United Nations Statistics Division.[4] In addition, there are significant variations in the level of response by geographical regions (see table). For example, 25 out of 48 countries and areas in Europe provided some data on the foreign-born population, while 15 out of 56 countries and areas in Africa provided such data.

There are 85 countries and areas that have provided data on population by citizenship since 1985. The percentage of countries that had provided population breakdowns by citizenship was similar across all continents in the 1990 census round, with Africa and Europe having had a slightly higher response rate than the other four continents. For the 2000 census round, about one quarter of the countries and areas in Asia and Europe reported population by citizenship, while the response rate for other continents was much lower. The low proportion of reporting countries in the 2000 census decade was associated with the fact that some countries either had not conducted their censuses or had not yet reported on the 2000 census round.

Most countries that have provided data on foreign-born population or population by citizenship since 1985 also provided those data disaggregated by sex. For example, among 90 countries and areas that have provided any data on foreign-born population since 1985, 83 countries (92 per cent) also provided the disaggregation by sex. Similarly, of 85 that have reported population by citizenship since 1985, 79 (93 per cent) also reported sex-disaggregated data.

In addition to the information requested through the *Demographic Yearbook* Population Census Questionnaires, the following tabulations are also recommended by the *Principles and Recommendations for Population and Housing Censuses, Revision 1:*

- Foreign-born population, by period of arrival, country of birth, age and sex
- Population, by country of birth and citizenship, age and sex
- Foreign-born population, by marital status, age and sex
- Foreign-born population ... years of age and over, by usual (or current) activity status, age and sex
- Economically active foreign-born population ... years of age and over, by period of arrival, occupation and sex
- Foreign-born population ... years of age and over, by education attainment, age and sex

Although the above additional tabulations are recommended by the United Nations, the level of response even to the most basic information about stocks of foreign-born or foreign citizens is still very low. For example, thus far only 90 out of the 230 countries and areas have been able to provide data on the size of foreign-born population, or data on population by citizenship (85 out of 230) since 1985. The fact that, among those that have not provided those data since 1985, 17 countries and areas have not had one census since 1985, further jeopardizes international comparisons. In addition, even for countries that that have had a census since 1985, some may not have asked questions about the foreign-born or citizenship of populations on their national census questionnaires, as already emphasized.

Continuing efforts have been made towards improving the data collection on international migration stock statistics. For example, the United Nations Statistics Division has been encouraging countries that have not had a census in the past 10 years to conduct a population and housing census. The Statistics Division is also involved in activities aimed at assisting countries and areas in conducting well-planned censuses, as well as in incorporating both traditional and newly emerging topics in national censuses. A census symposium will be conducted in September 2004, which will invite high-level officials in Governments to promote better planning, conducting and data processing for the 2010 round of population and housing censuses.

In addition, an Expert Group Meeting will be conducted in the same period to review the current *Principles and Recommendations for Population and Housing Censuses, Revision 1*. The review will take into consideration the newly emerging issues. For example in the area of international migration, variables of *place of birth* and *citizenship* are particularly relevant for the study of international migration. While one variable might be relevant in one country, the other might be used more in another country. For some countries, the focus is shifting towards place of birth owing to the problem of dual citizenship and also because it is difficult to track changes in citizenship, which would require an additional variable: *citizenship at birth*. Issues similar to this will be reviewed by the Expert Group Meeting so as to have national experiences reflected in the revised *Principles and Recommendations*. The ultimate goal is to provide the most relevant recommendations for consideration by countries when they are planning a census.

For those countries that have conducted censuses successfully, the United Nations Statistics Division is dedicated to improving their level of responses to the United Nations *Demographic Yearbook* Questionnaires. Efforts are being made to improve the *Demographic Yearbook* Questionnaires: an Expert Group Meeting on reviewing the *Demographic Yearbook* data-collection system was conducted in November 2003. In reviewing the *Demographic Yearbook* questionnaires the Expert Group Meeting produced a number of recommendations on how to better serve the needs of national Governments and international communities in respect of collecting and disseminating more comprehensive, comparable and timely data, while reducing the burden on countries in respect of filling out these questionnaires. Such general improvements will also facilitate the collection of migration statistics from countries and areas.

Data collection on migrant flows

Data on migrant flows describe the incidence of persons moving to a country other than that of his or her usual residence for a specified period of time of at least three months. It excludes the incidence of persons who move to a country for temporary travel abroad for purposes of recreation, holiday, visits to friends and relatives, and other such moves that do not change a person's country of usual residence (see box 1 in *Recommendations of Statistics of International Migration, Revision 1*). The main sources of flow data include border-crossing accounts, passenger surveys, population registers, visa applications, work permit applications, stay permit applications and asylum applications.

The responsibility for producing data for international migration statistics is often shared by different institutions such as the ministry of labour, the ministry of the interior, and the police. Therefore, the main challenge that national statistical offices face when collecting and compiling international migration data is associated with the variety of data sources and the degree of coordination required of the various institutions involved.

The United Nations Statistics Division has the mandate to communicate with and assist national statistical authorities in the area of data collection, compilation and dissemination. Therefore, it has been able to provide guidance to countries in collecting and compiling international migration statistics on stocks collected mainly from population censuses and samples surveys, as described in the previous section. Data on migrant flows, however, are often held by other ministries, such as the ministry of planning, the ministry of labour or the ministry of the interior.

Although it is rather difficult to collect migrant flows data without a clear international mandate for contacting relevant national agencies, the United Nations Statistics Division is making an effort to improve the response level and comparability of the data on migrant flows through its official contact with national statistical authorities.

The United Nations Statistics Division provides countries with technical support in the collection and compilation of data and in training statisticians on the application of the United Nations principles and recommendations on statistical concepts and methods. The Statistics Division also responds to requests from national statistics offices to provide technical assistance and advice.

In this context, the United Nations Statistics Division, in collaboration with the United Nations Conference on Trade and Development (UNCTAD), organized a Workshop on Improving the Compilation of International Migration Statistics which was held from 15 to 17 September 2003 in Geneva. The main objective of the workshop was to guide statisticians in the use of the *Recommendations on Statistics of International Migration, Revision 1*. Participants were introduced to the framework for compiling international migration statistics from available data sources as laid out in the *Recommendations*. The participants reviewed the requirements for and uses of international migration statistics; and explored ways to produce more complete and timely statistics so as to meet the growing demand for informed policy- and decision-making. Another workshop in the Economic and Social Commission for Asia and the Pacific (ESCAP) region is currently being planned to assist countries in the region in collecting and compiling migration statistics.

A trial International Travel and Migration Statistics questionnaire for the *Demographic Yearbook* system has been developed and a first testing was conducted during the above-mentioned 2003 Workshop. The trial questionnaire will also be tested in the Pacific islands community in addition to other regions and subregions of the world.

There is also a plan for the harmonization of national practices in the form of Web-based training modules. The purpose of this practice is to assist statistical offices in the collection of international migration statistics by exploring different national data sources and providing a harmonized approach to illustrative country practices.

Conclusion

International data collection on migration statistics as carried out throughout the past 50 years has been a difficult undertaking. For example, less than 40 per cent of countries and areas have provided some migrant stock data since 1985, while the response on flow data is even more scarce. Statistics on international migration suffer from a lack of harmonized concepts and definitions across countries. There is also a lack of resources, and a lack of coordination among various agencies within countries, as well as at the national and international levels.

The United Nations Statistics Division has actively worked to achieve agreement on internationally comparable concepts and definitions, through compilation of a series of recommendations on international migration statistics, as well as by improving national capacities through technical cooperation activities such as international and regional workshops and expert group meetings.

It is likely that more countries will be able to provide migrant stock data in the near future. However, owing to the specific mechanisms by which countries collect data on international migrant flows and the United Nations Statistics Division's lack of a clear international mandate with respect to collecting those data directly from the most relevant national authorities, improvements in this area will be limited. It remains unclear whether it is possible to create an international agreement to facilitate the collection of data on migrant flows through national authorities other than national statistical offices. In addition, the issue of how such an agreement would affect the current data-collection process needs further exploration.

Notes

1 See *Official Records of the Economic and Social Council, 1993, Supplement No. 6* (E/1993/26), para. 129 (d).

2 *Demographic Yearbook* is an annual publication that covers a wide array of demographic and social topics. International migration statistics are collected from national statistical authorities within the *Yearbook* data-collection system through questionnaires. The collected data are published in the *Yearbook.*

3 This new taxonomy replaces the one that was presented in table 1 of the *Recommendations on Statistics of International Migration* (United Nations, 1980).

4 The census questionnaires were sent out until March 2004 to all the countries that had conducted a census during the period 1995-2004. A special topic of the *Demographic Yearbook* on population censuses will be published in 2005.

Bibliography

Abella, Manolo I. (1997). *Sending Workers Abroad.* Geneva: International Labour Office.

Adams, J.D. (1997). *Technology, Trade and Wages.* National Bureau of Economic Research (NBER) Working Paper, No. 5940. Cambridge, Massachusetts: NBER.

Adams, R.H., Jr. (1989). Worker remittances and inequality in rural Egypt. *Economic Development and Cultural Change*, vol. 38, No. 1.

__________ (1998). Remittances, investment, and rural asset accumulation in Pakistan. *Economic Development and Cultural Change*, vol. 47, No. 1, p. 170.

__________ (2003). *International Migration, Remittances and the Brain Drain: A Study of 24 Labor-Exporting Countries.* World Bank Policy Research Working Paper, No. 3069. April. Washington, D.C.: World Bank.

Addy, D.N., B. Wijkström and C. Thouez (2003). Migrant remittances: country of origin experiences: strategies, policies, challenges and concerns. Paper prepared by the International Migration Policy programme (IMP). Geneva. Available from www.livelihoods.org/hot_topics/docs/REMITPAPER.doc (accessed 27 October 2004).

Adepoju, Aderanti (2000). Sub-Saharan Africa. In *World Migration Report 2000.* Geneva: International Organization for Migration, pp. 133-162.

__________ (2001). Regional organizations and intra-regional migration in sub-Saharan Africa: challenges and prospects. *International Migration*, vol. 39, No. 6, pp. 44-57.

African Centre for Technology Studies (ACTS) (2002). Return and reintegration of qualified African Nationals Programme (RQAN III) phase 3 report. Nairobi.

Alarcón, Rafael (2002). The development of home town associations in the United States and the use of social remittances in Mexico. Department of Estudios Sociales, El Colegio de la Frontera Norte, Baja California, Mexico. Available from http://www.thedialogue.org/publications/alarcon.pdf (accessed 1 November 2004).

Aleinikoff, T.A. (2003). International legal norms and migration: a report. In *Migration and International Legal Norms*, T. Alexander Aleinikoff and Vincent Chetail, eds. The Hague: T.M.C Asser Press.

Aleinikoff, T. Alexander, and Vincent Chetail, eds. (2003). *Migration and International Legal Norms.* The Hague: T.M.C. Asser Press.

Amuedo-Dorantes, C., and S. Pozo (2002). *On the Use of Differing Money Transmission Methods by Mexican Immigrants.* Working Paper, No. E2004/06. Sevilla, España: Fundación Centro de Estudios Andaluces, pp. 15-16. November.

Angrist, J.D., and A.D. Kugler (2001). *Protective or Counter-productive? European Labour Market Institutions and the Effect of Immigrants on EU natives.* NBER Working Paper, No. 8660. Cambridge, Massachusetts: NBER.

Appleyard, Reginald T. (1977). Major international population movements and policies: an historical review. In *International Population Conference*, México, 1977, vol. 2. Liège, Belgium: International Union for the Scientific Study of Population (IUSSP).

____________ (2001). International migration policies 1950-2000. *International Migration*, vol. 39, No. 6, pp. 7-18.

Armstrong, F. (1998). Migration of nurses: finding a sustainable solution. *Australian Nursing Journal*, vol. 11, No. 3.

Auerbach, A.J., and P. Oreopoulos (1999). Analyzing the fiscal impact of U.S. immigration. *American Economic Review: Papers and Proceedings*, vol. 89, No. 2.

Balán, Jorge (1992). The role of migration policies and social networks in the development of a migration system in the Southern Cone. In *International Migration Systems: A Global Approach*, Mary M. Kritz, Lin Lean Lim and Hania Zlotnik, eds. Oxford: Clarendon Press, pp. 115-130.

Barro, Robert and J.W. Lee (1996). *International Measurement of Schooling Years and Schooling Quality*. American Economic Review, Papers and Proceedings, vol. 86, No.2, pp. 218-223.

Bedford, Richard (2003). New Zealand: The politicization of immigration. Migration Information Source. Available from http://www.migrationinformation.org/Profiles/display.cfm?ID=86 (accessed 28 October 2004)

Beine, M., F. Docquier and H. Rapoport (2002). *Brain Drain and LDCs' Growth: Winners and Losers*. Working Paper, No. 129. Palo Alto, California: Center for Research on Economic Development and Policy Reform, Stanford University.

Bernard, W.S. (1982). A history of U.S. immigration policy. In *Immigration,* R.A. Easterlin and others, eds. Cambridge, Massachusetts: Harvard University Press.

Bhagwati, Jagdish (2003). Borders beyond control. *Foreign Affairs* (New York), vol. 82, No. 1 (January-February), pp. 98-104.

Bhagwati, J. (2004). *In Defense of Globalization*. New York: Oxford University Press, chap. 14.

Bilsborrow, Richard E., and others (1997). *International Migration Statistics: Guidelines for Improving Data Collection Systems.* Geneva: International Labour Office.

Boeri, Tito, and others (2001). *The Impact of Eastern European Enlargement on Employment and Labour Markets in the EU Member States: Final Report.* Berlin; and Milan, Italy: European Integration Consortium: Deutsche Institut für Wirtschaftsforschung, Center for Economic Policy Research, Trade Union Institute for Economic Research, Institute for Advanced Studies and Innocenzo Gasparini Institute for Economic Research.

Bollini, P., and H. Siem (1995). No real progress towards equity: health of migrants and ethnic minorities on the eve of the year 2000. *Social Science & Medicine,* vol. 41, No. 6, pp. 819-828.

Bonin, Holger (2002). Eine fiskalische Gesamtbilanz der Zuwanderung nach Deutschland. *Vierteljahrshefte zur Wirtschaftsforschung*, vol. 71.

____________, B. Raffelhüschen and J. Walliser (2000). Can immigration alleviate the demographic burden. *FinanzArchiv*, vol. 57, No. 1.

Borjas, George (1994). The economics of immigration. *Journal of Economic Literature*, (Nashville, Tennessee), vol. 32, No. 4 (December), pp. 1667-1717.

__________ (1995). The economic benefits from immigration. *Journal of Economic Perspectives*, vol. 9, No. 2.

__________ (1999). The economic analysis of immigration. In *Handbook of Labor Economics*, vol. 3A, Orley Ashenfelter and David Casel, eds. Dordrecht, Netherlands: North Holland.

__________ (2001). *Does immigration Grease the Wheels of the Labour Market?* Brookings Papers on Economic Activity, No. 1. Washington, D.C.: Brookings Institution.

__________ (2003). The labour demand curve is downward sloping: re-examining the impact of immigration on the labour markets. *The Quarterly Journal of Economics*, November 2003, pp. 1335-1374.

Bourgignon, François, and Christian Morrison (2002). Inequality among world citizens: 1820-1992. *American Economic Review*, vol. 92, No. 4 (September).

Boyd, Monica, and Elizabeth Grieco (2003). *Women and Migration: Incorporating Gender into International Migration Theory.* Washington, D.C.: Migration Policy Institute.

Buencamino, Leonides, and Sergei Gorbunov (2002). Informal money transfer systems: opportunities and challenges for development finance. DESA Discussion Paper, No. 26. ST/ESA/2002/DP/26. United Nations: New York.

Burney, N. (1987). Workers' remittances from the Middle East and their effect on Pakistan's economy. *The Pakistan Development Review*, vol. 26, No. 4.

Card, D. (1990). The Impact of the Mariel boatlift on the Miami labour market. *Industrial and Labour Relations Review*, vol. 43 (January 1990), pp. 245-257.

Cardenas, Enrique, José Antonio Ocampo and Rosemary Thorp, eds. (2000). *An Economic History of Twentieth Century Latin America*, vol. I, *The Export Age.* London: Palgrave.

Carlos, Reinaruth D. (2002). Determinants of international migration in the Philippines. *International Migration Review*, vol. 36, pp. 81-102.

Carrington, W. (1999). International migration and the "brain drain". *The Journal of Social, Political, and Economic Studies* (Washington, D.C.), vol. 24, No. 2.

__________, and P. deLima (1994). Large-scale immigration and labour markets: an analysis of the retornados and their impact on Portugal. Working paper. Baltimore, Maryland: Johns Hopkins University.

Carrington, W., and E. Detragiache (1998). *How Big is the Brain Drain?* IMF Working Paper WP/98/102. Washington, D.C.

Castles, Stephen (1999). International migration and the global agenda: reflections on the 1998 United Nations Technical Symposium. *International Migration* (Geneva) vol. 37, No. 1. pp. 5-20.

__________ (2000). International migration at the beginning of the twenty-first century: global trends and issues. *International Social Science Journal*, vol. 165, pp. 269-281.

__________ (2002). Migration and community formation under conditions of globalization. *The International Migration Review,* vol. 26, No. 4 (winter), pp. 1143-1168.

Centre d'Études et de Recherche sur la Population et le Développement (CERPOD) (1995). *Migrations et Urbanisation en Afrique de l'Ouest (MUAO): Résultats Préliminaires*. Bamako, Mali: CERPOD.

Chanda, Rupa (2003). Linkages between mode 4 and other GATS modes of supply. Paper presented during the OECD-World Bank-IOM Seminar on Trade and Migration, Geneva, 12-14 November 2003.

Chiswick, B.R. (2000). Are immigrants favorably self-selected? In *Migration Theory: Talking Across the Disciplines*, Caroline D. Brettell and James F. Hollifield, eds. New York, New York: Routledge.

Chiquiar, D., and G.H. Hanson (2002). *International Migration, Self-Selection, and the Distribution of Wages: Evidence from Mexico and the United States.* NBER Working Paper, No. 9242. Cambridge, Massachusetts: National Bureau of Economic Research.

Choo, Vivien (2003). Philippines losing its nurses, and now maybe its doctors. *The Lancet,* vol. 36, p. 1356.

Clark, K., and S. Drinkwater (2001). An investigation of household remittance behavior. School of Economic Studies, University of Manchester, Manchester, and Department of Economics, University of Surrey, Surrey, United Kingdom.

Collado, M.D., I. Iturbe-Ormaetxe and G. Valera (2003). Quantifying the impact of immigration on the Spanish welfare state. Mimeograph. University of Alicante, Alicante, Spain.

Commission of the European Communities (2003). Communication from the Commission to the Council, the European Parliament, the European Economic and Social Committee and the Committee of the Regions on immigration, integration and employment. 3 June. Brussels. P. 17.

Coppel, J., J.-C. Dumont and I. Visco (2001). Trends in immigration and economic consequences. OECD Economics Department Working papers, No. 284. Paris.

Cordero-Guzmán, Hector R., Robert Smith and Ramón Grosfoguel (2002). *Migration, Transnationalization, and Race in a Changing New York.* Philadelphia, Pennsylvania: Temple University Press.

Cortés-Conde, Roberto (2000). The vicissitudes of an exporting economy: Argentina (1875-1930). In *An Economic History of Twentieth Century Latin America,* vol. I, *The Export Age*, Enrique Cárdenas, José Antonio Ocampo and Rosemary Thorp, eds. London: Palgrave.

Council of Europe (2004). Convention on the Participation of Foreigners in Public Life at Local Level: status as of 22 October 2004. Available from http://conventions.coe.int/Treaty/Commun/ChercheSig.asp?NT=144&CM=8&DF=&CL=ENG (accessed 1 November 2004).

Crul, M., and H. Vermeulen (2002). The second generation in Europe. *The International Migration Review*, vol. 37, No. 4, pp. 965-987.

Crush, Jonathan, and Wade Pendleton (2004). Regionalizing xenophobia? Citizens' attitudes to immigration and refugee policy in Southern Africa. Southern African Migration Project.

Davis, K. (1951). *The Population of India and Pakistan.* Princeton, New Jersey: Princeton University Press.

de Braw, Alan, Edward J. Taylor and Scott Rozelle (2003). The impact of migration and remittances on rural incomes in China. Paper prepared with the sponsorship of the International Development Research Centre, the World Bank and the Ford Foundation. Beijing.

de Ferranti, D., and others (2003). Inequality in Latin America and the Caribbean: breaking with history? Washington, D.C.: International Bank for Reconstruction and Development/World Bank.

Delaunay, Daniel (1998). Le cas français. In *La mesure de la migration clandestine en Europe. Volume 2: Rapport des experts*, G. Tapinos and D. Delaunay, eds. Eurostat Working Papers (3/1998/E/no.7). Luxembourg.

Department of Trade and Industry, United Kingdom (2004). *Making Globalization a Force for Good.* Trade and Investment White Paper 2004. London: DTI. 7 July.

Desai, M.A., D. Kapur and J. McHale (2000). Sharing the spoils: taxing international human capital flows. Updated version of paper presented at the NBER-National Council of Applied Economic Research (NCAER) Conference on India's Economic Reforms.

Devan, Janamitra, and Parth S. Tewari (2001). Brains abroad. *The McKinsey Quarterley*, No. 4 (Emerging markets), p. 57.

Dialogue: Dial Newsletter (2003). No. 19 (June). Paris.

Doudeijns, M., and J.-C. Dumond (2003). Immigration and labour shortages: evaluation of needs and limits of selection policies in the recruitment of foreign labour. Paper prepared for the Conference on the Economic and Social Aspects of Migration, jointly organized by the European Commission and OECD.

Drinkwater, S., and others (2002). The economic impact of migration: a survey. Paper prepared for the second Workshop of the Fifth Framework Programme project entitled "European Enlargement: The Impact of East-West Migration on Growth and Employment". Vienna.

D'Sami, Bernard (2000). Migration patterns and challenges for Indians seeking work abroad: a special focus on South India, National Forum of Migrant Workers Rights. CARAM-Asia, Royapuram, Chennai, India. Available from http://aid-southasia.undp.org.in/publication/6TH%201CCAP/hiv_migration.htm (accessed 1 November 2004).

Duleep, Harriet O., and Mark C. Regets (1992). Some evidence on the effect of admission criteria on immigrant assimilation. In *Immigration, Language and Ethnicity: Canada and the United States*, Barry R. Chiswick, ed. Washington, D.C.: American Enterprise Institute.

Durand, J., and others (1996). International migration and development in Mexican communities. *Demography*, vol. 33, No. 2 (May), pp. 249-264.

__________, E.A. Parrado and D. Massey (1996). Migradollars and development: a reconsideration of the Mexican case. *International Migration Review*, vol. 30, No. 2. pp. 423-444.

Edwards, A.C., and M. Ureta (2001). Income transfer and children's schooling: evidence from El Salvador. California State University at Long Beach, Long Beach, California, and Texas A & M University, College Station, Texas. Revised June. NBER Inter-American Seminar on Economics, Monterrey, Mexico, November 2002.

Egan, Timothy (2004). Border desert proves deadly for Mexicans. *The New York Times*. 23 May.

Eurobarometer (1997). Opinion poll: racism and xenophobia in Europe. Eurobarometer Opinion Poll, No. 47.1, 1997.

European Commission (2001). The free movement of workers in the context of enlargement. Information note. 6 March. Available from http://europa.eu.int/comm/enlargement/docs/pdf/migration_enl.pdf

__________ (2003). Migration and social integration of migrants. Valorisation of research on migration and immigration funded under 4th and 5th European Framework Programmes of Research. Community Research. Proceedings of a dialogue workshop organized by DG Research, Brussels, 28 and 29 January 2002.

Ferenczi, I., and W.F. Willcox (1929). *International Migration*, vol. I., *Statistics*. New York: National Bureau of Economic Research.

Fetzer, Joel S. (2000). Economic self-interest or cultural marginality? Anti-immigration sentiment and nativist political movements in France, Germany and the USA. *Journal of Ethnic & Migration Studies*, vol. 26, No. 1, pp. 5-23.

Financial Times, (2004). April 28.

Freeman, Gary P. (2003). Immigration policies. In *Encyclopedia of Population,* Paul Demeny and Geoffrey McNicoll, eds. New York: Macmillan Reference USA.

Friedberg, R.M. (1997). The impact of mass migration on the Israeli labour market. Manuscript.

__________, and J. Hunt (1995). The impact of immigrants on host country wages, employment and growth. *Journal of Economic Perspectives*, vol. 9, No. 2.

Galenson, D.W. (1984). The rise and fall of indentured servitude in the Americas: an economic analysis. *Journal of Economic History*, vol. 44 (March).

Gammeltoft, P. (2002). *Remittances and other Financial Flows to Developing Countries.* Centre for Development Research Working Paper. Copenhagen.

Garson, Jean-Pierre, and Anaïs Loizillon (2003). Migration in Europe: trends and perspectives. Paper presented at the International Conference on the Economic and Social Aspects of Migration, jointly organized by the European Commission and OECD, Brussels 21and 22 January.

Gemery, H.A. (1994). Immigrants and emigrants: international migration and the US labor market in the Great Depression. In *Migration and the International Labor Market, 1850-1939,* T. J. Hatton and J. G. Williamson eds. London: Routledge.

Gieseck, A., U. Heilemann and H.D. von Loeffelholz (1995). Economic implications of migration into the Federal Republic of Germany, 1988-1992. *The International Migration Review*, vol. 29, No. 3.

Glaessel-Brown, E.E. (1998). Use of immigration policy to manage nursing shortages. *Journal of Nursing Scholarship*, vol. 30, No. 4.

Government of Canada (2003). Canada's view and proposals on transparency of horizontal Mode 4 commitments. Paper presented during the Expert Meeting on Market Access Issues in Mode 4 and Effective Implementation of Article IV on Increasing the Participation of Developing Countries. Geneva, 29-31 July 2003.

Grant, Oliver (2003). Globalisation versus de-coupling: German emigration and the evolution of the Atlantic labour market, 1870-1913. *Explorations in Economic History,* vol. 40, p. 390.

Grondin, Danielle (2004). Well-managed migrants' health benefits all. *Bulletin of the World Health Organization*, vol. 82, No. 8 (August), p. 561.

Guarnizo, Luis Eduardo (2003). The economics of transnational living. *The International Migration Review*, vol. 37, No. 3 (fall), pp. 666-699.

Hallock, J.A., S.S. Seeling and J.J. Norcini (2003). The international medical graduate pipeline. *Health Affairs*, vol. 22, No. 4.

Hansen, Randall (2003). Migration to Europe since 1945: its history and its lessons. In *The Politics of Migration: Managing Opportunity, Conflict and Change*, Sarah Spencer, ed. Oxford: Blackwell.

Hatton, T. J., and J. G. Williamson, eds. (1994). *Migration and the International Labor Market, 1850-1939.* London: Routledge.

Hatton, Timothy J., and Jeffrey G. Williamson (2005). *World Mass Migration: Two Centuries of Policy and Performance.* Cambridge, Massachusetts: The MIT Press.

Hendricks, L. (2002). How important is human capital for development? evidence from immigration earnings. *American Economic Review*, vol. 92, pp. 198-219.

Hille, Hubertus, and Thomas Straubhaar (2001). The impact of EU enlargement and economic integration: results of recent studies. In *Migration Policies and EU Enlargement: The Case of Central and Eastern Europe.* Geneva: International Labour Organization.

Hirschman, C. (2001). Immigration: public policy. In *International Encyclopedia of Social and Behavioral Science*, vol. 11, N.J. Smelser and P.B. Baltes, eds. Oxford, United Kingdom: Elsevier.

Hoddinott, J. (1996). A model of migration and remittances applied to Western Kenya. *Oxford Economic Papers*, vol. 46.

Huff, W.G. (1994). *The Economic Growth of Singapore: Trade and Development in the Twentieth Century.* Cambridge, United Kingdom: Cambridge University Press.

Hunt, J. (1992). The impact of the 1962 repatriation from Algeria on the French labour market. *Industrial and Labour Relations Review*, vol. 45. April.

Huttenback, R.A. (1976). *Racism and Empire: White Settlers and Colored Immigrants in the British Self-Governing Colonies, 1830-1910.* Ithaca, New York: Cornell University Press.

Hysenbegasi, A., and S. Poza (2002). What prompts workers to remit: evidence using a panel of Latin American and Caribbean nations. Citigroup, Irving, Texas, and Western Michigan University, Kalamazoo, Michigan. Available from http://homepages.wmich.edu/~pozo/what%20prompts.final.pdf (accessed 25 October 2004).

Institute of Public Affaris (2002). How Asian brain drain winds up benefiting Asia. *Review – Institute of Public Affairs*, vol. 54, No. 2 (June), p. 30.

Inter-American Development Bank (2001). Remittances to Latin America and the Caribbean: comparative statistics. Paper prepared by the Multilateral Investment Fund – Inter-American Development Bank for the Regional Conference on Remittances as a Development Tool. Washington, D.C.

International Labour Office (1936). *World Statistics of Aliens: A Comparative Study of Census Returns 1910-1920-1930.* Studies and Reports, Series O (Migration), No. 6. Geneva: International Labour Office.

International Labour Organization (2003). Migrant workers. *NATLEX* database on national laws and regulations concerning labour, social security, and related human rights, available from http://natlex.ilo.org.

__________ (2004a). *Towards a Fair Deal for Migrant Workers in the Global Economy.* Report VI, International Labour Conference, 92nd Session, 2004. Geneva: International Labour Office.

__________ (2004b). Provisional Record 22, International Labour Conference, Ninety-second session, Geneva, 2004. Available from www.ilo.org/public/english/standards/relm/ilc/ilc92/pdf/pr-22.pdf (accessed 24 November 2004).

International Migration Policy Programme (2000). *The International Migration Policy Conference for Central Asia, the Caucasus and Neighbouring States: Report and Conclusions.* Geneva.

__________ (2003). The international migration policy seminar for the Caribbean region: background paper. Geneva.

International Monetary Fund (2003). *Balance of Payments Statistics Yearbook, 2003.* Washington, D.C.

International Organization for Migration (IOM) (1996). Combating migrant trafficking through legislation. *Trafficking in Migrants: Quarterly Bulletin,* No. 12, pp. 1-3.

__________ (2002a). MIDA: Migration for development in Africa. Brochure. Geneva.

__________ (2002b). Managing migration at the regional level: strategies for regional consultation. Paper prepared for the Roundtable on Managing Migration at the Regional Level, held on 5 June 2002, Geneva. Available from http://www.iom.int.

__________ (2003a). Migrants' remittances in the Americas: trends and policy options for RCM countries. Intervention by Mr. Brunson McKinley, Director-General of IOM, during the VIII Regional Conference on Migration in Cancún, Mexico, 29 and 30 May.

__________ (2003b). Illustration of multilateral, regional and bilateral cooperative arrangements in the management of migration. In *Migration and International Legal Norms,* T. Alexander Aleinikoff and Vincent Chetail, eds. The Hague: T.M.C. Asser Press, pp. 305-333.

__________ (2003c). *World Migration 2003: Managing Migration: Challenges and Responses for People on the Move.* Geneva.

__________ (2003d). *Labour Migration in Asia: Trends, Challenges and Policy Responses in Countries of Origin.* Geneva.

__________, Council (2003). Migration in a globalized world. Eighty-sixth Session. 10 November. MC/INF/268.

__________, Office of Programme Evaluation (1999). *Evaluation of IOM Public Information Programmes.* Geneva.

International Organization for Migration (IOM) and United Nations (2000). *World Migration Report, 2000.* Sales No. E.00.III.S.3.

__________ (2002). *International Migration Report 2002.* Sales No. E.03.XIII.4. United Nations.

Iredale, Robyn, and Nicola Piper (2003). *Identification of the Obstacles to the Signing and Ratification of the UN Convention on the Protection of the Rights of All Migrant Workers: The Asia-Pacific Perspective.* Paris: UNESCO.

Issawi, C. (1966). *The Economy of the Middle East, 1800-1914.* Chicago, Illinois: University of Chicago Press.

Japan, Ministry of Justice (2001). *Immigration Control, 2001.* Tokyo.

Jaret, C. (1999). Troubled by newcomers: anti-immigrant attitudes and action during two eras of mass immigration to the United States. *Journal of American Ethnic History*, vol. 18, No. 3 (spring), pp. 9-39.

Joint United Nations Programme on HIV/AIDS and International Organization for Migration (2004). UNAIDS/IOM statement on HIV/AIDS-related travel restrictions. Geneva. June. Available from http://www.iom.int/en/pdf_files/hivaids/unaids_iom_statement_travel_restrictions.pdf (accessed 20 October 2004).

Kandil, M., and M.F. Metwally (1990). The impact of migrants' remittances on the Egyptian economy. *International Migration*, vol. XXVIII, No. 2.

Kapur, D. (2003). Remittances: the new development mantra? Paper prepared for the G-24 Technical Group Meeting, Harvard University, and Center for Global Development. UNCTAD/GDS/MDPB/G24/2004/5. New York: United Nations.

Kasasa, Aya (2001). Asylum and immigration: Europe's search for a common policy. *The Courier ACP-EU*, vol. 187, pp. 30-32.

Kenwood, A.G., and A.L. Lougheed (1999). *The Growth of the International Economy, 1820-2000*, 4th ed. London: Routledge.

Kesler, Christel (2004). Defining migrant status and assessing employment outcomes in Europe. May. Unpublished paper.

Kirk, Dudley (1946). *Europe's Population in the Interwar Years*. League of Nations. Princeton, New Jersey: Princeton University Press.

Klekowski von Koppenfels, Amanda (2001). *The Role of Regional Consultative Processes in Managing International Migration*. IOM Migration Research Series, No. 3. Geneva: IOM.

K. von Koppenfels, Amanda (2001). Informal but effective: regional consultative processes as a tool in managing migration. *International Migration*, vol. 39, No. 6, pp. 62-82.

Koc, I., and I. Onan (2001). The impact of remittances of international migrants on the standard of living of the left-behind families in Turkey. Conference Proceedings, XXIV IUSSP General Conference, Salvador, Brazil, 18-24 April 2001. Available from http://www.iussp.org/Brazil2001/s20/S26_03_koc.pdf (accessed 25 October 2004).

Kogan, I. (2004). Employment careers and unemployment dynamics of immigrants in Germany and Great Britain. Mannheim Centre for European Social Research, University of Mannheim, Mannheim, Germany. P. 18.

Koser, Khalid (2001). New approaches to asylum? *International Migration*, vol. 39, No. 6, pp. 85-99.

Kramer, Roger G. (2003). Development in international migration to the United States: 2003. Immigration Policy and Research, Working Paper 38. Washington, D.C.: United States Department of Labor, Bureau of International Labor Affairs.

Kule, D., and others (1999). *The Causes and Consequences of Albanian Emigration during Transition: Evidence from Micro Data*. Working Paper, No. 46. London: European Bank for Reconstruction and Development.

Labour Migration Ministerial Consultations for Countries of Origin in Asia (2004). Summary of statements and recommendations of the Ministers. Colombo.

Latham, A.J.H., and L. Neal (1983). The international market in rice and wheat 1868-1914. *Economic History Review*, vol. 36, pp. 260-275.

León-Ledesma, M., and M. Piracha (2001). *International Migration and the Role of Remittances in Eastern Europe*. Studies in Economics, No. 0113. Canterbury, United Kingdom: Department of Economics, University of Kent.

Lewis, W. Arthur (1978). *The Evolution of the International Economic Order*. Princeton, New Jersey: Princeton University Press.

Lewis, W.A. (1978). *Growth and Fluctuations 1870-1913*. London: Allen and Unwin.

Lim, Lin Lean (1996). The migration transition in Malaysia. *Asian and Pacific Migration Journal* (Manila), vol. 5, Nos. 2-3, pp. 319-337.

Lloyd, J. (2003). The closing of the European gates? the new populist parties of Europe. In *The Politics of Migration*, S. Spencer ed. Malden, Massachusetts, Blackwell Publishers, pp. 88-99.

Lowell, B. L. (2001). *Some Development Effects of the International Migration of Highly Skilled Persons.* International Migration Papers, No. 46. Geneva: International Labour Office.

__________, and R.O. de la Garza (2000). The developmental role of remittances in U.S. Latino Communities and in Latin American countries. Final project report prepared for the Thomás Rivera Policy Institute (TRPI), University of Texas, Austin, Texas, and the Inter-American Dialogue.

Lowell, B.L., and Allan Findlay (2001). *Migration of Highly Skilled Persons from Developing Countries: Impact and Policy Responses: Synthesis Report.* I nternational Migration Papers, No. 44. Geneva: International Labour Office.

Lowell, B.L., and Yvonne B. Kemper (2004). Transatlantic roundtable on low-skilled migration in the twenty-first century: prospect and policies. *International Migration*, vol. 42, No. 2, pp. 117-138.

Lucas, Robert E.B. (2001). Diaspora and development: highly skilled migrants from East Asia. Report prepared for the World Bank. November. Available from http://www.bu.edu/econ/ied/dp/papers/dp120.pdf (accessed 25 October 2004).

Lynch, James P., and Rita J. Simon (2003). *Immigration the World Over: Statutes, Policies, and Practices.* Lanham, Maryland: Rowman & Littlefield Publishers.

Maiden, Samantha (2004). Degrees come with a visa. *The Australian.* 25 February.

Mármora, Lelio (2003). Mutually agreed migration policies in Latin America. In *World Migration, 2003.* Geneva: ILO.

Martin, David A., and T. Alexander Aleinikoff (2002). Double ties: why nations should learn to love dual nationality. *Foreign Policy*, vol. 133, pp. 80-81.

Martin, Philip, and Elizabeth Midgley (2003). Immigration: shaping and reshaping America. *Population Bulletin,* vol. 58, No. 2.

Martin, Susan, Philip Martin and Patrick Weil (2002). Fostering cooperation between source and destination countries. Migration Information Source, Migration Policy Institute (MPI), Washington, D.C. Available from www.migrationinformation.org.

Martínez-Herrera, Enric, and Djaouida Moualhi (2004). Public opinion and immigration policies in five EU countries: accounting for (in)consistency between immigrants selection and integration policies and citizens' attitudes. Paper presented at the thirty-second European Consortium for Political Research (ECPR) Joint Sessions of Workshops, Uppsala, Sweden, 13-18 April 2004. Available from http://www.essex.ac.uk/ecpr/events/jointsessions/paperarchive/uppsala/ws16/Moualhi.pdf (accessed 20 October 2004).

Massey, Douglas S., Jorge Durand and Nolan Malone (2002). *Beyond Smoke and Mirrors: Mexican Immigration in an Era of Economic Integration.* New York, New York: Russell Sage.

Mattoo, Aaditya, Sumantha Chauduri, and Richard Self (2003). Liberalizing Mode 4: a possible approach. Paper presented during the OECD-World Bank-IOM Seminar on Trade and Migration, Geneva, 12-14 November 2003.

McClelland, C. (2002). South African brain drain costing $5 billion–and counting. *Canadian Medical Association Journal*, vol. 167, No. 7, p. 793.

McCormick, B., and J. Wahba (2003). Return international migration and geographical inequality: the case of Egypt. *Journal of African Economics*, vol. 12, No. 4, pp. 500-532.

Meyer, J.-B., and M. Brown (1999). Scientific diasporas: a new approach to the brain drain. United Nations Educational, Scientific and Cultural Organization (UNESCO) Management of Social Transformations Programme (MOST) discussion paper, No. 41, prepared for the World Conference on Science, UNESCO-International Council for Science (ICSU), Budapest, 26 June-1 July 1999.

Migration News (1998). Italy: North Africans, Kosovo. Vol. 5, No. 9 (September). Available from www.migration.ucdavis.edu.

Miller, Mark J. (1992). Evolution of policy modes for regulating international labour migration. In *International Migration Systems: A Global Approach*, Mary M. Kritz, Lin Lean Lim and Hania Zlotnik, eds. Oxford: Clarendon Press.

__________, and Philip L. Martin (1996). Prospects for cooperative management of international migration in the 21st century. *Asian and Pacific Migration Journal* (Quezon City, Philippines), vol. 5, Nos. 2-3, pp. 175-199.

Mosisa, Abraham T. (2002). The role of foreign-born workers in the U.S. economy. *Monthly Labor Review*, vol. 125, No. 5, pp. 3-14.

Mutume, Gumisai (2003). Reversing Africa's "brain drain". *Africa Recovery* (New York), vol. 17, No. 2.

National Science Foundation (1996). *Undergraduate Origins of Recent (1991-95) Science and Engineering Doctorate Recipients: Special Report.* Division of Science Resources Studies, Directorate for Social, Behavioral and Economic Sciences. Detailed Statistical Tables, NSF 96-334. Arlington, Virginia.

New Zealand Department of Labour (2003). *The Fiscal Impact of Migrants to New Zealand 2003.* Immigration Research Programme. April. Wellington.

Northrup, D. (1995). *Indentured Labor in the Age of Imperialism, 1834-1922.* Cambridge, United Kingdom: Cambridge University Press.

Ocampo, José Antonio, and Juan Martin, eds. (2003). *Globalization and Development.* Palo Alto, California: Stanford University Press/World Bank/ECLAC.

Okólski, Marek (1998). Regional dimension of international migration in Central and Eastern Europe. *GENUS* (Rome), vol. LIV, No. 1-2, pp. 11-36.

Omelaniuk, Irena (2003). Elements of a more global approach to migration management. In *World Migration 2003.* Geneva: ILO, pp. 271-289.

O'Neil, Kevin (2004). *Labor Export as Government Policy: The Case of the Philippines.* Washington, D.C.: Migration Policy Institute.

Organisation for Economic Co-operation and Development (2001). *International Mobility of the Highly-Skilled.* Paris: OECD.

__________ (2003). *Migration and the Labour Market in Asia: Recent Trends and Policies.* Paris.

O'Rourke, K.H., and J.G. Williamson (1999). *Globalization and History: The Evolution of a Nineteenth-Century Atlantic Economy*. Cambridge, Massachusetts: The MIT Press.

Pang, T., M.A. Lansang and A. Haines (2002). Brain drain and health professionals: a global problem needs global solutions. *British Medical Journal*, vol. 324 (2 March), pp. 499-500.

Parrado, Emilio A. and Marcela Cerrutti (2003). Labor migration between developing countries: the case of Paraguay and Argentina. *International Migration Review*, vol. 37, No. 1, pp. 101-132.

Passel, Jeffrey S. (2002). New estimates of the undocumented population in the United States. Mimeograph. In Migration Information Source, feature story, No. 19, 22 May. Available from www.migrationinformation.org (accessed 2 November 2004).

__________ (2004). Undocumented immigrants: facts and figures. Mimeo. Also available from http://www.urban.org/url.cfm?ID=1000587 (accessed 1 November 2004).

Piguet, E., and S. Losa (2002). *Travailleurs de l'ombre? Demande de main-d'oeuvre du domaine de l'asile et ampleur de l'emploi d'étrangers non déclarés en Suisse*. Zürich, Switzerland: Seisomo.

Plant, Roger (2002). Forced labour, migration and trafficking. *Labour Education*, vol. 4, No. 129. Available from http://www.-ilo-mirror.cornell.edu/public/english/dialogue/actrav/publ/129 (accessed 1 November 2004).

Poirine, B. (1997). A theory of remittances as an implicit family loan agreement. *World Development*, vol. 25, No. 4, pp. 589-611.

Portes, Alejandro (1995). Children of immigrants: segmented assimilation and its determinants. In *The Economic Sociology of Immigration*, A. Portes ed. New York, New York: Russell Sage, pp. 248-279.

Potts, Lydia (1990). *The World Labour Market: A History of Migration*. London: Zed Books.

Pries, Ludger (2003). Labour migration, social incorporation and transmigration in the New Europe: the case of Germany in a comparative perspective. Department of Social Sciences, Ruhr-University Bochum, Germany.

Puri, S., and T. Ritzema (1999). *Migrant Worker Remittances, Micro-finance and the Informal Economy: Prospects and Issues*. Working Paper, No. 21. Geneva: Social Finance Unit, International Labour Organization.

Ratha, Dilip (2003). Workers' remittances: an important and stable source of external development finance. In *Global Development Finance 2003: Striving for Stability in Development Finance*. Washington, D.C.: World Bank.

Rodrik, D. (2001). Comments at the Conference on Immigration Policy and the Welfare State. Paper presented at the Conference on Immigration Policy and the Welfare State, Trieste, Italy.

Rodrik, Dani (1997). *Has Globalization Gone too Far*? Washington, D.C.: Institute for International Economics.

__________ (2002). *Feasible Globalizations.* Centre for Economic Policy Research Discussion Papers, No. 3524. London: CEPR.

Rowthorn, R. (2004). The Economic Impact of Immigration. A Civitas Online Report. Available from http://www.civitas.org.uk/pdf/Rowthorn_Immigration.pdf (accessed 25 October 2004).

Rozelle, S., C. Pray and J. Huang (1998). Importing the means of production: foreign capital and technology flows in China's agriculture. Paper presented at the 1999 International Agricultural Trade Research Consortium Conference, San Francisco, California, 25 and 26 June 1999.

Ruhs, Martin (2003). *Temporary Foreign Worker Programmes: Policies, Adverse Consequences, and the Need to Make Them Work.* Geneva: International Migration Programme, International Labour Office.

Russell, M. (1984). Beyond remittances: the redistribution of cash in Swazi societies. *The Journal of Modern African Studies*, vol. 22, No. 4, pp. 595-615.

Russell, Sharon Stanton (1992). International migration and political turmoil in the Middle East. *Population and Development Review* (New York), vol. 18, No. 4, pp. 719-728.

Saggar, Shamit (2003). Immigration and the politics of public opinion. *Political Quarterly,* vol. 74, No. 1, pp. 178-194.

Salt, John (1999). Current trends in international migration in Europe. European Committee on Migration (CDMG), Council of Europe. CDMG (1999) 30. Mimeo.

__________ (2000). *Current Trends in International Migration in Europe*. Strasbourg, France: Council of Europe.

__________ (2002). Current trends in international migration in Europe. European Committee on Migration (CDMG), Council of Europe, CDMG (2002). Mimeo.

Sander, C. (2003). Migrant remittances to developing countries. Paper prepared for the United Kingdom Department for International Development (DFID), London.

__________, and S.M. Maimbo (2003). *Migrant Labour Remittances in Africa: Reducing Obstacles to Developmental Contributions*. World Bank Group Africa Region Working Paper Series, No. 64. Washington, D.C.: World Bank.

Santangelo Group (2004). Do visa delays hurt business? Washington, D.C. Available from http://www.nftc.org/default/visasurveyresults%20final.pdf (accessed 20 October 2004).

Schindlmayr, Thomas (2003). Sovereignty, legal regimes and international migration. *International Migration*, vol. 41, No. 2, pp. 109-123.

Shehu, Abdullahi (2003). The Asian alternative remittance systems and money laundering. *Journal of Money Laundering Control*, vol. 7, No. 2 (autumn), pp. 175-185.

Smith, James P., and Barry Edmonston, eds. (1997). *The New Americans: Economic, Demographic, and Fiscal Effects of Immigration.* Washington, D.C.: National Research Council, Commission on Behavioral and Social Sciences, and Education.

Solimano, Andrés (2003). *Development Cycles, Political Regimes and International Migration: Argentina in the Twentieth Century*. Macroeconomía del Desarrollo, Serie 22. Economic Development Division, Economic Commission for Latin America and the Caribbean (ECLAC), Santiago, Chile. Sales No. E.03.II.G.14. January.

Solimano, A. (2003a). Emigrants' remittances as a source of development finance. Paper prepared for the United Nations University/World Institute for Development Economics Research (UNU/WIDER) Conference on Sharing Global Prosperity, Helsinki.

__________ (2003b). *Remittances by Emigrants: Issues and Evidence*. Santiago, Economic Development Division, Economic Commission for Latin America and the Caribbean. October. Sales No. E.03.G.152.

__________, and Molly Pollack (2004). *International Mobility of the Highly Skilled: The Case between Europe and Latin America*. Working Papers Series, No. 1. January. Washington, D.C.: Inter-American Development Bank.

SOPEMI (Continuous Reporting System on Migration) (various years). *Trends in International Migration*. Paris: Organization for Economic Cooperation and Development.

__________ (1992). *Trends in International Migration: Annual Report, 1992 Edition*. Paris: Organization for Economic Cooperation and Development.

__________ (1994). *Trends in International Migration: Annual Report, 1993 Edition*. Paris: Organization for Economic Cooperation and Development.

__________ (1998). *Trends in International Migration: Annual Report, 1998 Edition*. Paris: Organization for Economic Cooperation and Development.

__________ (1999). *Trends in International Migration: Annual Report, 1999 Edition*. Paris: Organization for Economic Cooperation and Development.

__________ (2001a). *Trends in International Migration: Annual Report, 2000 Edition*. Paris: Organization for Economic Cooperation and Development.

__________ (2001b). *Trends in International Migration: Annual Report, 2001 Edition*. Paris: Organization for Economic Cooperation and Development.

__________ (2003). *Trends in International Migration: Annual Report, 2002 Edition*. Paris: Organization for Economic Cooperation and Development.

__________ (2004). Trends *in International Migration: Annual Report, 2003 Edition*. Paris: Organization for Economic Cooperation and Development.

South Africa, Chamber of Mines (1987). *Statistical Tables, 1987*. Johannesburg, South Africa: Chamber of Mines.

__________ (1993). *Statistical Tables, 1993*. Johannesburg, South Africa: Chamber of Mines.

South Africa, Ministry of Home Affairs, Task Team on International Migration (1999). White paper on international migration. Available from http://www.info.gov.za/whitepaper/1999/migrate.htm (accessed 2 November 2004).

Stahl, C.W., and A. Habib (1989). The impact of overseas workers' remittances on indigenous industries: evidence from Bangladesh. *The Developing Economies*, XXVII-3 (September), pp. 269-289.

Stalker, Peter (1994). *The Work of Strangers: A Survey of International Labour Migration.* Geneva: ILO.

__________ (2001). *The No-Nonsense Guide to International Migration*. London: New Internationalist/Verso.

__________ (2002). Migration trends and migration policy in Europe. *International Migration*, vol. 40, No. 5, pp. 151-179.

Stark, Oded (1991). Migration in LDCs: risk, remittances, and the family. *Finance and Development*, vol. 28, No. 4, pp. 39-41.

__________, and R.E.B. Lucas (1998). Migration, remittances and the family. *Economic Development & Cultural Change*, vol. 36, No. 3, pp. 465-481.

Stiglitz, Joseph E., and Andrew Charlton, with the Initiative for Policy Dialogue (2004). The development round of trade negotiations in the aftermath of Cancún. Report prepared for the Commonwealth Secretariat. London.

Taran, P., and E. Geronimi (2003). *Globalization, Labour and Migration: Protection is Paramount*. Geneva: International Labour Office.

Taylor, A.M., and J.G. Williamson (1997). Convergence in the age of mass migration. *European Review of Economic History*, vol. 1, pp. 27-63.

Taylor, J.E. (1999). The new economics of international migration and the role of remittances in the migration process. *International Migration*, vol 37, No. 1, pp. 63-88.

Teitelbaum, M.S. (2002). The role of the state in international migration. *The Brown Journal of World Affairs*, vol. VIII, Issue 2.

__________ (1959). International migration. In *The Study of Population: An Inventory and Appraisal*, Philip M. Hauser and Otis Dudley Duncan, eds. Bombay, India: Asia Publishing House, pp. 510-543.

Thomas, Brinley (1959). International Migration in *The Study of Population*, Philip M. Hauser and Otis Dudley Duncan, eds. Chicago, Illinois: University of Chicago Press, pp. 510-543.

Tilly, Charles (1998). *Durable Inequality*. Berkeley, California: University of California Press.

Timmer, A., and J.G. Williamson (1998). Immigration policy prior to the thirties: labor markets, policy interaction, and globalization backlash. *Population and Development Review*, vol. 24, No. 4 (December), pp. 739-771.

Tinker, H. (1974). *A New System of Slavery: The Export of Indian Labour Overseas, 1830-1920.* London: Oxford University Press.

Torres, F. (2002). Migrants' capital for small-scale infrastructure and small enterprise development in Mexico. Final report of a project undertaken by the World Bank in response to a request by Nacional Financiera (NAFIN). Washington, D.C.

Trindade, V., and J.E. Rauch (2000). Ethnic Chinese networks in international trade. Working Papers, 2002-007. Department of Economics, Syracuse University, Syracuse, New York.

Tsay, Ching-Lung (2000). Trends and characteristics of migration flows to the economy of Chinese Taipei. In *Proceedings of the International Workshop on International Migration and Human Resources Development in the APEC Member Economies, Chiba, Japan, 20-21 January 2000*. Chiba, Japan: Institute of Developing Economies, pp. 131-166.

__________, and Ji-Ping Lin (2001). Impacts of labour importation on the unemployment of local workers: an exploration based on survey data. In *Proceedings of the International Workshop on International Migration and Structural Change in the APEC Member Economies, Chinese Taipei, 19-20 October 2000*, Yasuko Hayase and Ching-Lung Tsay, eds. Chiba, Japan: Institute of Developing Economies-Japanese External Trade Organization, pp. 307-332.

Uh, SooBong (1999). Immigration and labour market issues in Korea. In *Migration and Regional Economic Integration in Asia*. Paris: OECD, pp. 153-164.

United Nations (1953). *International Migration Statistics*. Statistical Papers, No. 20. Sales No. E.53.XIII.10.

__________ (1954). *Treaty Series*, vol. 189, No. 2545.

__________ (1958). *Treaty Series*, vol. 89, No. 4300.

__________ (1967). *Treaty Series*, vol. 606, No. 8791.

__________ (1980). *Recommendations on Statistics of International Migration.* Statistical Papers, No. 58. Sales No. E.79.XVII.18.

__________ (1983). *Treaty Series*, vol. 1001, No. 14691.

__________ (1985). *World Population Trends, Population and Development Interrelations and Population Policies: 1983 Monitoring Report*, vol. I, *Population Trends*. Sales No. E.84.XIII.10.

__________ (1995). *Report of the International Conference on Population and Development, Cairo, 5-13 September 1994*. Sales No. E.95.XIII.18.

__________ (1996). *World Population Monitoring, 1993.* Sales No. E.95.XIII.8.

__________ (1997a). *International Migration and Development: The Concise Report.* Sales No. E.97.XIII.4.

__________ (1997b). Human *Rights: A Compilation of International Instruments*, vol. II, *Regional Instruments*. Sales No. E.97.XIV.1.

__________ (1998a). *International Migration Policies.* Sales No. E.98.XIII.8.

__________ (1998b). *Recommendations on Statistics of International Migration, Revision 1*. Statistical Papers, No. 58, Rev.1. Sales No. E.98.XVII.14.

__________ (1998c). Statistical Papers, No. 58, Rev.1. Sales No. E.98. XVII.14.

__________ (1998d). *Principles and Recommendations for Population and Housing Censuses, Revision 1*. Statistical Papers, No. 67, Rev.1. Sales No. E.98.XVII.8.

__________ (1998e). *World Population Monitoring, 1997: International Migration and Development.* Sales No. E.98.XIII.4.

__________ (1999). *World Population Prospects: The 1998 Revision*, vol. I, *Comprehensive Tables*, and vol. II, *Sex and Age*. Sales Nos. E.99.XIII.9 and E.99.XIII.8.

__________ (2001). *Replacement Migration: Is it a Solution to Declining and Ageing Populations?* Sales No. E.01.XIII.19.

__________ (2002a). *International Migration from Countries with Economies in Transition: 1980-1999.* United Nations Department of Economic and Social Affairs Population Division Working Paper No. ESA/P/WP.176, September.

__________ (2002b). *Report of the International Conference on Financing for Development, Monterrey, Mexico, 18-22 March 2002*. Sales No. E.02.II.A.7.

__________ (2003a). *Levels and Trends of International Migration to Selected Countries in Asia.* Sales No. E.03.XIII.2.

__________ (2003b). International migration and development: report of the Secretary-General. A/58/98. 1 July. Submitted to the General Assembly at its fifty-eighth session.

__________ (2003c). *Population, Education and Development: The Concise Report.* Sales No. E.03.XIII.11.

__________ (2003d). World population monitoring, 2003: population, education and development. Draft report prepared for the Commission on Population and Development at its thirty-sixth session, 31 March-4 April 2003, p. 158.

__________ (2003e). *World Population Prospects: The 2002 Revision*, vol. I, *Comprehensive Tables.* Sales No. E.03.XIII.6.

__________ (2004a). *Demographic Yearbook* review: national reporting of international migration data-implications for international recommendations. United Nations Department of Economic and Social Affairs Statistics Division Technical Report, No. ESA/STAT/2004/4. April.

__________ (2004b). Review and appraisal of the progress made in achieving the goals and objectives of the Programme of Action of the International Conference on Population and Development: report of the Secretary-General. E/CN.9/2004/3. 12 January. Submitted to the Commission on Population and Development at its thirty-seventh session, 22-26 March 2004.

__________ (2004c). *Trends in Total Migrant Stock: The 2003 Revision* (POP/DB/MIG/Rev.2003), database in digital form.

__________ (2004d). *Trends in Total Migrant Stock: The 2003 Revision. Diskette Documentation.* United Nations Department of Economic and Social Affairs Population Division Working Paper, No. ESA/P/WP.188.

__________ (2004e). *World Population Policies, 2003.* Sales No. E.04.XIII.3.

__________ (2004f). *2004 World Survey on the Role of Women in Development: Women and Migration.* Sales No. E.04.IV.4.

__________, European Commission, International Monetary Fund, Organisation for Economic Co-operation and Development, United Nations Conference on Trade and Development and World Trade Organization (2002). *Manual on Statistics of International Trade in Services.* Statistical Papers, No, 86. Sales No. E.02.XVII.11.

United Nations Conference on Trade and Development (2003). Report of the Expert Meeting on Market Access Issues in Mode 4 (Movement of Natural Persons to Supply Services) and Effective Implementation of Article IV on Increasing the Participation of Developing Countries, held at the Palais des Nations, Geneva, from 29 to 31 July 2003. TD/B/COM.1/64-TD/B/COM.1/EM.22/3. 27 November. Submitted to the Trade and Development Board, Commission on Trade in Goods and Services, and Commodities, at its eighth session, Geneva, 9-13 February 2004.

United Nations Development Programme (2004). *Human Development Report, 2004: Cultural Liberty in Today's Diverse World*. New York: UNDP.

United Nations High Commissioner for Refugees. Country of Origin Information (COI) database. Available from http://unhcr.ch.

__________ (various years). *The State of the World's Refugees*. Oxford and New York: Oxford University Press.

__________ (1993). *The State of the World's Refugees:The Challenge of Protection*. Middlesex, England: Penguin Books.

__________ (2000a). Annual theme: UNHCR at 50: from response to solutions. Report submitted to the Executive Committee of the High Commissioner's Programme at its fifty-first session. A/AC.96/938. 5 September.

__________ (2000b). *The State of the World's Refugees 2000: Fifty Years of Humanitarian Action*. Oxford, United Kingdom: Oxford University Press.

__________ (2002a). *Statistical Yearbook 2001*. Geneva.

__________ (2002b). *Statistical Yearbook, 2001: Refugees, Asylum-seekers and Other Persons of Concern–Trends in Displacement, Protection and Solutions*. Geneva: UNHCR. October.

__________ (2003a). *Global Report 2002: Strategies and Activities*. Geneva.

__________ (2003b). *Refugees by Numbers 2003*. Geneva.

__________ (2004a). *2003 Global Refugee Trend Overview of Refugee Populations, New Arrivals, Durable Solutions, Asylum-Seekers and Other Persons of Concern to UNHCR*. Geneva: Population Data Unit/PGDS, Division of Operational Support. 15 June. Available from http://www.unhcr.ch/statistics.

__________ (2004b). Protracted refugee situations. Document prepared for the 30th meeting of the Standing Committee of the Executive Committee of the High Commissioner's Programme. EC/54/SC/CRP.14. 10 June. Available from http://www.unhcr.ch/statistics.

United States Census Bureau (2001). Profile of the foreign-born population in the United States: 2000. *Current Population Reports*, Series P23-206. December. Washington, D.C.: United States Government Printing Office.

United States Commission for the Study of International Migration and Cooperative Economic Development (1990). *Unauthorized Migration: An Economic Development Response*. Washington, D.C.

United States Committee for Refugees. Worldwide Refugee Information database. Available from http://www.refugees.org/world/worldmain.htm (accessed 20 October 2004).

__________ (various years). *World Refugee Survey.* Annual. Washington, D.C.

United States, Department of Commerce Economics and Statistics Administration, Bureau of the Census (1997). *Census and You*, vol. 32, No. 6 (June). Available from http://www.census.gov.

United States Department of Homeland Security, Office of Immigration Statistics (2003). *2002 Yearbook of Immigration Statistics.* Washington, D.C.: United States Government Printing Office.

United States Department of Justice, Immigration and Naturalization Service (1991). *Statistical Yearbook of the Immigration and Naturalization Service.* Washington, D.C.: United States Government Printing Office.

__________ (1999). *Statistical Yearbook of the Immigration and Naturalization Service.* Washington, D.C.: United States Government Printing Office.

United States Immigration and Naturalization Service (2003). Estimates of the unauthorized immigrant population residing in the United States: 1990 to 2000. Office of Policy Planning. Available from http://uscis.gov/graphics/shared/aboutus/statistics/Ill_Report_1211.pdf (accessed 28 October 2004).

Villa, Miguel, and Jorge Martínez Pizarro (2001). Tendencias y patrones migratorios en las Américas. In *La Migración Internacional y el Desarrollo en las Américas. Simposio sobre migración internacional en las Américas, San José, Costa Rica, September 2000.* Santiago de Chile: CEPAL.

Voigt-Graf, Carmen (2003). Fijian teachers on the move: causes, implications and policies. *Asia Pacific Viewpoint*, vol. 44, No. 2, pp. 163-175.

Waddington, Clare (2003). International migration policies in Asia: a synthesis of ILO and other literature to manage the recruitment and protection of migrants, and facilitate remittances and their investment. Paper prepared for and presented at the Regional Conference on Migration, Development and Pro-Poor Policy Choices in Asia, 22-24 June 2003, Dhaka, Bangladesh, jointly organized by the Refugee and Migratory Movements Research Unit, Bangladesh, and the Department for International Development, United Kingdom. Available from http://www.livelihoods.org/hot_topics/docs/Dhaka_CP_10.pdf (accessed on 20 October 2004).

Wahba, S. (1991). What determines workers' remittances? *Finance & Development*, vol. 28, No. 4, p. 42.

Wallace, Claire (2000). Patterns of migration in Central Europe. Paper presented at Session 2: Potential Spillovers between the Labour Markets of EU and of Accession Countries, Conference on Economic and Social Dimensions of EU Enlargement, Belgium, 16 November 2000, Présidence française de l'Union européenne.

Weil, Patrick (2002). Towards a coherent policy of co-development. *International Migration* (Washington, D.C.), vol. 40, No. 3, pp. 41-55.

Williamson, J.G. (2000). Globalization, factor prices and living standards in Asia before 1940. In *Asia Pacific Dynamism 1500-2000,* A.J.H. Latham and H. Kawakatsu, eds. London: Routledge.

Williamson, Jeffrey G. (2004). The political economy of world mass migration: comparing two global centuries. American Enterprise Institute for Public Policy Research (AEI) Wendt Distinguished Lecture. Washington, D.C. 11 May.

Winkelman, R. (2000). The labour market performance of European immigrants in New Zealand in the 1980s and 1990s. *The International Migration Review*, vol. 34, No. 1, pp. 33-58.

Winters, L. Alan, and others (2002). *Negotiating the Liberalization of the Temporary Movement of Natural Persons*. Discussion Papers in Economics, No. 87. Brighton, United Kingdom: University of Sussex at Brighton. October.

Wöcke, Albert, and Saul Klein (2002). The implications of South Africa's skills migration policy for competitiveness. *Development Southern Africa*, vol. 19, No. 4, pp. 441-454.

Woolcock, Michael, and Deepa Narayan (2000). Social capital: implications for development theory, research, and policy. *World Bank Research Observer*, vol. 15, No. 2, pp. 225-249.

World Bank (2003). *Global Development Finance 2003*. Washington, D.C. chap. 7, pp. 165-166.

World Trade Organization (1999). *The Legal Texts: The Results of the Uruguay Round of Multilateral Negotiations*. Cambridge, United Kingdom: Cambridge University Press.

__________ (2000a). Communication from India: Proposed liberalisation of movement of professionals under the GATS. Submitted to the Council for Trade in Services of the World Trade Organization at its special session. S/CSS/W/12. 24 November.

__________ (2000b). Communication from the United States: Movement of natural persons. Submitted to the Council for Trade in Services of the World Trade Organization at its special session. S/CSS/W/29. 18 December.

__________ (2001a). Communication from the European Communities and their Member States: GATS 2000: Temporary movement of service suppliers. Submitted to the Council for Trade in Services of the World Trade Organization at its special session. S/CSS/W/45. 14 March.

__________ (2001b). Communication from Canada: Initial negotiating proposal on the temporary movement of natural persons supplying services under the GATS (Mode 4). Submitted to the Council for Trade in Services of the World Trade Organization at its special session. S/CSS/W/48. 14 March.

__________ (2001c). Communication from Japan: Movement of natural persons, supplement. Submitted to the Council for Trade in Services of the World Trade Organization at its special session. S/CSS/W/42/Suppl. 2. 6 July.

__________ (2002). GATS, Mode 4 and the Pattern of Commitments: background information prepared by the World Trade Organization Secretariat for the Joint World Trade Organization-World Bank Symposium on Movement of Natural Persons (Mode 4) under the GATS, World Trade Organization, Geneva, 11 and 12 April 2002.

__________ (2004). *World Trade Report 2004.* Geneva, Switzerland.

Wright, G. (1986). *Old South, New South.* New York: Basic Books.

Xu, Yu (2003). Are Chinese nurses a viable source to relieve the U.S. nurse shortage? *Nursing Economics*, vol. 21, No. 6 (Health Module), pp. 269-279.

Zachariah, K.C., and S. Irudaya Rajan (2001). Gender dimensions of migration in Kerala: macro and micro evidence. *Asia-Pacific Population Journal*, vol. 16, No. 3 (September), pp. 47-70.

Zegers de Beijl, R. ed. (2000). *Documenting Discrimination against Migrants in the Labour Market.* Geneva: International Labour Organization.

Zetter, Roger, and others (2003). *An Assessment of the Impact of Asylum Policies in Europe 1990-2000.* London: Home Office Research, Development and Statistics Directorate.

Zimmerman, K. F. (1995). Tackling the European migration problem. *Journal of Economic Perspectives*, vol. 9. No. 2.

Zlotnik, Hania (1998). International migration 1965-96: an overview. *Population and Development Review* (New York), vol. 4, No. 3 (September), pp. 429-468.

__________ (2003). The global dimensions of female migration. Under Data Insight, at Migration Information Source. Available from http://www.migrationinformation.org/Feature/display.cfm?ID=109 (accessed 1 November 2004).